Programming the Web with

ColdFusion MX 6.1 Using XHTML

Programming the Web with
ColdFusion MX 6.1 Using XHTML

Lakshmi Prayaga

University of West Florida

Hamsa Suri

University of Phoenix

Technology Education

Boston   Burr Ridge, IL   Dubuque, IA   Madison, WI   New York   San Francisco   St. Louis
Bangkok   Bogotá   Caracas   Kuala Lumpur   Lisbon   London   Madrid   Mexico City
Milan   Montreal   New Delhi   Santiago   Seoul   Singapore   Sydney   Taipei   Toronto

Technology Education

PROGRAMMING THE WEB WITH COLDFUSION MX 6.1 USING XHTML
Published by McGraw-Hill Technology Education, a business unit of The McGraw-Hill
Companies, Inc., 1221 Avenue of the Americas, New York, NY, 10020. Copyright © 2004 by The
McGraw-Hill Companies, Inc. All rights reserved. No part of this publication may be reproduced
or distributed in any form or by any means, or stored in a database or retrieval system, without
the prior written consent of The McGraw-Hill Companies, Inc., including, but not limited to, in
any network or other electronic storage or transmission, or broadcast for distance learning.

Some ancillaries, including electronic and print components, may not be available to customers
outside the United States.

This book is printed on acid-free paper.

1 2 3 4 5 6 7 8 9 0 DOC/DOC 0 9 8 7 6 5 4

ISBN   0-07-289032-0

Editor in chief: *Bob Woodbury*
Sponsoring editor: *Marc Chernoff*
Developmental editor: *Jennie Yates*
Marketing manager: *Andy Bernier*
Senior producer, Media technology: *Ed Przyzycki*
Senior project manager: *Christine A. Vaughan*
Senior production supervisor: *Sesha Bolisetty*
Lead designer: *Matthew Baldwin*
Supplement producer: *Matthew Perry*
Senior digital content specialist: *Brian Nacik*
Cover image: *©2003 Masterfile Corporation. Bill Frymire,* Globe with Arts and Technology
    Mosaic and Binary Code.
Typeface: *10/12 New Baskerville*
Compositor: *PreMediaOne/Black Dot Group*
Printer: *R. R. Donnelley*

Library of Congress Cataloging-in-Publication Data
Prayaga, Lakshmi.
    Programming the Web with ColdFusion MX 6.1 using XHTML /
Lakshmi Prayaga, Hamsa Suri.
        p. cm.
    Includes index.
    ISBN 0-07-289032-0 (alk. paper)
    1. ColdFusion. 2. Web databases. 3. Database design. 4. XHTML
(Document markup language). I. Suri, Hamsa. II. Title.
QA76.9.W43P73 2004
005.75'8–dc22

                                                                2003071093

www.mhhe.com

McGraw-Hill Technology Education

At McGraw-Hill Technology Education, we publish instructional materials for the technology education market—in particular, for computer instruction in post-secondary education that ranges from introductory courses in traditional four-year universities to continuing education and proprietary schools. McGraw-Hill Technology Education presents a broad range of innovative products—texts, lab manuals, study guides, testing materials, and technology-based training and assessment tools.

We realize that technology has created and will continue to create new mediums for professors and students to use in managing resources and communicating information to one another. McGraw-Hill Technology Education provides the most flexible and complete teaching and learning tools available and offers solutions to the changing needs of the classroom. McGraw-Hill Technology Education is dedicated to providing the tools for today's instructors and students, which will enable them to successfully navigate the world of Information Technology.

- McGraw-Hill/Osborne—This division of The McGraw-Hill Companies is known for its best-selling Internet titles, Harley Hahn's *Internet & Web Yellow Pages* and the *Internet Complete Reference*. For more information, visit Osborne at www.osborne.com.

- Digital Solutions—Whether you want to teach a class online or just post your "bricks-and-mortar" class syllabus, McGraw-Hill Technology Education is committed to publishing digital solutions. Taking your course online doesn't have to be a solitary adventure, nor does it have to be a difficult one. We offer several solutions that will allow you to enjoy all the benefits of having your course material online.

- Packaging Options—For more information about our discount options, contact your McGraw-Hill Sales representative at 1-800-338-3987 or visit our website at **www.mhhe.com/it.**

McGraw-Hill Technology Education is dedicated to providing the tools for today's instructors and students.

Preface

To the Instructor

Programming the Web with ColdFusion MX 6.1 Using XHTML has been designed to lead the student from the beginner's level all the way through the intricacies of Internet programming. The book also contains advanced topics that can be used as course material for students with some programming experience but who need to apply their knowledge to web programming. Two categories of students are targeted: one is the traditional CS/CIS major and the other, the interdisciplinary category with little or no training in programming.

Internet Programming Courses for CS/CIS Majors

The growth of the Internet over the past few years has exposed the scope and potential of web programming to impact every facet of life, which in turn has increased the need for Internet/web programmers. Many universities and community colleges have responded to this need by including Internet programming courses in their curriculum. *Programming the Web with ColdFusion MX 6.1 Using XHTML* provides a strong foundation to build dynamic web applications with an up-to-date introduction to ColdFusion MX 6.1 using XHTML. The textbook also includes chapters on advanced data types of ColdFusion MX 6.1 such as arrays and structures, custom tags, XML, charts and graphs, reusable components, modular coding, file processing, and database processing. These topics are highly suitable for an advanced course in Internet/web programming for traditional computer science or computer information science majors. The book walks students through a shopping cart project, gradually building up the shopping cart as the chapters progress. The end of the book completes a fully functional shopping cart application.

Internet Technologies for Interdisciplinary Students

The second set of students the book targets is the interdisciplinary students. These are typically non-CS majors. *Programming the Web* uses the simplicity of ColdFusion MX 6.1 to explain abstract traditional programming concepts with easy-to-understand, concrete examples. The simplicity of ColdFusion MX 6.1 makes it a natural choice to be used to teach programming to nontraditional computer science students. Chapters 1 through 7 can be very easily covered in one semester for this set of students. This part of the book covers all of the essential topics to build a ColdFusion application. These chapters help the students to build a simple version of the database-driven shopping cart application.

To the Student

This textbook is designed to introduce you to web programming with Cold Fusion MX 6.1 with a step-by-step approach. It includes a comprehensive yet simple discussion of ColdFusion MX 6.1 as a server-side technology. We have taken great care to introduce programming concepts related to web development one at a time. All the code segments in this book are complete hands-on exercises that illustrate various aspects of Internet programming that relate to CFMX 6.1. The end-of-chapter exercises, which include project building exercises that incrementally increase in complexity, reinforce the key concepts discussed in each chapter.

Key Features

Several key features have been included in *Programming the Web with ColdFusion MX 6.1 Using XHTML* to increase its pedagogical effectiveness:

- **Each code segment** is a complete working program, accompanied by screen shots of the code as displayed in a browser.

- **Tech Tip boxes and Important boxes** are placed where necessary to advise and draw students' attention to crucial aspects of that segment of code.

- **Complete discussions of database concepts** (from connectivity to dynamic SQL) demonstrate the crucial role played by a database in a web application.

- **Real-world examples** use built-in ColdFusion functions; complex data types such as lists, arrays, and structures; modular coding techniques such as custom tags; ColdFusion components; and user-defined functions.

- **Interesting topics** such as sending email, creating graphs, and generating XML through ColdFusion templates are made simple and easy to understand.

- **Comprehensive end-of-chapter material** is provided, including

  - Summary of the chapter.

  - Key Terms list.

  - Review Questions and True or False questions to help reinforce material discussed in the chapter.

  - Hands-on Programming Exercises that let students demonstrate their understanding of programming concepts discussed in the chapter.

- Project Building Exercises that introduce students to the steps involved in planning and creating a well-planned "interactive web application." Students are advised to complete this set of exercises after each chapter, since these exercises build on one another throughout the text.

- *Programming the Web with ColdFusion MX 6.1 Using XHTML* helps the student build two versions of the shopping cart application:

  - The first version guides the student through all phases of the application from the product-listing page to the final page where the customer's order is saved to the database. This version allows for the purchase and saving of an order with one item from the online store. The student can complete this version of the project by the end of Chapter 7.

  - The second version of the shopping cart application allows the purchase of multiple items from the online store. The students, on completion of Chapter 8, can complete a working version. The students can build a more sophisticated version using advanced ColdFusion MX 6.1 features in Chapters 9 and 10. A complete solution is provided in Chapter 11. Chapter 11 also gives suggestions on additional web applications with suggested design tips and techniques.

Appendices

Programming the Web with ColdFusion MX 6.1 Using XHTML includes two appendices to supply students with quick reference material for commonly used SQL statements and XHTML tags. These appendices by no means should be considered a complete discussion of SQL and XHTML.

- Appendix A contains coverage of SQL statements.

- Appendix B contains coverage of XHTML tags.

Instructor's Resource Kit

The Instructor's Resource Kit is a CD-ROM containing the Instructor's Manual in both MS Word and .pdf formats, ExamView Pro test-generating software, and accompanying test item files in both MS Word and .pdf formats for each chapter. Test Bank files are also available on the Instructor's Resource Kit.

Instructor's Manual

The Instructor's Manual contains the following teaching tools:

- Overview.

- Teaching tips and strategies.

- Lecture notes.

- Solutions to the end-of-chapter material.

- Example code to include URLs for images in a database.

The Test Bank

The Test Bank, which uses ExamView Pro testing software, contains 550 questions with page references to the text. There are 50 questions per chapter. The Test Bank consists of 20 multiple choice, 15 true/false, 10 fill-in-the-blank, and 5 short answer questions.

Custom Website

The course website, http://www.mhhe.com/webdev/prayaga, includes source code examples from the text, additional exercises for students, the instructor's resource kit, and other related information about the book.

About the Authors

Lakshmi Prayaga is an instructor in the Computer Science Department at the University of West Florida (UWF). Lakshmi holds a master's degree in software engineering from the University of West Florida; a master's in business administration from Alabama A&M University, Huntsville; and a master's in philosophy from the University of Bangalore, India. Lakshmi has designed and developed several courses and teaches courses such as Internet Programming, Software Methods for Remote Databases, and Web Design for E-Commerce (both in-class and online sections) at UWF. Lakshmi is currently working on her doctorate in education. She lives with her husband, Chandra Prayaga, who is chair of the Physics Department, UWF, in Pensacola, Florida.

Hamsa Suri holds a master's degree in Computer Science from the University of Manchester Institute of Science and Technology, Manchester, U.K. Hamsa currently works at Logitech Inc. in Fremont, CA. She has been involved in design and development of software and database applications for the past 10 years. Hamsa is also an online instructor at the University of Phoenix. She facilitates graduate and undergraduate computer science and management courses such as software engineering, project management, programming in various languages, web technologies, database management, and many others.

Acknowledgments

We would like to acknowledge the support and cooperation we have had from both our families, especially from our respective husbands, Chandra Prayaga and Prem Suri, for spending so many hours editing and correcting the text and providing us with their valuable inputs and soothing our frayed nerves. We thank them for solidly supporting us throughout this project and keeping their patience even when we lost ours.

Programming the Web with ColdFusion MX 6.1 Using XHTML has been reviewed and tested in several academic settings. It was class tested in the University of West Florida in fall 2002, spring 2003, and fall 2003 for several sections of students. It also was class tested at the National Computer Educator's Institute conference at the University of Central Oklahoma in the summer of 2003. We would like to take this opportunity to extend our thanks to all these participants for their valuable input that has contributed to the successful completion of this project.

We also would like to thank the following reviewers for their helpful suggestions:

- Rochelle Casolaro, Professor of Information Technology, University of Redlands

- Dr. Lei-da Chen, Assistant Professor of Information Systems and Technology, Creighton University

- Elizabeth Crane, Washtenaw Community College

- Dr. Stephen Floyd, Associate Professor of Management Information Systems, University of Alabama–Huntsville

- Dr. Edward J. Garrity, Associate Professor of Information Systems, Canisius College

- Gary Hackbarth, Professor of Management Information Systems, Iowa State University

- Jintae Lee, Professor of Information Systems, University of Colorado–Boulder

- Sathasivam Mathiyalakan, Assistant Professor of Management Information Systems, Syracuse University

- Dr. Robert Minch, Professor of Networking and Telecommunications, Boise State University

- Emily Powell, Senior Instructor of Computer Science Technology, Texas State Technical College–West Texas

- Vincent Ribiere, Assistant Professor, CAP Department, American University

- Dr. Andrew L. Wright, Assistant Professor of Computer Information Systems, University of Louisville

We also would like to thank the following technical editors for the time and effort they put into reviewing every piece of code in the book:

- Emily Powell, Senior Instructor of Computer Science Technology, Texas State Technical College–West Texas

- Jintae Lee, Professor of Information Systems, University of Colorado–Boulder

Brief Contents

Contents

CHAPTER 8

Complex Data Types   281

CHAPTER 9

Modular Code   317

ColdFusion MX 6.1

CHAPTER OBJECTIVES

1. Understand the difference between client- and server-side technologies.

2. Trace the history of ColdFusion.

3. Learn the architecture of web applications.

4. Install ColdFusion MX 6.1.

5. Create a "Hello world" program.

6. Navigate the ColdFusion Administrator.

This chapter gives an overview of ColdFusion MX 6.1. It traces the evolution of ColdFusion from the early version 1.0 to the most recent version ColdFusion MX 6.1. The chapter points out some of the new features of ColdFusion MX 6.1 as discussed in individual chapters in the book and the various applications that can be created and supported by ColdFusion MX 6.1.

Client/Server Technologies

The Internet has revolutionized the concept of accessing and transferring information. The method of exchanging information has moved away from a paper-based system to a more dynamic web-based technology. The Internet allows people to exchange vast streams of information beyond constraints of geographic locations. Information is available to anyone who has access to the Internet. But as time progressed, the demands on the type of information provided by the Internet changed. People were no longer satisfied with the passive or static information provided by the existing HTML technology. The demand arose for a technology that could provide more dynamic web content, react to user requests, and respond with appropriate result sets.

In response to this demand, a host of technologies such as ASP, Perl/CGI, JavaScript, and ColdFusion emerged. These technologies are broadly classified as **server side** or **client side,** based on whether the programs or technologies to process the user requests reside on the client's machine or on a remote server. JavaScript is typically a client-side technology, which means that as long as the client machine has JavaScript residing on it, any programs written in JavaScript can be executed on the client's machine. On the other hand, server-side technologies such as ColdFusion or ASP require that only the web host must have the technology and all applications written using that specific technology reside on it. There are no demands on the capabilities of the client's machine except that it have a browser. The client can access any of the information via a URL.

Client-versus Server-Side Technologies
Client-Side Technologies

- *Advantage:* Faster processing—Since the pages are processed on the client's machine, network traffic can be avoided, which results in faster processing of the code.
- *Disadvantage:* Less secure—The major disadvantage of client-side technologies is the transparency of code, which can lead to abuse by hackers.

Server-Side Technologies

- *Advantage:* Independent of client software—Since the software required to process all code is residing on the server, there are no extra software requirements that must be supported by the client machine; the client can access server-side resources such as databases.
- *Advantage:* Greater security—The code is opaque to the user, which means that the code cannot be tampered with.
- *Disadvantage:* The major drawback of this technology is the congestion caused by network traffic.

Tech Tip

When to Use Client or Server Technologies In general, use client technology such as JavaScript for applications or pages within an application that do not need heavy security, such as loading graphics. Use server-side technologies for applications that rely heavily on security.

Architecture and Dynamics of a Web Application

A web application is a set of web pages, static and dynamic, that work together to achieve a common purpose. An example of a web application is an electronic store. The components used in designing and creating a web application include a browser, a web application server such as ColdFusion MX 6.1,

CGI, ASP.Net, PHP, and a host of other such technologies. Web applications are usually developed based on a **tiered architecture.** The applications are categorized from a *one-tier* to an *n-tier* application. A brief discussion is given below.

A tiered application can be thought of as having separate tiers or layers where each layer performs a specific function of the application. Applications can have these tiers residing on the local machine and or in physically separate servers. The location of these tiers can be set up as mappings in the administrator section of the application server. An overview of ColdFusion MX 6.1 administrator is discussed later in the chapter.

The simplest kind of a tiered application is a **one-tier application.** This involves a single layer on a single machine where there is no logical separation of the functions being performed in the application. All the pieces that are required to run the application are bundled together. An example of this is a word processing or a spreadsheet application. A one-tier architecture is not suitable for designing a web application because it is limited to using a single machine for the entire application.

A **two-tier architecture** is a simple browser-to-server relationship. An example of this is a host server physically located someplace else that serves the browser's requests by returning the requested pages, where the client handles the presentation details and the server handles the business logic.

A more commonly followed architecture used by many web applications is a **three-tier architecture.** The three tiers in this architecture are the web browser (client), the application server (such as ColdFusion MX) to handle the business logic of the application, and the database layer (such as an Oracle or SQL database) to handle the database functions. Though the three-tier model offers some scalability and separation of basic functions into different modules in an application, it does not really separate the application into logically specialized functions. This logical separation of the different functions of an application increases the efficiency and performance of the application.

An **n-tier application** is one that has a number of tiers, where *n* represents the number of layers. An n-tier architecture expands from the simpler architectures to accommodate more flexibility and scalability for the application. It further separates the business logic into specialized modules, each one to perform a specific task, such as maintaining inventory, financial calculations, and so forth. ColdFusion MX 6.1 can be used to design n-tier applications because of its capabilities and interoperability with other applications.

An example of an n-tier web application is an electronic airline reservation system, which has the following tiers:

- **Client/browser tier:** This is the client layer. Since ColdFusion MX 6.1 can integrate with other applications such as Macromedia Flash MX, Dreamweaver, and Java, the client layer can present a rich and fulfilling experience to the user.

- **Presentation tier:** This layer is responsible for creating the dynamic content of your web page. This includes results from the database, Cold Fusion functions, and so forth. This tier is the glue that holds the entire application together. The tool for this tier is the application server, which in our case is ColdFusion MX.
- **Business logic tier:** This tier is responsible for the nitty-gritty details of your application. This includes tasks such as calculating totals, credit card processing, and so on.

Other tiers that can be used are

1. **Integration tier,** which provides an interface to talk to other tiers such as the business logic tier and the database tier. The advantage of having such a tier is that if anything changes in your business logic layer—for example, if you change your vendor for credit card processing or database provider—you can make the changes in the integration layer without having to change the code in all the pages that depend on this information.

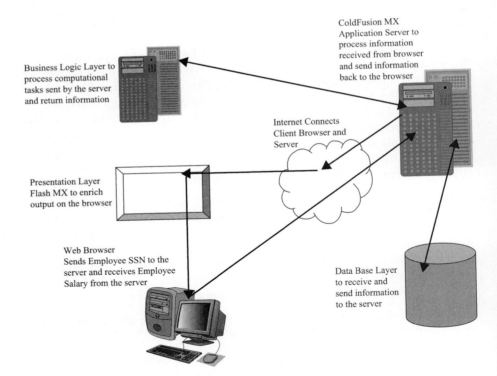

FIGURE 1.1   n-Tier Architecture

2. **Data tier,** which is created by database servers such as Oracle or MS SQL server. This tier ensures that data required by your web application is independent of any other tier, keeps the data from being corrupted, improves performance, and allows for scalability should the application require it. Figure 1.1 illustrates an n-tier architecture model.

History of ColdFusion

ColdFusion is a server-side technology. The first version of ColdFusion Markup Language (CFML) was released by Allaire in 1995. The main focus of this version was to provide a facility by which web developers could connect to databases and provide interaction with the database. Since then several versions of ColdFusion have been released, each offering more features such as allowing user-defined functions, extending server capabilities, and strengthening security features for files stored on the server. In the year 2000, Allaire merged with Macromedia and released ColdFusion version 5.0, which was the first version of ColdFusion that supported user-defined functions. This version also supported the concept of "querying a query," which strengthened its database interactivity feature.

ColdFusion MX

In the year 2002, Macromedia released ColdFusion MX. This was a major event since the merger of Allaire and Macromedia. This new product is the "next generation" software, a result of the synergy between the client-side design features of Macromedia products with the server-side features of Allaire products. This will, according to Macromedia, "create applications that combine the responsiveness and functionality of client/server applications with the reach and low-cost deployment of the Internet."[1] ColdFusion MX is available in two varieties for purchase: ColdFusion MX Server Professional Edition and the Enterprise Edition, which includes advanced security, performance, and management features that are important for mission-critical applications, and large-scale websites that rely on heavy security. Macromedia also offers a ColdFusion Developer Edition that is available as a free download. Instructions to download the Developer Edition are given later in the chapter. Some of the key features of ColdFusion MX include

- *Easy integration with XML:* ColdFusion MX allows you to integrate XML into your applications just as you would integrate any other data source (database, spreadsheets, or text documents).

---

[1] http://www.internetnews.com/dev-news/article.php/1023961.

- *ColdFusion Components (CFCs):* CFCs promote modularity in a whole new way. CFCs revolve around the theme of "write once, use many times." You can access them from a ColdFusion page, from a Flash client, or as a web service.

- *Easy-to-consume or publish web services:* The `<cfinvoke>` tag allows you to call web services from your ColdFusion application. You also can create web services with CFCs.

- *Creation of attractive and fully functional websites:* Easy integration between Flash clients and the ColdFusion MX server environment with the Flash Remoting Services provided with ColdFusion MX allows you to create compelling websites.

- *Enhanced* `<cfchart>` *tag:* ColdFusion MX now supports multiple data series, fully customizable output and report types, batch reporting, and drill-down functionality.

- *Unicode support:* Built-in Unicode support for languages such as Japanese, Korean, and Chinese allows you to create localized web applications.

- *Java Server Pages (JSP) and ColdFusion MX:* ColdFusion MX now allows you to import Java servlets and Java libraries into your ColdFusion applications.

- *Improved security:* The sandbox security available in ColdFusion administrator gives you greater control of your resources. A sandbox is an area consisting of files and directories in your website to which you want to apply some restrictions. This is particularly important in a shared environment where you need to restrict access to some of your critical database files and CF functions, preventing them from being tampered with.

- *ColdFusion MX as its own web server:* ColdFusion MX is a web server in itself. This is particularly suitable for development purposes, since it allows testing out applications independent of a host server technology.

- *ColdFusion MX for the J2EE application server:* ColdFusion MX is available in two varieties: ColdFusion MX as a standalone server and ColdFusion MX running on the J2EE application server. ColdFusion MX for the J2EE application server allows you to develop and deploy ColdFusion applications on other application servers such as IBM WebSphere, Macromedia JRun, and Sun One.

- *Creation of multiple instances of ColdFusion:* The stand-alone version of ColdFusion MX and other previous versions of ColdFusion caused server failure if the application failed. On the other hand, ColdFusion MX for the J2EE application server allows the administrator to create multiple instances of ColdFusion on a single machine. This ability provides a major advantage in the sense that it reduces the chances of a single instance of an application causing complete server failure.

Other advantages of ColdFusion MX for the J2EE server are

- It is compatible with all standard platforms such as the .net framework, WebSphere, Java, and J2EE.
- ColdFusion MX for the J2EE server combines the benefits of scalability, flexibility, and open standard architecture of the J2EE server technology with the rapid development environment of ColdFusion.

ColdFusion MX 6.1

In late summer of 2003, Macromedia released the next version of ColdFusion MX, which is ColdFusion MX 6.1. This version, according to Macromedia, "is an absolutely vital update to ColdFusion MX." In addition to all the above-mentioned features of ColdFusion MX, some of the main features of Cold Fusion MX 6.1 include

- *Simple installation and migration:* Provides greater backward compatibility than MX did and a web server configuration wizard.
- *Support for more operating systems:* Operating systems supported include Windows Server 2003 (and IIS 6), Redhat Linux 8 and 9, SuSE Linux 8, Solaris 9, and AIX 4.3.3 and 5.1.
- *Faster development time:* ColdFusion MX has a new compiler that compiles the ColdFusion code directly to Java byte code without the intermediate Java source code. This results in a very fast compile time, thus reducing the time for requests made during development to the CFML code.
- *Enhanced* `<cfmail>` *tag:* The `<cfmail>` tag is discussed in Chapter 10. ColdFusion MX 6.1 has improved the existing `<cfml>` tag in that it supports SMTP logins, which the SMTP servers use to prevent mail relaying. The `<cfmail>` tag has two new attributes, `USERNAME` and `PASSWORD`, to include login information within the tag. The new `<cfmail>` tag also allows developers to create multipart messages to accommodate both text and HTML within the same message and allows the support of multiple SMTP mail servers to accommodate for failure of the servers with an alternate SMTP server.
- *The* `wrap()` *function:* This tag allows you to insert breaks into text blocks to enforce wrapping. This removes the necessity to use escape mechanisms such as using two `<br>` tags to get the effect of one `<br>` within a block of text.

ColdFusion MX 6.1 is available in two versions:

- *ColdFusion Standard* (corresponds to the ColdFusion MX Professional).
- *ColdFusion Enterprise* (corresponds to ColdFusion MX Enterprise plus a full copy of Jrun 4 web server).[2]

---

[2] http://www.macromedia.com/software/coldfusion/productinfo/faq/cfmx61/#itemA-1.

Last but not least, ColdFusion MX 6.1 is a free upgrade to existing ColdFusion MX subscribers.

ColdFusion MX 6.1 Developer Edition

System Requirements

Windows

- Microsoft Windows 98 or higher

Hardware

- Pentium processor
- RAM minimum: 256 MB
- Hard-disk space: 400 MB to install and run ColdFusion MX

Browser

- Internet Explorer 5.x or 6
- Netscape 4, 6

Databases Supported by ColdFusion MX 6.1

- Microsoft SQL Server 7
- Oracle
- IBM DB2
- Sybase
- Informix
- Microsoft Access
- MySql
- MS SQL Server 7.0, 2000
- Sybase Adaptive Server 11.5 and higher
- Sybase Adaptive Server Enterprise 12.0 and 12.5

Instructions for Installing ColdFusion MX 6.1 (Developer Edition)

(The instructions given below assume installation of the trial version of Cold Fusion MX 6.1 from the Macromedia website at www.macromedia.com for Windows.) This version is available free from the Macromedia website, and it converts to a fully functional working development version after the 30-day period, again free of charge. This version can only be used to learn ColdFusion MX 6.1 or deploy your ColdFusion MX applications to third-party hosting providers.

IMPORTANT

At the end of the 30 days, the Trial Edition becomes the Developer Edition, a fully
functional server for local development purposes only that helps you learn ColdFusion
MX 6.1 or deploy to third-party hosting providers.

1. Visit the Macromedia website and download the trial version of Cold-Fusion MX 6.1 onto your local machine. Make sure you choose the version for English and Windows platform.

2. Double-click the icon for ColdFusion MX 6.1 to step through the installation process.

3. Click next on the **OK** button to confirm the version for English (Figure 1.2).

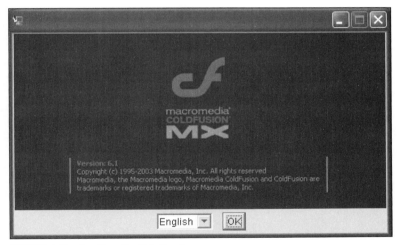

FIGURE 1.2   Confirm English Version

4. Click **Next** on the Introduction window (Figure 1.3).

5. Click the **I accept** button on the License Agreement screen (Figure 1.4).

6. From the next screen (Figure 1.5), choose the new version of Macro-media ColdFusion MX and click **Next**.

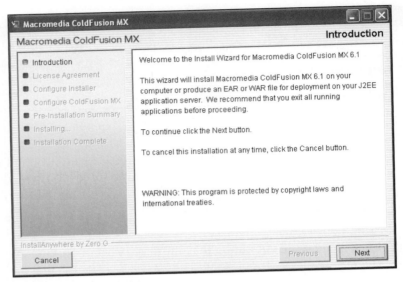

FIGURE 1.3   Introduction

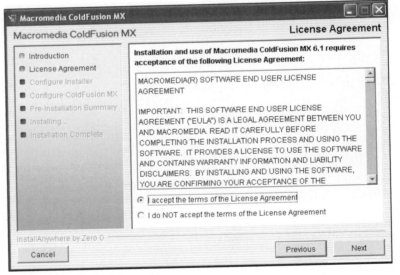

FIGURE 1.4   License Agreement

7. On the next screen (Figure 1.6), choose the **Server configuration** option to install ColdFusion MX as a self-contained server and click **Next**.

8. On the next screen (Figure 1.7), choose the directory in which to install ColdFusion MX. It is recommended that you use the default location, which is **C:\CFusionMX**, and click **Next**.

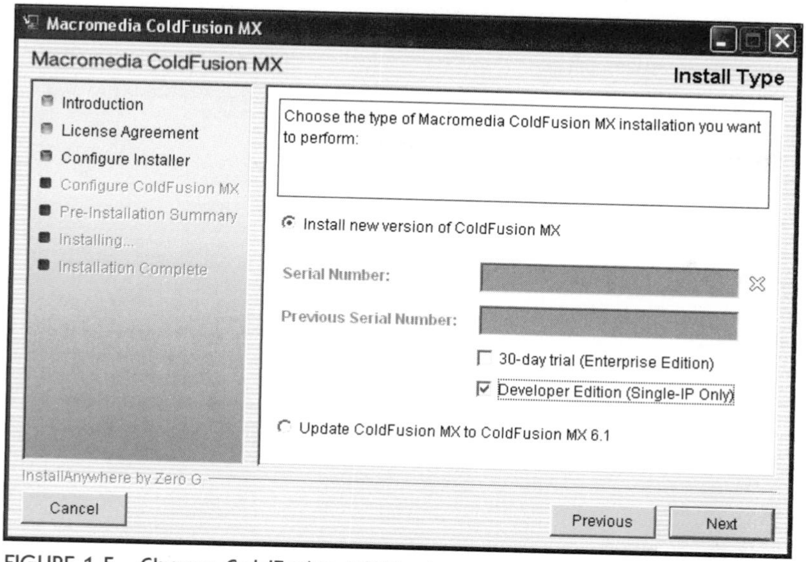

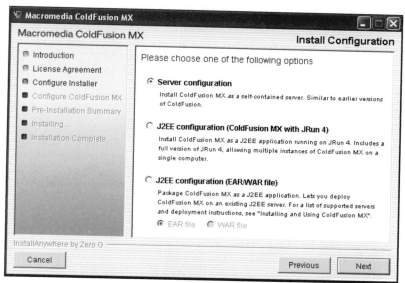

FIGURE 1.5   Choose ColdFusion MX Version

FIGURE 1.6   Choose Server Configuration

9. On the next screen (Figure 1.8), choose the web server to be configured for use with ColdFusion MX. Choose the **Built-in web server** option and click **Next**.

10. On the next screen (Figure 1.9), choose a password that you will use as an administrator and click **Next**.

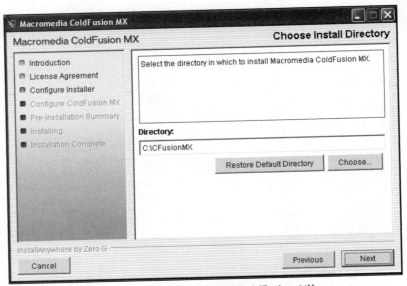

FIGURE 1.7   Choose the Directory to Install ColdFusion MX

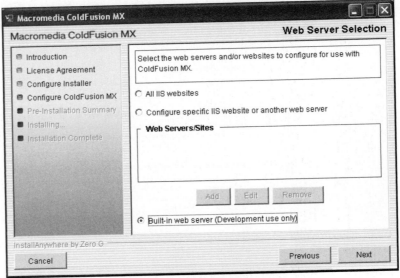

FIGURE 1.8   Choose Web Server to Configure

11. The next screen you see (Figure 1.10) is the Installation Confirmation window. Review the information and click **Install**.

12. The next screen (Figure 1.11) shows that Macromedia ColdFusion MX is being installed.

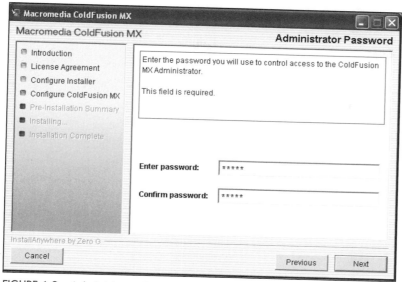

FIGURE 1.9   Administrator Password

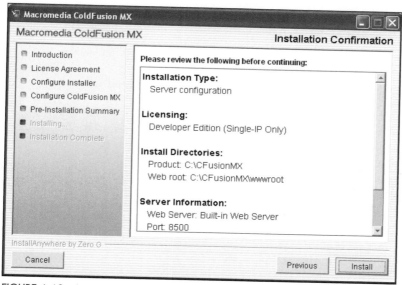

FIGURE 1.10   Installation Confirmation

13. The next screen (Figure 1.12) is the Installation Complete message. This completes the installation procedure for ColdFusion MX. Click **Done** to launch the configuration wizard in a default browser. This takes us to the second phase of the installation process.

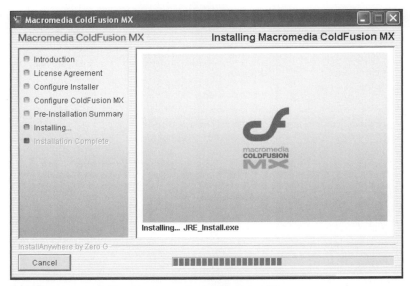

FIGURE 1.11   Installing Macromedia ColdFusion MX

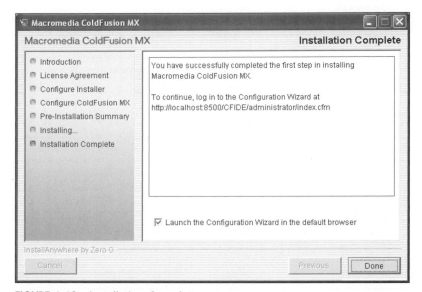

FIGURE 1.12   Installation Complete

ColdFusion MX 6.1 Installation: Configuration and Settings Wizard

14. ColdFusion MX 6.1 has a separate wizard to help you configure the web services required to run ColdFusion MX 6.1 templates on your machine. Figure 1.13 shows the Configuration and Settings Migration Wizard. At the prompt, enter the password that you used in step 10 above and press **Login**.

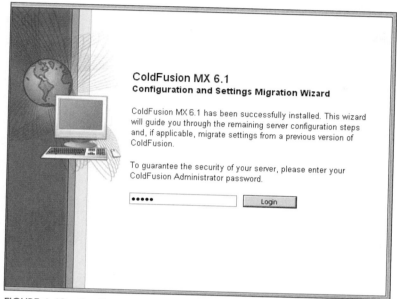

FIGURE 1.13   Configuration Wizard

15. The next screen (Figure 1.14) prompts you to enter a password for RDS (Remote Development Service). Type your password at the prompt and press **Next**.

16. Figure 1.15 shows the ODBC setup screen. This provides the necessary information for the database connectivity.

17. Figure 1.16 is a prompt to install ColdFusion example applications. Make your choice and press **Next**.

18. Figure 1.17 shows the Setup Complete window. This completes the entire installation process of ColdFusion MX 6.1. Click **OK** to open the ColdFusion MX Administrator window, which is discussed after the "Hello World Program." Close the ColdFusion MX Administrator window.

Writing a "Hello World" Program in ColdFusion

Before you start developing your ColdFusion applications, you should create a folder in which to save your programs. The **file path** to create your folder, called CFApps, is as follows:

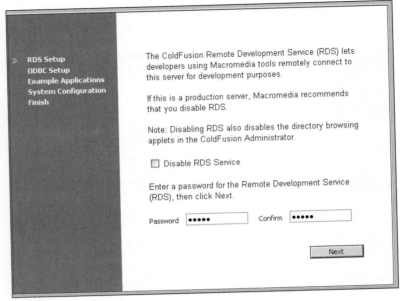

FIGURE 1.14   RDS Password

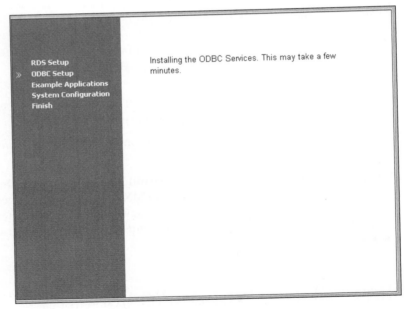

FIGURE 1.15   ODBC Setup

- Follow the path C:/CfusionM/wwwroot/.
- Create the folder called **CFApps** in the wwwroot folder.

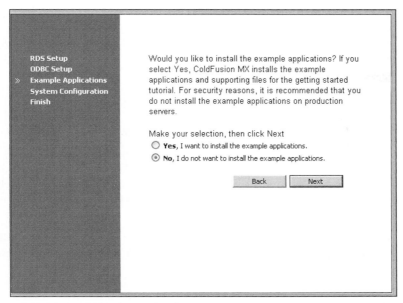

FIGURE 1.16   Example Applications

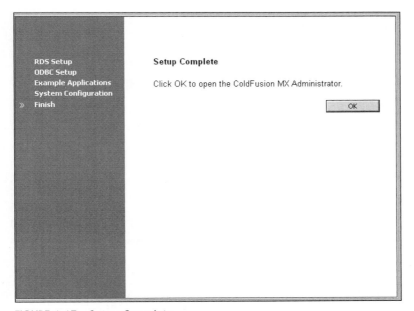

FIGURE 1.17   Setup Complete

There are many development environments such as Dreamweaver, Homesite, or ColdFusion Studio that will help you write your code. However, it is not necessary to use any of these environments to develop your ColdFusion applications. You can simply use Notepad or any text editor of your choice. This book presumes that you use Notepad to write your ColdFusion code. So, open Notepad and type the code given below:

Example 1.1

```
<html>
Hello! Welcome to the land of ColdFusion
</html>
```

Create a folder called **CH1** in the CFApps folder. (You will similarly create a folder for each chapter of this book to hold all the example files in that chapter.) Save the file as CH1Eg1.cfm in the CFApps/CH1 folder. All ColdFusion templates must be saved with a **.cfm** extension.

To browse the output of this file, open Internet Explorer and type the following URL: http://localhost:8500/CFApps/CH1/CH1Eg1.cfm. Your screen should now look like Figure 1.18.

FIGURE 1.18   Hello World Program

If your screen matches Figure 1.18, congratulations; you have just written your first ColdFusion template. We will work on more ColdFusion specific examples starting in Chapter 2.

During the installation process of ColdFusion MX, if you selected the standalone server in Windows, as the instructions prompted you to do, then, by default, the web server for ColdFusion MX runs on port 8500, which must be appended to the hostname or IP address of your machine. Therefore, the URL for browsing the ColdFusion template is **localhost:8500** followed by the path of the file. The rest of this chapter discusses ColdFusion Administrator and also gives you an overview of topics covered in the chapters of this book.

ColdFusion Administrator

ColdFusion Administrator offers a variety of functions that give you the ability to secure and access the features of ColdFusion MX. We will explore some of these functions in this section.

To open the ColdFusion Administrator, click on **Programs** and click on **Macromedia ColdFusion MX**, **Administrator**. If you look at the Administrator screen, you will find that there are five major categories listed on the left tab as shown in Figure 1.19. These are

- Server settings
- Data & services
- Debugging & Logging

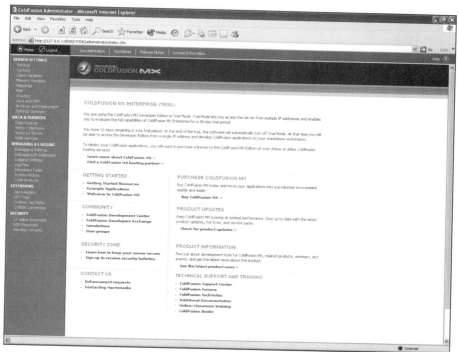

FIGURE 1.19   ColdFusion MX Administrator

- Extensions
- Security

Each of these categories has subtasks that are hyperlinks. These subtasks allow you to deal with specific functions, set up specific settings, and achieve the desired functionality. For our purposes, we will look at some of the frequently used tasks that can be performed from within the ColdFusion Administrator. For a detailed description on all categories and the subsections, visit http://macromedia.com. It is also a good idea to browse through each of these categories and see what these options offer.

Server Settings

The Settings link allows you to limit the maximum number of simultaneous requests to be processed by the server. The same link also allows you to set **time out** for requests made.

The Memory Variables link is used to enable **session** and **application variables** as shown in Figure 1.20. Once enabled, ColdFusion writes both application and session-level variables to memory and these can be accessed by any client using the application.

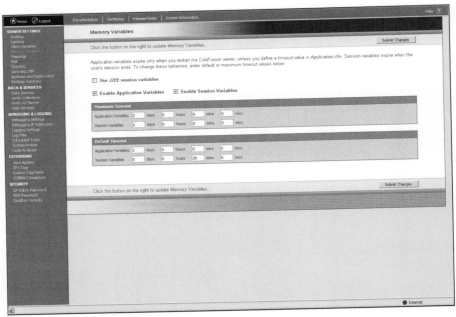

FIGURE 1.20   Memory Variables

The Mail link lets you specify the server name for sending dynamic **SMTP** messages.

The Charting option allows you to specify things like the maximum number of **charts** that can be stored in the cache and also the maximum number of chart requests that can be processed simultaneously.

Data & Services Settings

The Data Sources link allows you to set up your **data source,** which is the physical path to a database stored locally or on a remote server. This will be discussed in more detail in Chapter 5.

Debugging & Logging Settings

The Debugging Settings section allows you to select the features for which you would like to get **debugging reports.** These include debugging reports on database activity, variables, exception information, and so on.

The Debugging IP Addresses setting lets you set up the IP addresses that will receive the debugging reports. The default option is that all users will receive the reports.

The Logging Settings section allows you to choose the directory into which **logs** on the ColdFusion pages can be saved. The default setting is C:\CFusionMX\ logs. The files can log information about the processing speed of the ColdFusion pages, and they can keep track of all CORBA calls. You also can specify the maximum file size for the log files and the maximum number of log archives that ColdFusion must create.

Extensions Settings

The Extensions section allows you to access several enhanced features of ColdFusion MX.

The Java Applets section allows you to access Java applets from within your ColdFusion pages. Before you use Java applets, you must register them in this section. Similarly the section on Custom Tag Paths allows you to set file paths for the custom tags on your machine.

Security Settings

The Security section is a crucial part of the ColdFusion Administrator screen and the software itself.

The CF Admin Password section allows you to set up a password for the administrator who will basically control the software. Therefore, this password must be accessible only to trusted users.

The RDS Password similarly must be accessible only to trusted users since this password gives access to the ColdFusion server.

The Sandbox Security feature is a major development of ColdFusion MX. This section allows you to control access to ColdFusion resources based on the location of the files on the server. It is here that you can control access to files you want to be made visible to various users of the software. A sandbox is a directory or directories and their contents to which you can restrict access.

Organization of the Book

As stated previously, the book assumes

1. You will be using Notepad as your editor to type the code for your ColdFusion files.

2. We will be using XHTML as the standard markup language to be included with the ColdFusion template files. Please refer to Appendix A for commonly used XHTML tags.

3. You have a basic understanding of a relational database and SQL. Please refer to Appendix B for a list of commonly used SQL statements.

Chapter 2 presents a discussion on how variables are created, manipulated, and accessed using ColdFusion tags. We also look at some basic ColdFusion built-in functions.

Chapter 3 examines the control structures used in ColdFusion. We discuss conditional statements and looping structures used to optimize processing of ColdFusion templates.

Chapter 4 introduces the concept of creating dynamic web pages by using HTML forms to get user input and ColdFusion to respond to user requirements. We also discuss form data validation and the `wrap()` function, which is new to CFMX 6.1.

Chapters 5 and 6 explain the interaction between a database and ColdFusion. Chapter 5 presents a discussion on establishing a connection to a database, using SQL to send queries to a database, and presenting the results on a browser. Chapter 5 also briefly discusses security issues regarding MS Access database and ColdFusion. Chapter 6 looks into advanced database concepts such as using stored procedures, dynamic SQL, and transaction processing.

IMPORTANT

Sandbox Security is only available in ColdFusion Enterprise Edition.

Chapter 7 discusses some of the commonly used ColdFusion built-in functions. These include string manipulation, mathematical functions, date/time functions, dynamic evaluation, and system functions.

Chapter 8 presents complex data types in ColdFusion such as lists, arrays, and structures. A discussion on how to implement a shopping cart application as an array of structures will be presented in this chapter.

Chapter 9 includes a discussion on modularity in code using include files within CF templates, user-defined functions (UDFs), and Custom tags and paired tag. These features enable you to enhance your ColdFusion templates and make your code more efficient. We also present Components and CFFunction, which are new to ColdFusion MX and CFMX 6.1.

Chapter 10 includes a discussion on some of the cool and new features of ColdFusion MX such as <cfxml> to generate XML from database queries, <cfchart> to create different types of graphs and charts to enhance presentation of data, suppression of output with the <cfsilent> tag, exception handling, debugging, logging errors, and file handling. Chapter 10 also discusses the <cfmail> tag as enhanced in CFMX 6.1.

Chapter 11 presents a project of building a shopping cart application with ColdFusion MX. The project is designed to give an overview of all the important concepts of ColdFusion MX discussed in the text and includes suggestions on how the application can be further enhanced. One of the important features of the project is that it is built incrementally, right from the beginning of the book.

Each chapter, starting from Chapter 1, includes an exercise, based on the topics covered in the chapter, for the project. By the end of Chapter 7, the first version of the shopping cart is complete. This version is basically a proof of the concept so the student understands all the required elements of a shopping cart. Chapters 8, 9, and 10 build on the first version of the project and include some of the more advanced concepts that extend the functionality of the first version of the project. This section is particularly useful to professional programmers and challenging to the more industrious students.

Summary

This chapter discussed the history and evolution of ColdFusion MX 6.1 and presented some of the new and important features of ColdFusion MX and CFMX 6.1. ColdFusion MX 6.1 is a server-side technology that supports XML, Java servlets, charts, and other cool features that enhance web applications. ColdFusion MX makes it possible to build n-tiered applications that are scalable and efficient. ColdFusion MX 6.1 for the J2EE application server allows you to create multiple instances of ColdFusion on a single machine. This version is also compatible with all standard platforms, such as .net framework, WebSphere, Java, and J2EE.

Key Terms

application variables	file path	session variables
business logic tier	integration tier	SMTP
charts	localhost:8500	three-tier architecture
client side	logs	tiered architecture
client/browser tier	n-tier application	time out
data source	one-tier application	two-tier architecture
data tier	presentation tier	
debugging reports	server side	

Review Questions

1. What is the meaning of *client-side technology*? Give an example of a client-side technology.
2. What is meant by the term *server-side technology*? Give an example of a server-side technology.
3. What are the advantages and disadvantages of each of these technologies?
4. Define a tiered web application. What are the advantages of building a tiered application?
5. Open your ColdFusion Administrator and under the Settings tab click "Memory Variables" and check that the session and application variables are enabled.
6. Open your ColdFusion Administrator and under the Settings tab click "Settings Summary" and browse through the page. Identify the path listed under ColdFusion Mappings and write it down. Notice that this is exactly where you created your folder called CFAPPS to save your files.

True or False

State whether the following statements are true or false.

1. ColdFusion MX 6.1 is a client-side technology.
2. ColdFusion MX 6.1 has a built-in Unicode character support.
3. A tiered web application allows for scalability of the application.
4. In a tiered web application, all the resources required for each tier must physically reside on one single machine.
5. An n-tier application improves the performance of your web application.
6. ColdFusion MX 6.1 has an enhanced Chart tag that allows you to plot multiple series in a graph.
7. ColdFusion MX 6.1 is its own web server.
8. ColdFusion Administrator allows you to set server settings and enable session and application variables.

The goal of this section is to help you start the design and implementation of an electronic shopping cart application. The project will be phased out and built incrementally as you complete each chapter. The project has two phases. The first phase will be completed in Chapter 7, and the second phase in Chapter 10.

Your exercise in this chapter is to design a high-level flowchart that shows the functionality of an electronic shopping cart; that is, describe, in the form of a list, what happens in a typical online shopping cart procedure:

1. To get an idea, visit any online store, for example, amazon.com.
2. Try to make a fictitious purchase from that store.
3. Make a list of all the steps that you came across while making this purchase.
4. Describe the steps that you came across with short (one- or two-word) phrases. For example, list the items that you see on the home page of any website. Rewrite this step as: Show list of products. Do this for all the steps in your shopping list.
5. Enclose these phrases in small rectangular boxes, each showing a specific step of the transaction.
6. Now arrange these boxes in a chronological order and connect them with lines. This makes the high-level flowchart for the shopping cart application.

CHAPTER 2

ColdFusion: Basics

CHAPTER OBJECTIVES

1. Create a dynamic web page using the `<cfoutput>` tag.
2. Describe the `<cfset>` and `<cfparam>` tags to define and use variables.
3. Learn how to use basic built-in functions in ColdFusion.
4. List the different scopes of variables in ColdFusion.

In Chapter 1 you connected to your web server and wrote the "Hello World" program. Now you are ready to learn how ColdFusion can be used to create dynamic web pages and provide functionality to your web pages. This chapter explains how variables are created, manipulated, and accessed using ColdFusion tags to create dynamic web pages. We also look at some basic ColdFusion built-in functions. Understanding these preliminary concepts will lay a good background for the more detailed discussion of functions in the upcoming chapters.

Dynamic versus Static Web Pages

Unlike plain HTML, ColdFusion can be used to create **dynamic web pages,** which make websites more interesting and useful. A dynamic web page is one where the output, in the form of an HTML page, is generated only when the ColdFusion page is specifically requested by the user. A **static web page,** on the other hand, is one that was created and stored on the server. The content of the static web page is the same no matter when or how many times the user requests it. The code in Example 2.1 and the output in Figure 2.1 illustrate the concept of a static web page, and the code in Example 2.2 and the output in Figure 2. 2 illustrate the concept of a dynamic web page. Type the code in Examples 2.1 and 2.2 and save them as Ch2Eg1.cfm and Ch2Eg2.cfm.

Example 2.1

```
1. <?xml version = "1.0"?>
2. <!DOCTYPE html PUBLIC
3. "-//W3C//DTD XHTML 1.0 Transitional//EN"
4. "http://www.w3.org/TR/xhtml1/DTD/xhtml1-transitional.dtd">
5. <html xmlns = "http://www.w3.org/1999/xhtm">
6. <head>
7.    <title> Static Web page </title>
8. </head>
9. <body>
10.   <h1> Welcome to ColdFusion !</h1> <br />
11.   <h1> Today is Nov 29th 2003 </h1> <br />
12.   <h1> It is 6.30 PM </h1>
13. </body>
14. </html>
```

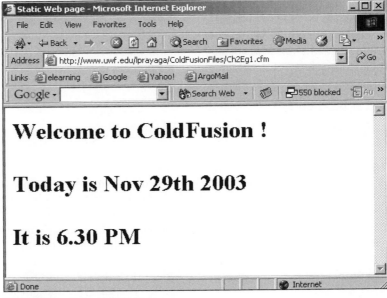

FIGURE 2.1   A Static HTML Page

How the Code Works

1. This is a very simple example. Lines 1 to 5 are the header and document type information required for an XHTML document.

2. Lines 10, 11, and 12 display a Welcome message along with precoded date and time values.

3. Lines 13 and 14 close the <body> and <html> tags.

4. Note that this is a static web page. Whenever the user requests the page, the same values for the date and time, namely, Nov 29th 2003 and 6.30 PM, are displayed.

Now let us look at the next example. This example uses two built-in **ColdFusion functions.** We will discuss functions in detail later, in Chapter 7. For the present, let us understand a function as something that takes one or more arguments that are constants, variables, or expressions and returns a value. For example, the function Max(2,3) takes two arguments, in this case, the two numbers 2 and 3, and returns the value 3, which is the maximum of the two arguments.

In Example 2.2, we use the DateFormat() and TimeFormat() functions of ColdFusion to create a dynamic web page. These values of date and time are not static, meaning that the values of date and time are not hard-coded as they were in the previous example. So they do not display the same preset values to users whenever the page is requested. Rather, these values are generated dynamically at the instant when the user requests the particular ColdFusion page, and thus the current values of date and time are displayed. Run the code a couple of times to see that the values for date and time change and are not static.

Example 2.2

```
1. <?xml version = "1.0"?>
2. <!DOCTYPE html PUBLIC
3. "-//W3C//DTD XHTML 1.0 Transitional//EN"
4. "http://www.w3.org/TR/xhtml1/DTD/xhtml1-transitional.dtd">
5. <html xmlns = "http://www.w3.org/1999/xhtm">
6. <head>
7. <title>Dynamic Page with ColdFusion</title>
8. </head>
9. <body>
10.    <h1> Welcome to ColdFusion !</h1>
```

```
11. <cfoutput>
12.    Today is #DateFormat(Now())# <BR>
13.    It is #TimeFormat(Now())#
14. </cfoutput>
15. </body>
16. </html>
```

FIGURE 2.2   A Dynamic Web Page

How the Code Works

1. Line 11 uses the `<cfoutput>` tag. ColdFusion uses the `<cfoutput>` tag to display the results of a database query or other operations on the browser. It has both an opening and a closing tag. Anything that is to be interpreted by the server, such as the value of a variable or the result of a query, and displayed on the browser must be nested within the `<cfoutput>` tag.

2. Line 12 uses the `DateFormat()` function. The `DateFormat()` function allows you to specify the way in which a date value should be displayed. The two arguments that it can take are the date value generated by a function or a variable having the date value, and an optional mask for displaying the date. In the example code, the

argument that is given to the `DateFormat()` function is another function called `Now()`, which returns the current date. The code uses the default formatting provided by the `DateFormat()`. You will see how to set and use masks for the `DateFormat()` function in Chapter 7.

3. Line 13 similarly uses the `TimeFormat()` function, which again takes another function `Now()` as its argument and returns the current time. Once again, the default formatting provided by the `TimeFormat()` function is used to display the result on the browser.

> **Tech Tip**
>
> The Use of # Signs Surrounding the Function Used to Display the Time and Date
> ColdFusion requires that variables, functions, or query names must be surrounded by # signs and embedded within the `<cfoutput>` tag.

As seen in Figure 2.2, the code was generated dynamically when the user requested the page. This feature of ColdFusion and other web programming languages to create dynamic web pages is what makes it so attractive. Later examples in this chapter and other chapters show how dynamic web pages can cater to the user's requests and create interesting web applications.

Variables, Expressions, and Operators

Variables, expressions, and operators are the building blocks of any programming language. First, we will discuss the concept of a variable. A **variable** can be thought of as a container that can hold a value. This container has two properties: a name and a value. The value for this variable can be

- Assigned by the programmer,
- Entered by the user, or
- Created by ColdFusion.

The value of the variable can later be retrieved by referencing its name. For example, if the name of the variable is firstname and its value is assigned to be "Joe", this value can later be retrieved by referencing the variable named firstname.

ColdFusion Variables

Variables can be classified in two different ways:

- According to the data type of the variable, which indicates the type of information a variable represents such as a string, number, or date.
- According to the scope of the variable, which indicates how long the variable persists and where the variable information is available.

This chapter discusses both these classifications in a broad fashion. Detailed examinations of specific aspects of these classifications are distributed throughout the book.

Creating Variables in ColdFusion

Most ColdFusion variables are created by assigning values to them. Different possible ways in which variables are created in ColdFusion are by

- The programmer using the `<cfset>` tag.
- CF tags that create other data objects. For example, the `<cfquery>` tag creates a query object variable.
- The `<cfparam>` tag, which creates a variable that can be assigned a default value. You will see the importance of such a variable in later sections of this chapter.
- Assignment statements in a `<cfscript>` tag.
- ColdFusion when it automatically generates some variables such as those that provide information of certain tags or operations.
- ColdFusion when it automatically creates variables in certain scopes like client and server variables. Refer to CFML references from www.macromedia.com for further information on these topics.

In this chapter we discuss creating variables using the `<cfset>` tag and the `<cfparam>` tag.

ColdFusion is said to be a **typeless** language, meaning that a data type is not necessary to be specified when declaring or creating a variable. If you are familiar with languages such as Visual Basic or C, a variable called fName would have to be declared as

- VB: `Dim num1 as integer`
- C: `int num1;`

The syntax for creating a variable in ColdFusion is

```
<cfset variable_name = expression>
```

The following statement creates a local variable fName with a value of "Joe":

```
<cfset fName = "Joe">
```

The following statement creates a local variable called max_count with a value of 25.

```
<cfset max_count = 25>
```

Notice that we did not have to specify the data type of fName or max_count. However, this does not mean that there are no data types in ColdFusion. ColdFusion variables must belong to one of the following data type catagories:

Data Type	Description
Simple	Variables that take a single value. Data types that fall under this category include strings, numbers, Booleans, and date-time.
Complex	Variables that can store more than one value. These include arrays, queries, XML objects, and structures.
Binary	Variables that can store raw data such as image files (gif, jpeg, etc.) or .exe files.
Objects	Variables that represent complex constructs such as COM, CORBA, ColdFusion Component, and Java.

Naming Rules for Variables in ColdFusion

1. A variable must begin with an alphabetic value (A–Z; case is not important).

2. It must contain only letters, numbers, and the underscore; no spaces are allowed.

3. It is not required to specify the data type of the variable in ColdFusion.

4. ColdFusion variables are not case sensitive, but consistent capitalization improves readability of code.

5. Queries and variables cannot have the same name in the same Cold-Fusion page. Queries in ColdFusion will be discussed in Chapter 5.

6. When using fields from a form in a query, make sure to match the form field names with the corresponding database field names. This concept will also be discussed in Chapters 5 and 6.

> **Tech Tip**
>
> Using descriptive names such as sum instead of x to hold the total of a given set of numbers makes your code more readable and easier to understand.

Using `<cfset>` and `<cfoutput>` Tags to Set and Display Values of Variables

The code given in Example 2.3 and the output shown in Figure 2.3 are an example of using the `<cfset>` and `<cfoutput>` tags. It also uses another ColdFusion built-in function, Max(). We will examine CF functions in more detail in Chapter 7. Type the code in Example 2.3, save it as Ch2Eg3.cfm and open it in your browser.

> **IMPORTANT**
>
> Code results in error if spaces or special characters are used in creating variables. Examples of invalid variable names are First Name, 5%, and 3rdPerson.

Example 2.3

```
1. <?xml version = "1.0"?>
2. <!DOCTYPE html PUBLIC
3. "-//W3C//DTD XHTML 1.0 Transitional//EN"
4. "http://www.w3.org/TR/xhtml1/DTD/xhtml1-transitional.dtd">
5. <html xmlns = "http://www.w3.org/1999/xhtm">
6. <head>
7. <title>Simple Addition</title>
8. </head>
9. <body>
10. <!-- Setting Variables -->
11.    <cfset num1 = "20">
12.    <cfset num2 = "30">
13.    <cfset sum = num1 + num2>
14.    <cfoutput>
15.       num1 is #num1#   <br />
16.       num2 is #num2#   <br />
17.       The sum of the two numbers is #sum# <br />
18.       Maximum of the two numbers is
19.       #Max(num1, num2)#
20.    </cfoutput><br />
21. </body>
22. </html>
```

How the Code Works

1. Line 10 shows how a **comment** is written in a ColdFusion template. The syntax is below

   ```
   < ! --- This is a comment --->
   ```

2. Lines 11, 12, and 13 use the `<cfset>` tag to create variables called num1, num2, and sum and assign values to them. Line 12 uses the + operator to add num1 and num2 and assign this value to the variable sum.

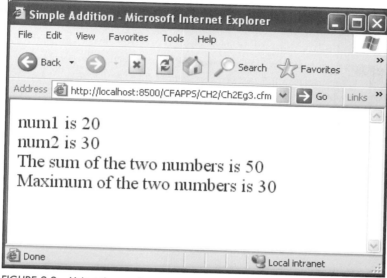

FIGURE 2.3   Using the `<cfset>` and `<cfoutput>` tags

3. Line 14 uses the `<cfoutput>` tag. This tag envelopes the values of variables num1, num2, and sum to be displayed on the browser. Notice that to display the value of a variable, the variable name must be enclosed within # signs.

4. Line 19 uses the built-in function `Max()` to find the maximum of the two numbers. The `Max()` function takes two numeric values as arguments and returns the larger of the two. The `Max()` function is nested within # signs and the arguments to the function are given within parentheses.

Using Pound (#) Signs in ColdFusion   Pound signs serve a special function in ColdFusion. Typically, pound signs are used to surround variables or functions. When ColdFusion encounters the pound signs, it verifies whether the text within the pound signs is a variable or a function. If so, it replaces the value of the variable or function and makes the value available for output or further manipulation. For example, when ColdFusion encounters the line `<cfoutput> #num1# </cfoutput>`, it replaces the value for the variable num1 and displays it on the browser.

Rules of Thumb for Using Pound Signs

1. Use pound signs to display values of variables using the `<cfoutput>` tag.

2. Use pound signs as delimiters to separate variables and functions from plain text.

3. Do not surround complex expressions such as $1 + 2$ by pound signs. It is not necessary to use pound signs when using the `<cfset>` tag to assign the value of one variable to another. For example:

   a. Version 1. `<cfset sum = num1 + num2>`

   b. Version 2. `<cfset sum = #num1# + #num2#>`

   Both versions are accepted by ColdFusion; however, version 2 is inefficient as processing by ColdFusion gets slower.

4. When using functions, surround the function name with pound signs; do not use pound signs around the argument for the function. For example:

   a. Version 1. `<cfset Textlen = "#Len(TheText)#">`

   b. Version 2. `<cfset Textlen = "#Len(#TheText#)#">`

   Version 1 is correct syntactically, whereas version 2 results in an error.

Using " " (Double Quotes) in ColdFusion

Surround all **literal** values within double quotes. A literal value is one that does not need to be evaluated by the ColdFusion server. It can include a string, numeric values, special characters, or a combination of all these. To be consistent, you can use this practice in all your assignment statements that deal with literal values.

Examples of Valid Assignment Statements

```
<cfset Num1 = "20">
<cfset City = "Pensacola">
<cfset NumItems = "45">
```

Example of Using Double Quotes When Dealing with Expressions in ColdFusion

```
<cfset Salary = "1100">
<cfset NewSalary = Salary + "200">
<cfoutput> #NewSalary# </cfoutput>
```

Example of Using " " as Part of a String

```
<cfset Message = ""This is a Quote"">
```

Points to Note from the Example Using Double Quotes

1. In the first assignment statement, the value 1100 is in " " because it is being treated as a literal. Since ColdFusion is a typeless language, it will convert the value to the proper data type when needed on the fly. So at this stage, the value 1100 is treated as a literal value.

2. In the second assignment statement, Salary is not enclosed in " " because it is a variable and it needs to be evaluated. Salary here is

not a literal so it must not be enclosed in " ". Doing so would make ColdFusion throw an error, because then it would take Salary to be a literal. The data type of "Salary" is a string and it will not allow ColdFusion to convert it to a numeric value. 200 is the new value that must be added to Salary; we treat it as a literal value and ColdFusion will convert it to the appropriate data type (numeric data type) when it needs to be evaluated.

3. The third statement is a <cfoutput> statement, and the variable whose value is to be displayed must be enclosed within # signs.

Escape Characters in ColdFusion

Occasionally you need to include either a pound sign, a double quote, or a single quote as part of the string that you want to output. We have already seen that these characters serve a special purpose in ColdFusion, so to include them as part of the string apart from their special purpose, ColdFusion provides an escape method. For example, when a pound sign must be used as part of a string as in #35, use two pound signs instead of one. The string should now look like this: "##35". This is also the case for single or double quotes. The code in Example 2.4 and the output in Figure 2.4 illustrate this concept. Type the code in Example 2.4 and save it as Ch2Eg4.cfm.

Example 2.4

```
1. <?xml version = "1.0"?>
2. <!DOCTYPE html PUBLIC
3. "-//W3C//DTD XHTML 1.0 Transitional//EN"
4. "http://www.w3.org/TR/xhtml1/DTD/xhtml1-transitional.dtd">
5. <html xmlns = "http://www.w3.org/1999/xhtm">
6. <head>
7. <title> CFISDEFINED CFIF </title>
8. </head>
9. <body>
10. <img src="Koalgif.gif" width="224" height="176"
       border="0" alt="">
11. <font size = "16">
12.   <cfset QuoteDouble = """"This is a cute Koala bear"""">
13.   <cfset QuotePound = "It costs 235##">
14.   <cfset QuoteSingle = '''Wow! That is a lot'''>
15.     <cfoutput>
```

16.   #QuoteDouble#

17.   #QuotePound#

18.   #QuoteSingle#

19.   </cfoutput>

20. </body>

21. </html>

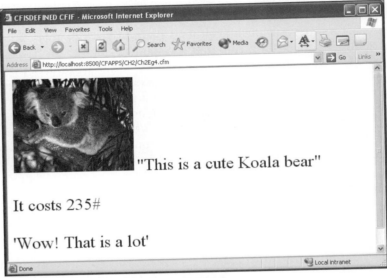

FIGURE 2.4   Escape Characters in ColdFusion

How the Code Works

1. Line 10 uses an HTML tag to insert an image.

2. Lines 12, 13, and 14 use the <cfset> tag to set values for variables QuoteDouble, QuotePound, and QuoteSingle.

3. Line 15 uses the <cfoutput> tag. This tag envelopes the values of the variables QuoteDouble, QuotePound, and QuoteSingle to be displayed on the browser.

Requesting an Undefined Variable

It is important that you declare a variable before requesting it in your Cold-Fusion page. ColdFusion will return an error message if an undefined variable has been requested. The code in Example 2.5 and the output shown in Figure 2.5 are a modification of the code given in Example 2.3 to illustrate this point. A little later in this chapter, you will see how you can prevent this error by using a special type of tag called <cfparam>. Type the code in Example 2.5 without the code in line 18. Save the file and then open the file in your browser. Your code should run fine, without any error messages. Now edit your code by adding the code given in line 18 and save it as Ch2Eg5.cfm. Before opening the file in your browser, see the Important note below and follow its instructions. Your screen should now look like Figure 2.5.

Example 2.5

```
1.  <?xml version = "1.0"?>
2.  <!DOCTYPE html PUBLIC
3.  "-//W3C//DTD XHTML 1.0 Transitional//EN"
4.  "http://www.w3.org/TR/xhtml1/DTD/xhtml1-transitional.dtd">
5.  <html xmlns = "http://www.w3.org/1999/xhtm">
6.  <head>
7.  <title>Undefined Variable Request</title>
8.  </head>
9.  <body>
10. <font color = "green">
11.   <cfset num1 = "20">
12.     <cfoutput> Num1 is #num1#</cfoutput> <br /> <br />
13.   <cfset num2 = "30">
14.     <cfoutput> Num2 is #num2# </cfoutput> <br /> <br />
15.   <cfset sum = num1 +  num2>
16.     <cfoutput> The sum of the two numbers is #sum#
17.     </cfoutput> <br /> <br />
18.     <cfoutput> Num3 is #num3# </cfoutput> <br /> <br />
19. </body>
20. </html>
```

IMPORTANT

To get this code to run correctly, first type the code excluding line 18 and save the file. Open the file in your browser. Now, go back and edit the file to include line 18, save the file again, and open it in your browser. Now your screen should look like Figure 2.5.

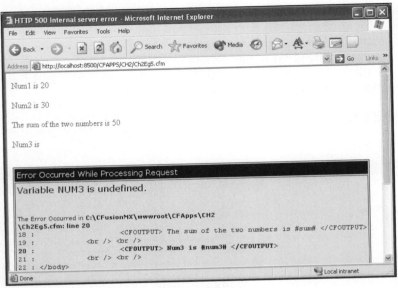

FIGURE 2.5   Requesting an Undefined Variable

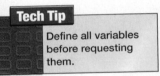

How the Code Works

Example 2.5 is very similar to Example 2.3, except that in line 18 the program attempts to display the value of #num3#, which was not defined earlier in the program. When ColdFusion encounters this line, it throws an exception and prints out an error message as seen in Figure 2.5.

Tech Tip

Define all variables before requesting them.

Operators and Operations

An operation is an action that can transform the contents of a variable. Operations that can be performed depend on the data type of the variable. The tables on page 41 give a list of **operators** and operations that can be performed on the specific data types.

Expressions

An **expression** is a combination of words and symbols that represent a value. For example, in the statement below,

```
<cfset AVERAGE = TOTAL / 15 >
```

the entire statement is an assignment statement. The two variables here are AVERAGE and TOTAL, and the = sign is the assignment operator. The right-hand side of the statement (TOTAL / 15) is the expression. An expression can

Mathematical and String Operators Supported by ColdFusion

Operator	Operation Performed
+	Addition
−	Subtraction
*	Multiplication
/	Integer division
\	Real number division
Mod	Modulo
^	Exponent
&	Concatenation of two strings

Logical Operators Supported by ColdFusion

Operator	Operation Performed
AND	Logical AND
OR	Logical OR
NOT	Logical NOT
EQV	Logical equivalence
IMP	Logical implication
XOR	Exclusive OR

Comparison Operators Supported by ColdFusion

Operator	Operation
IS, EQUAL, EQ	Equality
IS NOT, NEQ, NOT EQUAL	Inequality
LT, LESS THAN	Less than
GT, GREATER THAN	Greater than
GTE, GREATER THAN OR EQUAL TO	Greater than or equal to
LTE, LESS THAN OR EQUAL TO	Less than or equal to
CONTAINS	Has
DOES NOT CONTAIN	Does not have

include a literal value (such as a string or a number), another variable, math operations, string concatenations, and functions.

Creating an Expression Using String Concatenation

Example 2.6 shows how two string variables can be concatenated and the new value created is assigned to a third variable. We also embellish the code by adding a color attribute to the font displayed by HTML on the browser. Type the code in Example 2.6 and save it as `Ch2Eg6.cfm`. The output should be similar to Figure 2.6.

Example 2.6

```
 1. <?xml version = "1.0"?>
 2. <!DOCTYPE html PUBLIC
 3. "-//W3C//DTD XHTML 1.0 Transitional//EN"
 4. "http://www.w3.org/TR/xhtml1/DTD/xhtml1-transitional.dtd">
 5. <html xmlns = "http://www.w3.org/1999/xhtm">
 6. <head>
 7. <title>String Concatenation</title>
 8. </head>
 9. <body>
10.    <cfset auto1 = "Benz"> <font size = "14">
11.      <cfoutput> My first choice is a #auto1#
12.      </cfoutput> <br />
13.    <cfset auto2 = "BMW">
14.      <cfoutput> My second choice is a #auto2#
15.      </cfoutput> <br />
16.    <cfset auto3 = auto1 & " and a " & auto2> <br />
17. <font color = "Red">
18.      <cfoutput> But, My dream is to own a #auto3#
19.      </cfoutput>
20. </font size> </font color>
21. </body>
22. </html>
```

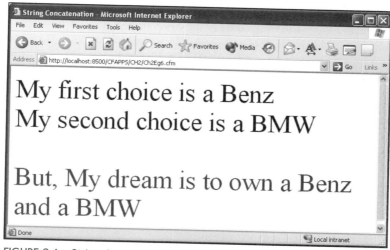

FIGURE 2.6   String Concatenation

How the Code Works

1. Lines 10 and 13 assign values of Benz and BMW to the string variables auto1 and auto2.

2. Line 16 concatenates the two variables created and assigns them to a third variable, auto3. Notice that we included words "and a" in quotes in this line between the two variables to make the sentence sound right. A word or words included in " " are called *literals*. If you did not want to include the literal in this line, you could have just said:

```
<cfset auto3 = auto1 & auto2>
```

The corresponding line in the output would then read:

```
But, My dream is to own a BenzBMW.
```

3. Line 17 uses an HTML color attribute for the color element.

4. Line 18 uses the <cfoutput> tag to display the value of the third variable on the browser.

Using Functions to Test the Value of Input

Since ColdFusion is a typeless language, it also means that the programmer has to be extra careful when performing operations on the data stored in the variables. ColdFusion does provide certain built-in functions that can identify the data type of a particular variable. Some of these functions include IsNumeric, IsBoolean, IsBinary, IsSimplevalue, IsQuery, and many more. Chapter 7 discusses how some of these functions can be used. These functions can be very helpful when trying to debug a large piece of code, where a particular value of a variable may not be exactly the type that a programmer intended the variable to have. The programmer can use such functions to know what data type was assigned to the variable by ColdFusion and then rewrite the code if a wrong data type was being given to the variable. Similarly, ColdFusion also has built-in functions such as ToString and ToBinary that can convert variable values to the data type specified by the functions. Given below is an example of how one such function, the IsNumeric function, works.

The IsNumeric function takes a single value as an argument and evaluates the argument. The function returns a value YES, equivalent to true, if the value of the argument evaluates to a number, or NO, equivalent to FALSE, if the value is not a number. Example 2.7 and the output in Figure 2.7 illustrate how the IsNumeric function works. Type the code in Example 2.7 and save it as Ch2Eg7.cfm and open it in your browser.

Example 2.7

```
1.  <?xml version = "1.0"?>
2.  <!DOCTYPE html PUBLIC
3.  "-//W3C//DTD XHTML 1.0 Transitional//EN"
4.  "http://www.w3.org/TR/xhtml1/DTD/xhtml1-transitional.dtd">
5.  <html xmlns = "http://www.w3.org/1999/xhtm">
6.  <head>
7.  <title>Is Numeric</title>
8.  </head>
9.  <body>
10. <font size = "6">
11.   <cfset A = "10">
12.   <cfset B = "Tom">
13.   <cfset ResultA = IsNumeric(A)>
14.     <cfoutput> Running the IsNumeric Function on
15.       value #A# returns #ResultA#
16.     </cfoutput> <br />
17.   <cfset ResultB = IsNumeric(B)>
18.     <cfoutput> Running the IsNumeric Function on
19.       value #B# returns #ResultB#
```

20.   `</cfoutput> <br />`

21. `</font>`

22. `</body>`

23. `</html>`

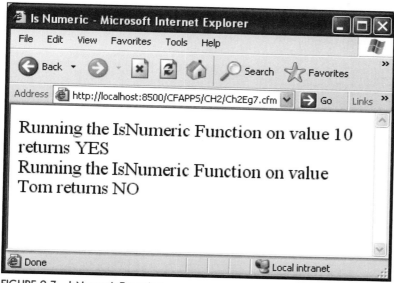

FIGURE 2.7   IsNumericFunction

How the Code Works

1. Lines 11 and 12 use `<cfset>` to set the values for variables A and B.

2. Line 13 assigns the result of function `IsNumeric` on its argument A to ResultA.

3. Line 14 uses the `<cfoutput>` tag to print the value of ResultA, which is a "Yes" because the value of A is a numeric data type.

4. Lines 17, 18, and 19 repeat the steps of lines 13 and 14, but on the argument B. This time the value of ResultB is No, because the value of B is not a numeric data type.

`<cfparam>` Tag

The second method to create variables is to use the `<cfparam>` tag. It is different from the `<cfset>` in two ways:

1. The `<cfparam>` creates a variable only if the variable was not created earlier by the `<cfset>` tag.

2. It also allows the programmer to set a default value to the variable if nothing else was supplied to it by some function or user input.

Example 2.8 shows how the $<$cfparam$>$ tag works. Figure 2.8 is the output of this code. Type the code in Example 2.8 and save it as Ch2Eg8.cfm and open it in your browser.

Example 2.8

```
1. <?xml version = "1.0"?>
2. <!DOCTYPE html PUBLIC
3. "-//W3C//DTD XHTML 1.0 Transitional//EN"
4. "http://www.w3.org/TR/xhtml1/DTD/xhtml1-transitional.dtd">
5. <html xmlns = "http://www.w3.org/1999/xhtm">
6. <head>
7. <title>CFPARAM Tag</title>
8. </head>
9. <body>
10.    <cfset num1 = "20">
11.    <cfparam Name = "num1" Default = "50">
12.    <cfparam Name = "num2" Default = "50">
13. <font color = "blue"> <font size = "8">
14.      <cfoutput> The value of num1 is #num1#
15.      </cfoutput> <br />
16.        because CFSET already created num1 and assigned
17.        a value of 20 to it. <br />
18.        So the CFPARAM did not create num1 and assign
19.        the default value to it. <br /> <br /></font>
            </font>
20. <font color = "magenta"> <font size = "8">
21.      <cfoutput> The value of num2 is #num2#
22.      </cfoutput> <br />
23.        because CFSET did not create num2, CFPARAM
24.        created it and used the default value for that
            variable.
```

25. `</body>`

26. `</html>`

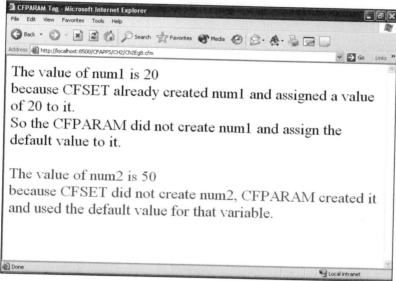

FIGURE 2.8 `<cfparam>` Tag

How the Code Works

1. Line 10 creates num1 with the `<cfset>` tag.

2. Lines 11 and 12 create num1 and num2 with `<cfparam>` tags.

3. Line 14 uses `<cfoutput>` for printing the value of num1. Notice that the value printed is 20, not the default value of 50 created by the `<cfparam>` tag. This is so because `<cfset>` already created the variable called num1 and assigned a value to it; hence, the `<cfparam>` did nothing in this case. As stated earlier, `<cfparam>` only creates a variable if it was not created earlier by the `<cfset>` tag.

4. Line 21 uses `<cfoutput>` for printing the value of num2. This time, since the `<cfset>` tag was not used to create the variable num2, `<cfparam>` creates this variable and assigns a value of 50 to it, which is the default value for num2.

Tech Tip

Using `<cfparam>` prevents suspension of the program when the program expects a value for a variable and cannot find it.

The `<cfparam>` tag is especially useful when the program expects an input to be assigned to a variable. If the input is not supplied, there is a danger of the program being terminated. This can be avoided by using the `<cfparam>` tag, which ensures that the variable is created and provides a default value to the program.

Variable Scoping in ColdFusion

In any programming language such as C or Visual Basic, the term **scope** refers to the visibility and accessibility of a variable. In other words, the scope determines where in the program the variable can be accessed. Usually, most programming languages talk about two types of variable scoping: **local** and **global.** A variable is said to have a global scope if it can be accessible anywhere within the code. On the other hand, if a variable is defined with a local scope, then that variable can be accessed only within the module it was defined in. Cold-Fusion has several scopes for variables. Some of the most commonly used scopes are listed in the table below. Each of the items (scope type) in the table may be used as a prefix to the variable name to refer to the scope this variable has. We will briefly discuss Variables scoping in ColdFusion as the last part of this chapter and present an example of using the client scope to set a cookie for the current client.

Scope Type	How Used/Prefix	Where/How Created	Where Available
Variables (local)	Optional, `variables`	On the current page using `<CFSET>` or `<CFPARAM>` tag	On the current page
Form	`form`	Upon submitting the HTML form via a post method	On the action page specified by the form
URL	`url`	In a query string	On the destination page of the URL
Cookies	`cookies`	With `<cfcookie>` tag	For one client, over multiple browser sessions
Client	`client`	With `<CFSET>` or `<CFPARAM>` tag	Over one template execution
Session	`session`	With `<CFSET>` or `<CFPARAM>` tag	Over one template execution

For a more complete listing of scoping types, refer to Macromedia CFML reference.

Using Variables Scoping to Output the Value of a Variable   In all the examples discussed in this chapter, Variables scope was implicitly used. For example, the output for the variable num1 on line 15 in Example 2.3 could be rewritten by using a prefix that specifies the scope of the variable as follows (this is the default scope used by ColdFusion, so it is not necessary to state it specifically):

```
<cfoutput>
  #Variables.num1#
</cfoutput>
```

The `Variables.` here refers to the page scope of the variable num1. The prefix is optional in this case.

Persisting Variables

Sometimes it is necessary to be able to access values of variables across pages and across sessions in a web application. ColdFusion offers different kinds of variable scopes (listed in the table above) that allow programmers to maintain data that persist beyond the scope of the current page. Let us see how some of these scoping techniques might be used in a web application.

Web Application Framework

A **web application** refers to a set of pages that work together. Examples of applications would include simple guest books, shopping carts, airline reservation systems, and so on. A ColdFusion web application is based on the following components:

- Application-level settings.
- Client, Session, Application, and Server scope variables.
- Web server security integration.
- Custom error handling.

Application-Level Settings

Application-level settings help you create, manage, and control variables and other features such as enabling `clientmanagement` and `sessionmanagement` that may be required across the application. The application-level variables are similar to global variables in other programming languages, because once these variables have been created, they are available within all levels of the application. Application-level settings should be defined in a file called `Application.cfm`. The application.cfm file must be saved in the same folder as all other .cfm files for that application. The purpose of an application.cfm file is to

- Set a name for an application.
- Declare application-level variables such as a data source name for accessing databases (discussed in Chapter 5).
- Enable or disable client and session management. This provides access to session, client, and application-level variables.

This is the first file that will be executed when the application starts. The code below gives an example application.cfm file:

```
<cfapplication name = "xyz"
   clientmanagement="yes"
```

```
        sessionmanagement="yes" >
<cfset application.dsn = "mydatabase">
```

Tech Tip

It is a good idea to create a separate folder for each of your web applications and save the corresponding application.cfm file within that folder. This is useful when you have more than one program in your folder that needs the application.cfm file. The choices in this case would be to include the variables and other information for all programs within the same application.cfm file or to have a separate application.cfm file for each of the programs with the required variables, data source information, and so forth for that program.

How the Code Works

1. Type the code above and save it as application.cfm file within a folder called XYZStore.

2. Line one creates the application with the `cfapplication` tag and sets the name of the application as `"XYZ"`.

3. Line two sets the value of `clientmanagement` to `"Yes"` and line three sets the value of `sessionmanagement` to `"Yes"`.

4. Line four is used to create a variable called dsn as an application-level variable so that the value of dsn can be accessed from any page within the application. The dsn here is just a name for a variable, conventionally used to refer to data source name. This is where you can give a reference to the data source that is created in the ColdFusion Administrator. It is important that the data source name in the ColdFusion Administrator be the same as that assigned to the variable application.dsn. In this example, the value `"MyDatabase"` is assigned to application.dsn. You will see how to create a data source in Chapter 5.

It is important to understand the particular meaning of enabling `clientmanagement` and `sessionmanagement` in relation to the application in which they are being used.

Client-Level Scoping

Client-level variables are persistent variables that allow you to keep track of a single user as he or she navigates through different pages in your web application. They also help you store information about the client for a long period of time and can be accessed at any time the client returns to this page. A typical example could be to save the user information as a cookie to help personalize information that could be presented to the user at a later time. Client variables, however, must be enabled in the file application.cfm by the state-

IMPORTANT

Since application-level variables are accessible to all levels and users of the application, sensitive information such as passwords and bank account numbers must not be stored in the application.cfm file.

ment `clientmanagement = "yes"` before being used. Once enabled, client-level variables can be created as shown below.

Syntax to Create a `Client` Variable

```
<cfset Client.favoriteMusic = "Rock">
```

Syntax to Use and Display This Variable in Another Page

```
<cfparam name = "Client.FavoriteMusic" default = "Rock">
<cfoutput>
  Your favorite type of music is #Client.FavoriteMusic#
</cfoutput>
```

Client-level variables can be stored in the web server's registry, in cookies, or in a database.

Setting a Cookie

Cookies are commonly used in web applications for tasks such as identifying customers when they return to visit your web application. Cookies are set on the client's machine as values of string variables by the server that is hosting the application. Cookies cannot be set for users who either choose not to accept cookies or have the cookies option disabled in their browsers. Example 2.9 shows how to set a cookie on a client's machine. The example also shows how ColdFusion deals with the different types of scopes associated with variables. The variable defined here, User_ID, is a cookie-level variable. Cookie-level variables persist beyond the life of the page; that is, the values of these variables can be retrieved even after the current program is terminated. The life spans of the values of these variables are determined by the value set for the cookie in its `expires` attribute. The values are available for access by the user during the lifespan of the cookie. In the example, the value assigned to the cookie-level variable User_ID, "`John Smith`", is available even after the program ends and the browser is shut down. The next time the user calls the page, provided it is within the one day as specified in the `expires` parameter, accessing the variable User_ID yields the value "`John Smith`". Figures 2.9A (first time the code is run) and 2.9B (the next time the code is run, before the cookie expires) are the output of this code. Type the code in Example 2.9 and save it as `Ch2Eg9.cfm` and open it in your browser.

Example 2.9

```
1. <?xml version = "1.0"?>
2. <!DOCTYPE html PUBLIC
3. "-//W3C//DTD XHTML 1.0 Transitional//EN"
4. "http://www.w3.org/TR/xhtml1/DTD/xhtml1-transitional.dtd">
5. <html xmlns = "http://www.w3.org/1999/xhtm">
```

6. `<head>`

7. `<title>Cookie Example</title>`

8. `</head>`

9. `<body bgcolor = cyan>`

10. `<H3>Cookie Example</H3>`

11.   `<cfif ISDefined("Cookie.User_ID")>`

12.   `<cfoutput> Welcome back #Cookie.User_ID#`

13.   `</cfoutput>`

14.   `<cfelse>`

15.   `Welcome to our site. Enjoy your visit!`

16.   `</cfif>`

17.   `<cfcookie name="User_ID" value = "John Smith"`

18.   `expires ="1">`

19. `</body>`

20. `</html>`

FIGURE 2.9A   SETTING A COOKIE

How the Code Works

1. Lines 17 and 18 set the cookie for this example by specifying the name of the cookie variable as User_ID and setting `value` = "John Smith" and `expires` = "1". We deliberately set the value to be for

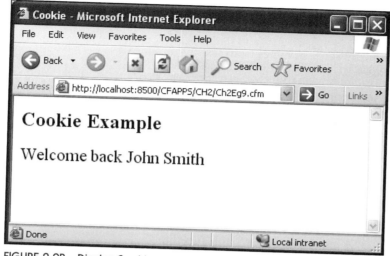

FIGURE 2.9B Display Cookie

one day so that you can experiment with the program after a day and check to see that you do not get the value of the cookie, but just get the original Welcome message as set in line 15.

2. Line 11 uses another ColdFusion built-in function, `IsDefined`, which checks to see if its argument was given a value in the program. The `IsDefined` function returns true if its argument evaluates to true, else it returns false.

3. Line 11 also uses a `cfif` function, which again executes a set of code statements if its argument, which is the result of `IsDefined(Cookie.User_ID)`, returns true. In this case, the first time the code is run, the cookie is not set, so the Welcome message from line 15 is displayed on the browser. Now, if the user hits the **Refresh** button on his or her browser, the cookie will be set so the `cfif` condition evaluates to true and the code in line 12, which is a Welcome back message with the value for the cookie.User_ID, is displayed on the browser.

Session-Level Variable Scoping

Session variables are used to keep track of all variables that are needed for a single session (from the time the user logs in until the time the user logs off from a website). A typical example would be to have an application keep track of all variables in an e-commerce shopping cart. Again, the session variables must be enabled in the application.cfm file, by the statement

```
sessionmanagement = "Yes"
```

Once enabled, the syntax to create a session variable is

```
<cfset session.NoOflaptops = 0>
<cfset session.NoOflaptops = #getLapTopStock.ProductQty#>
```

The syntax to retrieve values from session variables is

```
<cfoutput> Number of laptops in stock #session.
  NoOflaptops# </cfoutput>
```

The point here is that the value of the variable session. NoOflaptops is available as long as the session is on, and can be accessed from any page in your web application. In this example, the session variable is being used to record the quantity in stock for laptops from the database. In Chapter 5, you will see how information can be retrieved from the database using queries.

Application-Level Scoping

Application variables are again available to all pages within an application; that is, an application with the same application name. Application and session variables are written to memory and these variables are accessible to any user or client accessing the application. Therefore, this is a convenient place to store information about the application that the application needs irrespective of the client who is using it. The application name is set in the Application.cfm file. The syntax for creating an application name is <cfapplication name = "shopcart" >. Application variables, however, must be enabled from the ColdFusion Administrator as described in Chapter 1. Application variables expire either on the timeout values set in the Application.cfm file or when you restart the ColdFusion server.

Locking Shared-Scope (Session- and Application-Level) Variables

ColdFusion is a **multithreaded** application, meaning that multiple users can access a single application at any given point in time. This means that several users can access the application-level variables stored in memory, make modifications to these variables, and write them back to memory. Subsequent requests to these memory variables could experience problems and cause memory corruptions that, in turn, could crash the ColdFusion server. ColdFusion provides the <cflock> tag to avoid such problems. The two main types of locks that the <cflock> tag offers are

1. exclusive: Memory locations of a variable are accessed by single threads for the purpose of setting the value of that variable.

2. readonly: This ensures that the variable does not get an exclusive lock from another user until all read-only locks for that variable expire.

Syntax of the <cflock> tag is as follows:

```
<CFLOCK scope = "scope" type ="type" timeout ="seconds">
```

Example 2.10 is a consolidated example for using <CFLOCK> and session variables.

Example 2.10: Create the application.cfm File for This Application

```
1. <cfapplication name="john"
2. clientmanagement="yes"
3. sessionmanagement="Yes"
4. sessiontimeout = "#createtimespan(0,0,0,30)#">
```

Example 2.10A: Example Code for Setting a Session Variable

```
1.  <?xml version = "1.0"?>
2.  <!DOCTYPE html PUBLIC
3.  "-//W3C//DTD XHTML 1.0 Transitional//EN"
4.  "http://www.w3.org/TR/xhtml1/DTD/xhtml1-transitional.dtd">
5.  <html xmlns = "http://www.w3.org/1999/xhtm">
6.  <body>
7.      We are setting the color of a session variable
8.      <cflock scope="session" type="exclusive"
9.          timeout="#createtimespan(0,0,0,30)#">
10.     <cfset session.color = "green" >
11.     </cflock>
12. </body>
13. </html>
```

Example 2.10B: Example Code for Retrieving a Session Variable

```
1.  <?xml version = "1.0"?>
2.  <!DOCTYPE html PUBLIC
3.  "-//W3C//DTD XHTML 1.0 Transitional//EN"
4.  "http://www.w3.org/TR/xhtml1/DTD/xhtml1-transitional.dtd">
5.  <html xmlns = "http://www.w3.org/1999/xhtm">
```

6. `<body>`

7.   `This is the value of the session variable set in the previous page`

8.   `<cfoutput> Session.Color is #session.color#`

9.   `</cfoutput>`

10. `</body>`

11. `</html>`

The example code for the cflock has three files in it: 2.10, 2.10A, and 2.10B. Create a new folder called **cflock** within the CFApps/CH2 folder. Type Example 2.10 and save it in the cflock folder as `application.cfm`. Then type the code for Example 2.10A and save it as `Ch2Eg10A.cfm` in the cflock folder. Next, type the code for Example 2.10B and save it as `Ch2Eg10B.cfm` in the cflock folder.

Now open your browser and load Ch2Eg10A.cfm on it. Remember to include the path to the cflock folder in your URL. The output is shown in Figure 2.10A. Next, load Ch2Eg10B.cfm onto the browser. Make sure you load Ch2Eg10B.cfm immediately after Ch2Eg10A.cfm. Your screen should be similar to Figure 2.10B.

Now wait for 30 seconds and then refresh the browser on which you have Ch2Eg10B.cfm open. You should get an error on the screen as shown in Figure 2.10C.

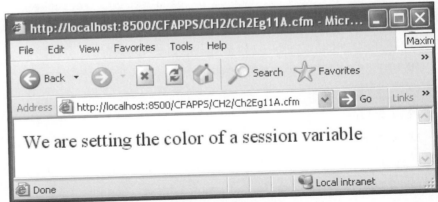

FIGURE 2.10A   Setting the Value for a Session Variable

How the Code Works
Example 2.10 (application.cfm)

1. This file creates the application.cfm file for this application. The `sessionmanagement` and `clientmanagement` attributes are set to "Yes".

FIGURE 2.10B   Display Value of the Session Variable

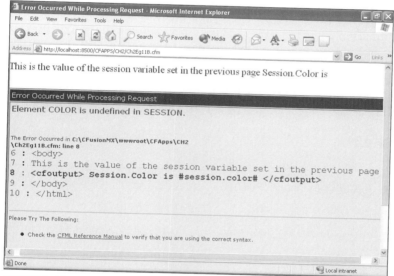

FIGURE 2.10C   Error Message after the Lock Expires

2. Line 4 is where a session `timeout` is set to 30 seconds using the function `createtimespan`. This function is a built-in function. It takes four arguments (days, hours, minutes, and seconds). The purpose of this timeout is to ensure that the session variables created in the individual pages in an application persist for the duration of the time set in the application.cfm file and perish thereafter.

Example 2.10A

1. This file creates the variable session.color and envelopes it within a `<cflock>` tag.

2. Lines 8 and 9 use the $<$cflock$>$ tag with the attributes of scope set to session, type set to exclusive, and timeout set to 30 seconds with the createtimespan function. The timeout here refers to the time period for locking the variable. This means that the session variable is locked on an exclusive type for a period of 30 seconds and loses the lock after that time period.

Example 2.10B   This file just retrieves the value of the session variable session.color in line 8.

Notice that we add the prefix session to color (session.color) to get the value of the session variable.

URL Variables

Another very commonly used method of passing variable values across pages within a ColdFusion application is via the **URL scope.** As stated in the table earlier, these variables are passed through a query string and are available on the destination page. Let us look at a simple example that shows how you can send a value of a variable called firstname through a URL variable using a form. At this stage don't worry about how a form and an action page work. You will learn about these concepts in Chapter 4. Type the code segments given in Examples 2.11A and 2.11B and save them as Ch2Eg11A.cfm and Ch2Eg11B.cfm.

Example 2.11A

```
1. <?xml version = "1.0"?>
2. <!DOCTYPE html PUBLIC
3. "-//W3C//DTD XHTML 1.0 Transitional//EN"
4. "http://www.w3.org/TR/xhtml1/DTD/xhtml1-transitional.dtd">
5. <html xmlns = "http://www.w3.org/1999/xhtm">
6. <head>
7. <title>URL variable Example</title>
8. </head>
9. <body>
10.    <cfset fname = "John">
11.       <a href = "Ch2Eg11B.cfm?FirstName=
             <cfoutput>#fname#</cfoutput>">
12.          Hi! Click to see how a URL variable works</a>
13. </body>
14. </html>
```

Example 2.11B

```
1.  <?xml version = "1.0"?>
2.  <!DOCTYPE html PUBLIC
3.  "-//W3C//DTD XHTML 1.0 Transitional//EN"
4.  "http://www.w3.org/TR/xhtml1/DTD/xhtml1-transitional.dtd">
5.  <html xmlns = "http://www.w3.org/1999/xhtm">
6.  <head>
7.  <title>URL variable response</title>
8.  </head>
9.  <body>
10.   <cfoutput> Welcome #URL.FirstName# </cfoutput>
11. </body>
12. </html>
```

The output of the code segments is shown in Figures 2.11A and 2.11B.

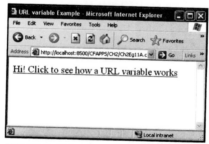

FIGURE 2.11A   Source Page to Provide a Link to a URL

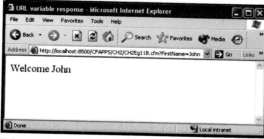

FIGURE 2.11B   The Destination Page

How the Code Works
Example 2.11A

1. Line 10 uses the `<cfset>` tag to create the variable fname and assign a value of "John" to it.

2. Line 11 creates the URL variable called firstname and uses the value of fname as its value. Notice the way a URL variable is created in line 11. Since this value is available only on the destination page, the destination page must be specified first. It must then be terminated by a question mark, followed by the URL variable name and its value. This is precisely what was done in line 11, where the destination page was given as `Ch2Eg11B.cfm` followed by a ?. Then the URL variable FirstName was created and its value was set to the value of the variable fname.

3. When the user clicks on the hyperlink text, he or she is redirected to the destination page.

Example 2.11B   Line 10 retrieves the value of the URL variable and displays it on the browser. Notice again that the variable FirstName was prefixed with the URL scope. If you just tried to output `#firstname#` without the `URL.`, ColdFusion would give you an error message that the variable was not defined.

Variable Scope and Performance

Though most variable types listed in the table do not need to be prefixed by the **scope identifier,** it improves the efficiency of program performance if the variable name is prefixed with the scope identifier. In the absence of the scope identifier prefix, ColdFusion evaluates and checks the scopes in the following order to find the variable:

1. Arguments
2. Variables
3. CGI
4. URL
5. Form
6. Cookie
7. Client

To access variables in other scopes, the variable name must be prefixed by the scope identifier.

Summary

ColdFusion is used to create dynamic web pages unlike pure HTML, which can only create static pages. ColdFusion can be mixed with XHTML elements to build impressive and interesting websites.

Variables are names for memory locations in a computer to store and access data. ColdFusion is a type-less language and so the data types for variables do not need to be declared while assigning values to variables.

ColdFusion uses different types of tags such as <cfset> and <cfoutput> to accomplish specific tasks. ColdFusion functions allow the programmer to perform different operations on expressions and format the output in an impressive manner.

ColdFusion has several types of variables with different scoping rules. Prefixing variables with the scope name improves the performance speed of the program.

Key Terms

application level
application variable
cflock
client level
ColdFusion function
comment
cookie
dynamic web page

expressions
global scope
literal
local scope
multithreaded
operators
scope
scope identifier

session variable
static web page
typeless
URL scope
variables
web application

Review Questions

1. State which of the following are invalid variable names: 1set, Zip Code, $Amount, name.
2. What is wrong with the following output statement, if the value of num1 is to be displayed?

   ```
   <cfoutput> num1 </cfoutput>
   ```
3. What is the purpose of using the <cfparam> tag?
4. What happens when you try to access a variable that was not defined in the template?
5. What is a literal? How do you write an assignment statement that assigns a value of 89 to a variable called score1?
6. When must you not use " " for expressions in ColdFusion?
7. What is the purpose of using pound signs in ColdFusion? Write a statement that displays the value of the variable Score1.
8. What is the default type of scoping rule used by ColdFusion?
9. How can you specify the scope of a variable in ColdFusion?
10. Is it necessary to use the scope prefix for a variable in ColdFusion? What is the downside of not using a scope prefix for a variable in ColdFusion?
11. What is the scope of application- and session-level variables?
12. What is the purpose of using the <cflock> tag?

State if the following statements are true or false.

1. All variables must be enclosed within pound signs irrespective of where they are being used.
2. Variable names must only contain alphabets and numbers.
3. ColdFusion is a strongly typed language.
4. The <cfparam> tag can be used to prevent runtime errors caused by requesting an undefined variable.
5. When assigning one variable of a numeric data type to another variable of a numeric data type, the variables being used must be enclosed within " " (double quotes).
6. ColdFusion requires that all variables be prefixed by their scope.
7. Application-level variables are written to memory locations.
8. Application-level variables cannot be used to store client-specific information.

1. Write a program that calculates the sum of salaries of five employees and displays their average. Use your own figures for the salaries.
2. Write a program that sets the height and width of a rectangle and calculates the area and perimeter of the rectangle. Use the table format with three columns and two rows to display the calculated values. In the first row, give column headings for Height/Width, Area, and Perimeter; in the second row display the dimensions used; and display the calculated results.

   Hint: HTML code to create a table with one row and two columns:

```
<table>
<tr>
<td width = "150" bgcolor = #33ccff> <cfoutput> <Font size = "5">
  <b> Decimal format </b> </cfoutput></td>
<td width = "150" bgcolor = #33ccff> <cfoutput> <Font size = "8">
  #DecimalFormat(40)# </cfoutput></td></tr>
</table>
```

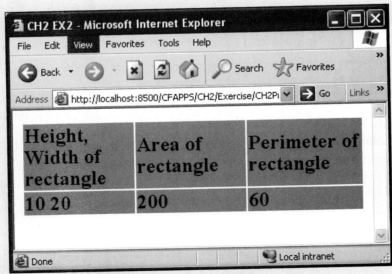

FIGURE 2.12   Table Display

3. Write a program that displays the price for a hat as $40 and then displays a tax rate of 7%. Now, calculate the tax on the price of the hat, then display a total price including the tax in currency format. For the time being, hard-code the currency symbol; you will learn about format options in Chapter 7. Use proper labels when displaying the information to the user.

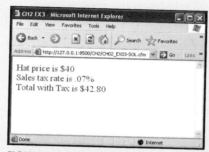

FIGURE 2.13   Display Total

4. Write a program that displays the FullName of an individual by concatenating two variables called FirstName and LastName and assigning values to them. Now modify the program so that it also displays a middle name, but use the `<cfparam>` tag to set the value for a middle initial.

FIGURE 2.14   Name Display

5. Correct the errors in the following code, save it, and run it in your browser.

```
<?xml version = "1.0"?>
<!DOCTYPE html PUBLIC
"-//W3C//DTD XHTML 1.0 Transitional//EN"
"http://www.w3.org/TR/xhtml1/DTD/xhtml1-transitional.dtd">
<html xmlns = "http://www.w3.org/1999/xhtm">
<head>
   <title>Simple Addition</title>
</head>
<body>
   <cfset emp1sal = "3000">
   <cfset emp2sal = "2000">
   <cfset emp3sal = "1500">
```

```
            <cfoutput> Employee 1 is #emp1sal# </cfoutput> <br />
            <cfoutput> Employee 2 is #emp2sal# </cfoutput> <br />
            <cfoutput> Employee 3 is #emp3sal# </cfoutput><br />
            <cfoutput> Total salaries is #total# </cfoutput><br />
    </body>
    </html>
```

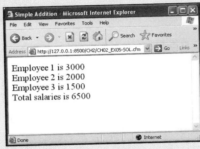

FIGURE 2.15   Debugged Code

Write a simple application.cfm file for the shopping cart application. Enable `sessionmanagement` and `clientmanagement`. Save the file in a folder called `Shoppingcart`.

CHAPTER 3

ColdFusion Control Structures (CFML Flow)

CHAPTER OBJECTIVES:

1. List and understand the three common types of control structures.

2. Understand syntax and use conditional statements to make and execute decisions in the programming environment.

3. Use loops as a tool to iterate through a set of statements to make code more efficient and concise.

This chapter examines the control structures used in ColdFusion. We discuss conditional statements and looping structures used to optimize processing of our ColdFusion templates. Conditional statements use test values to either stop code processing at a certain value or make a decision for the next set of statements to be executed. Looping structures are used to iterate through a set of program statements. Through the process of iteration, looping statements condense the code and also offer solutions to sticky problems.

Control Structures

Control structures allow programmers to control the flow of data within a program. There are three main types of control structures available in any programming language:

- Sequential structures—Statements execute in the order they have been written.
- Selection structures—A statement or a set of statements executes based on a condition being satisfied or not satisfied.
- Iterative structures—A set of statements is repeated for a certain number of times.

All the examples discussed in Chapter 2 are examples of sequential structures. Each line in the code is executed in order, one after the other, so there need not be a special discussion on this form of control structure here.

Selection Structures or Conditional Statements

Conditional statements provide a method to check if a particular condition is satisfied or not and return the result of true or false accordingly. The different types of conditional structures are

1. If . . . Then

2. If . . . Then
      Else

3. If . . . Then . . .
         ElseIf   Then
         ElseIf   Then
         . . .
      Else

4. Switch Case

Flowchart of If . . . Then Control Structure

The flowchart in Figure 3.1 shows the single If . . . Then control structure (it is the same when a <cfif> tag is used). The diamond symbol is used to indicate that a decision must be made at this juncture. In order for the code to make a decision, it needs an input, which is provided in the form of a **test condition.** The flowchart shows that there are two data flow lines (arrows) coming out of the test condition, one going to the right, showing what happens when the condition evaluates to true, and one coming down, indicating what needs to be done if the condition evaluates to false. The rectangular box is used to depict the action to be performed if the condition evaluates to true.

Flowchart of If . . . Then . . . Else Control Structure

The flowchart in Figure 3.2 uses the same symbols as the earlier one. The only difference here is that, in addition to specifying the action to be taken by the program when the condition evaluates to true, the figure also shows the action to be taken when the condition evaluates to false.

IMPORTANT

The syntax and flowcharts given in this chapter are independent of any programming language and, therefore, are applicable to ColdFusion too.

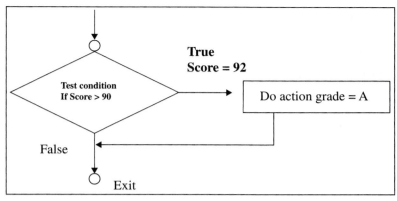

FIGURE 3.1   Flowchart of If . . . Then Control Structure

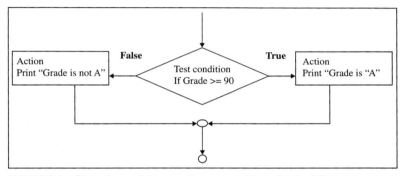

FIGURE 3.2   Flowchart of If . . . Then . . . Else Control Structure

Example 3.1 and the output given in Figure 3.3 show how conditional processing is implemented in ColdFusion. ColdFusion handles the conditional statements with the <cfif> and <cfelse> tags. The <cfif> tag checks to see if a certain condition evaluates to true or false. Type the code in Example 3.1 and save it as Ch3Eg1.cfm. Figure 3.3 shows the output of this code.

Example 3.1

```
1. <!DOCTYPE HTML PUBLIC "-//W3C//DTD HTML 4.0
     Transitional//EN">

2. <?xml version = "1.0"?>

3. <!DOCTYPE html PUBLIC

4. "-//W3C//DTD XHTML 1.0 Transitional//EN"

5. "http://www.w3.org/TR/xhtml1/DTD/xhtml1-transitional.
     dtd">
```

```
6.  <html xmlns = "http://www.w3.org/1999/xhtm">
7.  <head>
8.    <title>CFIF</title>
9.  </head>
10. <body>
11.   <cfset score = "80">
12.   <cfif score is "90">
13.      <font Size = "12"> Grade is A</font>
14.   <cfelse>
15.      <font Size = "12"> Grade is not A</font>
16.   </cfif>
17. </body>
18. </html>
```

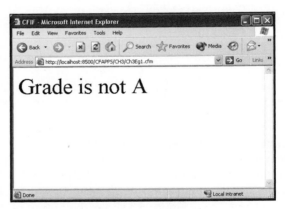

FIGURE 3.3   `<cfIf> . . . <cfelse>`

How the Code Works

1. Line 11 uses the `<cfset>` tag to declare a variable called score and set its value to 80.

2. Line 12 uses the `<cfif>` tag to test the value of score and specifies the condition to be satisfied. In this case, the condition is score is "90".

3. Line 13 executes if the condition in line 12 is satisfied by the value of score.

4. If the condition set for score is not satisfied, then the program shifts to line 14, which uses the `<cfelse>` tag to let the program execute the other action.

The `<cfif>` tag can be used for a number of practical purposes. An interesting application of the `<cfif>` tag is a situation where you ask the user to type in a password and use the `<cfif>` tag to verify if the password is correct. Of course, in the real world, the value for the form variable pwd would not be hard-coded in the program. The value would be checked in a database. If the value typed in by the user matches with the value in the database, the user will be granted permission to enter the site. Example 3.2A illustrates this by using a form to get the user input for the password and brings up an action page, Example 3.2B, to check if the password entered is correct. A detailed explanation on how the form and action pages work will be presented in Chapter 4. Type the code in Examples 3.2A and 3.2B and save them as Ch3Eg2A.cfm and Ch3eg2B.cfm. Figures 3.4A and 3.4B show the output of this code, where Figure 3.4A is the form page and Figure 3.4B is the action page.

Example 3.2A

```
1. <?xml version = "1.0"?>
2. <!DOCTYPE html PUBLIC
3. "-//W3C//DTD XHTML 1.0 Transitional//EN"
4. "http://www.w3.org/TR/xhtml1/DTD/xhtml1-transitional.dtd">
5. <html xmlns = "http://www.w3.org/1999/xhtm">
6. <head>
7.    <title> CFIF Form </title>
8.    <body>
9.    <form action = "Ch3Eg2B.cfm" method = "post">
10.       <input type = "Text" Name = "pwd" >
11.       <input type = "submit" value = "submit">
12.    </form>
13.    </body>
14. </html>
```

Example 3.2B

```
1. <?xml version = "1.0"?>
2. <!DOCTYPE html PUBLIC
3. "-//W3C//DTD XHTML 1.0 Transitional//EN"
```

```
4.   "http://www.w3.org/TR/xhtml1/DTD/xhtml1-transitional.dtd">
5.   <html xmlns = "http://www.w3.org/1999/xhtm">
6.   <head>
7.      <title> CFIF Action </title>
8.      <body>
9.      <cfparam name = "form.pwd" Default = "">
10.     <cfoutput> #form.pwd# </cfoutput>
11.        <cfif #form.pwd# IS "Hello">
12.          Welcome
13.        <cfelse>
14.          Sorry
15.        </cfif>
16.     </body>
17.  </html>
```

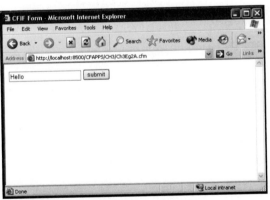

FIGURE 3.4A   Form to Get Password

How the Code Works
Example 3.2A

1. Line 9 specifies the page that must be opened when the user submits this page to the server (by clicking on the **submit** button).

2. Line 10 creates a text box with the name `pwd`.

3. Line 11 creates the **submit** button, with a value set to `"submit"`.

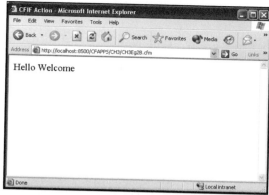

FIGURE 3.4B   Action Page to Check Password Submitted

Example 3.2 B

1. Line 9 uses the <cfparam> tag to create a variable called form.pwd, with a default value of an empty string.

2. Line 10 displays the value of the variable form.pwd. Notice the prefix of form to refer to form-level scope of the variable in question. This example shows how the form-level scope is used to retrieve the value of the variable pwd that was created in Example 3.2A.

3. Line 11 uses the <cfif> tag to check if the value of form.pwd is "Hello".

4. Line 12 is the program statement that must be executed if the condition in line 11 evaluates to true, which is to display a Welcome message.

5. Lines 13 and 14 cover the <cfelse> part of the <cfif> tag. If the value evaluates to false, a message saying "Sorry" will be displayed to the user.

Testing Multiple Conditions

ColdFusion uses the <cfif>, <cfelseif>, and <cfelse> tags to allow checking for more than one alternative and make decisions based on the outcome of the alternative being considered. The flowchart for this scenario is given in Figure 3.5.

Figure 3.5 shows that the If . . . ElseIf . . . Else control structure allows the program to evaluate more than one condition for a single variable and perform an action appropriate for the condition being tested.

The code segment in Example 3.3 and the output given in Figure 3.6 show how ColdFusion handles multiple-condition scenarios. The variable that is

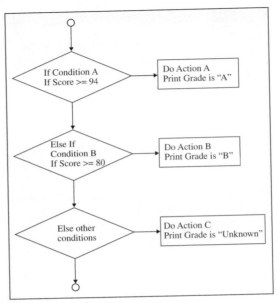

FIGURE 3.5 Flowchart for
`If . . . ElseIf . . . Else` **Control Structure**

being checked for its different possible values is score. Type the code in Example 3.3 and save it as `Ch3Eg3.cfm`. Figure 3.6 shows the output of this code.

Example 3.3

```
1. <?xml version = "1.0"?>
2. <!DOCTYPE html PUBLIC
3. "-//W3C//DTD XHTML 1.0 Transitional//EN"
4. "http://www.w3.org/TR/xhtml1/DTD/xhtml1-transitional.dtd">
5. <html xmlns = "http://www.w3.org/1999/xhtm">
6. <head>
7. <title> CFIF CFELSEIF </title></head>
8. <body>
9. <font Size = "6">
10. <cfset score = "70">
11.    <cfif score greater than "90">
12.       Grade is A
```

```
13.    <cfelseif score greater Than "80">
14.       Grade is B
15.    <cfelse>
16.       Grade is Unknown
17.    </cfif>
18. </font>
19. </body>
20. </html>
```

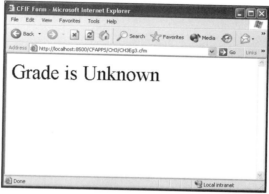

FIGURE 3.6   Multiple Conditions

How the Code Works

1. Line 10 sets the value of score to 70.

2. Line 11 checks if the value of score is greater than 90; if so, the program prints the statement Grade is A.

3. Line 13 checks for a value greater than 80 by the <cfelseif> tag. If the condition turns out to be true, the program prints the appropriate grade.

4. Line 15 uses the <cfelse> tag, which is the fallback that Cold-Fusion provides. This is used to assign a final value to the variable if all previous conditions turn out to be false.

Testing for a Compound Conditional Statement

The same <cfif> tag can evaluate an expression that has more than one condition along with Boolean operators. The code segment in Example 3.4 illustrates how ColdFusion evaluates a compound conditional expression.

IMPORTANT

It is important to use the <cfelse> tag after all the <cfelseif> tags have been completed. If the <cfelse> tag is not used, ColdFusion does not generate any output from the program.

This example is a simple calculator that determines an applicant's creditworthiness based on the applicant's debt-to-income ratio. Type the code in Example 3.4 and save it as ch3Eg4.cfm and open it in your browser. The output is shown in Figure 3.7.

Example 3.4

```
1.  <?xml version = "1.0"?>
2.  <!DOCTYPE html PUBLIC
3.  "-//W3C//DTD XHTML 1.0 Transitional//EN"
4.  "http://www.w3.org/TR/xhtml1/DTD/xhtml1-transitional.dtd">
5.  <html xmlns = "http://www.w3.org/1999/xhtm">
6.  <head></head>
7.  <title> Compound Condition Debt to Income ratio </title>
8.  <body>
9.    <cfset Income = "60000">
10.   <cfset Debt = "15000">
11.   <cfset Assets = "15000">
12.   <cfset Ratio = (Debt/Income) >
13.   <cfset RatioPercent = Ratio * 100>
14.   <cfif Ratio LT 0.30>
15.     <cfoutput> Your debt to Income Ratio is good, Your
16.       debt is #RatioPercent# % of your income<br />
17.       Congratulations! You are approved for the loan.
18.     </cfoutput>
19.   </cfif>
20.   <cfif Ratio GT 0.30 AND Assets GT Income * 0.30 >
21.     <cfoutput> Your debt to income ratio is
```

```
22.          falling short, Your debt is #RatioPercent# % of your
23.          Income<br />
24.          but you have assets worth #Assets#, you are
25.          approved for the loan.</cfoutput>
26.    </cfif>
27.    <cfif Ratio GT 0.30 AND Assets LTE Income * 0.15>
28.          Sorry we cannot qualify you at this time.
29.    </cfif>
30. </body>
31. </html>
```

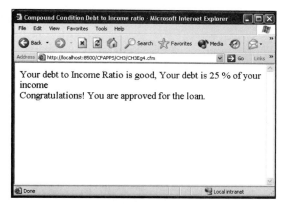

FIGURE 3.7   Compound Condition Debt to
Income Ratio Analysis

How the Code Works

1. Lines 9–12 create the variables Income, Debt, Assets, Ratio, and RatioPercent and assign values to them.

2. Line 14 uses a `<cfif>` to test if the value of Ratio is less than 30 percent.

3. If the result of the `<cfif>` in line 14 turns out to be true, then code in lines 15–17 are executed.

4. Lines 18 and 19 close the `<cfoutput>` and `<cfif>` tags.

5. Line 20 tests for the second case. This is a compound expression. The code checks for two conditions here:
   a. If the debt ratio is greater than 30 percent and
   b. If assets are greater than 30 percent of the income.

If both these conditions are true, then the code in lines 21 to 25 get executed.

6. Line 27 similarly tests for the next compound condition, which is if the debt ratio is greater than 30 percent and assets are less than 30 percent of the income. Here again, if both these conditions evaluate to true, then code in line 28 executes.

Try running the code with different values for Income, Debt, and Assets to see how the results of your code change.

<cfswitch> **and** <cfcase> **Tags**

The <**cfswitch**> and <**cfcase**> tags provide a more elegant way to deal with situations involving testing multiple values for a single variable. The flowchart for a Switch Case control structure is given in Figure 3.8.

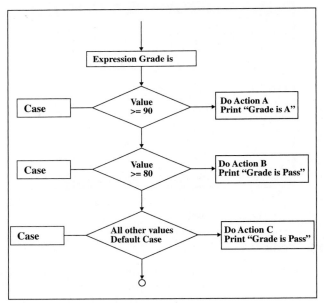

FIGURE 3.8　Flowchart of Switch Case

As shown in Figure 3.8, the Switch Case statement has the following elements:

1. The control structure uses an expression whose values are going to be tested against a set of values provided for in the program.

2. For each value, a set of action statements is also laid out in the code, so when a match occurs, the corresponding action statement or statements are executed by the program.

3. The last value to be tested is usually set up as a default case to accommodate any other value not specifically stated in the code and it has its own set of action statements to be executed. This scenario ensures that the program will not terminate if an uncovered value appears at run time; it is a good safeguard to use in programming.

The code in Example 3.5 is the same example discussed in the <cfelseif> section of Example 3.3 rewritten using the <cfswitch> and <cfcase> tags. Type the code in Example 3.5, save it as Ch3Eg5.cfm, and open it in your browser.

Example 3.5

```
1. <cfset score = "70">
2. <cfswitch Expression = "#score#">
3.    <cfcase value="90">
4.       Grade is A
5.    </cfcase>
6.    <cfcase value="80">
7.       Grade is B
8.    </cfcase>
9.    <cfcase value="70">
10.      Grade is C
11.   </cfcase>
12.   <cfdefaultcase >
13.      Grade is D
14.   </cfdefaultcase>
15. </cfswitch>
```

How the Code Works

1. The <cfswitch> tag takes an expression, which is score in the example code; evaluates the expression; and passes control to the appropriate case that matches the result of the expression.

2. In the example code, the value of the expression is set to 70 in line 1, so the control gets passed to the <cfcase> in lines 9–11, and the string in line 10 is printed as part of this <cfcase>.

> **IMPORTANT**
>
> It is invalid to test more than one value for a variable. The `<cfswitch>` tag allows you to test for only one value for a variable; attempting to test for more than one results in an error.

3. Lines 12–14 provide the `<cfdefaultcase>` case option to account for all other values of the expression not covered by the `<cfcase>` tags in the code.

Predicate Function isDefined

The **isDefined** function is a built-in ColdFusion function that is used to test if a particular variable exists. The function returns true if the variable is found and false if it is not found. This function can come in very handy to collapse code when creating forms and responses, as we shall see in Chapter 4. Example 3.6 shows the code and Figure 3.9 the output to illustrate how the isDefined function can be used in pages to check for a variable's value. Type the code in Example 3.6 and save it as Ch3Eg6.cfm. The output of this code is shown in Figure 3.9.

Example 3.6

```
1.  <?xml version = "1.0"?>
2.  <!DOCTYPE html PUBLIC
3.  "-//W3C//DTD XHTML 1.0 Transitional//EN"
4.  "http://www.w3.org/TR/xhtml1/DTD/xhtml1-transitional.dtd">
5.  <html xmlns = "http://www.w3.org/1999/xhtm">
6.  <head>
7.    <title> CFISDEFINED CFIF </title>
8.  </head>
9.  <body>
10. <Font color = "Blue", size = "6">
11.   <img src="Koalgif.gif" width="224" height="176"
         border="0" alt="">
12.   <cfset pet = "Koala">
13.     <cfif isDefined("pet")>
```

14.   My favorite pet is a `<b>` `<cfoutput>`
          `#pet#</cfoutput></b>`

15.   `<cfelse>`

16.   Your pet is not defined

17.   `</cfif>`

18.   `</body>`

19.   `</html>`

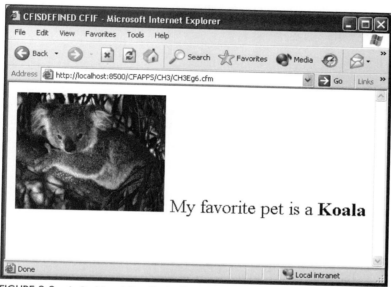

FIGURE 3.9   `isDefined` Predicate Function

How the Code Works

1. Line 11 uses an HTML tag for an image.

2. Line 12 uses the `<cfset>` tag to define the value of the variable pet as "Koala".

3. Line 13 uses the conditional keyword `<cfif>` and the predicate function `isDefined`.

4. The `isDefined` function takes "pet" as its argument and checks whether this variable was defined earlier in the code. It returns a value of true if it was defined earlier; if not, the function returns a value of false.

5. Line 14 gets executed if `isDefined` returns a true value; line 16 is executed if `isDefined` returns a false value.

Loop Structures

Loop structures allow you to repeat a set of program statements. ColdFusion allows you to use loops to repeat the program statements for a specified number of times, and also when you don't know the number of times in advance. The loop structure in ColdFusion is classified as a flow control tag called `<cfloop>`. It allows you to create five types of loops:

- Index loops
- List loops
- Conditional loops
- Query loops
- Collection loops

This book will discuss the first three types of loops in this chapter and query loops in Chapters 5 and 6.

Index Loops

The **index loop** allows you to iterate through (or repeat) a set of program statements for a specified number of times. It is similar to a FOR loop in other programming languages like Pascal or C. The `<cfloop>` tag takes four attributes to implement an index loop: `index`, `from`, `to`, and `step`. A flowchart for an index loop is given in Figure 3.10.

The flowchart shows the following:

1. The loop control or index variable is declared and its `from` (initial) and `to` (final) values are set.

2. After each iteration of the loop, the index is incremented by a specific amount called `step`. This specifies the number of times the loop must run. Now you can see that the index loop lets you decide how many times the loop will run.

For example:

1. If the initial value of `index` is 0, the final value is 10, and the `step` is 1 (the default), then the loop repeats 11 times. If the `step` is 2, the loop runs 6 times, corresponding to the index values 0, 2, 4, 6, 8, and 10.

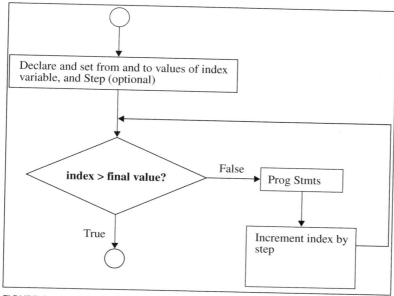

FIGURE 3.10   Flowchart of Index Loop

2. At the beginning of each iteration, the value of index is checked to see if it is greater than the to (final) value. If it is, the loop exits. If it is not, then the set of program statements are executed once more.

3. Next, the loop control variable is incremented by an amount equal to the step value, so the next iteration can start by going back to step 2 above.

The code in Example 3.7 and the output in Figure 3.11 illustrate how an index loop is implemented in ColdFusion. The code uses the index loop to repeat the program statements 10 times, to display the multiplication table for the number 2. Note that, since the value of step is not specified, the loop uses the default value of 1. Type the code in Example 3.7 and save it as Ch3Eg7.cfm.

Example 3.7

```
1. <?xml version = "1.0"?>
2. <!DOCTYPE html PUBLIC
3. "-//W3C//DTD XHTML 1.0 Transitional//EN"
4. "http://www.w3.org/TR/xhtml1/DTD/xhtml1-transitional.dtd">
```

```
5.  <html xmlns = "http://www.w3.org/1999/xhtm">

6.  <head>

7.  <title>Index Loop</title>

8.  </head>

9.  <body>

10.    <cfloop Index = "num"

11.      from = "1"

12.      to = "10">

13.    <cfset product = 2 * num>

14.    <cfoutput>

15.    <font Size = "6">

16.     2 * #num# = #product#

17.    </font>

18.    </cfoutput> <br />

19.    </cfloop>

20.  </body>

21.  </html>
```

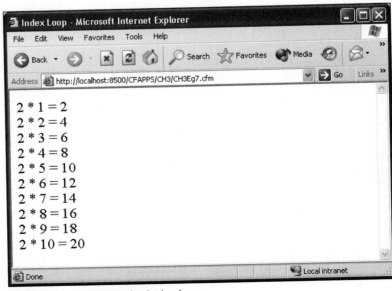

FIGURE 3.11   Example for Index Loop

How the Code Works

1. Line 10 uses the `<cfloop>` tag and specifies num as the index variable.

2. Lines 11 and 12 specify the `from` (initial) and `to` (final) values of the index variable num.

3. Since `step` is not specified, it takes the default value of 1.

4. Lines 13 and 16 are the program statements that must be executed during each iteration.

5. The process is as follows:

   a. When the `<cfloop>` is first started, the value of the index variable num is 1 (value of `from` as specified in line 11).

   b. The current value (1) of the index variable is checked to see if it is greater then the `to` value (10 from line 12). Since it is not, the next lines of code are executed.

   c. The code inside the `<cfloop>` (lines 13 and 16) are executed.

   d. The string value 2 * is printed,

   e. Followed by #num#, which prints the current value of #num# (which is 1),

   f. Followed by printing the symbol =,

   g. Followed lastly by printing the current value of #product#, which is set to be 2 * num.

   h. The process returns to the opening `<cfloop>` tag and increments the value of the index variable to the next number (2).

   i. The iterative process continues until the index variable num completes the last repetition, which is stated in line 12 to be 10. Once the iteration completes executing the program statements for the 10th time, the program terminates.

List Loops

In this type of loop, successive elements of a list of items are used in each iteration of the loop. The **list loop** takes three attributes: index, list, and delimiters (optional).

- index—The name of the variable to hold the value of each element in the list in each iteration.
- list—The name of the list to loop over or a list of elements separated by a delimiter.
- delimiters—(Optional) Separators between list elements.

Example 3.8A shows how the list loop works. Output of the code is shown in Figure 3.12. Type the code in Example 3.8A, save it as Ch3Eg8A.cfm, and open it in your browser.

Example 3.8A

```
1.  <?xml version = "1.0"?>
2.  <!DOCTYPE html PUBLIC
3.  "-//W3C//DTD XHTML 1.0 Transitional//EN"
4.  "http://www.w3.org/TR/xhtml1/DTD/xhtml1-transitional.dtd">
5.  <html xmlns = "http://www.w3.org/1999/xhtm">
6.  <head>
7.  <title>List Loop</title>
8.  </head>
9.  <body>
10. <font color = "Blue", size = "6">
11.    The seasons of the year are: <BR>
12.       <cfloop index = "seasons"
13.          list = "Spring; Summer; Autumn; Winter"
14.          delimiters = ";">
15.       <cfoutput>
16.          #seasons# <BR>
17.       </cfoutput>
18.       </cfloop>
19. </font>
20. </body>
21. </html>
```

How the Code Works

1. Line 12 sets the first attribute index of the <cfloop> to seasons.

2. Line 13 sets the second attribute list of the <cfloop> and inserts values into this list, separated by ; (semicolon).

3. Line 14 sets the delimiter of the list elements to be ; (a semicolon).

4. Line 15 uses the <cfoutput> tag.

5. Line 16 gives the value of the variable seasons (index variable) for each iteration of the loop to be printed by the <cfoutput> tag. As an example, the value of seasons in the first iteration would be

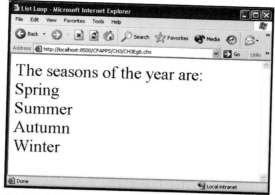

FIGURE 3.12   Example for Index loop

Spring, the value of seasons for the second iteration would be Summer, Autumn for the third, and so on.

A variation of writing the code above is given in Example 3.8B, where you use the <cfset> tag to set a variable to hold the list of items instead of listing them individually in the <cfloop> tag. Type the code in Example 3.8B, save it as Ch3eg8B.cfm, and open it in your browser.

Example 3.8B

```
1.  <?xml version = "1.0"?>
2.  <!DOCTYPE html PUBLIC
3.  "-//W3C//DTD XHTML 1.0 Transitional//EN"
4.  "http://www.w3.org/TR/xhtml1/DTD/xhtml1-transitional.dtd">
5.  <html xmlns = "http://www.w3.org/1999/xhtm">
6.  <head>
7.  <title>List Loop V2</title>
8.  </head>
9.  <body>
10. <font color = "Blue", size = "6">
11. The seasons of the year are: <br />
12.    <cfset seasons = "Spring; Summer; Autumn; Winter">
13.    <cfloop index = "SeasonNumber" list = "#seasons#"
           Delimiters = ";">
```

```
14.        <cfoutput>
15.           #SeasonNumber# <br />
16.        </cfoutput>
17.     </cfloop>
18.  </font>
19.  </body>
20.  </html>
```

How the Code Works

1. The code in Example 3.8B illustrates how the list variable can be set outside of the `<cfloop>` tag with the list values and be referenced by the list variable name within the `<cfloop>` tag.

2. Line 12 uses the `<cfset>` tag to declare the list variable seasons and sets four values as the list items.

3. Line 13 uses the `<cfloop>` tag and the second attribute, `list`, which takes seasons, set in line 12, as its value.

4. The rest of the code is similar to Example 3.8A.

Conditional Loops

The third type of loop that we discuss in this chapter is the **conditional loop.** This loop structure is similar to a `while` loop used in programming languages such as C and Visual Basic. The conditional loop iterates until a condition is no longer true. In other words, it iterates so long as a condition is true and terminates when the condition becomes false. If the condition evaluates to false upon ColdFusion's entry into the loop, the loop does not execute. The flowchart for a conditional loop is given in Figure 3.13.

The flowchart shows the following:

1. The conditional loop needs a condition to be tested.

2. If the condition is satisfied, the action to be performed gets executed.

3. If the condition is not satisfied, the program exits from the loop and the control is returned to the program.

Notice that unlike the index loop, in the conditional loop we do not know beforehand how many times the code will be executed. The code executes as long as the condition remains true and terminates once the condition is not satisfied. Example 3.9 and the output in Figure 3.14 illustrate how the conditional loop works. Type the code in Example 3.9, save it as `Ch3Eg9.cfm`, and open it in your browser.

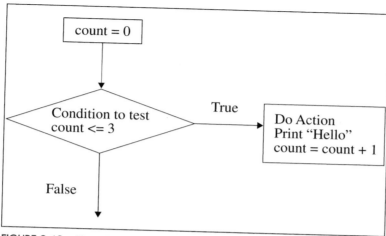

FIGURE 3.13   Flowchart for Conditional Loop

Example 3.9

```
1.  <?xml version = "1.0"?>
2.  <!DOCTYPE html PUBLIC
3.  "-//W3C//DTD XHTML 1.0 Transitional//EN"
4.  "http://www.w3.org/TR/xhtml1/DTD/xhtml1-transitional.dtd">
5.  <html xmlns = "http://www.w3.org/1999/xhtm">
6.  <head>
7.  <title>Conditional Loop</title>
8.  </head>
9.  <body>
10. <font color = "Blue", size = "6">
11.     While counter is Less Than or Equal to 10 the loop
            iterates to print the Counter <br />
12.         <cfset CountVar = 1>
13.            <cfloop condition = "CountVar LTE 10">
14.                Hello, This is number
15.                <cfoutput> #CountVar# </cfoutput> of the loop
                   iteration
16.            <cfset numsquare = CountVar * CountVar>
```

```
17.              The square of the number is
18.              <cfoutput>#numsquare# </cfoutput>
19.   <br />
20.              <cfset CountVar = CountVar + 1>
21.              </cfloop>
22. </font>
23. </body>
24. </html>
```

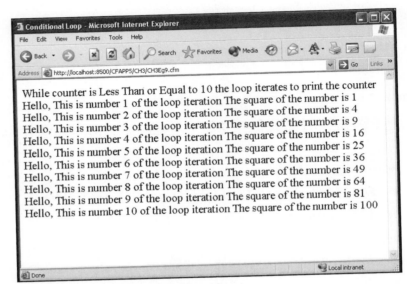

FIGURE 3.14   ColdFusion Conditional Loop

How the Code Works

1. Line 12 sets the conditional variable CountVar equal to 1.

2. Line 13 sets the condition to be tested; in this case, it is that CountVar is less than or equal to (LTE) 10.

3. Line 15 prints the value of CountVar in the first iteration of the loop; this is executed because the value of CountVar is LTE 10.

4. Line 16 sets another variable, numSquare, by multiplying CountVar by CountVar.

5. Line 18 prints the value of numSquare.

> **IMPORTANT**
>
> If the counter variable is not incremented, your loop does not terminate and you encounter the infinite loop, and the program must be manually terminated.

6. Line 20 increments CountVar by 1 and exits the current iteration.

7. Now when ColdFusion enters the loop again, the value of CountVar is 2, still LTE 10, so the steps in lines 15, 16, 18, and 20 execute. This process repeats till the value of CountVar becomes 10; at this point, ColdFusion exits the loop and the program terminates.

Summary

Control structures allow you to control the flow and execution of the code based on a certain value of a variable. In this chapter, we looked at two types of control structures:

• Selection structures/conditional statements.

• Iterative structures/looping structures.

Selection statements test for a certain value of a variable and return a true or a false result.

The two important types of conditional structures are

```
<cfif...>
<cfelseif...>
<cfelseif...>
  ...
  ...
<cfelse...>
</cfif>
```

ColdFusion also allows us to test for compound conditions by using comparison and Boolean operators. Iterative structures/looping structures provide a method to iterate through a set of program statements. In this chapter, we looked at three types of looping structures:

• Index loops

• List loops

• Conditional loops

```
<cfcase>
<cfelse>
<cfif>
<cfloop>
```

```
<cfswitch>
conditional loop
control structures
index loop
```

```
isDefined
list loop
loop structures
test condition
```

1. What is the main purpose of using control structures? Give an example of a situation that uses the `<cfif . . . > <cfelseif . . . > <cfelse> </cfif>` tag.

2. What is the error in the syntax below:

   ```
   <cfif . . . >
   <cfelseif . . . >
   <cfelseif . . . >
   </cfif>
   ```

3. Why and when is the `<cfswitch>` tag better than a multiple `<cfelseif>` scenario?

4. What is the main disadvantage of the `<cfswitch>` tag?

5. What are the three types of loops discussed in this chapter?

6. Name the attributes of index and list loops.

7. Which of the attributes listed in Question 6 is/are optional?

8. What are the conditions under which a `FOR` loop can be used?

9. Which of the three types of loops discussed in this chapter is similar to the `while` loop in other programming languages?

10. Under what circumstances can a `while` loop not execute?

11. What happens if a `<cfelseif . . . >` tag does not end with a `<cfelse>` tag?

State whether the following statements are true or false.

1. Selection structures allow you to iterate through a set of program statements.

2. A `FOR` loop requires a condition to be satisfied before executing the code for the loop.

3. A `WHILE` loop runs as long as the condition to be verified remains true.

4. A `CFSWITCH CASE` statement allows you to check for values for multiple variables.

5. A `FOR` loop is best suited to be used when the number of times to run the loop is known ahead of time.

6. The `index` attribute of the list loop specifies the name of the list to loop over.

7. Incrementing the loop counter variable is essential to ensure that the code does not enter an infinite loop situation.

1. Define two integer variables X and Y. Set the value of X to 5. Write a loop with Y ranging from 1 to 10; print X * Y in each loop. Your output should resemble Figure 3.15.

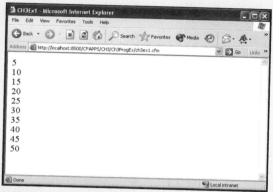

FIGURE 3.15

2. Define two integer variables X and Y. Set the value of X to 5. Write a loop with Y ranging from 1 to 10. In each loop, if Y <= X, print "Sorry!"; if Y > X, print "Great!". Your code should include text to indicate the number of loop iterations and also the value of Y. Your output should resemble Figure 3.16.

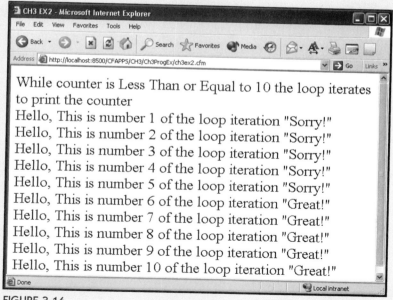

FIGURE 3.16

3. Define two integer variables X and Y. Set the value of X to 6. Write a `while` loop with Y starting from 1. Print the value of Y. Stop when Y >= (GTE) X. Your code should include text to indicate the number of loop iterations. Your output should resemble Figure 3.17.

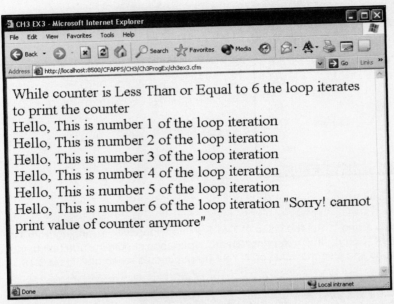

FIGURE 3.17

4. Use a list loop and print out the colors of the rainbow. Your output should match Figure 3.18.

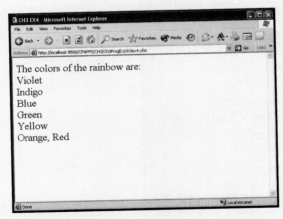

FIGURE 3.18

5. Design a program that uses a `<cfswitch>` and `<cfcase>` structure. Your program must use the ColdFusion built-in function `RandRange()` to generate a random number between the ranges of 1 and 4; assign this value to a variable called score. Your program must now display a separate message depending on the value of this score as generated by the RandRange function.

- If the value is 4, display the message "Grade is A".
- If the value is 3, display the message "Grade is B".
- If the value is 2, display the message "Grade is C".
- If the value is 1, display the message "Grade is D".

Your output should resemble Figure 3.19.

Hints: The `RandRange()` function returns an integer between two specified numbers. The syntax to use the `RandRange()` function is

```
RandRange(number1, number2)
```

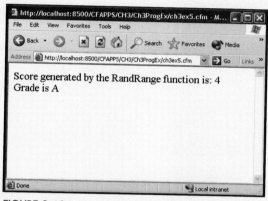

FIGURE 3.19

Open the high-level shopping cart designed in Chapter 1 and provide a detailed description of each page in the shopping cart with the help of a flow diagram. (Hint: For example, take the product listing page of the company and describe what you expect that page to do.)

What Is Visible to the User
1. Show a list of products from the database.
2. Show supplier information from the database.
3. Show the price of the products.
4. Have a button to add an item to the cart.

What Your Code Should Do
1. Extract appropriate information from the database.
2. Display hyperlinks to product details such as price and quantity in stock.
3. Add to cart hyperlinks with URL variables.

Project Building Exercises

CHAPTER 4

Forms

CHAPTER OBJECTIVES

1. Review HTML forms.
2. Create a ColdFusion form and use form elements.
3. Understand ColdFusion error messages.
4. Understand scope of form variables and create a ColdFusion action template to process forms.
5. Process form submissions using different form controls.
6. Prevent errors encountered while processing different form controls.
7. Use server-side validation of form fields using `hidden` form fields.
8. Enhance functionality of your web pages using ColdFusion form tags.
9. Use client-side validation of form fields.
10. Introduce the importance of ColdFusion forms and databases.

Now that you have a fairly good foundation on ColdFusion basics, you can proceed to learn how ColdFusion can be used to create multiple dynamic web pages by passing form variables between pages, thus enhancing the functionality of your web pages.

This chapter explains how Cold Fusion interacts with HTML forms. You will see how the value of a form field gets carried from one web page to another to enable you to produce a set of interactive web pages using different form controls. You will learn about form validation and you will use client-side and server-side validation. You will learn how to interpret the error messages produced by ColdFusion.

Finally, we will look at some special ColdFusion form tags that bring additional functionality to web forms.

Creating ColdFusion Forms

Web forms are used to gather input from the user and submit data to the web server for processing. Web forms are the computer equivalent of forms that we fill out manually, like an application form. At the end of a form, there is a submit button that sends all the data in the form to the server.

HTML Forms Overview

HTML forms are created using the `<form>` tag. The simplest form of this tag is given below:

```
<form method="post" action = "actionFileName">
```

This tag usually takes two parameters or tag attributes. The `action` attribute tells the server the name of the program or template to execute on submitting the form. To submit a form, you need to specify the name of the program or template that will process the form. This program or template will process the form's data and output HTML. The server then sends the output of that program back to the browser.

The `method` attribute specifies how the data are sent to the server. It specifies which HTTP method will be used to submit the form's data and how the data will be sent back to the web browser. Possible values for method are `get` and `post`. The default submission type is `get`. With the `get` method, the form data fields are passed as URL parameters. URL parameters are appended as `name=value` pairs to the URL after a question mark `?`. Each `name=value` pair is separated by an ampersand `&`, as you can see in the following URL: http://localhost/action1.cfm?name=kevin&id=12. This new URL is sent to the web server on form submission. Large amounts of form data passed as URL parameters using `get` may cause a problem since there is a limitation on URL length. Because of this limitation, the form can submit only a limited amount of data to the server using `get`. Using `post`, however, the form can send much more data to the server and URLs do not display form contents. The form data are attached to the end of the `post` request in its own object. In this way, `post` includes the form's data in the body of the form and sends it to the web server.

ColdFusion Forms

You are already aware that ColdFusion uses HTML-like tag syntax. HTML forms can be used within ColdFusion templates to submit data to other Cold-Fusion templates on the web server.

In ColdFusion, the form is submitted to a ColdFusion **template** (having a .cfm extension) for processing. This template is specified using the `action` attribute of the form. When the form is submitted to the server, the client's web browser sends an **HTTP request** to the **web server** via the Internet. The web server decides what to do with the data submitted by the client. It calls the ColdFusion template specified in the `action` attribute of the form. The **ColdFusion Application Server** processes this ColdFusion template. It interacts with database servers, file systems, and mail servers if required. The ColdFusion Application Server substitutes any CFML variables with actual values and dynamically generates an HTML page that is displayed on the client's web browser.

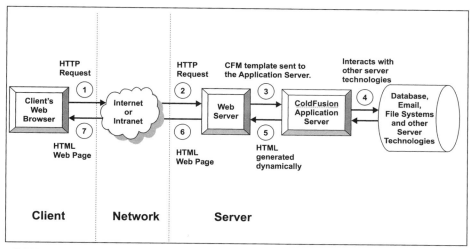

FIGURE 4.1   ColdFusion Template Processing

Figure 4.1 is a diagrammatic representation of this process. Thus, ColdFusion form processing replaces older methods such as CGI form processing that are much more complex to learn and use. The advantage of using ColdFusion for form processing is that it is easy to use and it gives you all the advantages of CGI with simple-to-create forms and **dynamic web pages.**

Form Elements

A form consists of controls such as text boxes, checkboxes, radio buttons, drop-down lists, and other input fields that are submitted through the form to another ColdFusion template that processes this input and generates another page in response. As we go along in this chapter, we will have a look at these field types and see how ColdFusion processes them.

Sometimes form field groups such as radio buttons or checkboxes could have the same name so that they can be submitted as a set of values for one variable. You will read more about this later in this chapter. Text fields may have the same name too, but, then, both sets of values are returned for a single field name, separated by a comma.

A form contains a **submit button** that submits the form to the web server when clicked. The submit button has a `value` attribute that specifies the text to be

Tech Tip

Generally, it is advisable for names of form fields to be unique, so that they can be individually validated and processed.

displayed in the button. The code snippet below creates a submit button with the text "Process" in it:

```
<input type="submit" name="submitbutton" value="Process">
```

The type of the input control is submit, which represents a button that instructs the form to be submitted. The optional name attribute can have any value that specifies the name of the control. If present, this element will be passed to the next page. The value attribute specifies the text label that will be displayed on the submit button. The name attribute is useful when you have two submit buttons in a form and you want to process the form elements differently depending on which one was clicked.

Example 4.2A is a simple form created in the ColdFusion template ex4-2a.cfm. This form just displays a text box form control to accept the user name and submits the form elements to the action template ex4-2b.cfm.

Example 4.2A   Text Boxes (Form) (ex4-2a.cfm)

```
1.  <!DOCTYPE html
2.  PUBLIC "-//W3C//DTD XHTML 1.0 Transitional//EN"
3.  "http://www.w3.org/TR/xhtml1/DTD/xhtml1-transitional.dtd">
4.  <html xmlns="http://www.w3.org/1999/xhtml">
5.  <head>
6.     <title>Welcome to HTML Forms!</title>
7.  </head>
8.  <body>
9.     <h2>Welcome to HTML Forms! </h2>
10.    <b>Enter Your Name:</b><br/>
11.    <form action="ex4-2b.cfm" method="post">
12.       <input type="text" size="30" name="username">
13.       <input type="submit" value="Go!">
14.    </form>
15. </body>
16. </html>
```

Figure 4.2A shows the form in Example 4.2A viewed through the web browser.

FIGURE 4.2A   An HTML Form Saved in a ColdFusion Template

How the Code Works

1. Line 11 uses the `<form>` tag to mark the beginning of an HTML form.

2. The `action` attribute in line 11 tells the server to execute ex4-2b.cfm (the action page) when the form is submitted.

3. The `method` attribute in line 11 has the value `post`. This enables the form with the input variable `username` to be sent to ex4-2b.cfm on the web server.

4. Line 12 uses the HTML `<input>` tag to display a text input field to accept `username`.

5. Line 13 shows the submit button that actually sends the form to the server. The text label displayed on the button (specified by the `value` attribute) is `"Go!"`

ColdFusion Error Pages

When ColdFusion cannot process a request, it generates an error. Cold Fusion errors can help you debug your application. If ColdFusion is not able to find the requested page on the server, it generates a **Missing Template error. Validation errors** occur when a user violates the server-side form field validation rules in a form being submitted. **Exceptions** occur when there is an error and an application's flow is interrupted. An error is generated when ColdFusion finds the template but cannot resolve a variable within the template. You will learn more about error handling throughout this chapter and in Chapter 10.

If you load ex4-2a.cfm and enter your name into the username field and submit the form, you will get a missing template error page like the one shown in Figure 4.2C. This is because ColdFusion cannot find the action template ex4-2b.cfm. We used the action attribute to specify that ColdFusion should run ex4-2b.cfm on submitting the form. This file should be present on the web server, but we have no such file yet.

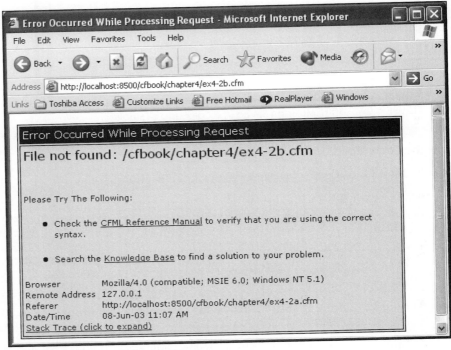

FIGURE 4.2C   Missing Template Error

Form Processing in ColdFusion

In Example 4.2A, we created a form that sent the form variable username that will be displayed in the action template. A form variable's **scope** is the **action page.** In other words, in the action template, you can refer to the elements defined in the form template. All form variables should be prefixed with the word form. when referencing them on the action page since they may conflict with other local variables having the same name. All variables are surrounded with the # (pound symbol). When the form was submitted, the form variable username was passed to the action template ex4-2b.cfm in which it can be accessed as #Form.username#. This variable will be displayed by ColdFusion if it is within the <cfoutput> and </cfoutput> tags. Example 4.2B is the code for the action template that displays the name submitted in the form in Example 4.2A. Save this code in a file called ex4-2b.cfm.

Example 4.2B   Text Box Processing (Action) (ex4-2b.cfm)

1. `<!DOCTYPE html`
2. `PUBLIC "-//W3C//DTD XHTML 1.0 Transitional//EN"`
3. `"http://www.w3.org/TR/xhtml1/DTD/xhtml1-transitional.dtd">`
4. `<html xmlns="http://www.w3.org/1999/xhtml">`
5. `<head>`
6. `   <title>Welcome to HTML Forms!</title>`
7. `</head>`
8. `<body>`
9. `   <h2>Welcome to HTML Forms! </h2>`
10. `   <cfoutput>`
11. `      <h2> Hello #Form.username# </h2>`
12. `   </cfoutput>`
13. `</body>`
14. `</html>`

When you load ex4-2a.cfm and click **Go!** you will see the action page ex4-2b.cfm as shown in Figure 4.2B.

How the Code Works

1. In line 11 the field username is fully qualified with field type (#form.username#) to prevent any name collisions. The pound signs (#) tell ColdFusion to evaluate the variable (form.username) they surround and replace it with its value (the username that is entered in the form).

2. Lines 10 and 12 show the <cfoutput> and </cfoutput> tags that tell ColdFusion to write the text between them to the web browser.

FIGURE 4.2B   ColdFusion Form Processing

Instead of #form.username#, let us say you had typed #form.firstname# in ex4-2b.cfm, where #firstname# is not a valid field in the form. You will receive an error page like Figure 4.2D. This is because ColdFusion cannot evaluate or resolve the value of the variable #form.firstname#. When you correct the form variable name in the action file, this error will disappear.

Processing Input from Radio Buttons

Tech Tip

You would use different names for radio button groups if you have more than one group of radio buttons on one page. Each group would then have a different name.

In the previous section, you saw how text fields are processed using Cold-Fusion. **Radio buttons** are form controls that are used to select one of two or more options (see Figure 4.3A). When you go to a payment processing web page, you are asked to select your credit card. You may be presented with a set of radio buttons to enable you to make your selection. If you want only one value selected, use the same name for each radio button that you want to group. If you want to allow more than one radio button to be selected, you can give each button a separate name, or you could use checkboxes instead.

We will build and expand Example 4.2A through the following sections to create and process different types of form fields. Example 4.3A adds radio buttons to the form to accept a credit card type from the user. Save the example code in a file called ex4-3a.cfm.

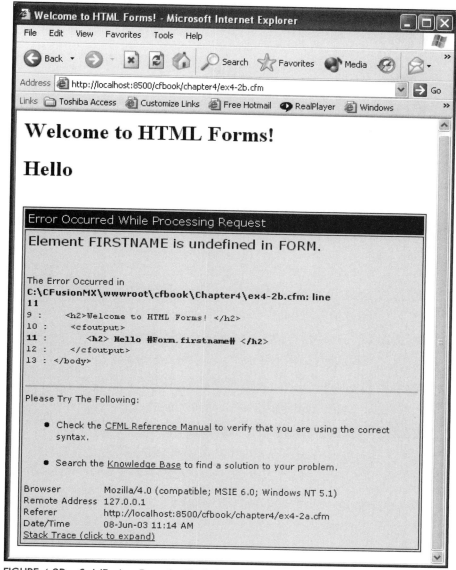

FIGURE 4.2D   ColdFusion Error for Undefined Variable

Example 4.3A   Radio Buttons (Form) (ex4-3a.cfm)

1. `<!DOCTYPE html`

2. `PUBLIC "-//W3C//DTD XHTML 1.0 Transitional//EN"`

3. `"http://www.w3.org/TR/xhtml1/DTD/xhtml1-transitional.dtd">`

```
4. <html xmlns="http://www.w3.org/1999/xhtml">
5. <head>
6.   <title>Welcome to ColdFusion Forms</title>
7. </head>
8. <body>
9.   <br />
10.   <b>Please fill in this form and click Process! </b>
11.   <hr />
12.   <form action="ex4-3b.cfm" method="post">
13.     <p />
14.     Please enter your name:
15.     <input type="text" size="40" name="customerName">
16.     <p />Please select your credit card type: <br />
17.     <input type="radio" name="creditCard"
18.        value="Visa"> VisaCard <br />
19.     <input type="radio" name="creditCard"
20.        value="Discover"> Discover Card <br />
21.     <input type="radio" name="creditCard"
22.        value="Master"> Master Card <br />
23.     <input type="radio" name="creditCard"
24.        value="Amex"> American Express <br /> <p />
25.     <input type="submit" value="Process">
26.   </form>
27. </body>
28. </html>
```

If you load this form in the browser, your window will look like Figure 4.3A.

How the Code Works

1. Let us look at the code used to create the radio buttons (lines 17 to 24). The four radio button fields have the same name attribute CreditCard to tell the browser that they all belong to the same field.

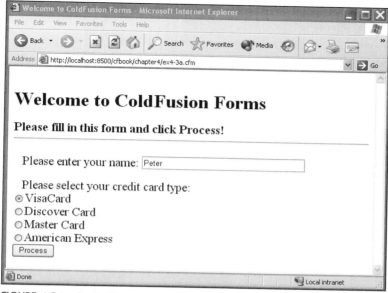

FIGURE 4.3A   Radio Buttons to Select Options

2. In lines 17 to 24, we pre-assign a value to each radio button. The value attribute tells the browser to return the value Amex in the field CreditCard if that radio button is selected.

3. If no radio button is selected, the field CreditCard will not exist on the action page.

Now let us see how to display the variable that was selected using the above radio buttons. Remember that since the same field name was used for each radio button in the form, the user will be allowed to select only one value. The action code is saved in a file called ex4-3b.cfm, which is the template name that we mentioned in the action attribute of the form ex4-3a.cfm in Example 4.3A. Example 4.3B shows how to display the value of the radio button in the action template.

Example 4.3B   Radio Button Processing (Action) (ex4-3b.cfm)

```
1. <!DOCTYPE html
2. PUBLIC "-//W3C//DTD XHTML 1.0 Transitional//EN"
3. "http://www.w3.org/TR/xhtml1/DTD/xhtml1-transitional.dtd">
4. <html xmlns="http://www.w3.org/1999/xhtml">
5. <head>
```

6.   `<title>Welcome to ColdFusion Forms!</title>`

7. `</head>`

8. `<body>`

9.   `<cfoutput>`

10.   `Hello <b>#Form.customerName#</b>,<br /> <br />`

11.   `You have selected your <b>#Form.CreditCard#</b> card!<br />`

12.   `</cfoutput>`

13. `</body>`

14. `</html>`

Now, load and fill the form ex4-3a.cfm. Select a credit card (say, VisaCard) and click on the **Process** button. The action page ex4-3b.cfm will be loaded and you should see your selected credit card in a page like Figure 4.3B.

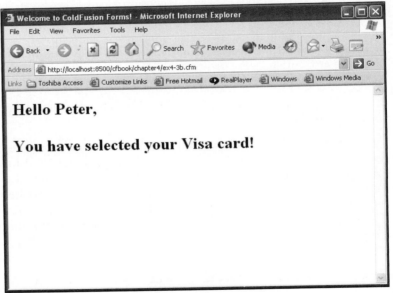

FIGURE 4.3B   Processing Radio Buttons

How the Code Works

1. The value of the form variable #Form.customerName# is displayed in line 10 using the `<cfoutput>` and `</cfoutput>` tags in lines 9 and 12. Note that this variable is fully qualified with the word Form. so that it is not confused with any other variable.

2. In line 11 the `CreditCard` radio button's selected value is displayed. The text `Visa` is displayed because that was the value of the form variable `#Form.CreditCard#` for the radio button.

Preventing Radio Button Processing Errors

If you noticed, when you loaded the form in Example 4.3A, no radio button was preselected. If radio buttons are coded this way, an error will occur if you leave the buttons unselected and submit the form. If no radio button is selected, no field is submitted to the server. To see the error, reload the page and submit the form without selecting any credit card. The action code tries to display the value of the radio button, but the field is not found. In this case, Cold-Fusion generates an error page like Figure 4.3C.

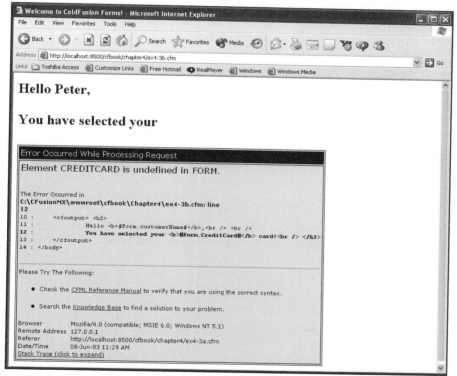

FIGURE 4.3C   Error Page When No Value Is Submitted for Radio Buttons

In the figure, you can see that ColdFusion was able to display "You have selected your". At this point it needs to substitute the variable `#form.CreditCard#` with its value and display it. But it cannot find this variable since we did not select any credit card in the form. This causes it to fail and produce the error.

If you read the error message in Figure 4.3C, ColdFusion clearly tells us in which line it finds the error and why the error occurred.

Preselection of Radio Buttons

The best way to prevent this error from occurring is to preselect a radio button option in the form to ensure that one value always gets submitted for this variable. To do this, just add the word `checked` against one of the buttons as shown below:

```
<input type = "radio" name = "CreditCard"
    value="Amex" checked> American Express
```

Amex now becomes the default value for this form field. Modify line 24 in Exercise 4.3A with the above statement and reload. This time, when you submit the form, you will see that a radio button is preselected. To deselect it, you need to select another radio button. This prevents the user from submitting the form without a radio button option selected. Now, when you submit the form, you will not see the error page any more.

Processing Input from Checkboxes

Checkboxes are used to select options that have two states: on or off. The user clicks on a checkbox to check it and clicks again to uncheck it. Checkboxes are form input elements of `type` `checkbox`. You can precheck a checkbox by using the word `checked` just as you did with radio buttons, as shown below.

```
<input type="checkbox" name="email" value="Yes" checked>
```

If the checkbox is selected, the value specified in the `value` attribute will be submitted. If multiple checkboxes exist with the same name, and more than one checkbox is checked, then ColdFusion will submit a comma-delimited list of values for that variable name, as shown in the following code snippet:

```
<input type="checkbox" name="interests"
    value="jobs">Jobs<br />
<input type="checkbox" name="interests"
    value="entertain">Entertainment<br />
<input type="checkbox" name="interests" value="dining">
    Dining Out<br />
```

If all three of the above checkboxes are checked, the form will submit jobs,entertain,dining to the server in the field `interests`. Let us modify the form in Example 4.3A by adding the above checkbox group before the submit button. We also will add another checkbox to ask the customer whether he or she would like to receive email offers from us. With the above changes, the new code will look like Example 4.4A.

Example 4.4A Checkboxes (Form) (ex4-4a.cfm)

```
1.  <!DOCTYPE html
2.  PUBLIC "-//W3C//DTD XHTML 1.0 Transitional//EN"
3.  "http://www.w3.org/TR/xhtml1/DTD/xhtml1-transitional.dtd">
4.  <html xmlns="http://www.w3.org/1999/xhtml">
5.  <head>
6.    <title>Welcome to ColdFusion Forms</title>
7.  </head>
8.  <body>
9.    <br />
10.   <h2>Welcome to ColdFusion Forms</h2>
11.   <b>Please fill in this form and click Process! </b>
12.   <hr />
13.   <form action="ex4-4b.cfm" method="post">
14.     <p />Please enter your name:
15.     <input type="text" size="40" name="customerName">
16.     <p />Please select your credit card type:<br />
17.     <input type="radio" name="creditCard"
             value="Visa">VisaCard<br />
18.     <input type="radio" name="creditCard"
             value="Discover">
19.       Discover Card<br />
20.     <input type="radio" name="creditCard"
21.         value="Master">Master Card<br />
22.     <input type="radio" name="creditCard" checked
23.         value="Amex">American Express<br />
24.     <p />Would you like to receive email offers?
25.     <input type="checkbox" name="email" value="Yes"
             checked>
26.     <p />
27.     Please select all your interests:<br />
28.     <input type="checkbox" name="interests"
```

```
29.              value="jobs"> Jobs<br />
30.         <input type="checkbox" name="interests"
31.              value="entertainment"> Entertainment<br />
32.         <input type="checkbox" name="interests"
33.              value="dining"> Dining Out<br />
34.     <p /><input type="submit" value="Process">
35.     </form>
36. </body>
37. </html>
```

The output of this code in a browser is shown in Figure 4.4A.

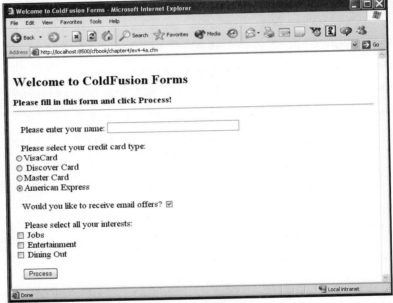

FIGURE 4.4A   Checkboxes to Accept Input

How the Code Works

1. An input form control of `type checkbox` has been created in line 25 to accept input from the user if he or she wants to get email offers. If the checkbox is checked, its value (in this case `Yes`) will be sent to ColdFusion by the browser. If the checkbox is not checked, this element is not sent at all.

2. Lines 28, 30, and 32 show the use of multiple checkboxes with the same name. Selection of multiple interests will submit multiple comma-separated values for the same variable (see Figure 4.4B).

This form is submitted to a template called ex4-4b.cfm shown in Example 4.4B. During this example, you will see problems that can occur with checkboxes similar to those you encountered with radio buttons. We have modified our previous action template by adding code that displays the appropriate text depending on the value of the `email` checkbox variable. We also display the interests selected in the form. Save this changed template as ex4-4b.cfm since the code in ex4-4a.cfm referred to this file in the `action` attribute of the `<form>` tag.

Example 4.4B   Checkbox Processing (Action) (ex4-4b.cfm)

```
1.  <!DOCTYPE html
2.  PUBLIC "-//W3C//DTD XHTML 1.0 Transitional//EN"
3.  "http://www.w3.org/TR/xhtml11/DTD/xhtml11-transitional.dtd">
4.  <html xmlns="http://www.w3.org/1999/xhtml">
5.  <head>
6.    <title>Welcome to ColdFusion Forms</title>
7.  </head>
8.  <body>
9.    <cfoutput>
10.      <h2>Hello #Form.CustomerName#,
11.      <br /> <p />
12.      You have chosen to use your
13.      <b>#Form.CreditCard#</b> card !
14.      <br /><p />
15.      <cfif #Form.email# is "Yes">
16.          You <i>will</i> be added to our mailing list
17.      <cfelse>
18.          You <i>will not</i> be added to our mailing list
19.      </cfif>
20.      <br /><p />
21.          Your interests are: <i>#form.interests#</i><br />
```

22.   `</h2>`

23.   `</cfoutput>`

24. `</body>`

25. `</html>`

In the form, enter a name, select the **American Express** card, and check the checkbox to receive emails. Select two interests and submit the form to see the result in the action template, ex4-4b.cfm. You will see a page like Figure 4.4B.

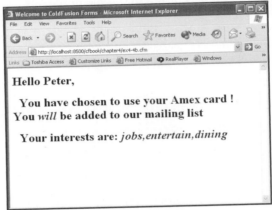

FIGURE 4.4B   Processing Checkboxes

How the Code Works

1. Lines 15 to 19 use conditional code to check the value of the form variable `#form.email#`. Note that the name being referenced is the same that we used in the form for the checkbox `email` element. Here we evaluate the value of the checkbox for email using the `<cfif>` tag.

2. If the checkbox is checked, the value `Yes` is sent to the server in the variable `#form.email#`. We can display an appropriate message to the user, in this case, telling the user that we will add him or her to our mailing list.

3. If the checkbox is not checked, we display that we will not add the user to our mailing list. There's a trick here since no `#form.email#` variable exists if that checkbox is not checked in the form. We'll look at ways to handle this problem shortly.

4. Line 21 displays a comma-delimited list of all the interests checked. If you selected only one, only that one will be displayed, and if you selected more than one, a comma-separated list that you selected will be displayed.

5. If no interests are selected, nothing is sent to the server. This is a problem since no `#form.interests#` variable will exist if none of the checkboxes is checked. The following section explains how we can resolve this problem.

Preventing Checkbox Processing Errors

If you uncheck a checkbox or all checkboxes in a checkbox group, nothing is sent to the server, just as with unselected radio buttons. For the Interests checkboxes, since they are one group, selecting even one will prevent an error, but if all interests are unchecked, no variable called `interests` is sent to the server. This is worse than the situation with radio buttons because even if we precheck the checkboxes in the form, the user can uncheck them anytime, unlike with radio buttons that enforce the selection of at least one option.

When the form is submitted, it tells the server to execute the template specified in the form's `action` attribute. The action template tries to display the checkbox variable by referring to it through the form that was submitted. In Example 4.4B, the action template tries to display the form variables `#form.interests#` and `#form.email#` presuming that these variables exist. If you uncheck the `email` checkbox and submit the form, ColdFusion will generate an error page like Figure 4.4C telling you exactly what the problem is.

There are two common ways to handle this problem, both of which are explained below.

Setting Parameters with Default Values

The best way to handle this problem is to set a default value in the action template by using the `<cfparam>` tag:

```
<cfparam name="form.email" default="">
<cfparam name="form.interests" default="">
```

The `<cfparam>` statements are added to the top of the action template before the variables are accessed in the code. This tag checks if the variable exists. If it does not exist, then it creates the variable and initializes it with the default value. If the variable already exists, that is, if the action template finds the variable, then it does nothing. Add the above lines to the top of your action template in ex4-4b.cfm (Example 4.4B). Now, reload the form ex4-4a. cfm (Example 4.4A). Uncheck all the checkboxes and submit the form. The new `<cfparam>` statements in the action template create the variables `#form.email#` and `#form.interests#` and sets them to empty strings. Now the action template is able to find these variables and ColdFusion continues processing without error. Since the `#form.email#` checkbox variable's value is not `Yes`, the `<cfelse>` part of the code is executed. For `#form.interests#`, since nothing is checked, an empty string is displayed since that is the value set by `<cfparam>`.

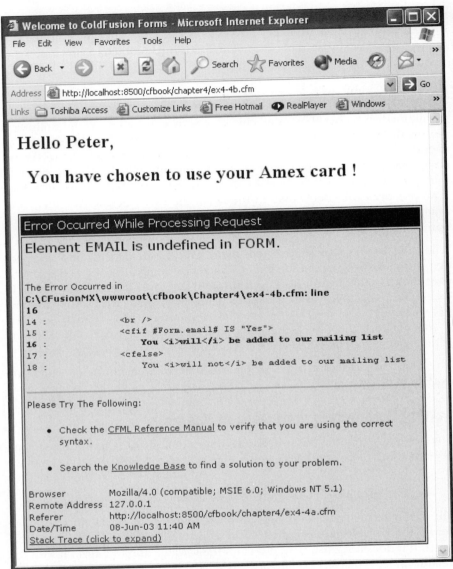

FIGURE 4.4C   Error Page if Checkbox Is Unchecked

You do not always have to assign the value Yes to a checkbox field in the form. In the above example, you could change the Yes value to will or anything else and the default parameter value to will not or any other string as given below:

```
<cfparam name="email" default="will not">
<input type="checkbox" name="email" value="will">
```

That way you can remove the conditional code completely. If the checkbox is checked, the value will is sent to the server. If it is not checked, the default value `will not` (as set by the `<cfparam>` tag) is sent. Now you can change the action template by just displaying the value of the variable as given below:

```
You <cfoutput> #form.email# </cfoutput> be added to our
    mailing list
```

Checking If Form Variables Are Defined before Using Them

It is a good idea to use the ColdFusion built-in function `isDefined()` to check if a variable exists before referencing it. This function is further explained in Chapter 7. The code snippet below checks if the form field `#form.email#` exists before it tries to use it. If ColdFusion does not find this variable defined, then it returns `False`.

In the code below, nothing is displayed if the `#form.email#` is not available. If it is available, then the value of the variable is checked. This prevents the ColdFusion error page from appearing.

```
<cfif IsDefined("form.email")>
<cfif form.email is "Yes">
You <i>will</i> be added to our mailing list
<cfelse>
   You <i>will not</i> be added to our mailing list
</cfif>
</cfif>
```

Processing Input from List Boxes

List boxes or **drop-down list** enable users to select one or more options from a list of available choices (see Figure 4.5). These are used when you don't have much room on the page for a checkbox group. They are normally used for selection from long lists such as countries or states.

Drop-down lists are defined by using the `<select>` tag. Nested inside this tag are `<option>` elements for each of the items in the list. Within the options, you could specifically preselect one of the elements in the list. The `selected` attribute allows you to specify which option is displayed and selected initially by default. If no option is selected, the first option in the list is displayed by default. The code snippet below shows how to create a drop-down list. Its output is shown in Figure 4.5.

```
<b>Please select the subject of your choice: </b><br />
<select name="subject">
  <option name="math">Mathematics</option>
  <option name="science">Science</option>
  <option name="social" selected>Social Studies</option>
  <option name="lang">Language Arts</option>
</select>
```

In Example 4.5, the `Social Studies` option is selected initially.

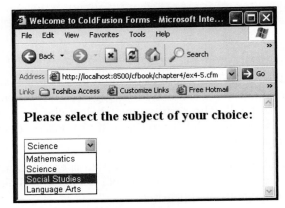

FIGURE 4.5   Drop-Down Lists

Tech Tip

If no value is specified in the `<option>` tag, the text between the `<option>` and `</option>` tags is sent to the action page.

Since no `value` attribute is specified, the display value `Social Studies` will be sent in this field if the option named `social` is chosen. Alternatively, we could have specified the optional `value` attribute as given below:

```
<option name="social" value="sst" selected>Social
    Studies</option>
```

In this case, the value `sst` will be sent to the action page. You can enable **multiple selections** in a list box by specifying `multiple` within the `<select>` tag as shown below:

```
<select name="subject" size=2 multiple>
```

Tech Tip

If a list box allows multiple selections, it could also allow you to deselect all; that is, no elements could be selected.

This will create a **scrolling list box** displaying two list elements and will allow multiple selections. If a list box is created to accept only one single selection, then there will be exactly one value returned to the server. If multiple items are selected, the form variable is set to a comma-separated list of values when submitted. If no item is selected, nothing is sent to the server.

We need to write code to protect against ColdFusion errors when the form field is not found in the action page, as you will see shortly. Example 4.5A adds a `states` selection list box to our previous example.

Example 4.5A   List Box (Form) (ex4-5a.cfm)

```
1. <!DOCTYPE html

2. PUBLIC "-//W3C//DTD XHTML 1.0 Transitional//EN"

3. "http://www.w3.org/TR/xhtml1/DTD/xhtml1-transitional.dtd">

4. <html xmlns="http://www.w3.org/1999/xhtml">
```

```
5.   <head>
6.     <title>Welcome to ColdFusion Forms</title>
7.   </head>
8.   <body>
9.     <br />
10.    <h2>Welcome to ColdFusion Forms</h2>
11.    <b>Please fill in this form and click Process! </b>
12.    <hr />
13.    <form action="ex4-5b.cfm" method="post">
14.      <p /><b>Please enter your name:</b>
15.      <input type="text" size="40" name="customerName">
16.      <p /><b>Please select your credit card
           type:</b><br />
17.      <input type="radio" name="creditCard"
18.        value="Visa">VisaCard<br />
19.      <input type="radio" name="creditCard"
20.        value="Discover">Discover Card <br />
21.      <input type="radio" name="creditCard"
22.        value="Master">Master Card<br />
23.      <input type="radio" name="creditCard" checked
24.        value="Amex">American Express<br />
25.      <p /><b>Would you like to receive email offers? </b>
26.      <input type="checkbox" name="email" value="Yes"> <p />
27.      </b>Please select all your interests:</b><br />
28.      <input type="checkbox" name="interests"
           value="jobs">Jobs<br />
29.      <input type="checkbox" name="interests"
30.        value="entertainment"> Entertainment<br />
31.      <input type="checkbox" name="interests"
32.        value="dining"> Dining Out<br />
33.      <p />
34.      <b>Please select the state of your choice:</b>
35.      <select name="state" size="4">
```

```
36.          <option value="Georgia">Georgia</option>
37.          <option value="Florida">Florida</option>
38.          <option value="California">California</option>
39.          <option value="Alabama">Alabama</option>
40.          <option value="Texas">Texas</option>
41.          <option value="Nevada" >Nevada</option>
42.          <option value="Oregon">Oregon</option>
43.    </select>
44.    <p /><input type="submit" value="Process">
45.  </form>
46. </body>
47. </html>
```

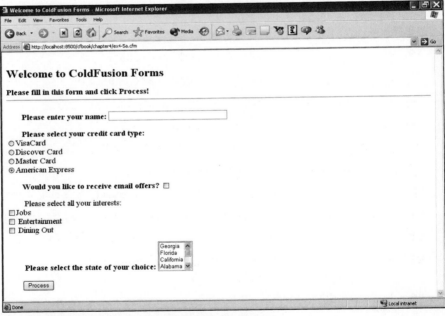

FIGURE 4.5A   Drop-Down Lists in ColdFusion Forms

If you load this code onto the browser, you will see a screen like Figure 4.5A. The states are populated in the drop-down list for states.

How the Code Works

1. Lines 35 to 43 set up the drop-down list with values for seven states.

2. On line 41, the keyword `selected` identifies Nevada as the prese-lected state, which is highlighted and displayed in the drop-down list.

Preventing Drop-Down List Processing Errors

When dealing with drop-down lists, if you enable multiple selections for drop-down lists, you should be aware that it is possible that no element is selected before submitting the form. Since this will cause no value to go to the server, you must always use the `<cfparam>` tag to give a default value to this element in the action template before accessing these variables. Alternatively, you could access these variables only if they are defined by using the built-in `isDe-fined()` function. The option you choose will depend on what you want to do.

The error protection code has been added to the action page using the `<cfparam>` tags as you can see in Example 4.5B. Make the modifications and save as ex4-5b.cfm.

Tech Tip

If you want to access the variables whether they come through the form or not, then `<cfparam>` is a good choice to set a default value for them. If you could ignore the variables if they are not available, then `isDefined()` is a good choice.

Example 4.5B List Box Processing (Action) (ex4-5b.cfm)

```
1.  <!DOCTYPE html
2.  PUBLIC "-//W3C//DTD XHTML 1.0 Transitional//EN"
3.  "http://www.w3.org/TR/xhtml1/DTD/xhtml1-transitional.dtd">
4.  <html xmlns="http://www.w3.org/1999/xhtml">
5.  <cfparam name="form.customername" default="">
6.  <cfparam name="form.email" default="">
7.  <cfparam name="form.interests" default="">
8.  <cfparam name="form.state" default="Nevada">
9.  <head>
10.    <title>Learning ColdFusion Forms</title>
11. </head>
12. <body>
13.    <cfoutput>
14.      <b>Hello #Form.customername#,   <br /> <p />
15.      You have chosen to use your
16.      <b>#Form.CreditCard#</b> card ! <br /><p />
17.      <cfif #Form.email# IS "Yes">
18.        You <i>will</i> be added to our mailing list
19.      <cfelse>
20.        You <i>will not</i> be added to our mailing list
```

```
21.      </cfif>

22.      <br />Your interests are:
             <i>#form.interests#</i><br />

23.          <br />Your preferred location is:
             <i>#form.state#</i><br />

24.      </b>

25.    </cfoutput>

26. </body>

27. </html>
```

To enable multiple selections of `state` in the form in Example 4.5A, you could modify line 35 in the code in Example 4.5A as shown below:

```
<select name=state multiple>
```

This also will enable you to deselect all states and submit the form. Load this modified form and fill it in. Do not select any state (i.e., deselect the selected state Nevada) and click on **Process**. Check to see that you don't get the error page. You will see that the default value for state, Nevada, is still displayed on your resulting page, even though you had a multiple selection drop-down list for state in your form and you had nothing selected before submission. The `<cfparam>` tags protected your code from failing when the undefined variable `#form.state#` was encountered. The resulting page will be as in Figure 4.5B.

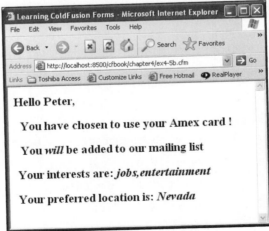

FIGURE 4.5B   Processing Drop-Down Lists

How the Code Works

1. Lines 5 to 8 use <cfparam> to set up parameters with default values. If the form fields are not present, these statements create and initialize these variables. If the form fields exist, these statements do nothing. Please note that sometimes you may want to give a specific default value as in state in line 8, and at other times you may want to give an empty string as in interests in line 7.

2. Line 22 displays the selected interests. If you uncheck all checkboxes, you still don't get any error. The default empty string is displayed because of the <cfparam> tag used for this variable in line 7.

3. Line 23 displays the selected state. If you don't select any state, you don't get any error. The default state, Nevada, is displayed because of the <cfparam> tag used for this variable in line 8. This way you can force a default value even in the case of multiple selection list boxes.

Processing Input from a textarea

A **textarea** allows you to enter multiple lines of free-form text and is created using the <textarea> tag. The field scrolls horizontally and vertically to enable users to enter more text. Typically these are used for comment fields. The size of the textarea field is specified with the row and column attributes as given below:

```
<textarea rows=10 cols=20 name="comment">
Default text goes here
</textarea>
```

Example 4.6A (saved in ex4-6a.cfm) shows how you would accept comments in a form using the <textarea> tag.

Example 4.6A Text Areas (Form) (ex4-6a.cfm)

1. <!DOCTYPE html

2. PUBLIC "-//W3C//DTD XHTML 1.0 Transitional//EN"

3. "http://www.w3.org/TR/xhtml1/DTD/xhtml1-transitional.dtd">

4. <html xmlns="http://www.w3.org/1999/xhtml">

5. <head>

6. <title>Welcome to ColdFusion Forms!</title>

```
 7.  </head>
 8.  <body>
 9.     <h2>Welcome to ColdFusion Forms! </h2>
10.     <b>Please enter your comments here:</b><br />
11.     <form action="ex4-6b.cfm" method="post">
12.       <center>
13.         <textarea rows=5 cols=30 name="comment">
14.         </textarea><br />
15.           <input type="submit" value=" Go! ">
16.       </center>
17.     </form>
18. </body>
19. </html>
```

Figure 4.6A shows how the textarea form field in the above code looks on the browser.

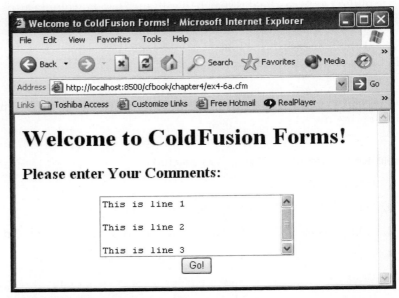

FIGURE 4.6A   Text Areas

How the Code Works

1. Line 13 creates the `textarea` input element.

2. The size of the `textarea` is 10 rows and 40 columns and its `name` is `comment`.

3. Note that the `<textarea>` tag has a closing `</textarea>` tag in line 13, unlike the form `<input>` tags.

The action template (ex4-6b.cfm) in Example 4.6B refers to this variable as `#Form.Comment#` just like any other form variable.

Example 4.6B   Text Areas (Action) (ex4-6b.cfm)

```
1. <!DOCTYPE html
2. PUBLIC "-//W3C//DTD XHTML 1.0 Transitional//EN"
3. "http://www.w3.org/TR/xhtml1/DTD/xhtml1-transitional.dtd">
4. <html xmlns="http://www.w3.org/1999/xhtml">
5. <head>
6.    <title>Learning ColdFusion Forms</title>
7. </head>
8. <body>
9.    <cfoutput>
10.       <br /><b>Your Comments:</b> <br />
11.       <i>#form.comment#</i><br />
12.    </cfoutput>
13. </body>
14. </html>
```

When you enter multiple lines of comments and submit the form, you will see that your comments are displayed in the action page ex4-6b.cfm, but none of your line breaks are preserved! See Figure 4.6B. This is a problem with `textarea` fields and the next section shows how this problem can be resolved.

How the Code Works

1. The comment that you entered in the form is output in line 11 by the action code.

2. If you entered multiple line breaks between lines, you will find that they are ignored and all your text appears as a single paragraph. The next section gives a solution for this problem with processing `textareas`.

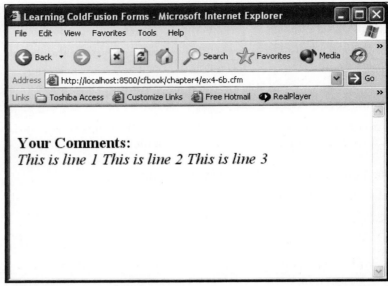

FIGURE 4.6B   Text Area Processing

Formatting and Wrapping a textarea

When you load the form that contains textarea input fields, try entering double line breaks in the textarea input box and then submit it (see Figure 4.6A, for example). When you click on **Go!** your line breaks disappear and your output will be like Figure 4.6B. This is because browsers ignore white-space characters and line-break characters are considered as white-space characters. That is why you lost all paragraph formatting in Example 4.6B. This problem can be resolved using two methods. The first method is by the using the ParagraphFormat() built-in function in ColdFusion. The second method is to use the wrap() built-in function introduced in ColdFusion MX 6.1.

Single line breaks are not replaced because ColdFusion has no way of knowing if the next line is a new paragraph or part of the previous one. First, let us see how to use the ParagraphFormat() function. Replace line 11 in Example 4.6B with the code given below:

```
<i>#ParagraphFormat(form.comment)#</i><br />
```

Now resubmit the form with double line breaks and see the result of the action page. It should be similar to Figure 4.6C, preserving all paragraph breaks.

Now let us see how to use the wrap() built-in function. The syntax of this function is

```
wrap(string, limit [, strip] )
```

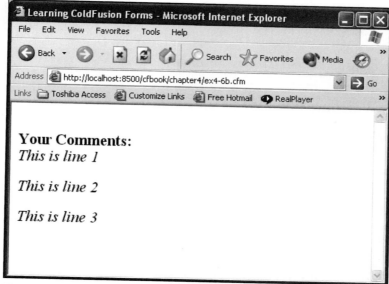

FIGURE 4.6C   Text Area Formatting Using `ParagraphFormat()`

This function takes the string or variable that contains the string, positive integer specifying the number of characters allowed on a line, and a Boolean value specifying whether to remove all existing new line and carriage return characters in the input string before wrapping the text. The default value is `False`. Now try replacing line 11 in Example 4.6B (ex4-6b.cfm) with the code given below and submit the form (ex4-6a.cfm) again to see the output.

```
<pre>#wrap(form.comment, 20, False)#</pre>
```

Figure 4.6D shows a sample form and Figure 4.6E shows how the `wrap()` function wraps the string output within the desired length. Make sure that you have more than 20 characters on one of the lines in your `textarea` field. Your output should show the line having more than 20 characters was split by the `wrap()` function.

Validation of Form Fields

Data validation is an important issue since forms accept data from customers and these data are often inserted into a database or used to modify data in the database. Range checks, required field validation, date validation, and numeric values validation are some checks that can be done before forms are processed to check that data entered through the form are the correct data type or range and to check that required fields are not left empty.

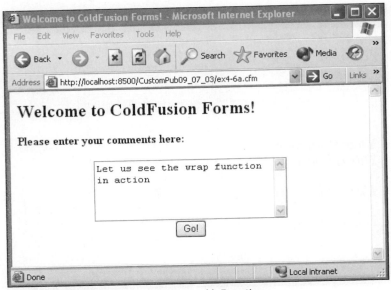

FIGURE 4.6D   Text Area for the `wrap()` Function

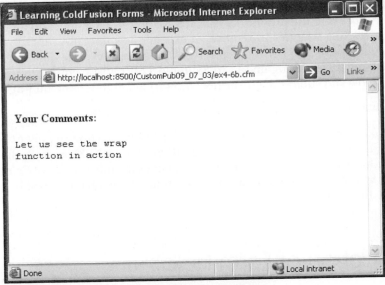

FIGURE 4.6E   `wrap()` Function to Format Text Areas

There are two types of data validation: **client-side validation** and **server-side validation.** Server-side validation takes place on the server once the form is submitted and client-side validation takes place on the client's machine before the form is submitted. While client-side validation is nice to have, not all users allow JavaScript to run on their browsers.

To ensure that data are always validated, we must combine the usage of server-side and client-side validation. Client-side validation will be covered in the next section along with the `<cfform>` tag. In this section, we will study about server-side validation in ColdFusion using `hidden` form fields.

Server-Side Validation in ColdFusion

`Hidden` input elements are very useful when you want to transparently pass along values from template to template. A `hidden` input type has a `name` and a `value`. These field values are carried along with all the other form variables to the action page. They are usually used when you do not require input from the user, but you want a value to be preset for a variable. For example, you could have a form that identifies a new user and passes that information through a `hidden` variable to the action page:

```
<input type ="hidden" name="newUser" value="Yes">
```

The action page now knows that this is a new user. You could add some conditional code in the action page to present a special welcome message for new users. This is all done in the background and is transparent to the user. The `hidden` variable can be accessed in the action page as `#form.newUser#` just like any other form variable.

HTML forms cannot validate a form field without the help of JavaScript or another scripting language. ColdFusion provides a way to validate form fields using `hidden` form variables by which you can validate the data type of the value entered, you can check if a number lies within a specific range, and you can specify that a field is required.

Required Field Validation

In ColdFusion, you can define an input field as `required` by adding a `hidden` field to the form with the same name as the field you want to validate. The `name` attribute of this field will have the value `fieldname_required`, where `fieldname` is the field to which you want to add required field validation followed by an underscore and the **validation rule**`_required`. For example, if we want to make sure that the `CustomerName` field in our earlier examples is never empty, that is, we want to make it a required field, we can just add the following line of code:

```
<input type="hidden" name="CustomerName_required">
```

This code will check if the `CustomerName` field is empty when you submit the form. As you may notice, you can use the `value` attribute of the `hidden` field to provide a customized error message to the customer. ColdFusion has its own default message that will be used if you do not supply this attribute. When the form is submitted, if the `CustomerName` field is empty, instead of the action page, a customized ColdFusion page is shown with the error message you entered in the `hidden` form field's `value` attribute. The resulting page would look like Figure 4.7.

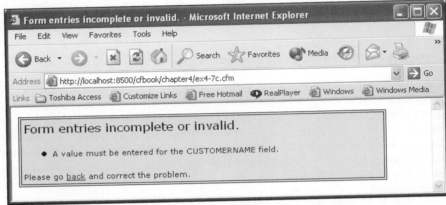

FIGURE 4.7   Server-Side Required Field Validation of Form Fields

ColdFusion checks if the field is empty before it decides which template to return to the client (the action template that you wrote or the customized error template). Since `hidden` fields are processed after the form is submitted to the server, we cannot tell the user about the invalid entry until the entire form has been submitted using server-side validation.

Data Type and Range Validation

Using ColdFusion you can validate data types and ranges of data entered through the form by simply adding `hidden` fields to the form. There are many validation rules that can be specified. A few of the commonly used ones are shown in the table on the next page.

A validation rule that checks the data type (e.g., `_integer`) does not check for required field validation. So required field validation needs to be done separately. Let us try an example. Example 4.7A combines validation for required fields and data types. The validation is done using hidden form fields. The form accepts two integers and the action page adds them. In this example, we will add three kinds of validation.

Code Snippets Using Validation Rules	Explanation of Code
`<input type="hidden" name="fieldname_integer">`	Verifies that the user entered a number. It rounds a floating point number to an integer.
`<input type="hidden" name="fieldname_float">`	Verifies that the user enters a number. No rounding off is done.
`<input type="hidden" name="fieldname_range" value="max=max value min=min value">`	Verifies that the numeric value is between the `min` and `max` values specified within the `value` attribute.

- Both fields should be validated for existence; that is, they are required fields.
- The first number should be any integer.
- The second number should be an integer between 1 and 10.

Type this in a file called ex4-7a.cfm.

Example 4.7A Server-Side Validation (Form) (ex4-7a.cfm)

```
1. <!DOCTYPE html
2. PUBLIC "-//W3C//DTD XHTML 1.0 Transitional//EN"
3. "http://www.w3.org/TR/xhtml1/DTD/xhtml1-
   transitional.dtd">
4. <html xmlns="http://www.w3.org/1999/xhtml">
5. <head>
6.   <title>Welcome to ColdFusion Forms</title>
7. </head>
8. <body>
9.   <br /><h2>Welcome to ColdFusion Forms</h2>
10.  <b>Please fill in this form and click Add!</b><hr />
11.  <form action="ex4-7b.cfm" method="post">
12.    <P>Please enter the first number:
13.    <input type="text" size="5" name="first">
14.    <P>Please enter the second number:
15.    <input type="text" size="5" name="second"><br />
16.    <input type="hidden" name="first_integer"
```

```
17.          value="The first number must be an integer">
18.      <input type="hidden" name="first_required">
19.      <input type="hidden" name="second_integer"
20.          value="The second number must be an integer">
21.      <input type="hidden" name="second_range"
22.          value="min=1 max=10">
23.      <input type="hidden" name="second_required">
24.      <input type="submit" value="ADD">
25.  </form>
26. </body>
27. </html>
```

The form when loaded will look like Figure 4.7A.

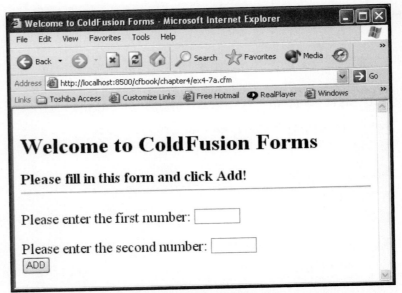

FIGURE 4.7A   Server-Side Range and Data Type Validation

How the Code Works

1. Lines 13 and 15 create input fields to accept numbers to add.

2. Line 16 creates a hidden field to validate that the first number is an integer.

3. Line 18 creates a `hidden` field to make the first number a required field.

4. Line 19 creates a `hidden` field to validate that the second number is an integer.

5. Line 21 creates a `hidden` field to supply a range, between 1 and 10, for the second number. A default ColdFusion error message will be displayed when the range check is violated with the minimum and maximum range that you specified in the `value` attribute. See Figure 4.7C.

6. Line 23 uses a `hidden` field to make the second number a required field.

Now let us write the action template. Example 4.7B is the action template that displays the sum of the numbers entered in the form. Save this code in a file called ex4-7b.cfm.

Example 4.7B   Server-Side Validation (Action) (ex4-7b.cfm)

```
1.  <!DOCTYPE html
2.  PUBLIC "-//W3C//DTD XHTML 1.0 Transitional//EN"
3.  "http://www.w3.org/TR/xhtml1/DTD/xhtml1-transitional.dtd">
4.  <html xmlns="http://www.w3.org/1999/xhtml">
5.  <head>
6.     <title>Welcome to ColdFusion Forms</title>
7.  </head>
8.  <body>
9.     <cfset result = #Form.first# + #Form.second#>
10.    <cfoutput>
11.      <h2> The sum of the two numbers
12.      #form.first# and #form.second# is #result# </h2>
13.    </cfoutput>
14. </body>
15. </html>
```

If you enter valid data, that is, integers within the appropriate range, and click on **ADD** in the form, you will see the action page as in Figure 4.7B.

If you enter invalid data, for example, if you violate the range check for the second field, and click **ADD** in the form, you will see a ColdFusion error page as in Figure 4.7C.

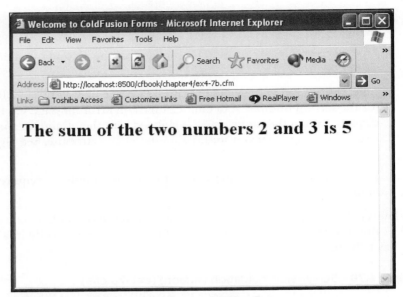

FIGURE 4.7B   Valid Form Data Produce Action Page

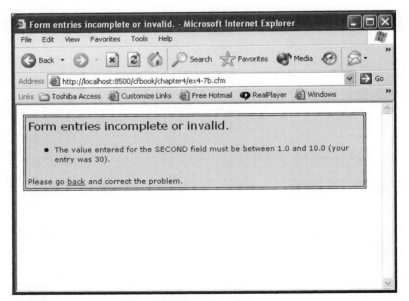

FIGURE 4.7C   Form Range Validation Error Page

How the Code Works

1. When you submit the form, ColdFusion scans the form fields for any validation rules, that is, `hidden` form field variables with the same name as the field name and a validation rule appended; for example, `first_required` or `first_range` where `first` is the field name.

2. ColdFusion applies these rules to analyze the input and, if any validation rules are violated, it sends an error message explaining the problem.

3. See Figure 4.7C for an error page when an out-of-range value is input into the form. You can then go back, correct the problem, and resubmit the form to get to the action page.

You can reload the form template, leave the number fields empty, and click on **ADD** to see the message change on the error page. You also can then try entering letters or numbers outside the range for the second number and see how the error page gives you the correct range. Only correct data will get you to the action page.

Hidden fields can be used with `textareas` also to validate for required fields. The following code shows how this is done:

```
<textarea rows=5 cols=30 name="comment"></textarea><br />
<input type="hidden" name="comment_required">
```

Enhancing Functionality with `<cfform>`

ColdFusion has special `<form>` tags that provide greater functionality than standard HTML form input elements and are simpler to code for validation. We will take a look at some of these tags below.

Creating Forms Using `<cfform>`

The tag `<cfform>` can be used to create dynamic forms in ColdFusion. The syntax of this tag is given below:

```
<cfform name="name"
   action="form_action"
   enablecab="yes/no"
   onsubmit = "JavaScript_name">
```

The `<cfform>` tag can be used in conjunction with other HTML code. If you replace the existing `<form>` tags with `<cfform>`, your pages should work fine. The forms that we have written until now required separate data validation that was executed on the server. The `<cfform>` tags enable us to use client-side data validation. In this book, we will learn only `<cfinput>` and `<cfselect>` tags and how they perform client-side data validation within a `<cfform>`.

`<cfinput>` as a Form Element

The `<cfinput>` tag is used to place radio buttons, checkboxes, text input boxes, and password entry boxes in a `<cfform>`. The `<cfinput>` tag is coded very much like the HTML `<input>` tag, but it has many more attributes that help with client-side data validation. The syntax of this tag is given below:

```
<cfinput
     type="input_type"
     name="name"
     value="default"
     required="yes/no"
     range="min_value, max_value"
     validate="data_type"
     onvalidate="javascript_function"
     message="validation_message"
     onerror="text"
     size="integer"
     maxlength="integer"
     checked="yes/no">
```

The table on the next page summarizes the purpose of each attribute.

> **Tech Tip**
>
> In the `<cfinput>` tag, do not put a line break in the message attribute's value. You'll get a JavaScript error.

The code below shows a password field created using the `<cfinput>` tag. Passwords, when entered, will be seen as XXXXX.

```
<cfinput name="password" required="yes" message="You must
    enter a password">
```

The following code shows how to use the `<cfinput>` tag for a radio button:

```
<cfinput type="radio" name="color" value="blue"> Blue
<cfinput type="radio" name="color" value="red"> Red
```

The following code shows how to use the `<cfinput>` tag for a checkbox.

```
<cfinput type="checkbox" name="color" value="blue">Blue
<cfinput type="checkbox" name="color" value="red">Red
```

Client-Side Validation Using `<cfinput>`

> **Tech Tip**
>
> Client-side validation takes place on the client's machine before the form is submitted to the ColdFusion server.

Client-side validation means that the validation code is executed on the client's browser and not by the server. The `<cfinput>` tag in ColdFusion enables us to perfom client-side validation on form data. The `<cfform>` tag automatically creates elaborate JavaScript validation code to validate your form fields as specified by you.

Now let us rewrite the code in Example 4.7A to use `<cfform>` and `<cfinput>` tags (using client-side validation) instead of HTML `<form>` tags and let's see the difference in the output between Example 4.7A and Example 4.8. Example 4.8 has the new form code saved as ex4-8.cfm. Note that the form in Example 4.8 still submits to ex4-7b.cfm. You need to change only the

`<cfinput>` Attribute	Optional/Required	Explanation
type	Optional	`text`: Creates a text entry box control (default) `password`: Creates a password entry control
name	Required	Name of the input element
value	Optional	Initial value for the input element
required	Optional	Required field or not Values: `Yes` or `No` with `No` being the default value
range	Optional	Minimum and maximum numeric values separated by a comma Entries that fall within that range will be accepted
validate	Optional	Uses JavaScript to validate data Some useful entries are • `date`—U.S. date • `float` • `integer` • `telephone`—formats ###-###-#### or ### ### #### • `zipcode`—5 or 9 digits in formats #####-#### or ##### ####. • `creditcard` • `social_security_number`—valid format ###-##-#### or ### ## ####
onvalidate	Optional	JavaScript function written to validate form input
message	Optional	Message to display if validation fails
onerror	Optional	JavaScript function to execute if data are invalid
size	Optional	Size of the input control Ignored for `radio` and `checkbox`
maxlength	Optional	Maximum length of text entered in the case of text boxes

form code and leave the action page code as it is. On loading this in the browser, you should see exactly the same output as you got when you loaded Example 4.7A (see Figure 4.7A). Before submitting the form, click on **View Source** (on the browser toolbar). You will see the elaborate JavaScript code that is generated by ColdFusion within your simple code.

Example 4.8_Client-Side Validation (Form) (ex4-8.cfm)

```
1. <!DOCTYPE html
2. PUBLIC "-//W3C//DTD XHTML 1.0 Transitional//EN"
3. "http://www.w3.org/TR/xhtml1/DTD/xhtml1-transitional.dtd">
```

```
4.  <html xmlns="http://www.w3.org/1999/xhtml">
5.  <head>
6.    <title>Welcome to ColdFusion Forms</title>
7.  </head>
8.  <body>
9.    <cfform action="ex4-7b.cfm" method="post">
10.     <br /><h2>Welcome to ColdFusion Forms</h2>
11.     <b>Please fill in this form and click Add!</b><hr />
12.     <P>Please enter the first number:
13.     <cfinput type="text" size="5" name="first"
14.         validate="integer"
15.         required="yes"
16.         message="Please enter an integer for the first
                number">
17.     <P>Please enter the second number:
18.     <cfinput type="text" size="5" name="second"
19.         validate="integer"
20.         required="yes"
21.         range="1,10"
22.         message="Please enter the second number between
                1 & 10 ">
23.     <br />
24.     <input type="submit" value="ADD">
25.   </cfform>
26.  </body>
27.  </html>
```

The only difference between the outputs of Example 4.8 and Example 4.7A is the validation part: Example 4.7A used server-side validation and Example 4.8 used client-side validation. Try leaving out the first number or enter letters instead of numbers and submit the form. You will see a JavaScript alert box pop up with the error message (see Figure 4.8) instead of the ColdFusion error page you saw in Figure 4.7C when we implemented server-side validation. Similarly, if you enter the first integer but go off the range for the second number or leave it out completely, you will see the other error message in an alert box telling you to enter the number within the specified range.

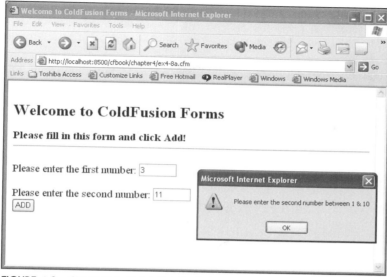

FIGURE 4.8   Client-Side Validation in ColdFusion

How the Code Works

1. Line 9 defines a form using the `<cfform>` tag. It looks exactly like the HTML `<form>` tag.

2. Lines 13 to 16 use the `<cfinput>` tag to accept the first number. Line 14 specifies to ColdFusion that the data entered in this field must be a valid integer. Line 15 specifies to ColdFusion that this is a required field so it must not be left empty. Line 16 is the `message` that will be displayed if any of the validation rules are violated.

3. Lines 18 to 22 use the `<cfinput>` tag to define the input field for the second number. Line 19 specifies that the second number should be an integer. Line 20 specifies that this is a required field. Line 21 specifies the `range` within which this number should be. Line 22 is the `message` that will be displayed if any of the above validation rules are violated.

Note that in the code in Example 4.8, there are no `hidden` fields, so no validation rules go to the server. All the validation is handled on the client's machine through the JavaScript that is generated by ColdFusion when the form is loaded. On submitting this form with correct data, that is, an integer for the first number and an integer between 1 and 10 for the second number, you should see exactly the same output for the action page as in the previous example (see Figure 4.7B).

In Example 4.8, you saw the JavaScript code that ColdFusion generated. This JavaScript validation code executes before the form is submitted to the server.

The <cfinput> tag includes the validate attribute that allows you to specify a valid data type entry for the control. When you specify an input type in the validate attribute, ColdFusion checks the data for the specified input type and submits the form data only if there is a successful match. Similarly, the required attribute does not allow you to leave the field empty. The validation we used in the <cfinput> tag in Example 4.8 is client-side validation because it is executed on the client machine before submitting the form.

In addition to native ColdFusion input validation using the validate attribute of the <cfinput> tag, the onvalidate attribute allows you to specify your own JavaScript function to handle your <cfform> input validation. In this book, you will not be learning how to write your own JavaScript code.

<cfselect> as a Form Element

The <cfselect> tag is used in a <cfform> to construct a drop-down list box. You can use the <option> elements or a database query to populate lists. We have an example of both these ways to populate drop-down list boxes. You should revisit the database example once you finish studying the chapters on databases. The syntax of this tag is as follows:

```
<cfselect
   name="name"
   message="text"
   onerror="text"
   size="integer"
   multiple="Yes/No"
   query="queryname"
   selected="column value"
   value="text"
   display="text">
</select>
```

The table on page 139 summarizes the attributes that can be used with the <cfselect> tag.

Example 4.9A is a simple piece of code that rewrites the states drop-down list introduced in Example 4.5A. Here, we use <cfselect> instead of the HTML <select> tag. Save this in a file called ex4-9a.cfm.

Example 4.9A_List Box Using <cfselect> **(Form) (ex4-9a.cfm)**

```
1. <!DOCTYPE html

2. PUBLIC "-//W3C//DTD XHTML 1.0 Transitional//EN"

3. "http://www.w3.org/TR/xhtml1/DTD/xhtml1-transitional.dtd">

4. <html xmlns="http://www.w3.org/1999/xhtml">

5. <head>
```

Attribute	Required/Optional	Explanation
name	Required	Selection box name
size	Required	Number of entries
required	Optional	If Yes, list element must be selected when the form is submitted; default is No
message	Optional	Message to display if required is Yes and no selection is made
onerror	Optional	JavaScript function to execute if validation fails
multiple	Optional	Yes or no field: Yes permits selection of multiple elements in the drop-down list box; default is No
query	Optional	Query to be used to populate the drop-down list
selected	Optional	Value that you want to preselect (applies only if list items are generated from a query)
value	Optional	Query column for the list element
display	Optional	Query column displayed

```
6.   <title>Welcome to ColdFusion Forms</title>
7.  </head>
8.  <body>
9.   <cfform action="ex4-9b.cfm" method="post">
10.     Please select a state<br />
11.     <cfselect
12.       name="states"
13.       required="yes"
14.       message="Please pick one or more states"
15.       multiple="yes">
16.        <option value="GA">Georgia
17.        <option value="CA">California
18.        <option value="AL">Alabama
19.        <option value="NV" >Nevada
20.        <option value="FL">Florida
21.        <option value="TX">Texas
```

22.   `</cfselect><br />`

23.   `<input type="submit" value="ADD">`

24.   `</cfform>`

25. `</body>`

26. `</html>`

You can now create a file called ex4-9b.cfm that displays the selected state using the form variable #form.states#. This code is shown in Example 4.9B.

Example 4.9B_List Box Processing (Action) (ex4-9b.cfm)

1. `<!DOCTYPE html`

2. `PUBLIC "-//W3C//DTD XHTML 1.0 Transitional//EN"`

3. `"http://www.w3.org/TR/xhtml1/DTD/xhtml1-transitional.dtd">`

4. `<html xmlns="http://www.w3.org/1999/xhtml">`

5. `<head>`

6. `<title>Welcome to ColdFusion Forms</title>`

7. `</head>`

8. `<body>`

9. `You selected <cfoutput>#form.states#</cfoutput>`

10. `</body>`

11. `</html>`

On loading the form (ex4-9a.cfm), you will see a simple drop-down list of states (see Figure 4.9A for the form and Figure 4.9B for the action page).

How the Form Code Works

1. Lines 11 to 22 use the `<cfselect>` tag to set up a drop-down list.

2. Line 12 specifies the name by which this element can be accessed in the action page.

3. Line 13 specifies that this is a required field.

4. Line 14 is the message used if you do not select any state.

5. Line 15 specifies that multiple selections may be made. This means that it will allow you to unselect all as well.

6. Then come the options, just like the HTML `<option>` tags, in lines 16 to 21 with each of the state names that we would like to show in

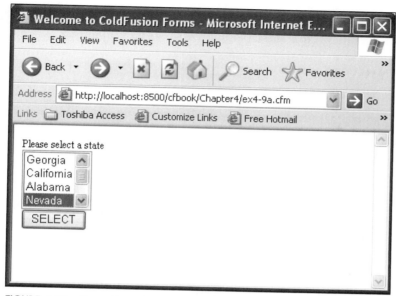

FIGURE 4.9A   Drop-Down List Using `<cfselect>` (Form)

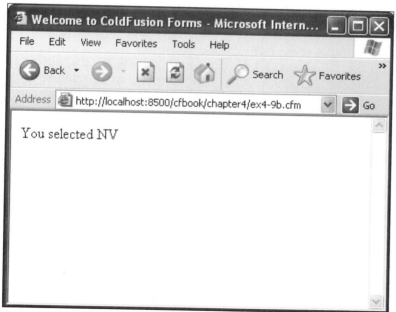

FIGURE 4.9B   Drop-Down List Selection (Action)

our list. In the database chapters (Chapters 5 and 6), you will see that this list can be populated from a database query as well.

7. Line 19 specifies that the selected state is Nevada.

8. Finally, we close the tag using </cfselect> on line 22.

How the Action Page Code Works

1. The action template executes when you submit the form.

2. It just has one line, line 9, which displays the selected state(s) using the form variable #form.states#; for example, You selected NV (if a single state was selected) or You selected NV,CA (if multiple selections were made). See Figure 4.9B.

ColdFusion Forms and Databases

Now that you know how to create and process forms in ColdFusion, you need to see how forms are used in business applications. Your action page needs to be able to store the information that is submitted through a form. Usually, data are stored in database tables. You may need to extract information from a database table in order to populate your form. For example, in a commercial environment, you would populate the states list in Example 4.9A from a database table using a query.

In the next two chapters, you will see how to manipulate data in your database through forms. In these chapters, we will revisit the <cfselect> tag and show you how a list box can be populated by a query. We also will take a look at the <cfgrid> tag, which is a Java-based form control that allows you to present a "spreadsheet" view of the data you query from your database.

Summary

In this chapter, we saw how to create forms and process different form variables to produce dynamic web pages. Using ColdFusion, we can provide our users with interactive pages that can easily pass parameters from one ColdFusion template to another. ColdFusion forms can be created using the <form> tag or the <cfform> tag. Depending on the type of tag use, you have a different range of functionality that can be performed in your form. If templates or form variables cannot be found, ColdFusion error pages are produced. Error pages are generated for checkboxes and radio buttons if nothing is selected in the form. It is important to check the existence of these variables before using them or to set a default value or force selection of such form fields. ColdFusion provides several attributes that help us to validate input data before submitting the data to the server. Client-side and server-side validation are possible using ColdFusion forms. We saw how ColdFusion forms have special tags that generate JavaScript code for us and make client-side validation really simple.

In the next chapter, we will look at database access through ColdFusion pages where we will see how forms can be populated with data or how form data can be used to manipulate data. We will revisit the <cfselect> and <cfgrid> tags to show you their power when used with a database query.

action page
checkbox
client-side validation
ColdFusion Application Server
data validation
drop-down list
dynamic web pages
exceptions

HTML forms
HTTP request
list box
Missing Template error
multiple selections
radio button
scope
scrolling list box

server-side validation
submit button
template
`textarea`
Validation error
validation rule
web forms
web server

1. Mention and explain three situations in which you think ColdFusion will throw an error page.
2. Why are ColdFusion error pages useful to developers?
3. Which two tags can you use to create forms in ColdFusion?
4. What is the scope of form variables?
5. Which qualifier do we use to qualify form variables? Explain why it is necessary to qualify variables.
6. If all radio buttons are unselected, what value is sent to the server?
7. What value is sent to the server if you allow more than one selection of a set of checkboxes that share a single name?
8. If we refer to the unchecked checkbox or unselected radio button in an action template, what does ColdFusion do?
9. Which form fields can be used to select from a list of options?
10. Which form fields can be used to send a yes/no answer for a question?
11. Which form field can be used to send multiple lines of free-form text to the server?
12. How can you make a text field called `qty` required in ColdFusion using server-side validation and client-side validation?
13. How do you validate a field called `counter` for an integer value using server-side validation and client-side validation?
14. How can you specify a range of values (1–100) for an integer input field called `age` using server-side validation and client-side validation?
15. Which element can you use to create a drop-down list box in a `<cfform>`?

State whether the following statements are true or false.

1. You can force selection of a radio button. _____
2. You can force the selection of a checkbox. _____
3. The action template should fully qualify the form variable. _____
4. You could not allow more than one selection in radio buttons even if you have different radio button groups in your form. _____
5. `<cfparam>` is used to define undefined variables and assign it a default value. _____
6. If a checkbox is unchecked, an empty string is sent to the server. _____
7. Validation using `hidden` fields is client-side validation. _____
8. `<cfinput>` can be used to place radio buttons, checkboxes, text input boxes, and password fields in a `<cfform>`. _____
9. Validation using JavaScript is server-side validation. _____
10. ColdFusion can handle both client-side and server-side validation. _____

1. Write a form to display months of the year as a list box. Enable multiple month selection and keep one month preselected. In the action page, display the months selected. Since all months can be deselected, you need to add some code that will prevent this form variable from being undefined in the action page or make it a required field in the form page. The screen shots in Figures 4.10A and 4.10B show sample form and action pages.

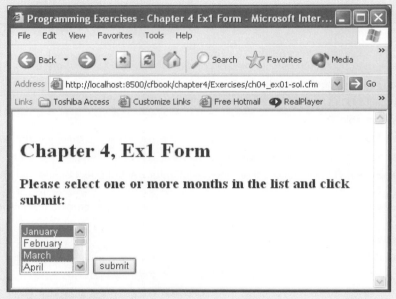

FIGURE 4.10A   Form

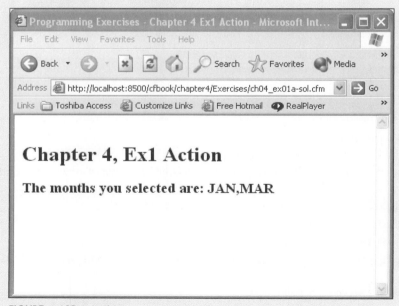

FIGURE 4.10B   Action

2. Write a form that accepts a number. The number is a required integer field and should be validated to be between 1 and 20. Use client-side validation. In the action page, loop between 0 and 12 and display the times table for that number. If the number is 3, your code should display:

$3 \times 0 = 0$
$3 \times 1 = 3$
$3 \times 2 = 6$
. . .
. . .
$3 \times 12 = 36$

For sample form and action page, look at Figures 4.11A and 4.11B.

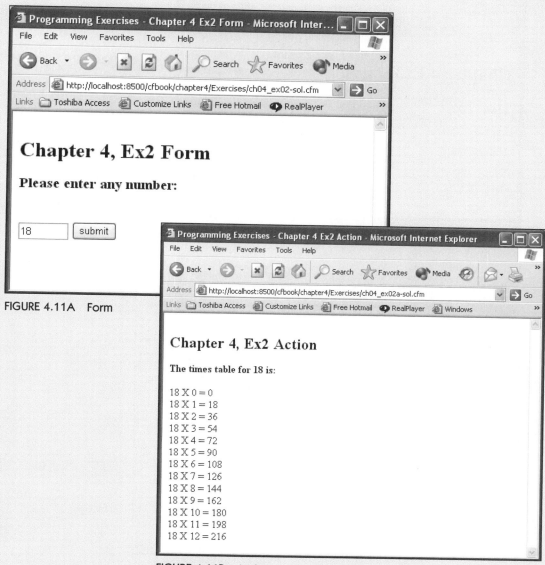

FIGURE 4.11A   Form

FIGURE 4.11B   Action

3. Write a form to accept a student's marks in four subjects: Math, Language, Science, and Social. Validate that marks entered are all integers between 0 and 100 and are required fields. Use server-side validation. In the action page, calculate the average mark for this student. Display the average to the user. For sample pages, look at Figures 4.12A and 4.12B.

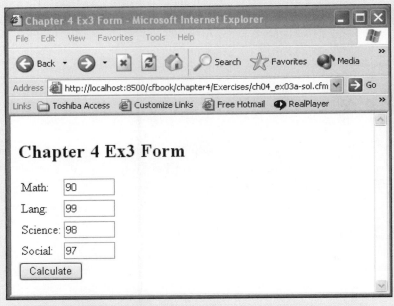

FIGURE 4.12A   Form

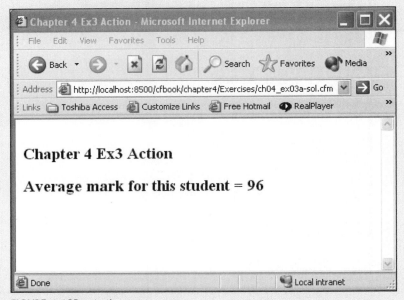

FIGURE 4.12B   Action

4. Modify the form in Exercise 3 to accept data for two students. Accept the student's name and marks in four subjects. Validate that marks entered are all integers between 0 and 100. All fields are required fields. In the action page, calculate and display the following:

a. Average marks for each student.

b. Student that got the maximum average.

c. Student that got the highest marks in each subject.

Sample form and action page are shown in Figures 4.13A and 4.13B.

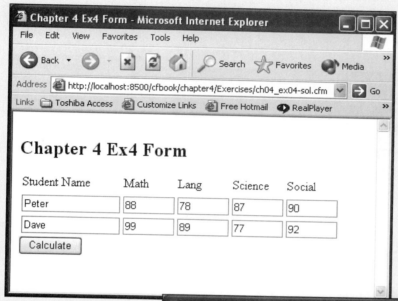

FIGURE 4.13A   Form

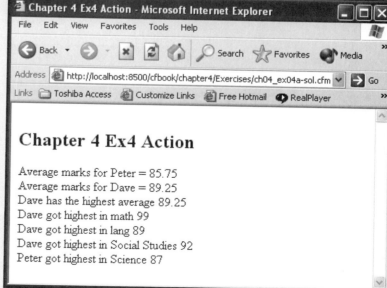

FIGURE 4.13B   Action

5. Write a ColdFusion template to display a Shipping Address form that accepts the following:
   a. User's name as a text box. Validate that this is not empty. Display an appropriate error message if it is empty.
   b. User's address as a text area. Validate that this is not empty. Display an appropriate error message.
   c. State as a pull-down list. Display any five states in the list box.
   d. Shipping method as radio buttons. The options for shipping method are Overnight, 1-day, 2-day. Preselect 2-day to force selection of at least one shipping method.

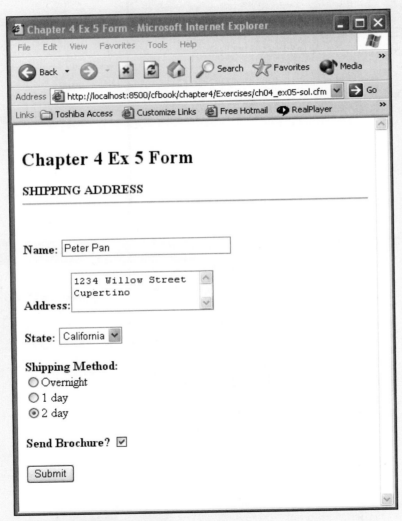

FIGURE 4.14A   Form

e. A checkbox to indicate whether the customer wants you to send him or her a company brochure. Write code to protect this field from generating an undefined variable error. Hint: Add a parameter in the action page to set a default value for this checkbox.

f. A submit button to invoke an action template.

Now write the action page that displays the inputs from the form. Preserve paragraph formatting in the address block. The action page should do the following:

a. Thank the user for his or her order.

b. Indicate the address to which the package will be mailed.

c. Indicate when the customer can expect the package to arrive.

d. Display whether a brochure will accompany the order.

Sample form and action page are given in Figures 4.14A and 4.14B.

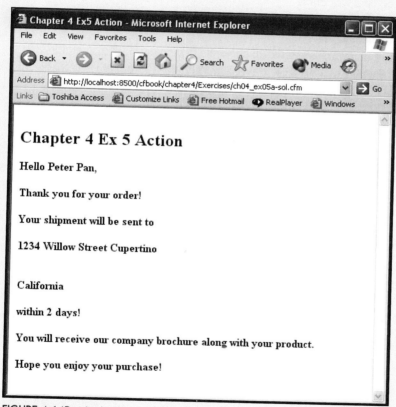

FIGURE 4.14B   Action

Customer Information Page

In this exercise, we are going to build the Customer Information page where you will collect customer address and payment information for a customer before the customer places his or her order. Design a form that accepts the customer's billing and shipping details, shipping method, and payment details. Use client-side and server-side validation where you need to. The requirements for this page are as follows:

1. Page title and heading: "Your Address and Payment Information"
2. Billing address:
    a. First name: text box, required field validation.
    b. Last name: text box, required field validation.
    c. Street address: text box, required field validation.
    d. City: text box, required field validation.
    e. State: text box, required field validation.
    f. Zip: text box, required field validation, zip code validation.
    g. Email: text box, required field validation.
    h. Put a red asterisk in front of all required fields to show the customer that they are required.
3. Shipping address (inform the customer to enter this only if it is different from the billing address):
    a. First name: text box.
    b. Last name: text box.
    c. Street address: text box.
    d. City: text box.
    e. State: text box.
    f. Zip: text box.
    g. Email.
4. Shipping method:
    a. Ground, Air, Overnight: radio buttons; preselect Overnight.
5. Payment details:
    a. Visa, Master, Discover: radio buttons; preselect Visa.
    b. Credit card number: text box, add credit card validation, required field validation.
    c. Expiration date: text box, date validation, required field validation.

6. Submit button:
   a. Display the text "Review Order" on the submit button.
   b. The form should submit to another template called Review.cfm. We will develop this action page (Review.cfm) in Chapter 7.

   The Customer Information page (form) should look like the screen shot in Figure 4.15 below:

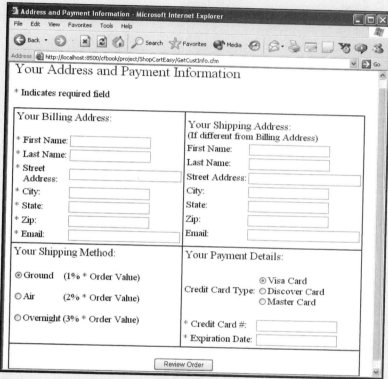

FIGURE 4.15 Customer Information Page

DataBase Basics: Connectivity, Simple Queries, and Security Issues

CHAPTER OBJECTIVES

1. Understand ColdFusion and database interaction.

2. Understand database connectivity and create data sources.

3. Use SQL with ColdFusion:
   a. SQL SELECT
   b. <cfquery>
   c. SQL INSERT and <cfinsert>
   d. SQL UPDATE
   e. SQL JOIN
   f. SQL DELETE

4. Use <cfselect>.

5. Use <cftable>.

6. Use Security options.

7. Create SQL VIEW.

Now that you are equipped with the necessary tools to understand how a Cold-Fusion page is processed, it is time to enhance your skills and apply them to real-world situations and get some meaningful results. The real world is a vast sea of information, most of it redundant. It is the programmer's job to extract relevant information from this sea and present it in a manner that is useful to the customer. One way a programmer can make this happen is to use a database system. Database systems allow you to store data in an organized manner and provide mechanisms such as queries, forms, and reports to extract relevant information and present it in a (systematic and organized) orderly manner. There are several types of database systems such as relational databases, object-oriented databases, distributed database systems, and so forth. We will use the relational database model in this book. Appendix A describes the relational database model and how to build relations (tables). The appendix also gives a set of common queries that can be designed using the Structured Query Language (SQL). These queries can be used to extract information from the tables.

Relational database systems are used very widely; some of the popular relational database management systems (RDBMS) include Microsoft Access, Oracle, and SQL Server. Since the advent of the Internet, there has been a strong demand for instant access to information including that from databases being made available on the web. This demand created the need for technologies that could retrieve the information stored in databases and present it on the web. The result of this is the emergence of technologies like ColdFusion, ASP, Perl/CGI, and a host of other packages, which offer good mechanisms to meet the new demand. In this chapter, we will see how ColdFusion interacts with databases and renders information from the tables on the browser.

ColdFusion and Database Interaction

ColdFusion is an excellent tool that allows users to dynamically interact with databases and provide information from the databases located locally or remotely and output this information on the browser. There are many types of databases that ColdFusion supports, including Oracle, Microsoft Access, Fox-Pro, and SQL Server. In this book, we will deal with the interaction of Cold-Fusion with the Microsoft Access database system.

Open Database Connectivity (ODBC) is a popular application program interface (API) that is used to communicate with the database. ODBC provides an abstract layer in the sense that it allows you to communicate with the database without knowing all details of how the specific type of data source such as a database or a spreadsheet works.

As shown in Figure 5.1, ColdFusion connects to the data source (in this case the Access database) by the ODBC tool, which acts as the translator that translates your SQL queries being sent to the database.

The steps necessary to set up the data source using ODBC are discussed next.

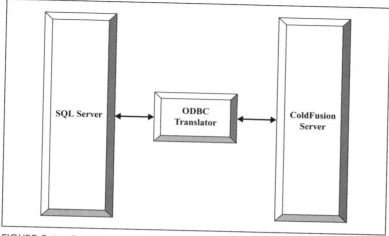

FIGURE 5.1   ColdFusion and Database Server Interaction

Creating a Data Source

Before proceeding further, we must first create a **data source** for the database that we wish to use for our programming purposes. The purpose of the data source is to tell ColdFusion two things:

* The type of database system being used.
* The location of the database on your local machine or on a remote server.

Setting Up a Connection to an Access Database Stored Locally

1. Open ColdFusion Administrator and click **Data Sources**, found under the Data & Services tab on the left pane of the window. Your screen should look like Figure 5.2.

2. In the textbox next to Data Source Name, type in **nwind**. (This is just a name, you can give your data source any name you like, but it is

IMPORTANT

We will be using the Northwind database that comes with Microsoft Access and is stored in the default directory C:\Program Files\Microsoft Office\Office\Samples. Locate the database on your machine before you start working on the examples.

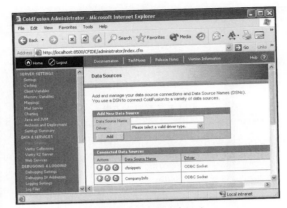

FIGURE 5.2   ColdFusion Administrator

advisable to give it some descriptive name, so it becomes easier to know what it means later on. This name serves as an alias to your actual database.)

3. Click the arrow in the box that asks you to select a driver and choose **Microsoft Access** as the driver. See Figure 5.3.

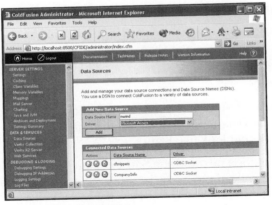

FIGURE 5.3   Choose Driver

4. Click on the **Add** button.

5. The next screen you see will need some more information on the location of the database on your system or stored remotely on another machine. If you are using MicroSoft Access, then your screen must look like Figure 5.4.

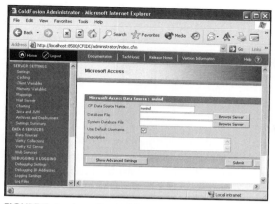

FIGURE 5.4   Location of Database

6. Click on the **Browse Server** button and browse to the location where you have the Northwind database saved.

7. Click on the **Apply** button.

8. Check that the **Use Default Username** box is checked; if it is not, check the box.

9. Click on the **Submit** button.

If everything went right, your screen should look like Figure 5.5 and you have established the data source. You will be using this data source for any queries that you send to your database.

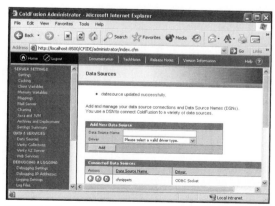

FIGURE 5.5   Data Source Confirmation

Accessing the Data Source via SQL Select, `<cfquery>`, and `<cfoutput>` to Retrieve and Display Data

Once the data source is set up, a database would be no good if the information were just stored without providing a mechanism to view this information. **Structured Query Language (SQL)** is a standard tool supported by database systems. We will use SQL to view and manipulate the information stored in the database.

The `<cfquery>` Tag and SQL `Select`

We will use ColdFusion as the front-end tool to help display the information on the browser. This means that our code will have both an SQL element and a ColdFusion element to it. The SQL is used to send the query to the database, and ColdFusion is the technology that helps display the result of the query on the browser. `<cfquery>` is the ColdFusion tag within which the SQL is embedded. So, let us look at an example. Example 5.1 uses a very common **SQL** `Select` statement. The `Select` statement of SQL is a query used to extract the specified information from the appropriate tables in the database and display it on the screen. Type the code segment below and save it as `CH5Eg1.cfm`. Open this file in your browser. Your output should be similar to Figure 5.6.

Example 5.1

```
1.  <?xml version = "1.0"?>
2.  <!DOCTYPE html PUBLIC
3.  "-//W3C//DTD XHTML 1.0 Transitional//EN"
4.  "http://www.w3.org/TR/xhtml1/DTD/xhtml1-transitional.dtd">
5.  <html xmlns = "http://www.w3.org/1999/xhtm">
6.  <head>
7.  <title> Select * Example </title>
8.  </head>
9.  <body>
10.    <cfquery name = "getEmpList" datasource="nwind">
11.      select * from Employees
```

```
12.    </cfquery>
13.    <cfoutput query ="getEmplist">
14.        #getEmplist.LastName#
15.        #getEmplist.FirstName#<br />
16.    </cfoutput>
17. </body>
18. </html>
```

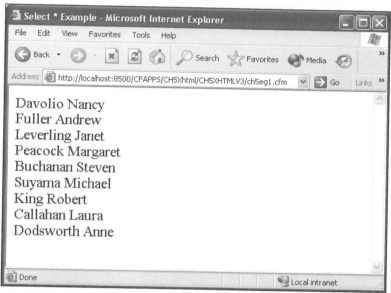

FIGURE 5.6   SQL Select

How the Code Works

1. Line 10 of this code segment starts with a <cfquery> tag. The
   <cfquery> tag is a mechanism by which ColdFusion passes any SQL
   statement to the database. The <cfquery> tag has many attributes
   such as name, datasource, username, and maxrows. This example
   uses two of the required attributes of the <cfquery> tag. The first
   attribute is the name attribute, which is the name of the query you
   are running. The name attribute will contain any results returned by
   the query that can be referenced later for other purposes such as displaying, deleting, and updating records. The second attribute is the
   name of the datasource, which you set up earlier in this chapter.

2. Line 11 is the standard SQL statement `select *`, which gets all the information (contained in all columns/all rows) from the Employees table. (The Employees table is found in the data source nwind specified in line 10.)

3. Line 12 closes the <cfquery> tag.

4. Line 13 starts the <cfoutput> tag with the `query` attribute. The `query` attribute has a built-in mechanism that returns all the data for each record that it contains. It works like a loop structure without the necessity of using the <cfloop> tag.

5. Lines 14 and 15 ask for the specific fields for which we want the output. Notice the syntax used here: we prefix each field name with the name of the query followed by a . (dot). It is important to follow the syntax, so ColdFusion knows which query the information must be retrieved and printed from. The advantage of having such a notation is that if your ColdFusion page has more than one query and you need to get information from one or all of these queries, it is just a matter of specifying the name of the query, followed by a dot and the field name from that table.

The above example is a very simple query and uses the default settings to display the data. This is fine for a start, but it is a very inefficient method to get the data from the table because the SQL statement `Select *` would select the entire contents of the table and store the data in the <cfquery> tag. This holds up a lot of memory if we were looking at a table with thousands of records, and the user may not need all this information. This method is also inefficient in terms of the time the query takes to retrieve the result, and this can be further delayed if the network traffic is heavy. To make this selection process more efficient, the same query can be modified to select specific fields from the table. Example 5.2 and output in Figure 5.7 illustrate the selection of specific fields from the Employees table, and also include the XHTML table tags to display the information in a more presentable manner.

Type the code shown in Example 5.2, save it as `CH5Eg2.cfm`, and open the file in the browser. The output of this code is shown in Figure 5.7.

Example 5.2

```
1. <?xml version = "1.0"?>
2. <!DOCTYPE html PUBLIC
3. "-//W3C//DTD XHTML 1.0 Transitional//EN"
4. "http://www.w3.org/TR/xhtml1/DTD/xhtml1-transitional.dtd">
5. <html xmlns = "http://www.w3.org/1999/xhtm">
6. <head>
```

```
7.  <title> Select specific fields </title>

8.  </head>

9.  <body>

10. <font size="+2" color="Blue">Welcome to our Employee
    list! </font><br /><br />

11.     <cfquery name = "getEmpList" datasource ="nwind">

12.         select LastName, FirstName, Title, HireDate, City

13.         from Employees

14.     </cfquery>

15. <table border = "1" cellspacing = "0">

16. <tr>

17.     <td width= "20%" bordercolor = "red">Last Name</td>

18.     <td width= "20%" bordercolor = "red">First Name </td>

19.     <td width= "20%" bordercolor = "red">Title</td>

20.     <td width= "20%" bordercolor = "red">Hire Date</td>

21.     <td width= "20%" bordercolor = "red">City</td>

22. </tr>

23.     <cfoutput query ="getEmplist">

24. <tr>

25.     <td width= "20%" bordercolor = "red" >#getEmplist.
        LastName#</td>

26.     <td width= "20%" bordercolor = "red">#getEmplist.
        FirstName#</td>

27.     <td width= "20%" bordercolor = "red">#getEmplist.
        Title#</td>

28.     <td width= "20%" bordercolor = "red">#getEmplist.
        HireDate#</td>

29.     <td width= "20%" bordercolor = "red">#getEmplist.
        City#</td>

30. </tr>

31.     </cfoutput>

32. </table>
```

33. `</body>`

34. `</html>`

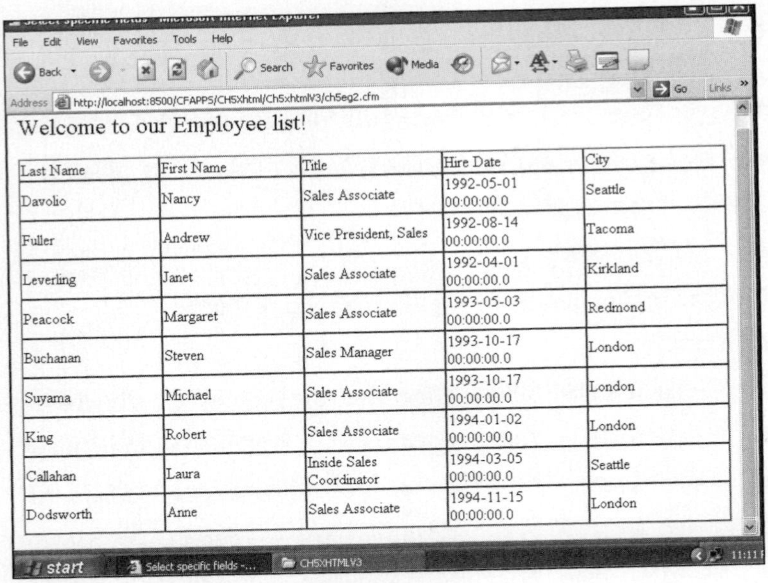

FIGURE 5.7   `<cfquery>` and HTML Table

How the Code Works

1. Line 11 specifies the name of the query and the name of the data source.

2. Line 12 is what makes this query different from the previous example. It is here that we specify the field names for which we want the values from the table. As you can see, this approach offers flexibility in terms of being able to get as little or as much information from the table as you want. We also specify the name of the table in the database.

3. Line 15 starts the XHTML table definition, with lines 17 through 21 creating the column headings.

4. Line 23 uses the `<cfoutput>` tag to display the results of the query "`getEmplist`".

5. Line 24 creates the first row, and lines 25 through 29 create a column/cell for each row.

6. The `<cfoutput>` tag with the `query` attribute prints out values for each record into the created columns of each row.

The `<cfquery>` tag also gives information about the query object it creates, via query variables such as `recordcount`, `currentrow`, and `columnlist`.

These attributes give us more information about the record set that has been returned by the <cfquery> tag. For example, the recordcount attribute gives us the total number of records returned by the <cfquery> tag. These attributes are discussed in Example 5.9.

The <cftable> Tag

The <cftable> tag is a built-in ColdFusion tag that presents the data from the query as preformatted text or as an HTML table with the HTMLTable attribute. The main advantage is that this tag can be used when you don't want to write the HTML code to create a table. Example 5.3 shows how a <cftable> tag can be used with an HTMLTable attribute. Type the code in Example 5.3 and save it as Ch5Eg3.cfm. Figure 5.8 shows the output of this code.

Example 5.3

```
1.  <?xml version = "1.0"?>
2.  <!DOCTYPE html PUBLIC
3.  "-//W3C//DTD XHTML 1.0 Transitional//EN"
4.  "http://www.w3.org/TR/xhtml1/DTD/xhtml1-transitional.dtd">
5.  <html xmlns = "http://www.w3.org/1999/xhtm">
6.  <head>
7.  <title> CFTABLE </title>
8.  </head>
9.  <body>
10. <cfquery name = "getEmpList" datasource="nwind">
11. Select * From Employees
12. </cfquery>
13. <cftable query ="getEmpList"
14. border = "yes"
15. HTMLTable>
16. <cfcol header = "LastName"
17. text = "#getEmpList.LastName#">
18. <cfcol header ="FirstName"
19. align=center text="#getEmpList.FirstName#">
20. </cftable>
```

21. `</body>`

22. `</html>`

How the Code Works

1. Lines 10 through 12 create the query with the `<cfquery>` tag. The results of this query will be displayed in a table format with the `<cftable>` tag.

2. Line 13 starts the `<cftable>` tag. The `query` attribute, which is a required attribute for the `<cftable>` tag, specifies the name of the query, which is `getEmpList`, which was created earlier.

3. Line 14 sets the `border` attribute equal to `"yes"`, which ensures that the cells in the table have a border.

4. Line 15 uses the `HTMLTable` attribute to display the data as an HTML table and not as preformatted text.

5. Lines 16 and 18 specify the columns to be displayed from the query with the `<cfcol>` attribute. Note the use of the `header` attribute. The value of this `header` attribute is what will be displayed as the column header in the table.

6. Line 19 uses the `align` attribute to specify the alignment of text.

7. Line 20 closes the `<cftable>` tag.

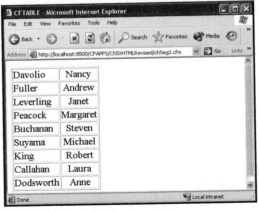

FIGURE 5.8   `<cftable>`

Partial Record Sets

Just as you could specify the columns you need in the query, you also can specify the number of rows that you want to be displayed by the query. The function that allows you to do this is **Maxrows**. The `Maxrows` function takes an attribute of an integer type and returns the number of rows starting from row one in your query and ending with the row number provided for this attribute. Example 5.4 and the output of Figure 5.9 illustrate the usage of the Maxrows tag. Type the code in Example 5.4 and save it as Ch5Eg4.cfm.

Example 5.4

```
1.  <?xml version = "1.0"?>
2.  <!DOCTYPE html PUBLIC
3.  "-//W3C//DTD XHTML 1.0 Transitional//EN"
4.  "http://www.w3.org/TR/xhtml1/DTD/xhtml1-transitional.dtd">
5.  <html xmlns = "http://www.w3.org/1999/xhtm">
6.  <head>
7.  <title> Using MaxRows </title>
8.  </head>
9.  <body>
10.   <cfquery name = "getEmpList" datasource ="nwind">
11.     select * from Employees
12.   </cfquery>
13.   <cfoutput query ="getEmplist" Maxrows = 3>
14.     #getEmplist.LastName#
15.     #getEmplist.FirstName#<br \>
16.   </cfoutput>
17. </body>
18. </html>
```

FIGURE 5.9   Maxrows

How the Code Works

Line 13 uses the `Maxrows` attribute and specifies the number of rows (three in this case) to be displayed on the browser. The rest of the code is straightforward and has been explained in Example 5.3.

Using `Where` and `Like` Clauses to Select Partial Records

Another way to select partial records is to use **SQL** `Where` and `Like` clauses. This is particularly useful when you want a partial list of records based on some criterion and not a numeric value. Take a look at the code segment below:

```
SELECT Employees.FirstName
FROM Employees
WHERE (((Employees.FirstName) Like "A*"));
```

This example selects a partial number of records based on the criterion specified. The criterion here is that the first name starts with the letter A, followed by a *. The * (star) is a wild character that represents all characters following "A". This means that you are looking for all names starting with A. Modify one of the above examples to include this `Select` statement and see what your code returns as output. You should get a list of all employees whose first names start with the alphabetic letter A followed by any other letters.

The `<cfgrid>` Tag

Another useful and easy control that helps present the data returned by the query in a table format is the`<cfgrid>`. The `<cfgrid>` control is a Java applet that is programmed to display the results of the query that it receives in a table format. The `<cfgrid>` tag must be used inside `<cfform>` tags. The `name` attribute of the `<cfgrid>` control is a required attribute. The `<cfgrid>` control has several other attributes such as `width`, `height`, `color`, `columnHeader`, and so forth. If you do not specify the columns/fields as values for the `cfgridcolumn` attribute to be displayed, then all the columns returned by the query will be displayed in the grid. The code given for Examples 5.5 and 5.6 shows how the `<cfgrid>` tag can be used. The output of these examples is shown in Figures 5.10 and 5.11. Type the code in Example 5.5 and save it as `Ch5Eg5.cfm`. Type the code in Example 5.6 and save it as `Ch5Eg6.cfm`.

Example 5.5

1. `<?xml version = "1.0"?>`

2. `<!DOCTYPE html PUBLIC`

3. `"-//W3C//DTD XHTML 1.0 Transitional//EN"`

4. `"http://www.w3.org/TR/xhtml1/DTD/xhtml1-transitional.dtd">`

5. `<html xmlns = "http://www.w3.org/1999/xhtm">`

6. `<head>`

7. `<title> Using CFGRID </title>`

8. `</head>`

9. `<body>`

10. `<cfquery name = "getCustList" datasource="nwind">`

11. `select * from Customers`

12. `</cfquery>`

13. `<cfform name = "custgrid" >`

14. `<cfgrid name = "custlist" width = "500" query = "getCustList">`

15. `</cfgrid>`

16. `</cfform>`

17. `</body>`

18. `</html>`

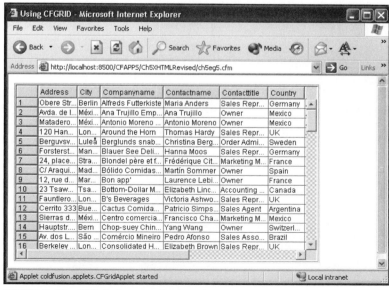

FIGURE 5.10   SQL Select and cfgrid

How the Code Works

This example uses a query to populate the `<cfgrid>` control.

1. Line 11 gives the `select` statement to get all fields from the Customers table.

2. Line 13 creates the `<cfform>` tag, since the `<cfgrid>` tag must be nested within the `<cfform>` tag.

3. Line 14 creates the `<cfgrid>` tag. Like the `<cfquery>` tag, this control also supports many attributes. The `name` attribute is required. The `query` attribute supplies the name of the query, which provides data for the `<cfgrid>` control.

4. Since no other attributes of the `<cfgrid>` control are specified, the control displays the entire table with all its columns and rows.

Now let's look at Example 5.6, which specifies the columns to be displayed by the `<cfgrid>` tag.

Example 5.6

```
1.  <?xml version = "1.0"?>
2.  <!DOCTYPE html PUBLIC
3.  "-//W3C//DTD XHTML 1.0 Transitional//EN"
4.  "http://www.w3.org/TR/xhtml1/DTD/xhtml1-transitional.dtd">
5.  <html xmlns = "http://www.w3.org/1999/xhtm">
6.  <head>
7.  <title> CFGRID with Selected Columns </title>
8.  </head>
9.  <body>
10.    <cfquery name = "getCustMin" datasource="nwind">
11.      select * from Customers
12.    </cfquery>
13.    <cfform name = "custgrid" >
14.      <cfgrid name = "custlist" Query = "getCustMin"
            selectmode = "Edit" >
15.      <cfgridcolumn name ="ContactName" Header =
            "Contact Name">
```

```
16.     <cfgridcolumn name ="ContactTitle" Header =
            "ContactTitle">
17.     </cfgrid>
18.   </cfform>
19. </body>
20. </html>
```

FIGURE 5.11   Specific Columns with `<cfgrid>`

How the Code Works

This example specifies a set of columns to be displayed by the `<cfgrid>` control. The ability to control and specify the columns you need to be displayed obviously offers more flexibility and control to the programmer.

1. Lines 10 through 12 set up the `<cfquery>` tag with the SQL query included. Notice that line 11 still uses a `select *`, and not any specific fields from the table Customers.

2. Lines 13 through 18 use the `<cfform>` and `<cfgrid>` tags.

3. Line 14 sets up the `<cfgrid>` and values for its attributes. Notice that the `selectmode` is set to `Edit`, so users can edit the data on the screen.

4. Lines 15 and 16 use the `<cfgridcolumn>` name attribute to specify the fields to be selected from the query and displayed. The Header attribute of the `<cfgridcolumn>` tag is optional but can be used to specify the name of the column heading. If the Header value is not specified, the default value is the value given to the `<cfgridcolumn>` name attribute earlier in your code.

5. Lines 19 and 20 close the `<body>` and the `<html>` tags.

Tech Tip

The `selectmode` should not be set to "Edit" unless you want the data to be edited by the users.

Managing Data: Insert, Update, and Delete Records

The next item that needs attention is the capability to add records to the tables in the database. Of course, you can manually open the table and key in the information, but as a programmer you want to make sure that the database is protected and not exposed to the user, and any insert, delete, or update operations are done in a manner controlled by the programmer, via forms.

The <cfinsert> Tag

The <cfinsert> tag is a built-in ColdFusion tag and is a very easy way to insert a single record into a table. The syntax of the tag is

Version 1

```
<cfInsert Datasource="nwind"
    Tablename ="employees"
    Formfields="LastName, FirstName">
```

Version 2

```
<cfInsert Datasource="nwind"
    Tablename ="employees">
```

The two required attributes for the <cfinsert> tag are Datasource, which specifies the location of the database, and Tablename, the name of the table into which the record must be inserted. The Formfields attribute is optional; if this attribute is not used, then ColdFusion will insert all values submitted via the form, building the columns and their values dynamically. Version 2 given above is an example of not using the Formfields attribute. The Formfields attribute is required when you want to submit only some of the field values collected in the form.

Requirements for the <cfinsert> Tag

1. The two attributes Datasource and Tablename are required.

2. The form variable names must match the table names in the database.

3. All information must be submitted via a form.

4. The Formfields attribute is required when you want to insert values into specific fields of the table.

The example code segments in Examples 5.7A and 5.7B show how the <cfinsert> tag works. We have a form to collect the information from the user that must be added to the database table, and we have the action page that inserts the data into the specified table. Type the code in Examples 5.7A and 5.7B and save the files as CH5Eg7A.cfm and CH5Eg7B.cfm, respectively. The output of these two examples is shown in Figures 5.12A amd 5.12B.

Example 5.7A   Form Code

```
1. <?xml version = "1.0"?>
2. <!DOCTYPE html PUBLIC
3. "-//W3C//DTD XHTML 1.0 Transitional//EN"
4. "http://www.w3.org/TR/xhtml11/DTD/xhtml1-transitional.dtd">
5. <html xmlns = "http://www.w3.org/1999/xhtm">
6. <head>
7. <title> CFINSERT Example </title>
8. </head>
9. <body>
10. Please enter info to be added to the table
11.    <form action = "CH5Eg7B.cfm" Method = "post">
12.       <b> Enter Last Name: <Input type = "text"
              name="LastName"></b><br />
13.       <b> Enter First Name: <Input type = "text"
              name="FirstName"></b><br />
14.    <b><Input type = "submit" value="submit">
15.    </form>
16. </body>
17. </html>
```

Example 5.7B   Action Page Code

```
1. <cfInsert Datasource="nwind"
2.    Tablename ="employees"
3.    Formfields ="LastName, FirstName">
4. Record added
```

FIGURE 5.12A   <cfinsert> Form

FIGURE 5.12B   <cfinsert> Action

How the Form Code Works

1. The form code is straightforward. Line 11 specifies the action page that must be activated upon submission of the form.

2. Lines 12 and 13 use input boxes to collect the required information from the user. Note that the names of these input boxes are the same as the field names of the table in the database.

3. Line 14 has the **submit** button for the form.

How the Action Page Code Works

1. Line 1 uses the <cfinsert> tag followed by the Datasource name.

2. Line 2 specifies the Tablename into which the Formfields values will be inserted.

3. Line 3 specifies the Formfields attribute followed by the specific fieldnames—LastName and FirstName—of the table into which these values must be inserted.

4. Line 4 is just to get a confirmation that the record was added to the table.

Tech Tip

It is very important that your Formfields names match the field/column names of the database table.

Constraints of the `<cfinsert>` Tag

1. The `<cfinsert>` tag can be used only for values received from a form.

2. Form data cannot be manipulated with the `<cfinsert>` tag.

3. It is also considerably slower in execution compared to the SQL `Insert` statement.

SQL `Insert` Statement for ColdFusion

The above-mentioned constraints can be overcome by using the **SQL** `Insert` statement. Examples 5.8A and 5.8B are the form and action page that contain the SQL `Insert` including the required ColdFusion tags. Type the code in Examples 5.8A and 5.8B and save the files as `CH5Eg8A.cfm` and `CH5Eg8B.cfm`.

Example 5.8A Form Code

```
1. <?xml version = "1.0"?>
2. <!DOCTYPE html PUBLIC
3. "-//W3C//DTD XHTML 1.0 Transitional//EN"
4. "http://www.w3.org/TR/xhtml1/DTD/xhtml1-transitional.dtd">
5. <html xmlns = "http://www.w3.org/1999/xhtm">
6. <head>
7. <title> SQL Insert </title>
8. </head>
9. <body>
10. Please enter info to be added to the table
11.    <form action = "Ch5Eg8B.cfm" Method = "post">
12.       <b> Enter Last Name: </b><Input type = "text"
          name="LName"><br />
13.       <b> Enter First Name: </b><Input type = "text"
          name="FName"><br />
14.    <Input type = "submit" value="submit">
15. </form>
16. </body>
17. </html>
```

Example 5.8B   Action Page Code

```
1. <cfquery Datasource="nwind">
2.    insert into employees(LastName, FirstName)
3.       values ('#LName#', '#FName#')
4. </cfquery>
5. Record added
```

After running CH5Eg8A.cfm in your browser, you should now see a screen that shows the message `Record added`.

How the Form Code Works

1. The form code is straightforward. Line 11 specifies the action page that must be activated upon submission of the form.

2. Lines 12 and 13 use input boxes to collect the required information from the user. Note that the names of these input boxes are not the same as the field names of the table in the database. The restriction of form fieldnames matching the table field names does not apply when using an SQL `Insert` statement. The reason for this will become clear when we examine the code for the action page.

3. Line 14 has the **submit** button for the form.

How the Action Page Code Works

1. Line 1 uses the `<cfquery>` tag since we are sending an SQL instruction to the database. It also specifies the `Datasource` name.

2. Line 2 uses the SQL `Insert` statement. Notice that the table name and the field names are specified here. The field names here are the exact same names as the fields in the database table.

3. Line 3 is also part of the SQL `Insert` statement, except that the parameters for the values are coming from the form. The values that are given here get inserted into the fields specified in line 2. Since these are values and not the field names that are being passed to the SQL statement, it is not necessary that the field names used in the form match the field names in the database table.

SQL Update

The **SQL** `Update` command is used to edit information for a column in a table. To see how this command works, suppose that your manager asks you to change the title of Sales Representative to Sales Associate in the Employees table. It would be very painstaking to manually change this value for every record in the table. SQL's Update command makes this task very easy. Example 5.9 (the output doesn't show "before" the update) illustrates how the Update command works. Type the code in Example 5.9 and save it as Ch5Eg9.cfm. The output of this code is shown in Figure 5.13.

Example 5.9

```
1. <?xml version = "1.0"?>
2. <!DOCTYPE html PUBLIC
3. "-//W3C//DTD XHTML 1.0 Transitional//EN"
4. "http://www.w3.org/TR/xhtml1/DTD/xhtml1-transitional.dtd">
5. <html xmlns = "http://www.w3.org/1999/xhtm">
6. <head>
7. <title> Update command </title>
8. </head>
9. <body>
10. List of Employees Before Update<br /><br />
11.    <cfquery name = "getEmpList" Datasource="nwind">
12.       select * From Employees
13.    </cfquery>
14.    <cfoutput query ="getEmplist">
15.       #getEmplist.LastName#
16.       #getEmplist.Title#<br />
17.    </cfoutput>
18. <br /> <br />
19. List of Employees after Update <br /><br />
20.    <cfquery Datasource="nwind">
21.       update Employees
22.       set Title = 'Sales Associate'
23.       where Title = 'Sales Representative' OR Title =
             'Sales Rep'
24.    </cfquery>
25.    <cfquery name = "getTitles" Datasource="nwind">
26.       select * from Employees
```

```
27.    </cfquery>
28.    <cfoutput query ="getTitles" >
29.      #getTitles.LastName#
30.      #getTitles.Title#
31. <br />
32.    </cfoutput>
33.    <cfquery name = "getTitlesNum" Datasource = "nwind">
34.      select Employees.Title
35.      from Employees
36.      where Employees.Title='Sales Associate'
37.    </cfquery>
38. <br /> <br />
39.    <cfset Total = #getTitlesNum.recordcount#>
40.    <cfoutput>The total number of Records Updated with
         Title being set to Sales
41.      Associate is #Total#
42.    </cfoutput> <br /> <br />
43.    <cfset FieldNames = #getEmpList.ColumnList#>
44.    <cfoutput> Fields in table Employee are :
         #fieldNames# <br />
45.    </cfoutput>
46. </body>
47. </html>
```

How the Code Works

1. Lines 11 through 17 are routine by now. We use a <cfquery> to
   send an SQL statement and use a <cfoutput> to display the results
   of the query.

IMPORTANT

The actual number of records displayed on your browser depends on the number of records you have in your table.

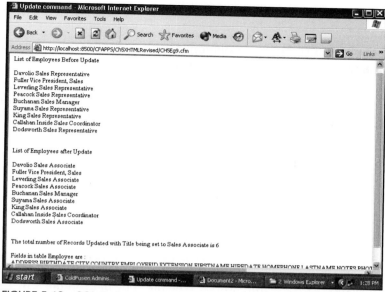

FIGURE 5.13 SQL Update

2. Lines 21 through 23 are using the SQL Update command. The Update command needs the table name, the new value that replaces the old value, and the old value that needs to be replaced. We use the set statement to supply the new value and a where statement to identify the old value.

3. Lines 25 through 32 are again a repeat of lines 11 through 17, except that this time the output shows that all titles for Sales Rep or Sales Representative have been changed to Sales Associate, the result of the Update command.

4. Lines 33 through 36 create another <cfquery> but use a where clause to select records where the value of Title is Sales Associate.

5. Line 39 is interesting. We look at another attribute of the <cfquery> tag. As mentioned earlier in the chapter, the <cfquery> tag has other attributes and also gives information about the query object itself, which can be accessed by three query variables:

   a. *Query_name*.Recordcount, which returns the number of records in the query result.

   b. *Query_name*.CurrentRow, which returns the current row being processed by the <cfoutput>.

   c. *Query_name*.ColumnList, which returns a comma-delimited list of column names from the table.

6. The *Query_name*.`RecordCount` is set to the variable called `Total` and is printed out by line 41.

7. In line 43 *Query_name*.ColumnList is set to the variable `FieldNames` and is printed out by line 44.

These properties of the <cfquery> tag are useful for rendering statistical information and can be very valuable to people in managerial positions for purposes of data analysis. A simple example would be to write a query that would tell the manager how many people exceeded their sales quota or vice versa.

SQL Delete

The **SQL** Delete command is a simple and useful command. As the name implies, this command is used to delete a record in the table based on a specified condition. The Delete command can come in handy in situations where you might want to delete some fields from your tables and it is expensive to redesign your entire database so that it reflects these changes. Example 5.10 shows how the Delete feature works. Type the code in Example 5.10 and save it as Ch5Eg10.cfm. Figure 5.14 is the output of this code.

Example 5.10

```
1.  <?xml version = "1.0"?>
2.  <!DOCTYPE html PUBLIC
3.  "-//W3C//DTD XHTML 1.0 Transitional//EN"
4.  "http://www.w3.org/TR/xhtml1/DTD/xhtml1-transitional.dtd">
5.  <html xmlns = "http://www.w3.org/1999/xhtm">
6.  <head>
7.  <title> DELETE Command </title>
8.  </head>
9.   <cfquery name = "DisplayNames" Datasource="nwind">
10.     select * from Employees
11.  </cfquery>
12.  <cfoutput query ="DisplayNames">
13.     #DisplayNames.LastName#
14.     #DisplayNames.FirstName# <br />
15.  </cfoutput>
16.  <cfquery Datasource="nwind">
```

```
17.      delete from Employees
18.      where LastName = 'Fuller' and FirstName = 'Andrew'
19.  </cfquery>
20. <br /><br /> Record deleted<br /><br />
21.  <cfquery name = "getNames" Datasource="nwind">
22.    select * from Employees
23.  </cfquery>
24.  <cfoutput query ="getNames">
25.    #getNames.LastName#
26.    #getNames.FirstName# <br />
27.  </cfoutput>
28. <br /><br />
29. </html>
```

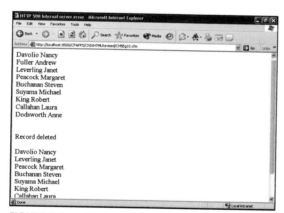

FIGURE 5.14   SQL Delete

How the Code Works

1. As you can see, we have just added extra code to show you the results from the table before the delete operation (lines 9 through 15) and again after the delete operation (lines 21 through 27).

2. The most important part of this code segment lies in lines 17 and 18, where the SQL Delete command is used along with the conditions under which this operation must be performed as shown by the where clause on line 18.

In Chapter 6 you will look at an example that shows you what must be done when you want to delete fields from one table that have a relation to other tables. This kind of a situation is more involved than the example discussed here.

SQL Join

The **SQL** Join operation comes in handy when information required can be obtained only from a combination of two or more tables. Appendix A gives the syntax and explanation of the SQL Join command. An example situation would involve wanting the names of the products and their corresponding suppliers from the Northwind database. By looking at the Northwind databse, you realize that this information (both the fields) is not available in one table, but it can be obtained from two tables: Products (has the product name) and Suppliers (has the company name). So this situation calls for a join of both these tables, where the common key to connect both the tables is SupplierID, which is present in both the tables. The code in Example 5.11 shows the SQL Join operation. Type the code in Example 5.11 and save it as CH5Eg11.cfm. Figure 5.15 shows the output of this code.

Example 5.11

```
1.  <?xml version = "1.0"?>
2.  <!DOCTYPE html PUBLIC
3.  "-//W3C//DTD XHTML 1.0 Transitional//EN"
4.  "http://www.w3.org/TR/xhtml1/DTD/xhtml1-transitional.dtd">
5.  <html xmlns = "http://www.w3.org/1999/xhtm">
6.  <head>
7.  <title> JOIN COMMAND </title>
8.  </head>
9.  <body>
10.    <cfquery name = "JoinProdSupp" Datasource="nwind">
11.       select [Products].[ProductName],
12.       [Products].[UnitPrice], [Suppliers].[CompanyName]
13.       from Suppliers inner join Products on
```

> **IMPORTANT**
>
> The Join operation requires that there is one common key (also known as the primary key), or field, in the tables that will be joined.

14.   `[Suppliers].[SupplierID]=[Products].[SupplierID]`

15.   `</cfquery>`

16. `List of CompanyNames, Products and Unit Prices given below:<br /> <br />`

17.   `<cfform Name = "Joingridfrm" >`

18.   `<cfgrid Name = "JoinGrid" Query = "JoinProdSupp">`

19.   `</cfgrid>`

20.   `</cfform>`

21. `</body>`

22. `</html>`

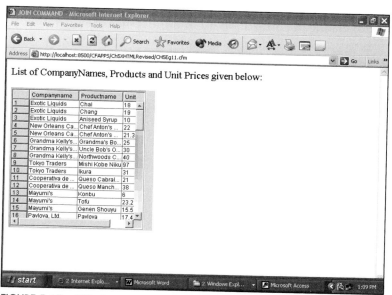

FIGURE 5.15 SQL Join

How the Code Works

1. Line 11 specifies the `Select` statement with the required fields from each table specified. Notice that the field name is prefixed by the table name to specify to the program the name of the table that contains this particular field. The [ ] are used just to improve readability; they are not required.

2. Line 13 specifies the `join` condition (the common field in both the tables). Refer to Appendix A for syntax and explanation of the SQL Join.

3. Lines 18 and 19 use the `<cfgrid>` to print out the results from this query onto the browser.

The `<cfselect>` Tag

The `<cfselect>` tag creates a drop-down list control within a `<cftemplate>`. The drop-down list control can be populated either by the results of a query that can be assigned to the `query` attribute of the `<cfselect>` tag or by using the option tags. The syntax for setting the values of option tags is similar to setting the values for option tags in an HTML page. Refer to Chapter 4 for a review of this material. Examples 5.12A and 5.12B illustrate the usage of the `<cfselect>` tag with the `query` attribute. Type the Examples 5.12A and 5.12B and save them as CH5Eg12A.cfm and CH5Eg12B.cfm. The output of this code is shown in Figures 5.16A and 5.16B. Example 5.12A is the form being used to perform two actions:

1. Populating the drop-down list with the results of a query (`getEmpList`).

2. Passing the value of a selected item to the action page.

Example 5.12B is the action page that takes the input returned by the form page, uses the value in another query (`getEmpTitle`), and displays the results of this query.

Example 5.12A   Form Code

```
1. <!DOCTYPE html PUBLIC
2. "-//W3C//DTD XHTML 1.0 Transitional//EN"
3. "DTD/xhtml1-transitional.dtd">
4. <html xmlns="http://www.w3.org/1999/xhtml">
5. <Title> CFSELECT </title>
6. <body>
7. <cfquery name = "getEmpList" Datasource="nwind">
8. Select * From Employees
9. </cfquery>
10. <cfform action="CH5Eg12B.cfm" method="post" enablecab="Yes">
11. <cfselect name = "employees"
12. message = "You must select an employee"
13. query = "getEmpList"
```

```
14. value = "lastname">
15. </cfselect>
16. <input type = "submit" name = "submit" value = "submit">
17. </cfform>
18. </body>
19. </html>
```

Example 5.12B Action Page Code

```
1. <!DOCTYPE html PUBLIC
2. "-//W3C//DTD XHTML 1.0 Transitional//EN"
3. "DTD/xhtml1-transitional.dtd">
4. <html xmlns="http://www.w3.org/1999/xhtml">
5. <Title> CFSELECT Action page </title>
6. <body>
7. <cfset empLastName = #Form.employees#> <br \>
8. <cfquery name = "getEmpTitle" Datasource="nwind">
9. select Employees.Title
10. from Employees
11. where Employees.LastName = '#empLastName#'
12. </cfquery>
13. <cfoutput query ="getEmpTitle">
14. The Title of the person with the lastname #empLastname#
        you selected is:
15. #getEmpTitle.Title#
16. </cfoutput>
17. </body>
18. </html>
```

How the Form Code Works

Example 5.12A is the form being used to get the last name of the employee for whom the title is being searched.

1. Lines 7 through 9 use the <cfquery> tag to contain the select query, which is a basic Select * from the Employees table.

FIGURE 5.16A   Get Employee Last Name

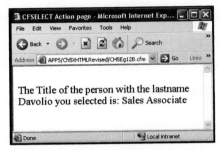

FIGURE 5.16B   Return Employee Title

2. Line 10 has the details of the action page that must be opened upon submission of the form page.

3. Lines 11 through 15 use the <cfselect> tag. Line 11 has the name attribute (a required attribute) of the <cfselect> tag set to "employees".

4. Line 12 is an alert message to the user to select an employee from the drop-down list.

5. Line 13 has the query attribute of the <cfselect> tag set to getempList used in lines 7 through 9.

6. Line 14 has the value attribute of the <cfselect> tag to which is assigned the field name or column name from the query getempList, which will be used to populate the drop-down list.

7. Line 15 closes the <cfselect> tag.

How the Action Page Code Works

Example 5.12B takes the last name of the employee given by the form page and returns the title of this employee.

1. Line 7 creates a variable called empLastName and assigns the value returned by the form.

2. Lines 8 through 12 create the query getEmpTitle, which will use the empLastName as the parameter for the where clause to search for the title of the employee.

3. Lines 13 through 16 use the <cfoutput> tag to display the title for the employee being searched.

4. Lines 17 and 18 close the <body> and <html> tags.

The topics discussed above describe a list of common SQL queries and commands that, when used within ColdFusion, present the data returned on the browser. Chapter 6 will discuss more advanced features of ColdFusion and SQL commands such as Aggregate, Group By, dynamic SQL, and <cftransaction>.

Security Issues of Databases on the ColdFusion Server

It is very important that the databases stored on the server are secured so that hackers do not gain access to them and destroy valuable information. There are basically two ways by which the security issue can be addressed: (1) look at the security offered by the database system in use and (2) check into the security features offered by the ColdFusion server. In this chapter, we will look at the security features offered by the database system (MicroSoft Access) and one method offered by ColdFusion to maintain database integrity.

Security Provided by Database Systems

Most database systems offer two broad categories of security features that can be enforced to the databases that are being built:

1. Administrator-level securities

2. Design-time securities

Administrator-Level Securities

For example, if you were working in MS Access 2000, you could set up security features such as

1. Establish a password and allow access to the database only if the password matches.

2. Use the file system security features of the operating system to secure the data access page that connects to the database, by restricting unauthorized users, and also control the levels of access to users.

In a multi-user environment, replication of a database is a very serious problem since any one of the users can replicate the database and use it for malicious purposes. Access allows the administrator to set up user-level permissions to restrict users from replicating the files. User-level permissions will not allow access to replicate database information; replication is possible only by an administrator.

Design-Time Securities in MS Access

Creating SQL views is a very good way to ensure protection of data within the database tables. Views can be thought of as partial tables. You could think of situations where you would only want a portion of the table visible to the users and not to expose the rest of the data. For example, suppose that a medical office has a database application to keep track of their business. The medical office has several people working and all of them using the database. It would not be wise to expose the entire database to all users. Such a situation is ideal for and warrants a view. As a designer, you could design different views of your database and save them in your database. You could then set up passwords for different users, and each time a user logs into the system, you could make a particular view (set of tables relevant to that user) visible and restrict access to the other tables.

Create Views in Ms Access

Example 5.13 creates a view in Access and runs a query on the view created. Type the code in Example 5.13 and save it as `Ch5Eg13.cfm`. The output is shown in Figure 5.17.

Example 5.13

```
1. <?xml version = "1.0"?>
2. <!DOCTYPE html PUBLIC
3. "-//W3C//DTD XHTML 1.0 Transitional//EN"
4. "http://www.w3.org/TR/xhtml1/DTD/xhtml1-transitional.dtd">
5. <html xmlns = "http://www.w3.org/1999/xhtm">
6. <head>
7. <title> Create View </title>
8. </head>
9. <body>
10. <form>
11.    <cfquery name = "getCustomers" Datasource = "nwind">
12.       create View Vget_Customers AS
```

```
13.      select CompanyName

14.      from Customers

15.    </cfquery> <br />

16.    <b>The view named Vget_Customers has been created
       </b><br />

17.    <b>Here is the list of companies that start with
       alphabet A </b><br />

18.    <cfquery Name = "getCust" Datasource = "nwind">

19.      select CompanyName FROM Vget_Customers Where

20.      CompanyName Like 'A%'

21.    </cfquery>

22.    <cfoutput query = "getCust">

23.      #CompanyName# <br />

24.    </cfoutput>

25.  </form>

26.  </body>

27.  </html>
```

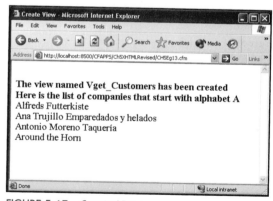

FIGURE 5.17   Create View

How the Code Works

1. Line 12 is the heart of this code. The SQL command create View in line 12 is used to create a view called Vget_Customers, and the SQL statement in line 13 specifies the fields to be included in this view.

2. Once the view is created, you can send queries to that view just as you would to any table. Lines 18 through 21 use a `<cfquery>` to get the list of all companies that start with the letter A. For an explanation of the SQL `Like` command, refer to Appendix A.

3. Lines 22 through 24 are the usual statements to output the results of the query.

Security Provided by ColdFusion to Maintain Database Integrity

ColdFusion provides a `<cfqueryparam>` tag, which serves two purposes:

1. It offers greater security to your database.

2. It makes your code more efficient in terms of speed of execution.

Greater Security

The `<cfqueryparam>` tag ensures that the correct data type is sent as a query parameter to the database so no malicious hackers can break the integrity of the database. To see the `<cfqueryparam>` tag in action, let us rewrite `CH5Eg8B.cfm` as in Example 5.14A. The output of the code will be the same as in Figure 5.12B.

Example 5.14A   Form Code

```
1. <?xml version = "1.0"?>
2. <!DOCTYPE html PUBLIC
3. "-//W3C//DTD XHTML 1.0 Transitional//EN"
4. "http://www.w3.org/TR/xhtml1/DTD/xhtml1-transitional.dtd">
5. <html xmlns = "http://www.w3.org/1999/xhtm">
6. <head>
7. <title> SQL Insert </title>
8. </head>
```

> **IMPORTANT**
>
> The code to create a view must be run only once. Attempting to run the code after the view has been created results in an error.

9. `<body>`

10. `Please enter info to be added to the table`

11. `<form action = "Ch5Eg8B.cfm" Method = "post">`

12. `<b> Enter Last Name: </b><Input type = "text" name="LName"><br />`

13. `<b> Enter First Name: </b><Input type = "text" name="FName"><br />`

14. `<Input type = "submit" value="submit">`

15. `</form>`

16. `</body>`

17. `</html>`

Example 5.14B   Action Plan Code

1. `<cfquery Datasource="nwind">`

2. `insert into employees(LastName, FirstName)`

3. `values`

4. `(<cfqueryparam cfsqltype="cf_sql_varchar" value="#LName#">,`

5. `<cfqueryparam cfsqltype="cf_sql_varchar" value="#FName#">)`

6. `</cfquery>`

7. `Record added`

How the Code Works

Example 5.14A is exactly the same as Example 5.8A. It is a form to collect user input for the first and last names of the employee. Example 5.14B is different from Example 5.8B. Notice that line 4 uses the `<cfqueryparam>` tag. The required attributes for this tag are the `value` and a separator, which is a comma that separates values in a query. The `cfsqltype` specifies the data type for the value being passed as a parameter. In this example, the data type being passed is a char type and is specified by the `cf_sql-varchar` description.

Examples of other data types commonly used are given below:

```
"cf_sql_float" value = "taxrate"
"cf_sql_int" value = "productid"
"cf_sql_date" value = "startDate"
```

For a more complete listing of `cfsqltype` data types and how they can be used, refer to CH11 (saveorder.cfm) file.

Enhances Efficiency of Code Execution

The second benefit of using the <cfqueryparam> tag is that it converts the data being passed to the database to the native code that the database expects, and thus performs a data binding. This avoids the task of the database having to parse the plain text that it normally receives, thus speeding up the processing phase.

Macromedia advises that all query parameters be sent using the <cfqueryparam> tag to enhance execution speed and also maintain the integrity of the database.

Summary

This chapter has laid the groundwork to understand how ColdFusion interacts with databases, specifically MS Access. We have seen how ODBC is used as a tool to connect to the data source and translate the information being sent from a program such as ColdFusion to the database.

SQL is the standard language used to extract and manipulate data from the database. This chapter discussed how to use common and simple SQL statements to extract exactly the information that we need and present it on the browser. SQL commands such as Select, Where, Like, Update, Delete, and Insert give us quite a lot of flexibility to get the required information from the tables, but SQL provides us with a lot more features that are more powerful in manipulating data, which we will look into in Chapter 6.

Database systems enable both the administrator and the designer to establish security options to the database being used. Some of the techniques that can be used include passwords, user-level permissions, and views.

Key Terms

<cfgrid>	data source	SQL Join
<cfinsert>	Maxrows	SQL Like
<cfquery>	Open Database Connectivity (ODBC)	SQL Select
<cfqueryparam>		SQL Update
<cfselect>	SQL Delete	SQL Where
<cftable>	SQL Insert	Structured Query Language (SQL)

1. What is the role of the ODBC API?
2. What are the main purposes of a data source?
3. Why is SQL not enough to retrieve information and display it on the browser?
4. What is the <cfquery> tag used for? What does the <cfquery> tag do?
5. Why is a Select * not a good idea when dealing with large databases? What methods can be used to improve this performance in terms of program efficiency?
6. What is the default performance of a <cfgrid> tag?
7. What is the difference between the two versions of <cfinsert> given below?

   Version 1:

   ```
   <cfInsert Datasource="nwind"
   Tablename ="employees"
   Formfields="LastName, FirstName">
   ```

   Version 2:

   ```
   <cfInsert Datasource="nwind"
   Tablename ="employees">
   ```

8. What are the constraints of the <cfinsert> tag and how can they be alieviated?
9. What is the requirement for a Join condition in SQL?
10. What are the different ways in which a database can be secured?

State whether the following statements are true or false.

1. The <cfquery> tag may be used as a general purpose tag to send any type of information to the database. _____
2. The datasource is a required attribute for the <cfquery> tag. _____
3. One way to get partial recordsets is by using the Maxrows attribute within the <cfquery> tag. _____
4. The <cfgrid> tag must be used within a <cfform> tag. _____
5. Controlling access to the database to maintain security can be done only by the administrator. _____

Contact.mdb is the database that will be used for these exercises.

1. Create a new data source called Contact for the Contacts database that can be found on your local machine. (If necessary, use the **search** button from the **Start** menu to locate the database and also the path to it.)
2. Design a query to get the list of CompanyName, Address, and City from the Company table of the Contacts database.
3. Design a form to insert a new record into the Company table. Provide a form to the user to enter the company name, address, and city. Once the form is submitted, show an action page to the user that shows the message, "Record Added". Use the default <cfinsert> method.
4. Design a CF template that uses an SQL Join to show the CompanyName from the Company table and the Title, LastName, and FirstName from the Contacts table. Display the results in a <cfgrid>.
5. Correct the errors in the following code:

```
<?xml version = "1.0"?>
<!DOCTYPE html PUBLIC
"-//W3C//DTD XHTML 1.0 Transitional//EN"
"http://www.w3.org/TR/xhtml1/DTD/xhtml1-transitional.dtd">
<html xmlns = "http://www.w3.org/1999/xhtm">
<head>
   <title> Using CFGRID </title>
</head>
<body>
   <CFQUERY NAME = "getContacts" datasource="Contact">
      SELECT Contacts.FirstName, Contacts.LastName, Contacts.Title,
         Company.CompanyName, Company.City
      FROM Company INNER JOIN Company ON Company.CompanyID =
         Contacts.CompanyID;

   </CFQUERY>
      <CFGRID NAME = "Titlelist" width = "500" QUERY = "getContacts">
         </CFGRID>
   </body>
</html>
```

Project Building Exercises

1. In this exercise, we are going to design the shopping cart database. The following are the tables that we require to save information pertaining to our store and for orders placed for items that we sell on-line.

PRODUCT TABLE

Productid	Autonumber	Primary key
Supplierid	Number	Foreign key to supplier table
Productname	Text	Name of the product
Productqty	Number	Quantity in stock
Productprice	Currency	Sale price of item
Productdescription	Text	Description

SUPPLIER TABLE

Supplierid	Autonumber	Primary key
Suppliername	Text	Name of supplier (brand)

CUSTOMER TABLE

Addressid	Autonumber	Primary key
AddressType	Text	Customer's address type. Possible values are "billing" for billing address and "shipping" for shipping address
Firstname	Text	Customer's first name
Lastname	Text	Customer's last name
City	Text	City
State	Text	State
Zip	Text	Zip code
Email	Text	Email address

ORDER TABLE

Orderid	Autonumber	Primary key
BillingAddressId	Number	Foreign key to address table
ShippingAddressId	Number	Foreign key to address table
OrderDate	Date/time	Date order is placed
OrderAmount	Currency	Sum of ItemAmounts
PaymentType	Text	Credit card type Options: Visa, Discover, Master
CreditCardNumber	Text	Encrypted credit card number
ExpirationDate	Date/time	Expiration date of the credit card
ShippingMethod	Text	Shipping method Options: Ground, Air, Overnight
ShippingCost	Currency	Shipping charge: Ground—1% of OrderAmount Air—2% of OrderAmount Overnight—3% of OrderAmount
Taxes	Currency	Tax amount 7% of OrderAmount
OrderStatus	Text	Order status; every new order will have status "New"

ORDERITEM TABLE

Orderid	Number	Foreign key to Order table
ItemNumber	Number	Line number for this item in the order
ProductId	Number	Foreign key to Product table
ProductQty	Number	Quantity ordered
ItemAmount	Currency	ProductPrice * ProductQty

a. Create the five tables that have been given above.

b. Figure 5.18 is the entity relationship diagram for the ShoppingCart database. Create the relationships in your database.

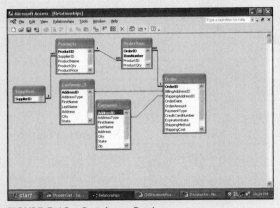

FIGURE 5.18   Database Design

c. Now enter some data into your Product and Supplier tables.

d. Create a data source called ShoppingCart for this database using the ColdFusion administrator interface.

2. Design a product-listing template to show all the items in the Product table. The fields that need to be shown for each product are the following:

a. Query the Product and Supplier tables (join by SupplierID) to get the following fields
(Query_name = getlist)

```
ProductID
Productname
Suppliername
ProductQty
Productprice
Productdescription
```

b. Add To Cart hyperlink: This hyperlink should go to a page called shoppingcart.cfm (this will be created later). Pass the following URL parameters to the shoppingcart page:

```
ProductId
Productname
Brand (Suppliername)
Productprice
QtyAvail (ProductQty)
Qty (ordered quantity - 1)
```

Hint: Your Add To Cart hyperlink will look something like this with the URL parameters:

```
<a href = "shoppingcart.cfm?productid=#getlist.productid#
    &productname=#getlist.productname#&brand=#getlist.suppliername#
    &price=#getlist.productprice#&qty=1&qtyAvail=#getlist.ProductQty#">
    Add to Cart </a>
```

See Figure 5.19 for a sample product listing page.

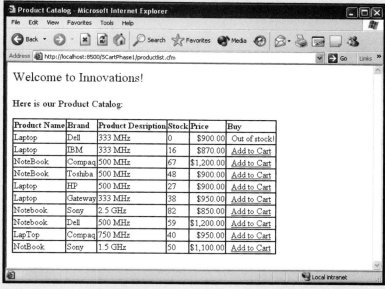

FIGURE 5.19   Productlist.cfm

Advanced Database Features

CHAPTER OBJECTIVES

1. Understand SQL aggregate functions.
2. Use the Group `attribute` and column aliases.
3. Understand transaction processing.
4. Create and use stored procedures.
5. Learn to generate dynamic SQL.
6. Process SQL with forms.

In Chapter 5 we looked at simple database concepts and saw how ColdFusion can interact with databases and provide the user with meaningful and relevant information. In this chapter we will explore further into the advanced features of databases such as aggregate functions, grouping of attribute values, transaction processing, stored procedures, and dynamic SQL. We also will also see how ColdFusion can interact with the features offered by the database system and provide the user with dynamic web content.

SQL Aggregate Functions

SQL has some built-in commands (functions) that can be used to return aggregate values to the user. Some of the common aggregate functions available in SQL are listed in Table 6.1.

TABLE 6.1

Name of Aggregate Function	Description
Count	Returns the number of rows in a column Note: Using `Distinct Count` excludes duplicate values from the count
Min	Returns the smallest value from the list of values in a column
Max	Returns the largest value from the list of values in a column
Avg	Returns the average value of all the values in a column
Sum	Adds all the values in a column and returns the result

Min and Max Aggregate Functions

These SQL functions are performed on a column in a table and the result returned is a single value for each function. Type the code in Example 6.1 and save it as `Ch6eg1.cfm`. Example 6.1 is a segment of code that illustrates the usage of the **aggregate functions** listed above. It also uses the concept of column **aliases,** which become very crucial in real-world business applications. The method of using aliases for field names or column names can come in very handy, especially when the field names in question are cryptic or lengthy. Once you create an alias, you will be able to use the alias instead of the original field name. For example, in your output tag you could say

```
<cfoutput #minPrice#>
```

where the alias `minPrice` stands for the minimum value in the column `UnitPrice` (refer to Appendix A for an explanation of aliases). Figure 6.1 is the output of this code segment.

Example 6.1

1. `<?xml version = "1.0"?>`
2. `<!DOCTYPE html PUBLIC`
3. `"-//W3C//DTD XHTML 1.0 Transitional//EN"`
4. `"http://www.w3.org/TR/xhtml1/DTD/xhtml1-transitional.dtd">`
5. `<html xmlns = "http://www.w3.org/1999/xhtm">`
6. `<head>`
7. `<title>Aggregate functions V2</title>`
8. `    <cfquery Name = "getLowHigh" Datasource = "nwind">`
9. `    select count ('ProductName')as Item_Count,`
   `        Min(UnitPrice) as minPrice,`
   `        Max(UnitPrice) as maxPrice`

```
10.         from Products
11.     </cfquery>
12.     <cfoutput query ="getLowHigh">
13.       The Total number of products carried in our
              inventory is #Item_Count# <br />
14.       The Lowest Price is #minPrice#<br />
15.       The Highest Price is #maxprice#<br />
16.     </cfoutput>
17.  </html>
```

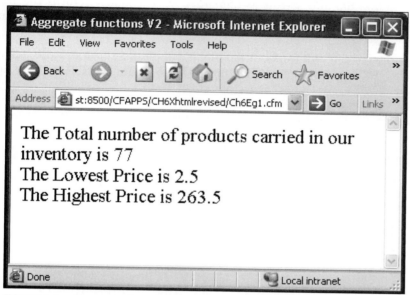

FIGURE 6.1   Aggregate Function

How the Code Works

1. Line 9 uses the `Count` function to return the total number of products in the column `ProductName`. The result is stored in `Item_Count`.

2. Line 9 also uses the `Min` and `Max` functions to return the lowest and highest prices in the column `UnitPrice`. The results are stored in `minPrice` and `maxPrice`.

3. The common thread in all these lines of code is that
   a. Each of these lines makes use of an alias for a column name.
   b. Each line uses a different function, which takes an argument, the column name, and returns a single result.

4. The rest of lines 12 through 16 are old hat by now, where the
   <cfoutput> tag is used to display the results of the query. Note that
   the aliases have been used as variables in the <cfoutput> statement.

The Group By/Order By Command

The SQL **Group By** command allows you to organize and categorize records in
the table based on a certain criterion (value in a column). Grouping enables
the presentation of data returned by the query in an organized manner.
Group By works well with server-based database systems such as ORACLE or
SQL Server. Appendix A gives the generic syntax of the SQL Group By statement. In MS Access, the command **Order By** gives the same result. The code
segment given in Example 6.2 illustrates the use of Order By. Type the code
in Example 6.2 and save it as Ch6Eg2.cfm. The query returns the list of
employees and their titles, grouped or ordered by city. Figure 6.2 is the output
of this code segment.

In Access, Group By works differently. Example 6.3 illustrates the usage of
Group By in MS Access. Type the code in Example 6.3 and save it as
Ch6eg3.cfm. Figure 6.3 is the output of this code.

In MS Access, Group By works only in conjunction with an aggregate function.

Example 6.2

```
1. <?xml version = "1.0"?>
2. <!DOCTYPE html PUBLIC
3. "-//W3C//DTD XHTML 1.0 Transitional//EN"
4. "http://www.w3.org/TR/xhtml1/DTD/xhtml1-transitional.dtd">
5. <html xmlns = "http://www.w3.org/1999/xhtm">
6. <head>
7.    <title>Order By City</title>
8. </head>
9. <body>
10.    <cfquery name = "nwindGroup" datasource="nwind">
11.       select * from Employees Order by city
12.    </cfquery>
13.    <cfoutput query="nwindgroup" GROUP="city">
14.       <b> Employees in city: #city# </b><br />
15.    <cfoutput>
```

16.   `<b> FirstName: </b> #FirstName#<br />`

17.   `<b>Title: </b> #title#<br /><br />`

18.   `</cfoutput>`

19.   `</cfoutput>`

20. `</body>`

21. `</html>`

FIGURE 6.2   Order By City

How the Code Works

This is a Select query on the Employees table. It returns the list of employees, Title, and City.

1. Line 11 does the major work in this example. The SQL Select statement selects the fields and uses one of the fields of the table as the criterion by which to group (order) the records. The result contains the records, categorized and grouped according to the City field, since that was the grouping criterion.

2. Lines 13 through 19 perform the usual <cfoutput> task. We used a nested <cfoutput> here, to get the output structured such that we first get the name of the city followed by an output of employees for

that city, then loop through the result set so that we do this for each city in the result set.

3. Line 13 is important here. Notice that we have first given the query name and next used the GROUP parameter of the <cfoutput> tag. This tag takes the value of the grouping criterion by which we want our records to be grouped in the output. The value of this tag must be equal to the value given to the Order By clause in the SQL used in the code. In our example, line 11 specifies the value of Order By to be city, and that is what is also given as the value to the GROUP parameter in the <cfoutput>, as seen in line 13 by the statement <cfoutput query="nwindgroup" GROUP="city">. This allows the <cfoutput> tag to display the data grouped according to the group parameter.

Example 6.3

1. ```
   <?xml version = "1.0"?>
   ```

2. ```
   <!DOCTYPE html PUBLIC
   ```

3. ```
   "-//W3C//DTD XHTML 1.0 Transitional//EN"
   ```

4. ```
   "http://www.w3.org/TR/xhtml1/DTD/xhtml1-transitional.dtd">
   ```

5. ```
   <html xmlns = "http://www.w3.org/1999/xhtm">
   ```

6. ```
   <head>
   ```

7. ```
   <title>Group By With Aggregate</title>
   ```

8. ```
   </head>
   ```

9. ```
   <body>
   ```

10. ```
    <cfquery name = "groupByCat" datasource = "nwind">
    select Avg(Products.UnitPrice) as AvgOfUnitPrice,
    Categories.CategoryName from Categories inner
    join Products on Categories.CategoryID =
    Products.CategoryID group by Categories.
    CategoryName;
    ```

11. ```
    </cfquery>
    ```

12. ```
    Here is the list of Categories of products we carry,
    and the average price of products for each of these
    categories <br /> <br />
    ```

13. ```
    <table border = "2" width = "50%"><th width = "10%">
    Category Name </th> <th width = "10%"> Average Price
    </th>
    ```

14. ```
    <cfoutput query ="groupByCat" >
    ```

15. `<tr><td width = "10%">#CategoryName# </td>`
`<td width = "10%"> #DollarFormat(AvgofUnitPrice)#`
`</td></tr></cfoutput></table>`

16. `</body>`

17. `</html>`

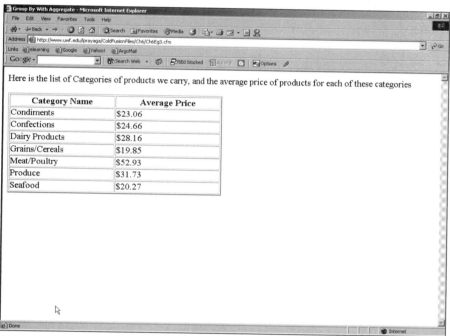

FIGURE 6.3   Group By Category with Aggregate Function

How the Code Works

This example groups products according to their category and returns the average unit price for each category.

1. Line 10 does the selection. Note the use of an alias for the average unit price.

2. The `Select` statement in line 10 uses an aggregate function `Avg` that returns the average of the `UnitPrice` for each category as specified by the rest of the query.

3. Line 10 also specifies the tables from which the required fields must be extracted. Notice that a join on two tables is being performed here because the information required is not available in one table.

4. The last part of line 10 specifies the grouping field to be
   `CategoryName`. This is what ensures that all products are sorted
   according to the category they belong to.

5. Lines 13 through 15 use the table tags to display the output in a
   table format. Refer to Appendix B for XHTML tags and their description.

Transaction Processing and Security of the Database

Transaction processing is the process of grouping together a set of queries
sent to the database via the server. This process serves two main purposes:

1. To ensure that a group of queries succeed or fail in totality. The benefit here is that the database will not be altered until all steps
   required to be completed are completed, thus maintaining the
   integrity of the database.

2. To provide a mechanism for locking the records of the table when
   the table is being used, thus not allowing multiple users to manipulate and modify the data at the same time.

The `<cftransaction>` Tag

ColdFusion uses the `<cftransaction>` tag to achieve the two purposes mentioned above. The `<cftransaction>` tag has two optional attributes:

1. `Action`. This attribute has three options:
   a. `Begin` is the default value. It marks the starting point of the
      block of code to be executed in sequence.
   b. `Commit` commits the set of pending queries or code segments to
      be executed.
   c. `RollBack` rolls back the set of pending queries or code seg-
      ments to be executed.

2. `Isolation`. This attribute supports four levels:
   a. `Serializable`, the highest level, allows exclusive locking; that
      is, nobody other than the current user can modify the data
      being read.
   b. `Repeatable Read` allows the ability to insert data by other SQL
      statements.
   c. `Read Committed` allows the ability to both read and insert data.
   d. `Read Uncommitted` is similar to SQL `Commit`, but readers can see
      the changes prior to `Commit`.

Tech Tip

It must be noted that ColdFusion cannot directly lock a data-base, but it provides a method via the `<cftransaction>` `isolation` attribute.

Syntax of the `<cftransaction>` Tag

1. `<cftransaction>`
2. `<cfquery name = "qry1" datasource = "test">`
3. `</cfquery>`
4. `<cfquery name = "qry2" datasource = "test">`
5. `</cfquery>`
6. `more queries . . .`
7. `<cftransaction action = "rollback">`
8. `</cftransaction>`

Points to Note from the `<cftransaction>` Syntax

1. The `<cftransaction>` tag is the first tag in the code segment.

2. The collection or transaction set starts with the very next ColdFusion tag that appears after the `<cftransaction>` tag.

3. The transaction ends with the `</cftransaction>` tag, which marks the end of the code segment.

> **Tech Tip**
>
> All ColdFusion tags within a `<cftransaction>` must use the same Datasource.

Let us take the Categories table from the Northwind database. Suppose your company no longer wants to carry any of the products that fall under the category Beverages. So we need to delete the category called Beverages from all the tables that refer to this category. Here comes the tricky part. To be able to maintain referential integrity of the tables (see Appendix A for a discussion on referential integrity and the `cascade delete` process), we need to make sure that every row in every table that refers to this category, either directly or indirectly through foreign keys, is deleted. In order to accomplish this task, the design of the tables must be edited. The changes required are listed below. (Note that we are using a Microsoft Access database and the steps listed are specific to this database system. Appendix A gives a generic SQL statement to accomplish the same goal.)

1. Open Microsoft Access and open the Northwind database.

2. On the tool bar, click the **relationships** icon.

3. The tables that are of direct interest to us are Categories, Products, Order Details, and Orders. This is so because these are the only tables that have a reference to the `CategoryName` either directly, as in the table Categories, or indirectly, as in Products, Order Details, and Orders via foreign keys.

4. Right-click on the line connecting Categories and Products and click on **Edit Relationships**. Click in the checkbox next to **Cascade Delete**

Related Records. Do the same for the line connecting Products and Order Details, and the line connecting Order Details and Orders. When the delete query is performed on the main table (Categories), the related records from the other tables having information about this category also get deleted, thus preserving referential integrity.

5. Figure 6.4 shows how your database looks like while editing the relationships between the tables. Figure 6.5 shows your database after the code in Example 6.4 is executed.

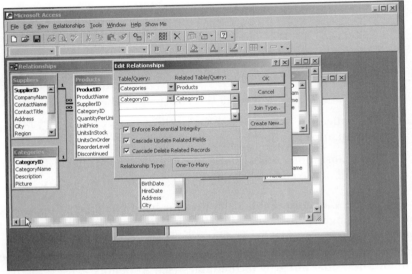

FIGURE 6.4   Cascade Delete Screen in Access

After you complete Step 4, your screen should look similar to Figure 6.4. Figure 6.5 is what your categories table should look like after running Example 6.4.

Now, you can close or minimize Northwind and work on the ColdFusion part of the example. The code in Example 6.4 illustrates the usage of <cftransaction>. Type the code given in Example 6.4 and save it as Ch6eg4.cfm. Figures 6.6 and 6.7 show the output of Example 6.4.

Example 6.4

```
1. <?xml version = "1.0"?>
2. <!DOCTYPE html PUBLIC
3. "-//W3C//DTD XHTML 1.0 Transitional//EN"
4. "http://www.w3.org/TR/xhtml1/DTD/xhtml1-transitional.dtd">
```

```
5.  <html xmlns = "http://www.w3.org/1999/xhtm">
6.  <head>
7.  <title>CFTransaction</title>
8.  </head>
9.  <body>
10. <cftransaction>
11. <cfquery name = "getCatList" datasource="nwind">
12. select * from Categories
13. </cfquery>
14. List of items in the Category table <br /> <br />
15. <cfoutput query ="getCatlist" >
16. #getCatlist.CategoryName# <br />
17. </cfoutput>
18. <cfquery name = "Delcat" datasource = "nwind">
19. delete Categories.CategoryName
20. from Categories
21. where Categories.CategoryName='Beverages'
22. </cfquery>
23. List of items in the Category table after deleting
        Beverages Category <br /><br />
24. <cfquery name = "getCatList" datasource="nwind">
25. select * from Categories
26. </cfquery>
27. <cfoutput query ="getCatlist" >
28. #getCatlist.CategoryName# <br />
29. </cfoutput>
30. <cftransaction Action = "Rollback" />
31. List of items in the Category table after Restoring
        Beverages
32. Category <br /><br />
33. <cfquery name = "getCatList" datasource="nwind">
34. select * from Categories
```

```
35. </cfquery>
36. <cfoutput query ="getCatList" >
37. #getCatlist.CategoryName# <br />
38. </cfoutput> <br /><br />
39. Now, we will be using Commit to commit the delete
       transaction
40. <br /><br />
41. <cfquery name = "Delcat2" datasource = "nwind">
42. delete Categories.CategoryName
43. from Categories
44. where Categories.CategoryName='Beverages'
45. </cfquery>
46. List of items in the Category table after deleting Beverages
47. Category for the second time <br /><br />
48. <cfquery name = "getCatList" datasource="nwind">
49. select * from Categories
50. </cfquery>
51. <cfoutput query ="getCatlist" >
52. #getCatlist.CategoryName# <br />
53. </cfoutput>
54. <cftransaction Action = "Commit" />
55. List of items in the Category table after Committing
       the deletion
56. of Beverages Category <br /><br />
57. <cfquery name = "getCatList" datasource="nwind">
58. select * from Categories
59. </cfquery>
60. <cfoutput query ="getCatList" >
61. #getCatlist.CategoryName# <br />
62. </cfoutput>
63. </cftransaction>
```

64. `</body>`

65. `</html>`

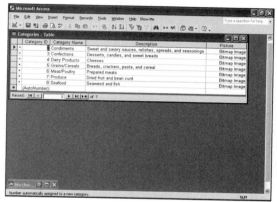

FIGURE 6.5   Categories Table after Deletion of Beverages

Notice that Figure 6.5 now does not have the listing for Beverages under the Category Name in the Categories table. This is the final product of your database after running Example 6.4.

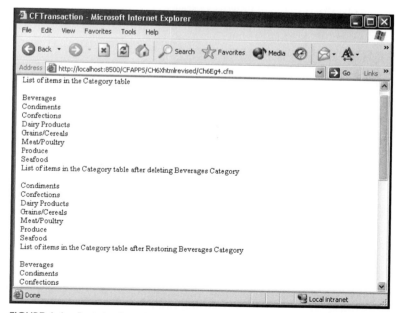

FIGURE 6.6   Part 1 of `<cftransaction>` Example

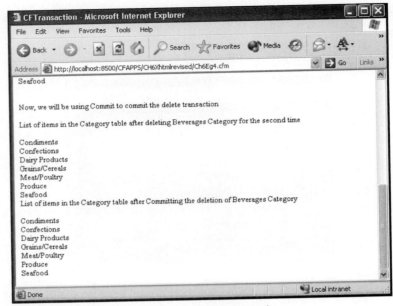

FIGURE 6.7   Part 2 of `<cftransaction>` Example

This is a rather large piece of code, but most of it has already been discussed in the earlier chapters and we have repeated the basic code block several times in the example. The main purpose of the example is to demonstrate how the `<cftransaction>` tag works.

How the Code Works

By glancing at the code, you will see that the code contains a set of `<cfquery>` tags. That is the very purpose of the `<cftransaction>` tag: to provide the facility to execute a set of queries in sequence and accommodate `rollback` and `commit` actions. These attributes give you the flexibility to either `commit` and complete a set of transactions you grouped together or let you `rollback` to the original state. In this example, we show how you can first delete the category Beverages, revert back by using `rollback`, then delete it again, and finally `commit` the delete operation.

1. Line 10 starts the transaction (set of SQL statements to be executed) with the `<cftransaction>` tag required by ColdFusion.

2. Lines 11 through 13 set up the `<cfquery>` getCatList, with the appropriate SQL statement to select all fields from the Categories table. Lines 15 through 17 use the `<cfoutput>` to display the results from this query. Figure 6.6 shows this output. To follow the example in full detail, you should open the database in Access and note some of the Products under the category of Beverages.

3. Lines 18 through 22 use another <cfquery>, Delcat, to perform a delete operation on the Categories table. This is where the category Beverages is being deleted from the table as specified by the where clause in line 21.

4. Lines 24 through 26 use the <cfquery> getCatList again to retrieve the information from the Categories table after the delete operation. Lines 27 through 29 use the <cfoutput> to display the current list of items from the Categories table. The list displayed now does not have the Beverages category. Figure 6.6 shows this output. If you now check the Products table, you will note that the Products belonging to the category Beverages have been deleted automatically because of the Cascade Delete option that you set up in the relationships in the database. Figure 6.5 shows that the Categories table now does not have the category called Beverages in it.

5. Line 30 plays an important role. We set the <cftransaction> action attribute's value to rollback. This will undo the previous delete command and restore the original data into the table.

6. Lines 33 through 35 again use the <cfquery> getCatList to retrieve the data from the Categories table and lines 36 through 38 use the <cfoutput> to display the output from this query. Figure 6.6 shows that Beverages has been restored and lists the categories again.

7. Lines 41 through 53 again run the delete command within the <cfquery> and display the output as before.

8. In line 54, we set the <cftransaction> action attribute's value to commit. This command physically deletes the record from all the tables that have a reference to the category Beverages. This action cannot be restored. The last part of Figure 6.7 shows the records after using the rollback and commit commands.

9. Lines 57 through 62 run the <cfquery> getCatList and <cfoutput> tags again for the last time to retrieve and display the information from the Categories table. As you can see from the output in Figure 6.7, the category Beverages is no longer listed.

10. Line 63 closes the <cftransaction> tag and line 65 closes the <html> tag.

Note that we used the same <cfquery> getCatList and the <cfoutput> for this query several times within this block of code. Is that really necessary? Not at all. In Chapter 9, you will learn to use other features such as <cfinclude>, functions, and procedures, which will allow you to avoid repeating the same block of code, and thus improve functionality and efficiency of your code.

Wow, that was a long example, but hopefully it was well worth your time.

Stored Procedures

A **stored procedure** is just a query created earlier and called when necessary. Stored procedures have a number of benefits such as

1. Avoiding traffic via the network and providing speed of execution. Since the query is already built and saved in the database, database access is minimized; thus, the processing time speeds up.

2. Enabling reuse. Once created, stored procedures allow for the concept of reuse, which is a very crucial component of efficient and good programming.

3. Promoting modular and team programming. Since stored procedures can be thought of as individual blocks, they can be developed as modules, where each module can be developed by different members of the team, thus benefiting from the advantages of modular and team programming concepts.

Stored procedures are supported by database systems such as Oracle, SQL Server, and other server-based database programs. **File-based systems** such as Access do not support stored procedures in the strict sense, but have equivalent components (queries that can be built earlier and saved) that behave like stored procedures. We will give an example to show how ColdFusion interacts with a saved query in MS Access. To see how ColdFusion uses a stored procedure using the <cfstoredproc> tag, visit the companion website for the book to get a list of references on this topic.

ColdFusion and MS Access Querying a Query

With ColdFusion 5, developers of ColdFusion templates have access to a new feature called querying a query. The concept is similar to a stored procedure and is very simple to use. Example 6.5 illustrates the usage of querying a query; Figure 6.8 is the ouput of this code. Type the code given in Example 6.5 and save it as Ch6Eg5.cfm.

Example 6.5

```
1. <?xml version = "1.0"?>
2. <!DOCTYPE html PUBLIC
3. "-//W3C//DTD XHTML 1.0 Transitional//EN"
4. "http://www.w3.org/TR/xhtml1/DTD/xhtml1-transitional.dtd">
5. <html xmlns = "http://www.w3.org/1999/xhtm">
6. <head>
7. <title>Querying a Query</title>
```

```
 8.  </head>
 9.  <body>
10.   <cfquery name = "qryByQry1" DATASOURCE = "nwind">
11.      SELECT * FROM qryByqry1
12.   </cfquery>
13.   <cfquery name = "orderbyCity" DBTYPE = "query">
14.      SELECT LastName, FirstName, City, Title FROM qryByqry1
15.      ORDER BY City
16.   </cfquery>
17.   Ordering records by City<BR>
18.   <cfoutput query = "orderbyCity" >
19.     City is #City# <br />
20.     NAME of Employee is: #LastName# #FirstName# <br />
21.     Title: #Title# <br /><br />
22.   </cfoutput>
23. <br />
24.   Ordering Records by Title<br /><br />
25.   <cfquery name = "orderbyTitle" DBTYPE = "query">
26.     SELECT LastName, FirstName, Title FROM qryByqry1
27.     ORDER BY Title
28.   </cfquery>
29.   <cfoutput query = "orderbyTitle" >
30.     Title is #Title# <br />
31.     NAME of Employee is: #LastName# #FirstName#
        <br /><br />
32.   </cfoutput>
33. </body>
34. </html>
```

How the Code Works

Prior to typing this code, you need to create a query in the Northwind database and save it as qrybyqry1 (this is what we have named it; you can save it with any name), which is the name we will be using in line 5 as the stored

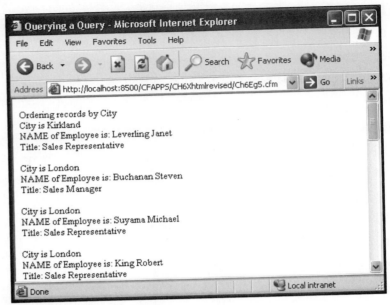

FIGURE 6.8   Query by Query

query from which we wish to extract the relevant information. The code for the query to be created in the Northwind database is a `select` query and is given below:

```
SELECT Lastname, FirstName, Title, City
FROM Employees;
```

Once this query is created, for all practical purposes it can be treated as a table in the database.

1. Line 10 uses `qryByqry1` as the name of the query from which the `SELECT` is being done.

2. Line 13 defines a new query called `orderbyCity` and replaces the usual word `datasource` with `DBTYPE`, which has the value `query`. So we see that the source for this new query is the first query created, which uses a `Select *`, so it contains all the information. Now, the advantage here is that subsequent queries can extract the required information just from this query, thus avoiding returning to the database. This helps improve the speed of execution, since the network traffic and congestion can be avoided.

3. The two queries in this code, `orderbyCity` and `orderbyTitle`, use `qryByqry1` as their data source and extract required information

from the query. Line 15 uses `ORDER BY City`, which sorts the records by the name of the city in ascending order; line 27 orders the results by title.

4. The rest of the code is just used to output the results of the query in an appropriate fashion.

Dynamic SQL

Technologies such as ColdFusion have become so popular because of their ability to generate dynamic web content. This feature becomes all the more important when dealing with databases stored on the server. The power of web-based database applications becomes evident only if the user can specify the information he or she wants, and then the application reacts dynamically and returns only the required information. The SQL command sent to the server is said to be dynamic, because the database will not know the SQL statement being sent to it until runtime.

Dynamic SQL works like this. For example, suppose the user would like to know the different products carried by a particular company. The user enters the name of the company into a form, which is passed to the action page of the form. The code in the action page then builds the SQL command with the name of the company included in it and passes it to the database, which then responds with the result set. It is not difficult to imagine the scope and potential of such a facility. Applications such as electronic shopping carts, electronic banking, and electronic libraries are all examples of such dynamic web-based database applications.

The information required by the database to complete the query processing is sent by form. The code segments in Examples 6.6A and 6.6B and the output in Figures 9.9A and 9.9B illustrate the concept of dynamic SQL. Example 6.6A is a form that displays the names of companies from the Suppliers table in Northwind. The user enters the name of the company into the form. This user input is passed to the action page. Example 6.6B shows the code for the action page. This code uses the passed value to complete the SQL query, passes it to the database, and displays the returned result. Type the code in Examples 6.6A and 6.6B and save the files as `Ch6Eg6A.cfm` and `Ch6Eg6B.cfm`.

Example 6.6A Form

```
1. <?xml version = "1.0"?>
2. <!DOCTYPE html PUBLIC
3. "-//W3C//DTD XHTML 1.0 Transitional//EN"
```

4. `"http://www.w3.org/TR/xhtml1/DTD/xhtml1-`
   `transitional.dtd">`

5. `<html xmlns = "http://www.w3.org/1999/xhtm">`

6. `<head>`

7. `<title>Dynamic SQL Form</title>`

8. `</head>`

9. `<body>`

10. `<form action = "Ch6Eg6B.cfm" Method = "post">`

11. `<cfquery name = "SupplierNames" datasource = "nwind">`

12. `select distinct CompanyName from Suppliers`

13. `</cfquery>`

14. `Here is the list of Companies we trade with.`

15. `<cfoutput query = "SupplierNames">`

16. `#CompanyName# <br />`

17. `</cfoutput>`

18. `<b> Enter CompanyName to get a list of products they carry:`

19. `<Input type = "text" name="CompanyName"> </b><br />`

20. `<Input type = "submit" Value = "submit">`

21. `<form>`

22. `</body>`

23. `</html>`

Example 6.6B Action Page

1. `<?xml version = "1.0"?>`

2. `<!DOCTYPE html PUBLIC`

3. `"-//W3C//DTD XHTML 1.0 Transitional//EN"`

4. `"http://www.w3.org/TR/xhtml1/DTD/xhtml1-transitional.dtd">`

5. `<html xmlns = "http://www.w3.org/1999/xhtm">`

6. `<head>`

7. `<title>Dynamic SQL Action</title>`

8. `</head>`

```
9.  <body>
10. These are the products made by the company
11.   <cfoutput> #Form.CompanyName# </cfoutput><br /><br />
12.   <cfquery name = "SupplierNames" datasource = "nwind">
13.     select Suppliers.CompanyName, Products.ProductName
14.     from Suppliers inner join Products ON
           Suppliers.SupplierID =
15.     Products.SupplierID
16.     WHERE (Suppliers.CompanyName)=('#Form.CompanyName#');
17.   </cfquery>
18. Products:<br />
19.   <cfoutput query = "SupplierNames">
20.   #ProductName#<br />
21.   </cfoutput>
22. </body>
23. </html>
```

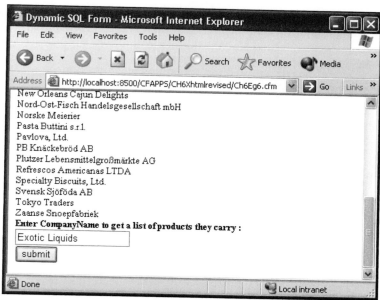

FIGURE 6.9A   Form to Get Company Name

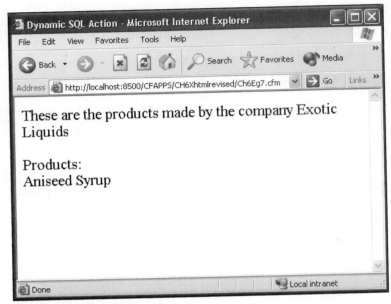

FIGURE 6.9B   Display Products

How the Form Code Works

1. This is a form to collect information (company name) from the user. Lines 11 through 13 run the query `SupplierNames`, which gets the list of company names from the Suppliers table. Notice that we used `distinct` to ensure that any duplicate names of suppliers would not be taken into the result set.

2. Lines 15 through 17 use the `<cfoutput>` to display the result set.

3. Lines 18 and 19 collect the information from the user and store it in the textbox `CompanyName`.

How the Action Page Code Works

1. Lines 12 through 17 run the query `SupplierNames`. Line 13 specifies the fieldnames to be selected from the tables. This query is a join of the tables Products and Suppliers. The join condition (common fieldname between the two tables) is specified on line 14; it is part of the `select` statement.

2. Line 16 is the crucial part of this query. This is where the information collected in the form is passed to the query with the statement

```
WHERE (Suppliers.CompanyName)=('#Form.CompanyName#')
```

This statement specifies that the CompanyName selected in line 13 must be equal to the value typed by the user into the textbox (CompanyName) in the form.

3. Lines 19 through 21 are just using <cfoutput> to display the result set onto the browser.

Working with Dates

Dates are always sticky data types, because each database system requires the dates to be formatted in a specific manner. So passing them to a SQL statement becomes tricky. Let us see how ColdFusion sends date values to a MS Access database. Code segments in Examples 6.7A and 6.7B illustrate this. Figures 6.10A and 6.10B show the ouput of this code.

Type the code in Example 6.7A and save it as Ch6Eg7A.cfm. Example 6.7A is a form to collect user input for three parameters: LastName, StartDate, and EndDate. Type the code in Example 6.7B and save it as Ch6Eg7B.cfm. Example 6.7B is the action page, which takes these three values and substitutes them into the SQL query. The query looks up the order history of this employee between the start and end dates as specified by the user.

Example 6.7A Form

```
1.  <?xml version = "1.0"?>
2.  <!DOCTYPE html PUBLIC
3.  "-//W3C//DTD XHTML 1.0 Transitional//EN"
4.  "http://www.w3.org/TR/xhtml1/DTD/xhtml1-transitional.dtd">
5.  <html xmlns = "http://www.w3.org/1999/xhtm">
6.  <head>
7.  <title>Dynamic SQL Dates Form</title>
8.  </head>
9.  <body>
10. <cfform action = "Ch6Eg7B.cfm" Method = "post">
11.    <b> Complete the information on this form to search
```

12.   `for the order history of Employee </b><br /><br />`

13.   `<b> Enter Employee Last Name`

14. `<cfinput type = "text" name="empLastName"></b><br />`

15.   `<b> Enter StartDate in the format mm/dd/yyyy`

16. `<cfinput type = "text" name="StartDate" Validate ="date"`

17.   `Message ="Sorry, Please Enter date mm/dd/yyyy."> </b><br />`

18.   `<b> Enter EndDate in the format mm/dd/yyyy`

19. `<cfinput type = "text" name="EndDate" Validate ="date"`

20.   `Message ="Sorry, Please Enter date mm/dd/yyyy.">`

21.   `</b><br />`

22. `<Input type = "submit" Value = "submit">`

23. `</cfform>`

24. `</body>`

25. `</html>`

Example 6.7B Action Page

1. `<?xml version = "1.0"?>`

2. `<!DOCTYPE html PUBLIC`

3. `"-//W3C//DTD XHTML 1.0 Transitional//EN"`

4. `"http://www.w3.org/TR/xhtml1/DTD/xhtml1-transitional.dtd">`

5. `<html xmlns = "http://www.w3.org/1999/xhtm">`

6. `<head>`

7. `<title>Dynamic SQL Dates Action</title>`

8. `</head>`

9. `<body>`

10. `Here is the order history for Employee:`

11.   `<cfoutput> #Form.empLastName# </cfoutput><br />`

12.   `<cfset new_date1 = #createodbcdate(#Form. StartDate#)#>`

```
13.    <cfset new_date2 = #createodbcdate(#Form.
          EndDate#)#>

14.    <cfquery name = "OrderDetails" datasource = "nwind">

15.       select Employees.EmployeeID, Employees.LastName,

16.          Employees.FirstName, Orders.OrderID, Orders.
             OrderDate

17.       from Employees INNER JOIN Orders ON Employees.
          EmployeeID =

18.          Orders.EmployeeID

19.       where ((Employees.LastName)='#form.empLastName#') AND

20.          (Orders.OrderDate)

21.       between #new_Date1# And #new_Date2#

22.    </cfquery>

23. <cfform name = "Catgrid" method = "post">

24.    <cfgrid name = "getEmpDetails" Query = "OrderDetails" >

25.       <cfgridcolumn name="Lastname">

26.       <cfgridcolumn name="FirstName">

27.       <cfgridcolumn name="OrderID">

28.       <cfgridcolumn name="OrderDate" width = "80">

29.    </cfgrid>

30. </cfform>

31. </html>
```

How the Form Code Works

1. Line 10 is using a <cfform> tag so that it can later be used to accommodate <cfinput> tags. It specifies the action page Ch6Eg7B.cfm that must be accessed upon submission of this form.

2. Lines 14 through 19 use <cfinput> tags to collect user input into textboxes. Notice that in lines 16 and 19 we have used the Validate attribute of the <cfinput> tag and provided date as the type that the input must be validated against. In the event of a wrong input by the user, the message box attribute of the <cfinput> tag pops up with an error message. This is a good way to ensure that the user inputs valid data into the provided textboxes.

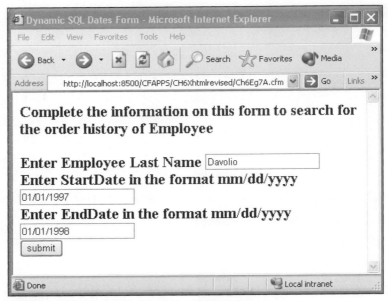

FIGURE 6.10A   Get Date Inputs for Order History

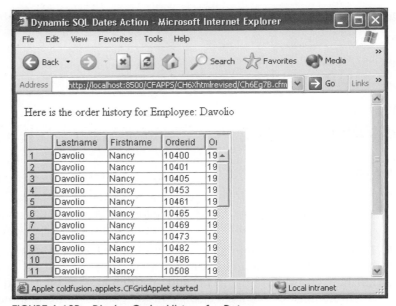

FIGURE 6.10B   Display Order History for Dates

The rest of the code is similar to what we have seen in earlier examples.

How the Action Page Code Works

1. Lines 12 and 13 use the function `createodbcdate` to convert the dates, entered by the user into the `StartDate` and `EndDate` textboxes, into a format that is understood by the database. These converted values are saved in variables `new_date1` and `new_date2`.

2. Line 14 specifies the `name` and `datasource` of the query being used.

3. Lines 15 through 18 form the first part of the SQL statement that specifies the requirements to select `EmployeeID`, the employee's `LastName`, and so forth from the two tables Employees and Orders with the join condition.

4. Lines 19 through 21 are the crux of this query. They specify the `where` condition of the SQL query, which requires three inputs: `LastName`, `StartDate`, and `EndDate`. This is where the input collected in the forms gets passed to these fields. It is important to notice that we are using the `new_date1` and `new_date2`—not `Form.StartDate` and `Form.EndDate`—as inputs for `StartDate` and `EndDate`. As stated earlier, this is an easy way to handle tricky date conversions peculiar to different database systems.

5. Lines 24 through 29 use the `<cfgrid>` to display the results from the query. Notice that we have specifically selected the fields we would like to be displayed from the result set instead of the entire data returned by the SQL statement. Lines 25 through 28 demonstrate the method of selecting individual fields by specifying the fieldname as the value for the `name` attribute of the `<cfgridcolumn>` tag.

Summary

We have covered a lot of ground in this chapter. We saw how the combination of ColdFusion and databases can be a powerful tool in generating dynamic web applications that are applicable to the real world.

Features such as aggregate functions and grouping certainly enable a more organized presentation of data that is appealing and easy to comprehend. The `<cftransaction>` tag allows us to maintain integrity of databases by either processing all the queries grouped within the `<cftransaction>` tag or not processing the whole set if even a single query fails for some reason.

The concepts of stored procedures and querying queries are very useful to promote efficiency of code execution, since they help avoid trips to the database over the network, thus reducing network traffic.

The last part of the chapter discussed dynamic SQL, which is the heart of any web-enabled application. This is the element that allows you to use all the concepts discussed earlier and present relevant information to the user.

Key Terms

aggregate function	dynamic SQL	`Order By`
aliases	file-based system	stored procedure
`<cftransaction>`	`Group By`	

Review Questions

1. What is the advantage of using a column alias in an SQL statement?
2. Are the aggregate functions performed on a row or a column?
3. How many results can an aggregate function return?
4. What is the purpose of the `Group By` clause?
5. What are the two purposes of transaction processing?
6. What are the attributes of the `<cftransaction>` tag?
7. Can ColdFusion directly lock a database?
8. Can you use different data sources within a `<cftransaction>` tag?
9. What is the one design time operation that must be done in MS Access to ensure that all related records in different tables do get deleted when you issue a `Delete` SQL command via ColdFusion?
10. What are stored procedures? What are the advantages of stored procedures? How does MS Acess address this issue?
11. What is the meaning of dynamic SQL?
12. Illustrate one example of a commercial application where you have dynamic SQL in action.

True or False

State whether the following statements are true or false.

1. A `<cftransaction>` is said to be successful if at least one of the queries in the transaction set runs successfully. _____
2. The `Rollback` and `Commit` are locking mechanisms provided by the `<cftransaction>` tag. _____
3. Aggregate functions allow you to organize your data in a column based on some criterion from the column. _____
4. Stored procedures must be created in the database before they can be used in your code. _____
5. Dynamic SQL is the idea of generating SQL at design time. _____

Use the Northwind and Contact databases for these exercises.

1. Use the Employees table in Northwind for this exercise. Assume that your manager wants to know the employees hired between two given dates. Provide him with a form that asks him to enter the start and end dates to search the database for. Upon submitting the form, your action page should contain the required code and SQL to retrieve the records of employees that were hired between these two dates. Display the names of the employees and their titles. (Look at the database and decide what tables are needed for this project.)

2. Use the Northwind database for this exercise. In MS Access, design a query that will retrieve information for `ProductName`, `UnitPrice`, and `CompanyName`. The two tables you will need here are Products and Suppliers. Save this query as `qry1`. Now create a ColdFusion template that will use a <cfquery> `qry2` that will use `qry1` and retrieve and display just the `ProductName` and `UnitPrice`.

3. Use the Northwind database for this exercise. Design a <cftransaction> scenario that will update the `UnitPrice` of Products `Where Category = Beverages`. Next, use a `rollback` to revert back to the original price. Finally, run the `update` command again to increase the price and commit the <cftransaction>.

4. Look at the code given below and debug the code so the code displays the results in a table format. The code should display the `CallDate`, `Subject`, `FirstName`, and `LastName` in a <cfgrid>. (Use the Contact database for this question. The two tables you will need are Calls and Contacts.) Your screen output should resemble Figure 6.11. Here is the code:

```
1.  <!DOCTYPE html PUBLIC
2.  "-//W3C//DTD XHTML 1.0 Transitional//EN"
3.  "DTD/xhtml1-transitional.dtd">
4.  <html xmlns="http://www.w3.org/1999/xhtml">
5.  <CFQUERY NAME = "getCallDetails" datasource = "Contact">
6.  SELECT Calls.CallDate, Contacts.Subject, Contacts.LastName,
           Contacts.FirstName
7.  FROM Contacts INNER JOIN Calls ON Contacts.ContactID =
           Calls.Contactid;
8.  </CFQUERY>

9.  <CFFORM NAME = "Catgrid" METHOD = "post">
10. <CFGRID NAME = "CallDetails" Query = "getCallDetails" >
11. <CFGRIDCOLUMN NAME="Calldate width = "100">
12. <CFGRIDCOLUMN NAME="Subject" width = "100">
13. <CFGRIDCOLUMN NAME="Lastname"
14. <CFGRIDCOLUMN NAME="Firstname" >
15. </CFGRID>
16. </CFFORM>
17. </html>
```

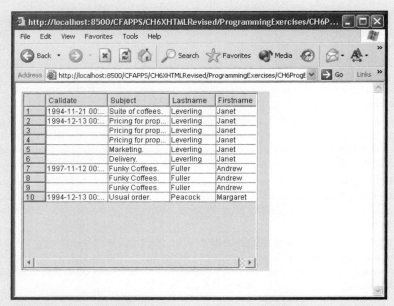

FIGURE 6.11   Call Date History

Shopping Cart Page

In this exercise, we will build the shopping cart page. In this simple shopping cart, we are going to enable only a single item to be ordered. Each additional item will overwrite the first one. This is so that we can get through the shopping cart without adding any complexity to the code. In a later chapter, you will build a fully functional shopping cart with multiple line items and the capability to add, delete, or update the quantity. Here we are only going to build the quantity update feature of the shopping cart.

The following are the steps that you need to follow:

1. This form will have two buttons, one **Proceed to Checkout** and another **update**. Set the action of the form to submit to itself since we need to handle the **update** differently from the **Proceed to Checkout**.

2. If `form.update` and `form.submit` do not exist (i.e., you came to this page via the product list page), then you will have only the URL variables available to you. Set all the URL variables into the session. Note the URL parameters that are sent to this page through the URL in Figure 6.12.

    a. `url.productid`: Product ID.

    b. `url.qty`: Quantity ordered.

    c. `url.productname`: Product name.

    d. `url.price`: Product price.

    e. `url.qtyAvail`: Quantity in stock.

3. If the form was submitted using a **submit** or **update** button, first set the quantity ordered (`form.qty`) into the session. This is so that we have the updated quantity and our other totals will be correct in case the user changed the quantity in his or her order using the quantity textbox in the form. See Figure 6.12.

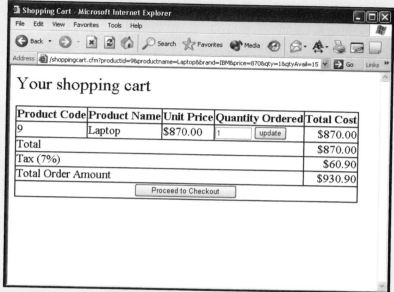

FIGURE 6.12   Shopping Cart Page

4. Now do the following calculations and set the results in the session as separate variables.

   a. `Itemtotal = price * qty`

   b. `OrderTotal = ItemTotal` (for now we will do only one item in the shopping cart)

   c. `Tax = OrderTotal * 0.007`

   d. `TotalOrderAmount = OrderTotal + Tax`

5. Set all of the above values into the session.

6. With these calculations done, check which button was clicked: **Proceed to Checkout** or **update**. If it is **update**, continue with this page; otherwise relocate the user to the customer information page (which will be built later). To relocate the user to another page, use the following code:

```
<cflocation url="getCustInfo.cfm">.
```

You will learn about this in a later chapter.

Built-In Functions

CHAPTER OBJECTIVES

1. Manipulate strings using string functions.

2. Justify strings within a field.

3. Wrap strings to limit output width.

4. Encrypt and decrypt sensitive data.

5. Extract parts of strings.

6. Search strings for characters or substrings.

7. Use mathematical functions to process numeric data.

8. Manipulate dates using date and time functions.

9. Understand the power of dynamic evaluation.

10. Use system functions to manipulate files and directories.

In Chapters 5 and 6 we looked at how ColdFusion interacts with databases. In this chapter we will learn some of the numerous built-in functions that can be used in ColdFusion to manipulate data. The following pages will give a short description of a few functions from each category so that you understand their usage with the help of examples. Some functions have already been introduced in earlier chapters.

Built-in functions in ColdFusion are used to perform tasks such as manipulating strings and dates, formatting data, determining the datatype of a variable, performing mathematical operations, getting system information, and so on. Built-in functions are frequently used in a $<cfset>$ or $<cfoutput>$ tag to prepare data for display or further use. ColdFusion MX has introduced some new functions for XML parsing. We will discuss these in Chapter 10. The new `wrap()` function introduced in ColdFusion MX 6.1 was explained in Chapter 4 to format text areas. It will be revisited here.

All functions return a value. In ColdFusion, the return value can be a number; string; Boolean; date and time object; or lists, arrays, structures, queries, or COM objects. Data are passed to functions via arguments or parameters. Most functions take at least one parameter, but there are some functions that take no parameters. ColdFusion allows you to write your own functions called user-defined functions (UDFs) that can be called from anywhere in your code. We will learn about UDFs in Chapter 9.

String Manipulation

A **string** is a set of **characters** that can be manipulated as a group. These characters can be enclosed in single or double quotes. In our applications, we may want to display strings, split them, search for substrings, trim strings, or encrypt them. String functions are used to manipulate strings.

Trimming Strings

ColdFusion provides built-in functions that remove extra spaces on the left, right, or both sides of a string. These functions take a single parameter—that is, the string to be trimmed—and they return the trimmed string.

- Ltrim(*String*) trims leading spaces, that is, spaces from the beginning of the string.
- Rtrim(*String*) trims the trailing spaces, that is, spaces from the end of the string.
- Trim(*String*) trims the leading and trailing spaces, that is, spaces from the beginning and end of the string.

Example 7.1 (save as trim.cfm) displays a form that accepts a string. On submission of the form, the action part of the code shows the effects of ltrim(), rtrim(), and trim() on the string.

Example 7.1   String Functions (trim.cfm)

```
1. <?xml version = "1.0"?>
2. <!DOCTYPE html
3. PUBLIC "-//W3C//DTD XHTML 1.0 Transitional//EN"
4. "http://www.w3.org/TR/xhtml1/DTD/xhtml1-transitional.dtd">
5. <html xmlns="http://www.w3.org/1999/xhtml">
6. <head>
```

```
7.    <title>Ltrim(), Rtrim() and Trim()</title>

8.  </head>

9.  <body>

10.   <h3>Ltrim(), Rtrim() and Trim()</h3>

11.   <form action = "trim.cfm" method = "POST">

12.     Type in some text, with spaces to the left and
          right.<br>

13.     <input type = "Text" name = "myText" value =
        "   Test String     ">

14.     <br /><br />

15.     <input type = "Submit" name = "submitButton"
          value="Trim String">

16.     <br />

17.   </form>

18.   <cfif IsDefined("form.submitButton")>

19.     <cfoutput>

20.       <pre>

21.         Original string:
              "#form.myText#"

22.         LTrim (trims leading spaces):
              "#ltrim(form.myText)#"

23.         RTrim (trims trailing spaces):
              "#rtrim(form.myText)#"

24.         Trim (trims leading & trailing spaces):
              "#trim(form.myText)#"

25.       </pre>

26.     </cfoutput>

27.   </cfif> <hr />

28. </body>

29. </html>
```

When you first load this page, you will see a screen like Figure 7.1A. The string is prepopulated.

Click on **Trim String** and you will see the results of the above trimming functions as in Figure 7.1B.

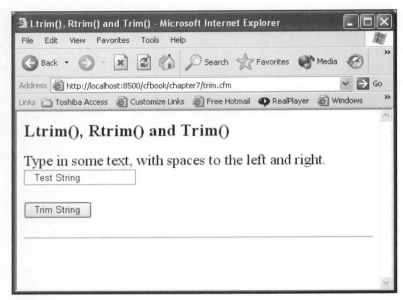

FIGURE 7.1A   Accept a String to Trim

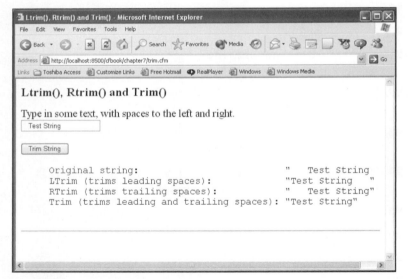

FIGURE 7.1B   Trimming Strings

How the Code Works

1. In the code, line 13 takes in a text string, the initial value of which is set to **"   Test String   "** (four leading and trailing spaces).

2. Line 15 displays a **submit** button for submitting the form to the same file.

3. A conditional statement in line 18 executes the action part of this page only if the **submit** button is defined.

4. Line 22 shows how `ltrim()` modifies the text by deleting leading spaces from the left of the string.

5. Line 23 shows how `rtrim()` modifies your text by removing trailing spaces from the right of the string.

6. Line 24 shows how `trim()` modifies your text by removing leading spaces from the left and trailing spaces from the right of the string.

Justifying Strings

You can position or align a string to the left, right, or center of a field using ColdFusion's built-in string justification functions. These functions take two parameters: the string to process and the desired string length. They return the justified string.

- `Ljustify(String, length)`: Left aligns a string within a field of a specified length. It does this by padding spaces after the specified string.
- `Rjustify(String, length)`: Right aligns a string within a field of a specified length. It does this by padding spaces before the specified string.
- `Cjustify(String, length)`: Centers a string within a field of a specified length. It does this by padding spaces before and after the specified string.

Example 7.2 accepts a string and aligns it appropriately in the field using `Cjustify()`, `Rjustify()`, and `Ljustify()`. Save this code in a file called `justify.cfm`.

Example 7.2   String Functions (justify.cfm)

```
1. <?xml version = "1.0"?>
2. <!DOCTYPE html
3. PUBLIC "-//W3C//DTD XHTML 1.0 Transitional//EN"
4. "http://www.w3.org/TR/xhtml1/DTD/xhtml1-transitional.dtd">
5. <html xmlns="http://www.w3.org/1999/xhtml">
6. <head>
7.   <title>Cjustify(), Ljustify() and Rjustify()
        Example</title>
8. </head>
9. <cfparam name="form.myString" default="test">
10. <body>
```

```
11.    <h3>Center, Left and Right Justification</h3>
12.    <form action = "justify.cfm" method = "post">
13.      <br />Enter a string (5-6 characters):
14.      <input type = "Text" size = "10" name = "myString"
15.        value ="<cfoutput>#form.myString#</cfoutput>">
16.      <br /><br />
17.      <input type = "Submit" name = "submitButton" value
             = "Justify String">
18.    </form>
19.    <cfif isDefined("form.submitButton")>
20.        <br />Left Justified     :
21.        <input type = "Text" size = "10" name = "lString"
22.          value = "<cfoutput># ljustify("#form.
             myString#", 20)#</cfoutput>">
23.        <br />Right Justified  :
24.        <input type = "Text" size = "10" name = "rString"
25.          value = "<cfoutput># rjustify("#form.
             myString#", 20)#</cfoutput>">
26.        <br />Center Justified:
27.        <input type = "Text" size = "10" name = "cString"
28.          value = "<cfoutput># cjustify("#form.
             myString#", 20)#</cfoutput>" >
29.    </cfif>
30.  </body>
31.  </html>
```

On loading the above code in your browser, a screen like Figure 7.2A will be visible.

Enter a string into the textbox and click on **Justify String**. You can see the effect of string justification in Figure 7.2B.

How the Code Works

1. The <cfparam> tag in line 9 enables us to use the variable #form.myString# to give a value to the input string in line 15. If the form is not submitted, #form.myString# will not be available, so

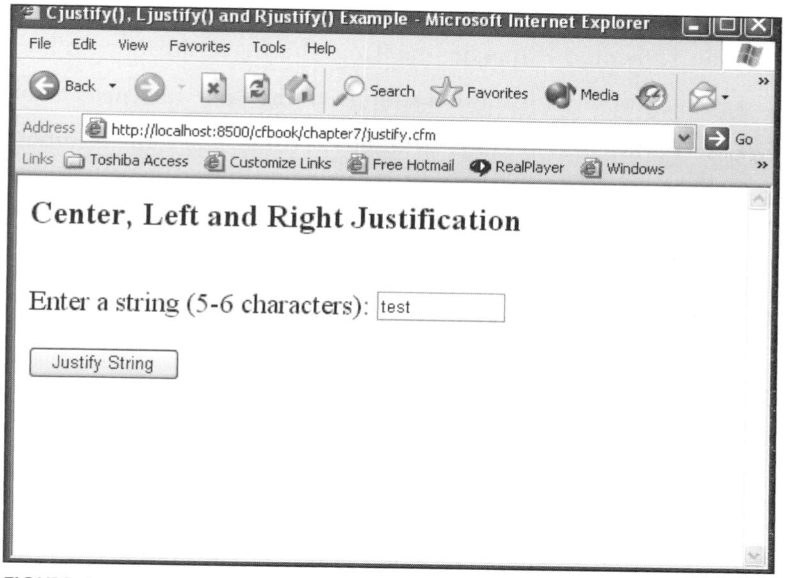

FIGURE 7.2A   Accept String to Justify

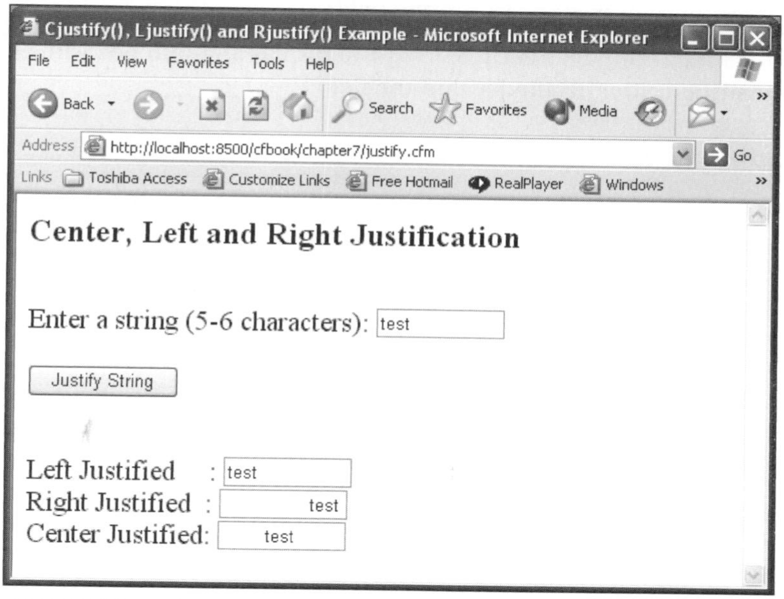

FIGURE 7.2B   String Justification

<cfparam> creates it and gives it the value test. Once the form is submitted, #form.myString# has whatever value you entered in the form. This is just a little trick to retain values entered into form

input elements even after the form is submitted. To simplify this code, you could eliminate line 9 and the `value` attribute in line 15.

2. Line 12 displays a form that submits to the same file (justify.cfm).

3. Line 14 displays a textbox to accept a string. The value is initialized to the variable `#form.myString#`, which is the string you entered in the form if the form is already submitted. If the form is loading for the first time, the value set by the `<cfparam>` tag in line 9, `test`, is displayed.

4. Line 17 displays a **submit** button called `submitButton` with `Justify String` displayed on it.

5. We need conditional code to determine if the form is submitted and if we should process the action part of the code. That is what line 19 does. It checks for the existence of the form field `#form.submitButton#`, which is the **submit** button of our form. If it finds this variable, it processes the code between the `<cfif>` and `</cfif>` tags.

6. Lines 21 and 22 use `ljustify()` to display an input box with the string left justified within the field.

7. Lines 24 and 25 use `rjustify()` to display an input box with the string right justified within the field.

8. Lines 27 and 28 use `cjustify()` to display an input box with the string center justified within the field.

Changing String Case

ColdFusion has built-in functions that enable us to change a string to lower-case or uppercase characters. These functions take one parameter: the string to be converted. They return the converted string.

- `Lcase(String)` converts a string to lowercase characters.
- `Ucase(String)` converts a string to uppercase characters.

The following lines of code show the usage of `Lcase()` and `Ucase()` to change a string to lower- or uppercase. These lines could be integrated with Example 7.2 (after line 28) to view the results in the browser.

```
<cfoutput>#Lcase(form.myString)#</cfoutput>
<cfoutput>#Ucase(form.myString)#</cfoutput>
```

Wrapping Strings

As mentioned in Chapter 4, `wrap()` is a new function introduced in Cold-Fusion MX 6.1 that enables you to limit the number of characters per line. The syntax of this function is

```
Wrap(string, limit[, strip])
```

It takes three parameters: the string to wrap, the number of characters to limit the length of the line to, and a Boolean (optional; default is `False`) specifying whether or not to remove new line characters before wrapping the text. The following code shows the usage of this function.

```
<cfoutput><pre>#wrap("Let us see the wrap function in
    action", 20, False)#</pre></cfoutput>
```

The output of this line of code is shown in Figure 7.2C. Each line is limited to 20 characters. Chapter 4 shows how a text area field of a form can be formatted using this function.

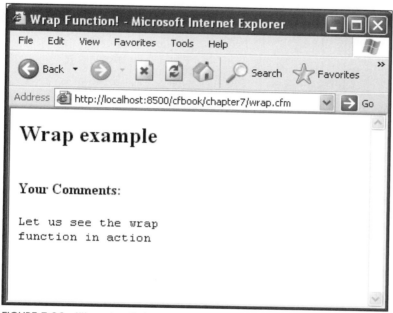

FIGURE 7.2C   Wrapping Strings

String Encryption and Decryption

Encryption protects confidential and private data by using a mathematical algorithm to disguise the string to be encrypted. Very often we need to encrypt data before storing it in files or databases in order to preserve the privacy of the data. ColdFusion has built-in functions that we can use to encrypt and decrypt strings of data.

`Encrypt(String, seed)` uses a symmetric key-based algorithm in which the **key** used to encrypt a string is the same one that is used to decrypt the string. The security of the encrypted string is dependent on keeping the key private.

This function takes two parameters: the string to be encrypted and a **seed** that is used to generate the 32-bit key used to encrypt the string.

Decrypt(*EncryptedString, seed*) decrypts the string (reverses the encryption) using the same key that was used to encrypt the string. It takes two parameters: the encrypted string and the key or seed that is used to generate the 32-bit key used to encrypt the string.

Example 7.3 encrypts the code you enter and then decrypts it.

Example 7.3   String Functions (encrypt.cfm)

```
1.  <?xml version = "1.0"?>
2.  <!DOCTYPE html
3.  PUBLIC "-//W3C//DTD XHTML 1.0 Transitional//EN"
4.  "http://www.w3.org/TR/xhtml1/DTD/xhtml1-transitional.dtd">
5.  <cfparam name="form.myString" default="">
6.  <html xmlns="http://www.w3.org/1999/xhtml">
7.  <head>
8.    <title>Encrypt() and Decrypt() Example</title>
9.  </head>
10. <body>
11.   <h3>Encrypt() and Decrypt() Example</h3>
12.   <p />This example encrypts and decrypts a string.
13.   Enter a string and a key of your choice and click on
          "Encrypt"
14.   <form action = "encrypt.cfm" method = "post">
15.     <br />Input your key:
16.     <br /><input type = "Text" name = "myKey" value = "">
```

```
17.    <br /><br />Input string to encrypt:
18.    <br /><textarea name = "myString"
19.        cols = "40" rows = "5" wrap = "virtual">
20.      </textarea>
21.    <br /><input type = "Submit" name="submitButton"
       value = "Encrypt">
22.  </form>
23.  <cfif isDefined("form.submitButton")>
24.    <cfset string = form.myString>
25.    <cfset key = form.myKey>
26.    <cfset encrypted = encrypt(string, key)>
27.    <cfset decrypted = decrypt(encrypted, key)>
28.    <cfoutput>
29.      <table>
30.        <tr><td><b>The string:
           </b></td><td>#string#</td></tr>
31.        <tr><td><b>The key:
           </b></td><td>#key#</td></tr>
32.        <tr><td><b>Encrypted:
           </b></td><td>#encrypted#</td></tr>
33.        <tr><td><b>Decrypted:
           </b></td><td>#decrypted#</td></tr>
34.      </table>
35.    </cfoutput>
36.  </cfif>
37. </body>
38. </html>
```

Save this code in a file called encrypt.cfm and load it in a browser to see a screen like the one in Figure 7.3A. It will prompt you for a key and a string to encrypt.

Enter any key and string to be encrypted and click on **Encrypt**. Your text is encrypted using the key specified by you. The text is also decrypted using the same key and displayed as you can see in Figure 7.3B.

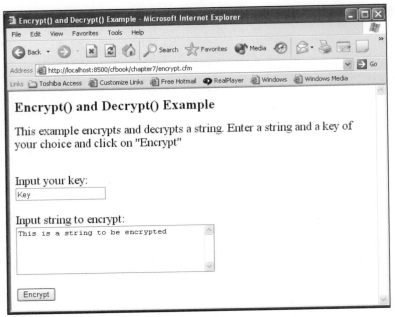

FIGURE 7.3A   Accept String to Encrypt

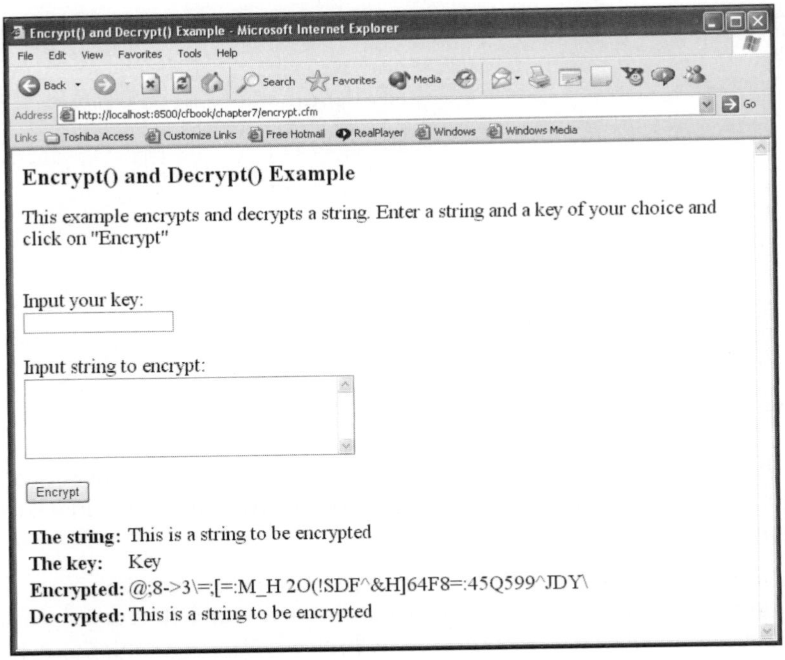

FIGURE 7.3B   String Encryption

How the Code Works

1. Line 14 creates a form with a textbox in line 16 to accept the key. Normally the key is stored in a database table and not accepted through the interface. You can type in any word here; for example, `testkey`.

2. Lines 18 through 20 accept the text to be encrypted in a `textarea`. You can type in a couple of sentences here.

3. Line 23 checks if the variable `form.submitButton` is present (i.e., the form is submitted). If so, then lines 24 through 35 are executed.

4. Lines 24 and 25 set the string and key form variables to local variables just for convenience.

5. Line 26 uses `encrypt()` to encrypt the string using the key entered in the form.

6. Line 27 uses `decrypt()` to decrypt the encrypted string using the same key.

7. The original string and key are displayed in lines 30 and 31.

8. Lines 32 and 33 display the encrypted and decrypted strings.

Extracting Substrings

Substrings are parts of strings. ColdFusion has some built-in functions that enable us to extract parts of a string, to split strings into substrings, or to remove some characters in the string. Very often in our real-world applications, we accept data or read data from files in a specific format.

For example, we may have a date string in the format `mmddyyyy` in which the first two characters stand for the month, the third and fourth stand for the day, and the last four characters stand for the year. From this format we may want to extract the month, day, and year separately. The following built-in functions that ColdFusion offers us help us achieve tasks like this.

`Len(String)` returns the length of the string. It takes one parameter, the string of which we want the length. The length of a string is the number of characters in the string.

`Left(String, count)` and `Right(String, count)` return the specified number of characters from the left or right of the string, respectively. They take two parameters: the string from which to extract these characters and the number of characters to extract.

`Mid(String, startingPosition, Count)` returns the specified number of characters from anywhere in the string. It takes three parameters: the string from which to extract the characters, the starting position from which to start extracting the characters, and the number of characters to extract. The index

> **Tech Tip**
>
> Use substring functions when you want to extract parts of a string and when you know how many characters to extract and where to start the extraction from within the string.

of the first character in the string is 1. If the starting position is 1, the number of characters specified by the variable Count are extracted starting from the first character of the string.

RemoveChars(*String, startingPosition, Count*) returns a string with the specified number of characters removed from it. It is the exact opposite of the Mid() function. It takes three parameters: the string from which to remove the characters, the position from which to start removing the characters, and the number of characters to remove. If the starting position is 1, the characters are removed starting from the first character of the string.

Example 7.4 shows how a string can be split by using the functions len(), left(), right(), mid(), and removeChars(). Save this code in a file called substring.cfm. In the example, we will extract the month, day, and year as separate strings from a date string in the format mmddyyyy.

Example 7.4   String Functions (substring.cfm)

```
1. <?xml version = "1.0"?>
2. <!DOCTYPE html
3. PUBLIC "-//W3C//DTD XHTML 1.0 Transitional//EN"
4. "http://www.w3.org/TR/xhtml1/DTD/xhtml1-transitional.dtd">
5. <html xmlns="http://www.w3.org/1999/xhtml">
6. <head>
7.    <title>Len(), Left(), Right(), Mid() and
         RemoveChars() Example.</title>
8. </head>
9. <body>
10.   <h3>Len(), Left(), Right(), Mid() and RemoveChars()
         Example</h3>
11.   <cfset mydate="08112004">
12.   Original String: "<cfoutput>#mydate#</cfoutput>".
13.   <br />String Length =
14.     <cfoutput> #len(mydate)# </cfoutput>
15.   <br />Month (leftmost 2 characters) =
16.     "<cfoutput>#left(mydate,2)#</cfoutput>".
17.   <br />Day (2 characters starting from the 3rd
         character) =
```

```
18.        "<cfoutput>#mid(mydate,3,2)#</cfoutput>".
19.    <br />Year (rightmost 4 characters)=
20.        "<cfoutput>#right(mydate,4)#</cfoutput>".
21.    <br />String after removing 6 characters starting
           from the 3rd character =
22.        "<cfoutput>#removeChars(mydate,3,6)#</cfoutput>".
23. </body>
24. </html>
```

On loading this code in your browser, you will see a screen like the one in Figure 7.4.

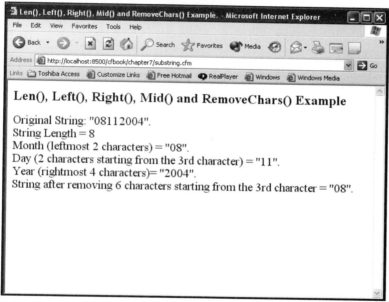

FIGURE 7.4   Strings and Substrings

How the Code Works

1. Line 11 sets a variable called mydate to the value 08112004. We want to extract 08 as month (August), 11 as day, and 2004 as year.

2. Line 14 uses the len() function to show the number of characters in the variable mydate.

3. Line 16 shows the month (the first two characters) using the `left()` function to display the leftmost two characters of the string.

4. Line 18 shows the day (the third and fourth characters) using the `mid()` function to display characters from the middle of the string.

5. Line 20 shows the year (the rightmost four characters) using the `right()` function to display the last four characters of the string.

6. Line 22 shows the month (the first two characters) using the `removeChars()` function to remove all the characters starting from the third character.

Searching and Replacing Strings

ColdFusion offers some built-in functions that help us find or replace strings within strings. For example, we may want to ensure the email address entered by a user is valid by searching the email address to determine it has the characters "@" and "." in it. Or we may want to mask (find and replace) the first few digits of the credit card number using "X" and show only the last four digits to the customer.

`Find(substring, string [, start-position])` and `FindNoCase(substring, string [, start-position])` are used to perform a search for a substring within a string. Both functions return the position of the first occurrence of the substring if it is found and 0 if the substring is not found in the string. Both functions take three parameters: the substring to search for, the string to be searched, and an optional position from which to start the search. `Find()` performs a case-sensitive search and `FindNoCase()` performs a case-insensitive search. If the optional argument `start-position` is not specified, the entire string is searched; otherwise, the search starts from the position specified. In ColdFusion, the index of the first character of a string is 1.

`FindOneOf(set, string [, start-position])` returns the position of the first occurrence of any of the characters in a specified set. Optionally, this search could be starting from a specified start position. The search is case sensitive. If no member of the set is found in the string, it returns 0. `FindOneOf()` takes three parameters: the string containing the set of characters to search for, the string to search, and, optionally, the start position of the search. If the optional argument, `start-position`, is not specified, the entire string is searched.

`Replace(string to search, old substring, new substring [, scope])` and `ReplaceNoCase(string to search, old substring, new substring [, scope]` are used to replace occurrences of a string with another string. These functions return the new string after the substitution has taken place. They take three parameters: the old substring, the new substring, and an optional scope that can be `one` or `all`, which will determine whether the first or all occurrences will be replaced. By default, the first occurrence is replaced. Replace() is a case-sensitive search-and-replace function and ReplaceNoCase() is a case-insensitive search-and-replace function.

Example 7.5 finds occurrences of characters in a string and replaces characters in the string using the case-sensitive and insensitive functions explained above. Save the code in a file called find.cfm.

Example 7.5   String Functions (find.cfm)

```
1. <?xml version = "1.0"?>
2. <!DOCTYPE html
3. PUBLIC "-//W3C//DTD XHTML 1.0 Transitional//EN"
4. "http://www.w3.org/TR/xhtml1/DTD/xhtml1-transitional.dtd">
5. <html xmlns="http://www.w3.org/1999/xhtml">
6. <head>
7.   <title>find(), findnocase(), findoneof()
         example</title>
8. </head>
9. <body>
10.   <cfoutput>
11.     <cfset stringToSearch = "The cow jumped over the moon">
12.     <h4>find, findnocase and findoneof example</h4>
13.     Original String: #stringToSearch#
14.     <hr /><b>find: Case sensitive search</b><br />
15.     Position of "the": #find("the",stringToSearch)#<br />
16.     Position of "the" after 15th character:
17.         #find("the",stringToSearch,15)#<br />
18.     Position of "not found":
            #find("not found",stringToSearch)#
19.     <hr /><b />findnocase: Case insensitive
         search</b><br />
20.     Position of "THE": #findnocase
            ("THE",stringToSearch)#<br />
21.     Position of "THE" after the 5th character:
```

```
22.        #findnocase("THE",stringToSearch,5)#<br />

23.      Position of "not found": #findnocase
           ("not found",stringToSearch)#

24.      <hr /><b>findoneof: Multiple search</b><br />

25.      Position of any of "aeiou":
           #findoneof("aeiou",stringToSearch)#<br />

26.      Position of any of "aeiou" after the 4th character:

27.        #findoneof("aeiou",stringToSearch,4)#<br />

28.      Position of any of "xyz": #findoneof
           ("xyz",stringToSearch)#<br />

29.      <hr /><b>Replace - case sensitive</b><br />

30.      Replacing one "the" with "a":

31.        #Replace(stringToSearch, "the", "a", "one")#<br />

32.      <hr /><b>Replace - case insensitive</b><br />

33.      Replacing one "the" with "a":

34.        #ReplaceNoCase(stringToSearch, "the", "a",
           "one")#<br />

35.      Replacing all "the" with "a":

36.        #ReplaceNoCase(stringToSearch, "the", "a",
           "all")#<br />

37.   </cfoutput>

38. </body>

39. </html>
```

On loading this page, you will see the functionality of the above functions on the screen like the one in Figure 7.5.

How the Code Works

1. Line 11 sets the value of the variable stringToSearch to the string The cow jumped over the moon.

2. Line 15 uses the function find() to search for the position of the substring the within the string. Since find() is a case-sensitive search, it does not pick up the first The but goes to the 21st character.

3. Line 17 searches for the same string the starting from the 15th position. The output of this search is 21 because that is the first occurrence after position 15.

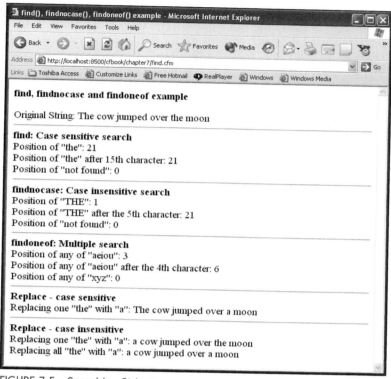

FIGURE 7.5 Searching Strings

4. Line 18 tries to search for the string not found, which does not exist in the string, so the output is 0.

5. Line 20 uses the FindNoCase() function to search for the string THE in the original string. This is a case-insensitive search and so it gets The in position 1.

6. If a start position of 5 is specified as in line 22, the second occurrence of THE is searched for and the output is 21.

7. In line 23, FindNoCase() returns 0 because the string not found is not found.

8. Line 25 searches for any of the vowels aeiou in the original string. It returns the first occurrence, that is, 3, since the letter "e" occurs in the third position in the string.

9. If a start position is specified, say 4, as in line 27, the search starts from the fourth position and returns 6, the position of the letter "o".

10. In line 28, FindOneOf() searches for one of the characters xyz, none of which exists in the original string, so the output is 0.

11. In line 31, the `Replace()` function replaces the first occurrence of `the` with `a` (note that the scope parameter is `one`). Since this is a case-sensitive function, `the` in position 21 is replaced and not `The` in position 1.

12. In line 34, `ReplaceNoCase()` replaces the first occurrence of `the` with `a`. Since this is a case-insensitive function, the first `The` is replaced.

13. Line 36 replaces all occurrences of `the` (case insensitive) with `a`. The string `The cow jumped over the moon` is thus changed to `a cow jumped over a moon`.

Decision or Boolean Functions

Decision functions return true or false.

`IsNumeric(String)` returns true if a string can be converted to a number. Otherwise it returns false. We may want to check if a string is numeric before using it in any mathematical functions. In the code snippet given below, if the child's age entered in the form is numeric, then the mother's age is calculated; otherwise, an error message is displayed.

```
<cfif isNumeric(form.childAge)>
   <cfset motherAge = form.childAge + 25>
<cfelse>
   Child's age is invalid.
</cfif>
```

`isDefined("variable name")` returns true if the named variable exists. Otherwise it returns false. We have been using this function in many examples to check if our form has been submitted or not. If the form has not been submitted, we display the form; if it has, we perform the action. That way the same template can do both the form and the action part.

```
<cfif isDefined("form.submitButton">
   <!-- perform action -->
<cfelse>
   <!-- display form -->
</cfif>
```

Mathematical Functions

Mathematical functions help us perform mathematical operations on variables. We may want to find the smaller or larger of two numbers or the square root of a number or we may want to round numbers to the nearest whole number. We also can find random numbers using built-in functions. Let us look at some of these functions below:

Min(*num1*, *num2*) returns the smaller value of two numbers. Max(*num1*, *num2*) returns the larger value of two numbers. Both functions take two parameters: the numbers to be compared.

Round(*num*) rounds a number to the closest integer. It takes one parameter: the number to round.

Sqr(*num*) returns the square root of a number. It takes one parameter: the number for which we need the square root.

Abs(*num*) returns the absolute value (a number without its sign) of a number. It takes one parameter: the number for which the absolute value is needed.

Rand() and Randrange(*num1*, *num2*) return random numbers. Rand() returns a random number in the range 0 to 1, including 0 and 1. It takes no parameters. Randrange(*num1*, *num2*) returns a random number within a range. It takes two parameters: the numbers that specify the range between which we need random numbers. *Num1* and *Num2* are included in the range.

NumberFormat() formats the display of numbers. It creates a number value in the format specified by the **mask,** which indicates the format of the number and the way it should be displayed. If no mask is specified, it returns the number as an integer with a thousands separator. Masks can be one or more of the following:

Mask	Explanation
_ (underscore)	Digit placeholder
9	Digit placeholder
.	Specifies location of decimal point
0	Pads with zeros
( )	Negative numbers are parenthesized
+	+ in front of positive numbers, - in front of negative numbers
-	Space in front of positive numbers, - in front of negative numbers
,	Thousands separated with commas
L,C	Left or center justify a number within the width of the mask column; default is right justified
$	$ sign placed in front of the number; $ should be the first character of the mask
^	Separates left from right formatting

If you put a $ sign on the left side of the number format, then ColdFusion will display the symbol on the left edge; if you put the sign on the right side, then it will display on the right. The same goes with the minus sign with negative numbers, as you can see in the table below. The underscore character decides whether the symbol is placed in the far or near position.

Example	Output
`<cfoutput>#NumberFormat("4.56", "$___.__")#</cfoutput>`	$ 4.56
`<cfoutput>#NumberFormat("4.56", "_$___.__")#</cfoutput>`	$4.56
`<cfoutput>#NumberFormat("-4.56", "-___.__")#</cfoutput>`	- 4.56
`<cfoutput>#NumberFormat("-4.56", "_-___.__")#</cfoutput>`	-4.56
`<cfoutput>#NumberFormat("-456", "C(__^__)")#</cfoutput>`	(456)
`<cfoutput>#NumberFormat("-456", "C__(^__)")#</cfoutput>`	(456)
`<cfoutput>#NumberFormat("-456", "C(__^)__")#</cfoutput>`	(456)
`<cfoutput>#NumberFormat("-456", "C__(^)__")#</cfoutput>`	(456)

Example 7.6 demonstrates the use of the mathematical functions by performing these functions on a set of numbers. This example lets you observe the results and the effects of mathematical functions. Save this code in a file called math.cfm.

Example 7.6   Mathematical Functions (math.cfm)

```
1. <?xml version = "1.0"?>
2. <!DOCTYPE html
3. PUBLIC "-//W3C//DTD XHTML 1.0 Transitional//EN"
4. "http://www.w3.org/TR/xhtml1/DTD/xhtml1-transitional.dtd">
5. <html xmlns="http://www.w3.org/1999/xhtml">
6. <head>
7.    <title>Mathematical Functions Example</title>
8. </head>
9. <body>
10.    <h3>Mathematical Functions Example</h3>
11.    <cfset num1 = 4>
12.    <cfset num2 = 16>
13.    <cfset num3 = 9.23>
```

```
14.    <cfset num4 = 9.99>

15.    <cfset num5 = 9001.89>

16.    <cfset alpha1 = "Apple">

17.    <cfoutput>

18.        Minimum of #num1# and #num2# is:
               #Min(num1,num2)#<br />

19.        Maximum of #num1# and #num2# is:
               #Max(num1,num2)#<br />

20.        Rand() is #Rand()#<br />

21.        RandRange(#num1#, #num2#) is #RandRange(num1,
               num2)#<br />

22.        Round(#num3#) is #Round(num3)# and

23.        Round(#num4#) is #Round(num4)#<br />

24.        Sqr(#num1#) is #Sqr(num1)# and

25.        Sqr(#num2#) is #Sqr(num2)#<br />

26.        Abs(#num1#) is #Abs(num1)# and

27.        Abs(-#num2#) is #Abs(-num2)#<br />

28.        Number format ($ and thousands separator) for
               #num5# is

29.        #NumberFormat(num5, "$_,___.__")#<br />

30.        <cfif isNumeric(num1)>1 is numeric</cfif><br />

31.        <cfif not isNumeric(alpha1)>#alpha1# is not
               numeric</cfif>

32.    </cfoutput>

33. </body>

34. </html>
```

After loading this code in your browser, you can see the result of the mathematical functions in Figure 7.6.

How the Code Works

1. Lines 11 through 16 set numbers num1, num2, num3, num4, and num5 and string alpha1.

2. Functions Min() and Max() in lines 18 and 19 compare two numbers—4 and 16—and identify the minimum and maximum of the two.

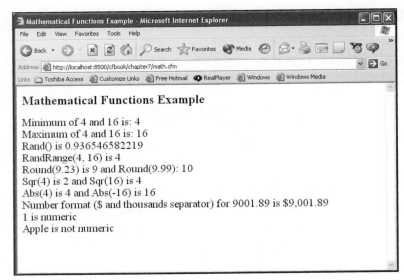

FIGURE 7.6   Mathematical Functions

3. Line 20 uses function Rand() to get a random number between 0 and 1.

4. RandRange() in line 21 gets a random number between 4 and 16. Each time you reload this page, Rand() and RandRange() will get different numbers.

5. Lines 22 and 23 round decimal numbers using the function Round().

6. Lines 24 and 25 get the square root of 4 and 16 respectively using the function Sqr().

7. Lines 26 and 27 show the result of the Abs() function on positive and negative numbers.

8. Line 29 formats a number using the $ sign and thousands separator using the NumberFormat() function.

9. Lines 30 and 31 use the decision function isNumeric() to check whether a value is a number or not.

Tech Tip

Use date and time functions when you want to create or manipulate date/time objects, or format date objects for display.

Date and Time Functions

Date and time functions allow you to perform manipulations on date/time form fields.

Creating Date/Time Objects

A date/time object in ColdFusion is the representation of a complete date and time accurate to the second and is used to pass date/time information between functions. The ranges are given in the table below.

Period	Range
Year	100–9999
Month	1–12
Day	1–31
Hour	1–23
Minute	0–59
Second	0–59

CreateDate(*year, month, day*) and CreateDateTime(*year, month, day, hour, minute, second*) returns a valid date/time object. CreateDate() takes parameters year, month, and day, which are integers. CreateDateTime() takes in additional integers for time—hour, minute, and second.

CreateODBCDate(*date*) and CreateODBCDateTime(*date*) return a valid date/time object in ODBC date format. They take one parameter: a date/time object.

Formatting Dates

To display a date/time object, we can use one of the date/time formatting functions.

DateFormat(*date* [, *mask*]) returns the date/time formatted as specified in the mask or format. The default mask is dd-mmm-yy. Parameters are a date/time object and the mask, which shows how to display the date. The mask is specified for day, month, and year in the following manner:

Mask for Day	• d—day of month as digits • dd—day of month as digits with leading 0 • ddd—day of week as 3-letter abbreviation
Mask for Month	• m—month as digits • mm—month as digits with leading 0 • mmm—full month name
Mask for Year	• y—year as last two digits • yy—year as last two digits with leading 0 • yyyy—year as 4 digits

`DatePart()` returns part of a date as an integer. The parameters are the part of the date to return and the date/time object. Part of date can be one of the following:

DatePart	Explanation
Yyyy	Year
Q	Quarter
M	Month
Y	Day of year
D	Day
W	Weekday
WW	Week
H	Hour
N	Minute
S	Second
L	Millisecond (introduced in ColdFusion MX 6.1)

Date Arithmetic

`DateAdd(datepart, number, date)` returns the date to which a period has been added. Parameters are `datepart` (part of the date to add), the number of units of `datepart` to add to the date (if positive) or subtract from the date (if negative), and `date`—date/time object.

`DateDiff(datepart, date1, date2)` returns the number of intervals in units of `datepart` by which dates differ; `datepart` here can be any of the parts of the date, as in the above table.

Functions to Extract Parts of Dates

- `Day(date)` returns the numeric day of the month ranging from 1 through 31.
- `Week(date)` returns the numeric week of the year ranging from 1 through 53.
- `Month(date)` returns the month of the year ranging from 1 through 12.
- `Year(date)` returns the year of the date.
- `Quarter(date)` calculates and returns the quarter in which the date falls, ranging from 1 through 4.
- `Hour(date)` returns the numeric value for hour in the range 0 through 23.
- `Minute(date)` returns the numeric value for minute in the range 0 through 59.

- Second(*date*) returns the numeric value for second in the range 0 through 59.

All these functions take the date/time object as a parameter.

Other Date Functions

- DaysInYear(*date*) returns the number of days in a year.
- DaysInMonth(*date*) returns the number of days in the month.
- DayOfWeek(*date*) returns the numeric day of the week (e.g., 1 for Sunday).
- DayOfYear(*date*) returns the numeric day of the year.

All these functions take the date/time object as a parameter.

DayOfWeekAsString(*day_number*) returns the name of the day of the week number. The parameter is the numeric day of the week; that is, a number from 1 (Sunday) to 7 (Saturday).

MonthAsString(*month_number*) returns the name of the month corresponding to the month number. It takes one parameter: the numeric month ranging from 1 through 12.

Now() returns the current date and time as a date/time object. The Cold-Fusion server date is used.

Decision or Boolean Date Functions

Boolean functions return true or false.

IsDate(*String*) returns true if the string is a valid date string. It takes a string as a parameter.

IsLeapYear(*Year*) returns true if the year is a leap year. It takes a numeric year as a parameter.

Example 7.7 shows the use and output of each of the above date functions. Save this code in a file called datetime.cfm.

Example 7.7   Date Functions (datetime.cfm)

```
1. <!DOCTYPE html
2. PUBLIC "-//W3C//DTD XHTML 1.0 Transitional//EN"
3. "http://www.w3.org/TR/xhtml1/DTD/xhtml1-
   transitional.dtd">
4. <html xmlns="http://www.w3.org/1999/xhtml">
5. <head>
6.   <title>Date/Time Functions Examples</title>
7. </head>
```

8. `<body>`

9.   `<h4>Date/Time Functions Examples</h4>`

10. `<cfoutput>`

11.   `<b>Using Now():</b>#now()#`

12.   `<cfset thismonth = month(now())>`

13.   `<cfset thisday = day(now())>`

14.   `<cfset thisyear = year(now())>`

15.   `<cfset thishr = hour(now())>`

16.   `<cfset thismin = minute(now())>`

17.   `<cfset thissec = second(now())>`

18.   `<cfset thisDate = CreateDate(thisyear, thismonth, thisday)>`

19.   `<br /><b>CreateDate:</b>#thisDate#`

20.   `<br /><b>Current month, day and year:</b>`

21.   `#thismonth#/#thisday#/#thisyear#`

22.   `<br /><b>Current hour, minute and second:</b>`

23.   `#thishr#:#thismin#:#thissec#`

24.   `<br /><b>CreateDateTime:</b>`

25.   `#CreateDateTime(thisyear, thismonth, thisday, thishr, thismin, thissec)#`

26.   `<br /><b>CreateODBCDate:</b> #CreateODBCDate(thisDate)#`

27.   `<br /><b>CreateODBCDateTime:</b>`

28.   `#CreateODBCDateTime(thisDate)#`

29.   `<br /><b>Format mmm d, yyyy from ODBCDate:</b>`

30.   `#DateFormat(CreateODBCDate(thisDate), "mmmm d, yyyy")#<br />`

31.   `<b>Using DatePart to get year from the date:</b>`

32.   `#DatePart("yyyy", thisDate)#<br />`

33.   `<b>Day of Week as number:</b>#DayOfWeek (thisDate)#<br />`

34.   `<b>Day of Week as String:</b>`

35.   `#DayofWeekAsString(DayOfWeek(thisDate))#<br />`

```
36.        <b>Month as number:</b> #Month(thisDate)#<br />
37.        <b>Month as string:</b> #MonthAsString
           (Month(thisDate))#<br />
38.        <b>Day of month as number:</b> #Day(thisDate)#<br />
39.        <b>Number of days in month:</b> #DaysInMonth
           (thisDate)#<br />
40.        <b>Week of year as number:</b> #Week(thisDate)#<br />
41.        <b>Year as number:</b> #Year(thisDate)#<br />
42.        <b>Day of year as number:</b> #DayOfYear
           (thisDate)#<br />
43.        <b>Number of days in year:</b> #DaysinYear
           (thisDate)#<br />
44.        <b>Quarter of year:</b> #Quarter(thisDate)#<br />
45.        <b>Leap year :</b>
46.        <cfif IsLeapYear(Year(thisDate))>This is a leap year
47.        <cfelse>This is not a leap year
48.        </cfif>
49.    </cfoutput>
50.    <hr />
51. </body>
52. </html>
```

Load this page in your browser to see a screen like Figure 7.7.

How the Code Works

1. We use the now() function to get the current date/time object in line 11.

2. We then set individual variables for each part of the date/time object by using the month(), day(), year(), hour(), minute(), and second() functions in lines 12 through 17.

3. These values are passed to the createDate() function in line 18 and createDateTime() function in line 25. The ODBC date is created in line 26 using this date/time object and is displayed.

4. The date is formatted in line 30 with the dateformat() function. Any format mask may be used here. We have used mmmm d, yyyy, which will display the date in the following format: March 9, 2003.

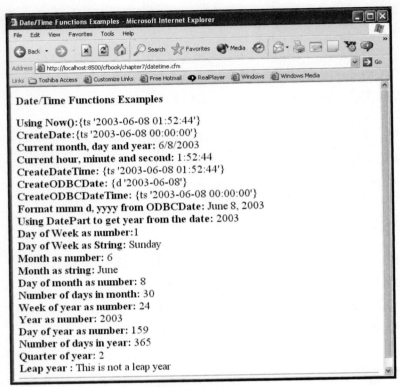

FIGURE 7.7   Date and Time Functions

5. The year part of the date is extracted using the `DatePart()` function in line 32.

6. The day of week is extracted as a number in line 33 and as a string in line 35 and displayed.

7. The month is extracted as a number in line 36 and as a string in line 37 and displayed.

8. The day of month is extracted as a number in line 38 and displayed.

9. The number of days in the month is extracted by line 39 and displayed.

10. Line 40 displays the week of the year as a number.

11. Line 41 displays the year as a number.

12. Line 42 shows the day of the year as a number.

13. Line 43 displays the number of days in the year.

14. Line 44 displays the quarter of the year.

15. Lines 46 through 48 check if this year is a leap year or not and display an appropriate message.

Evaluation of Expressions

Dynamic evaluation is the process of evaluating a string expression. It is an advanced technique in ColdFusion that allows expressions to be created dynamically using string operations that are evaluated as needed. Dynamic expressions are created using string expressions (surrounded with quotation marks). The actual expression is determined at run time, when ColdFusion looks up and replaces the variables with their values, calling any functions, and performing any required operations.

ColdFusion provides us several dynamic expression evaluation functions such as `Evaluate()`, `IIF()`, and `DE()`. We will look at `Evaluate()` below.

`Evaluate()` as a Dynamic Evaluation Function

`Evaluate()` evaluates arguments, from left to right, and returns the result of evaluating the last argument. This function takes as parameters string expressions that are to be evaluated. It returns the evaluated result. The syntax of this function is given below.

```
Evaluate(string expression1 [, string expression2 [, ... ] ] )
```

Look at the examples below to see the simplest usage of `evaluate()`.

```
Evaluate("4*5")
```

The above code will evaluate the product of 4 and 5 and the result will be 20.

```
Evaluate("sqr(4)")
```

The above code will evaluate the mathematical function `sqr()` and return 2.

If quotes are not escaped around the string expression, that is, the string expression is not within quotes, then the `evaluate()` function will look a level deeper to evaluate. This is called **double evaluation** since it is two levels deep. See Example 7.8 for an example of `evaluate()` with single and double evaluation. Save this code in a file called `eval.cfm`.

Example 7.8_Dynamic Evaluation (eval.cfm)

```
1. <!DOCTYPE html
2. PUBLIC "-//W3C//DTD XHTML 1.0 Transitional//EN"
3. "http://www.w3.org/TR/xhtml1/DTD/xhtml1-transitional.dtd">
4. <html xmlns="http://www.w3.org/1999/xhtml">
```

```
5. <head>
      <title>Evaluate example</title>
6. </head>
7. <body>
8.    <cfset var2 = "yes">
9.    <cfset var1 = "var2">
10.   <h3>
11.   <cfoutput>Evaluation of 1 + 2 - escaping quotes:
12.   #Evaluate("1+2")#</cfoutput><br />
13.   <cfoutput>Evaluation of var1 - escaping quotes:
14.   #Evaluate("var1")#</cfoutput><br />
15.   <cfoutput>Evaluation of var1 - no escaping quotes:
16.   #Evaluate(var1)#</cfoutput><br />
17.   </h3>
18. </body>
19. </html>
```

When you load this page in your browser, you will see a screen like Figure 7.8.

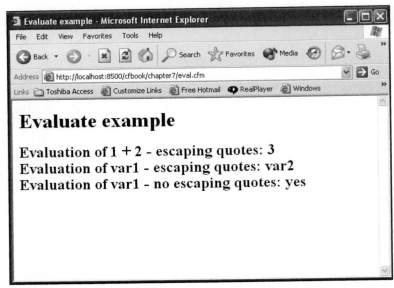

FIGURE 7.8   Dynamic Evaluation

How the Code Works

1. Line 12 evaluates the expression "1+2" to give the output 3. The sum is evaluated or calculated.

2. Line 14 evaluates the value of `var1` as `var2` and displays `var2`. Since quotes are escaped (quotes are around `var1`), single-level evaluation takes place. The expression is evaluated to `var2` because line 9 sets `var1` to the string `var2`.

3. In line 16, since quotes are not escaped (i.e., no quotes around `var1`), ColdFusion evaluates `var1` as `var2` and then evaluates `var2` as `yes`. The value of `var2`—that is, `yes`—is ultimately displayed on the screen. This is double evaluation.

Business Example for `Evaluate()`

Variable names can be built dynamically and evaluated using the `Evaluate()` function.

This is best explained using an example. Example 7.9 demonstrates this use of the `Evaluate()` function in a common business application. The code sets up an order form with four input fields to accept four product names and four quantity fields to accept quantities for each product. The template handles both the form and action, so the form is submitted to the same template. The action part of this template loops through each item on the order form, dynamically evaluating the variable name, and gets the four product names and quantities entered in the form. Type and save this code in a file called `evalbusiness.cfm`.

> **Tech Tip**
>
> The `Evaluate()` function is useful for forming one variable from multiple variables.

Example 7.9   Dynamic Evaluation (evalbusiness.cfm)

```
1.  <!DOCTYPE html
2.  PUBLIC "-//W3C//DTD XHTML 1.0 Transitional//EN"
3.  "http://www.w3.org/TR/xhtml1/DTD/xhtml1-transitional.dtd">
4.  <html xmlns="http://www.w3.org/1999/xhtml">
5.  <head>
6.    <title>Dynamic Evaluation Business Example</title>
7.  </head>
8.  <body>
9.    <cfif not isDefined("Form.submitbutton")>
10.     <h3>Order Form</h3>
```

```
11.   <form name="evaluateForm" method="post"
      action="evalBusiness.cfm"><br />

12.   <table>

13.   <tr>

14.     <td><b>S.No.</b></td>

15.     <td><b>Product Name</b></td>

16.     <td><b>Quantity</b></td>

17.   </tr>

18.   <tr>

19.     <td>1) </td>

20.     <td><input type="text" name="Item_1"
        value="Computer"></td>

21.     <td><input type="text" size="4" name="qty_1"
        value="0"></td>

22.   </tr>

23.   <tr>

24.     <td>2) </td>

25.     <td><input type="text" name="Item_2"
        value="Monitor"></td>

26.     <td><input type="text" size="4" name="qty_2"
        value="0"></td>

27.   </tr>

28.   <tr>

29.     <td>3) </td>

30.     <td><input type="text" name="Item_3"
        value="Keyboard"></td>

31.     <td><input type="text" size="4" name="qty_3"
        value="0"></td>

32.   </tr>

33.   <tr>

34.     <td>4) </td>

35.     <td><input type="text" name="Item_4"
        value="Mouse"></td>
```

```
36.        <td><input type="text" size="4" name="qty_4"
              value="0"></td>
37.     </tr>
38.     <tr>
39.       <td colspan=3 align=center>
40.         <input type="submit" name="submitbutton"
              value="Go!">
41.       </td>
42.     </tr>
43.     </table>
44.     </form>
45.   </cfif>
46.   <cfif isDefined("Form.submitbutton")>
47.     <h3>You ordered the following items:</h3>
48.     <cfset varname1 = "Item">
49.     <cfset varname2 = "Qty">
50.     <table>
51.     <tr>
52.       <td><b>S.No.</b></td>
53.       <td><b>Product Name</b></td>
54.       <td><b>Quantity</b></td>
55.     </tr>
56.     <cfloop from=1 to=4 index="i">
57.       <cfoutput>
58.       <tr>
59.         <td>#i#)</td>
60.         <td>#Evaluate("form.#varname1#_#i#")#</td>
61.         <td>#Evaluate("form.#varname2#_#i#")#</td>
62.       </tr>
63.       </cfoutput>
64.     </cfloop>
```

65.   `</table>`

66.   `</cfif>`

67. `</body>`

68. `</html>`

On loading this page you will see a screen similar to the one in Figure 7.9A.

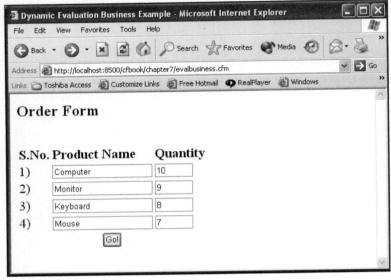

FIGURE 7.9A   Business Example Using `Evaluate()` (Form)

The form has not yet been submitted, so you see only the form as in Figure 7.9A. If you click on **Go!** you will see a screen like Figure 7.9B. Change the product names and quantities and click **Go!** again to see the list below the action page changing your order.

How the Code Works

1. If you look at the conditional code in line 9, the form is displayed only if it is not submitted yet. So once the form is submitted, only the action part of the page is displayed (see line 46).

2. Line 11 creates the form. The form is submitted to the same template (evalBusiness.cfm), which handles the action page too. We will see this shortly.

3. Lines 13 through 17 display the table headers—S.No. (Serial Number), Product Name, and Quantity.

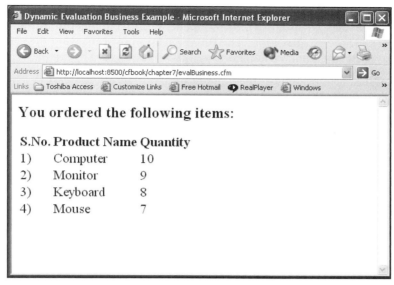

FIGURE 7.9B   Business Example Using `Evaluate()` (Action)

4. Lines 18 through 37 display the input boxes `item_1`, `item_2`, `item_3`, and `item_4` to accept the names of the four products. The values are initialized to "Computer," "Monitor," "Keyboard," and "Mouse" to make it easier for you. The input boxes `qty_1`, `qty_2`, `qty_3`, and `qty_4` accept the four quantities for these products (initially set to 0).

5. Line 40 displays a submit button that says `Go!` When you click on this, the action part of the form is executed because `form.submitbutton` is now available.

6. Lines 48 and 49 set `varname1` and `varname2` to `Item` and `Qty` to make it convenient to build the variable name for items and quantities.

7. Lines 51 through 55 display the table heading for the action page.

8. Line 56 starts a loop from 1 to 4 since we must get the value of each of the four items by first generating the four variable names dynamically.

9. Line 60 shows how to dynamically build the variable name `Item_1`, `Item_2`, and so on and to get the value of this variable using the `Evaluate()` function. Within the loop to create the value of the form variable, we use the base variable value `Item`, which we have stored in the variable `varname1`. We add the underscore _ and then the value of the loop variable, `i`, at the end using pound signs: `#varname1#_#i#`. This process gives us one of the variable names that we've passed through the form, but we need the contents of the variable also, not only the name. For this we need to use the `Evaluate()` function. The full expression for retrieving the value of the dynamic variable is `#Evaluate(#varname1#_#i#)#`.

10. Similarly, in line 61, the code `#Evaluate(#varname2#_#i#)#` gets us the value for each quantity in the loop. The item names and quantities are displayed once evaluated in the action part of the page.

System Functions

System functions are used to access files and directories on the server. First, let us understand what **absolute** and **relative paths** are. Let us imagine that our current directory is `c:/cfusionmx/cfbook/chapter7/` and our images directory is `c:/cfusionmx/cfbook/images/`.

The path `c:\cfusionmx\cfbook\chapter7\system.cfm` is the absolute path for the file `system.cfm`.

You can use a slash (/) or backslash (\) in a relative path. For example, we can refer to a file in the images directory by using the relative path `..\images\logo.gif`.

`ExpandPath(relative_path)` converts a relative directory reference (.\ and ..\) to an absolute path. The function throws an error if this argument or the resulting absolute path is invalid. This function takes one parameter: the relative path. The code below converts the relative path `../images/logo.gif` and returns the absolute path `c:/cfusionmx/cfbook/chapter7/images/logo.gif`. If any directory or the file is missing, then ColdFusion will throw an error.

```
ExpandPath("../images/logo.gif")
```

`GetDirectoryFromPath(path)` extracts the directory (with a backslash) from a fully specified path. This function takes one parameter: the path, which is the drive, directory, filename, and extension. The code below returns `c:/cfusionmx/cfbook/chapter7/images/`, that is, just the directory part of the path.

```
GetDirectoryFromPath("c:/cfusionmx/cfbook/chapter7/
    images/logo.gif")
```

`GetFileFromPath(path)` extracts the filename from a fully specified path. It takes one parameter: the fully qualified path, that is, the drive, directory, filename, and extension. The example code below returns the file name `logo.gif`:

Tech Tip

The absolute path is the entire path of the file with no directory names left out. It is not relative to the current directory.

Tech Tip

The relative path leaves out some directory names and uses the ..\ syntax to refer to files. The path is relative to the current directory path.

```
GetFileFromPath("c:/cfusionmx/cfbook/chapter7/images/logo.
   gif")
```

DirectoryExists(*absolute_path*) returns yes if the directory specified in the argument does exist; otherwise, it returns no. It takes the absolute path as a parameter. The example below returns yes if the images directory exists; otherwise it returns no.

```
DirectoryExists("c:/cfusionmx/cfbook/chapter7/images/")
```

FileExists(*path*) returns yes if the file specified in the argument exists; otherwise it returns no. It takes the absolute path as a parameter. The example below returns yes if the logo.gif file exists; otherwise it returns no.

```
FileExists("c:/cfusionmx/cfbook/chapter7/images/logo.gif")
```

GetBaseTemplatePath() gets the absolute path of an application's base page. This function takes no parameters.

Example 7.10 demonstrates the system functions described above. It accepts the relative path of a file on your system and displays the expanded path and directory path. It checks if your directory exists on the system and also displays the base template path of your code. Type this code and save it in a file called system.cfm.

> **Tech Tip**
>
> GetBaseTemplate Path() is useful when you want to access the absolute path of the current template from within your code.

Example 7.10   System Functions (system.cfm)

```
1.  <!DOCTYPE html
2.  PUBLIC "-//W3C//DTD XHTML 1.0 Transitional//EN"
3.  "http://www.w3.org/TR/xhtml1/DTD/xhtml1-transitional.dtd">
4.  <html xmlns="http://www.w3.org/1999/xhtml">
5.  <head>
6.    <title>System Functions Example</title>
7.  </head>
8.  <body>
9.    <H3>System Functions Example</H3>
10.   <form name="systemForm" method="post"
         action="system.cfm">
11.     Please type in a file name using relative path: <br>
12.     <input type="text" name="path" size="30"
13.        value="./system.cfm">
14.     <br><input type="submit" name="submitButton"
           value="Go">
```

```
15.    </form>
16.    <cfif isDefined("Form.submitButton")>
17.      <cfset thisPath = ExpandPath(#form.path#)>
18.      <cfset thisDirectory = GetDirectoryFromPath
             (#thisPath#)>
19.      <cfoutput>
20.        The expanded path is: #thisPath#<br>
21.        The directory of the path is:
             #thisDirectory#<br>
22.        <cfif DirectoryExists(thisdirectory)>
23.          Your directory #thisDirectory# exists!
24.          <cfif FileExists(thisPath)>
25.            <P>Your file exists in this directory
                 #thisDirectory#
26.            <br>You entered the correct file name,
27.            #GetFileFromPath("#thisPath#")#
28.          <cfelse>
29.            <P>Your file does not exist here
                 #thisDirectory#
30.            <br>You entered the incorrect file name,
31.            #GetFileFromPath("#thisPath#")#
32.          </cfif>
33.        <cfelse>
34.          Your directory #thisDirectory# does not exist!
35.        </cfif>
36.      </cfoutput>
37.    </cfif>
38.    <p>Base Template Path: <cfoutput>#GetBaseTemplate
             Path()#</cfoutput>   </p>
39. </body>
40. </html>
```

Figure 7.10A shows what this form looks like in the browser when the page is loaded. The value in the textbox defaults to ./system.cfm, which is the relative path of the file that holds the above code (the template that contains our code is `http://localhost:8500/cfbook/system.cfm`). You can give any file name here with its path relative to the current template's directory.

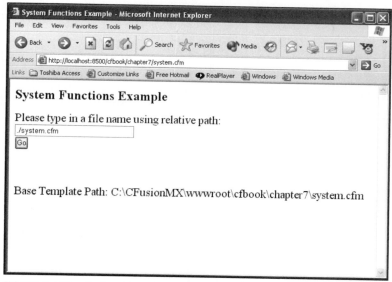

FIGURE 7.10A   System Functions—Relative Path

After you type in a relative directory path and filename that exist on your system, click on **Go**. You will see a page like Figure 7.10B.

How the Code Works

1. A form is created in line 10 that displays an input box on line 12 to accept the relative path of a file. The default value is set as `./system.cfm`. You can type any existing filename along with its relative path and submit the form. This form is submitted to the same file `system.cfm` that does the action part too.

2. If the form is submitted, `form.submitbutton` is available on line 16, and the action part between lines 16 and 37 is executed.

3. If the form is not yet submitted, the control jumps to line 38, which just displays the base template path of the current template being loaded.

4. Line 17 uses `ExpandPath()` to get an absolute path from the relative path we got through the form. This absolute path is assigned to the variable `thisPath`. Line 20 displays the expanded path.

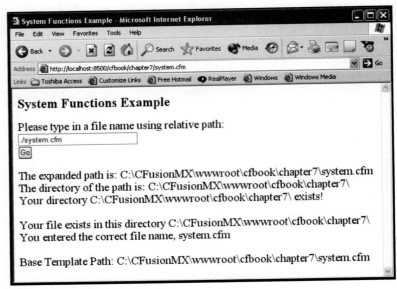

FIGURE 7.10B   System Functions

5. Line 18 uses `GetDirectoryFromPath()` to get the absolute directory path of the relative path given in the relative path field. Line 21 displays the path of the directory.

6. Line 22 uses the function `DirectoryExists()` to check if this directory exists in your system. If it does not, then the code within that condition is not executed. Line 34 is executed, which tells you that your directory does not exist.

7. If the directory exists, then line 23 tells you that your directory exists.

8. Line 24 uses the function `FileExists()` to check if the file exists in the directory (it uses the expanded path) on your system. If your directory/file does not exist, the code displays the appropriate messages on lines 29 and 30.

9. If the file exists, line 27 gets the filename from the expanded path using `GetFileFromPath()`.

10. Line 38 gets the base template path of your template using the function `GetBaseTemplatePath()`.

Summary

In this chapter, we saw some of the broad categories of functions and we also looked at some functions from these categories. ColdFusion has built-in functions that help to process and manipulate strings by trimming, justifying strings, changing case, encrypting, and decrypting. We can extract substrings and search for substrings within strings using built-in functions. ColdFusion MX 6.1 introduced the new `wrap()` function to wrap strings within a specified width. Mathematical functions enable us to perform mathematical operations within our template and date and time functions are very convenient to perform any date and time manipulations or formatting. Display and formatting functions have been touched on while we learned mathematical, date/time, and string functions; for example, `dateformat()`, `numberformat()`, and justification functions are formatting functions since they control the display of dates, numbers, and strings. Dynamic evaluation functions help us evaluate dynamic expressions. We learned only the `Evaluate()` function here. There are other functions such as `IIF()` and `DE()`, which are out of the scope of this book. System-level functions perform actions on directories and paths.

ColdFusion provides many more built-in functions that we have not covered here. The aim of this chapter was to give you an introduction to the basic functions and their usage. In ColdFusion we can even create our own functions, called user-defined functions. We will cover this in Chapter 9. In the next chapter, we will study about complex data types such as arrays, lists, and structures and their related functions.

The project building exercises at the end of this chapter should help you to complete Phase 1 of the shopping cart application.

Key Terms

absolute path
characters
double evaluation
dynamic evaluation
encryption
key
mask
relative path
seed
string
substring
system functions

Review Questions

1. What is the purpose of trim functions on strings? When would you normally use a trim function? What is the difference between `ltrim()`, `rtrim()`, and `trim()`?
2. What do the justification functions do and when would you use them? Name three justification functions and state their purpose.
3. Give three instances when you would find case changing useful in string manipulation. Name two case-changing functions in ColdFusion.
4. Give three instances when you feel that substrings may be useful. Name and state the purpose of two substring extraction functions in ColdFusion.
5. Give an instance when you feel that searching strings can be useful. Name and state the purpose of two functions used to search strings.
6. Name three mathematical functions and give their purpose.
7. Write the function to display a number `num` with a dollar sign in front and two decimal places.
8. What is the `DatePart()` function used for? Give one example of its usage.
9. Name and state the purpose of two functions used to do date arithmetic.

10. What is the purpose of dynamic evaluation?

11. State the purpose and one example of the `Evaluate()` function.

12. Name and state the purpose of two system functions.

13. How would you get the path of your code template?

14. What are the parameters of string encryption functions? What is the security of string encryption dependent on?

15. Explain the purpose of `isDefined()`. State two situations in which you have found this function useful.

True or False

State whether the following statements are true or false.

1. In the function `GetFileFromPath(path)`, *path* is an absolute path. _____

2. If you encrypt a string using a key, you need to use the same key to decrypt the string. _____

3. `DatePart()` is a function used for formatting dates for output. _____

4. `Rtrim()` trims leading spaces in strings. _____

5. To extract the leftmost characters from a string, we can use the `Mid()` function. _____

6. `Replace()` is a case-insensitive function that replaces a substring with another substring. _____

7. The code `#evaluate("sqr(36)")#` outputs the string sqr(36). _____

8. System functions act on the client files and directories. _____

9. String indices start from 1 in ColdFusion. _____

10. `DateFormat()` is used for formatting dates for output. _____

Programming Exercises

1. Write a ColdFusion template in which you have a form that accepts names, ages, and joining dates of two employees. See Figure 7.11A for a sample form.

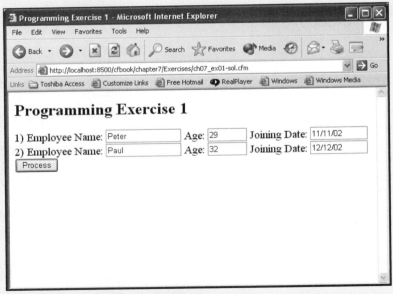

FIGURE 7.11A   Employee Age—Form

Submit the form to the same template. In the action part of the template, display the following results:

a. Using simple conditional statements, find the older employee's age and name. State whether the employees are the same age.

b. Using functions `Min` and `Max`, find the older and younger employees' ages.

c. Find the employee who has been with the company longer and display the number of months between the two employees' joining dates. (Hint: Use `DateDiff()` between the joining dates.)

d. Display how many months each employee has worked in the company. (Hint: Use `DateDiff()` between the joining date and the current date.)

See Figure 7.11B for a sample action screen.

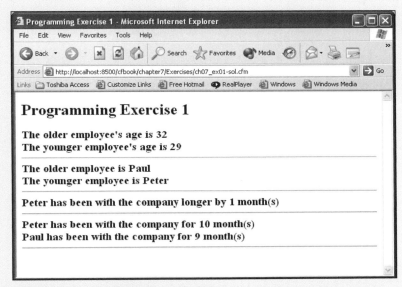

FIGURE 7.11B   Employee Age—Action

2. Simulate a lottery drawing. Accept five numbers from the user. See Figure 7.12A for a sample form. Validate that the numbers lie in the range 1 through 10.

Your form should be submitted to the same file that will do the lottery drawing. Your action code should pick a random number within the range.

If none of the numbers chosen by the user matches the lucky number, ask the user to try again next time. See Figure 7.12B for a sample action screen to be shown if the user did not win.

If the user had entered even one number that matches the lucky number, congratulate him or her on winning the lottery! See Figure 7.12C for a sample winner screen.

3. Create a template with a variable set to the following string: "The Big Bad Wolf". Write code snippets for the following:

a. Extract the four rightmost characters.

b. Replace "Wolf" with "Fox".

c. Display the position of "Bad".

d. Display the string in uppercase letters.

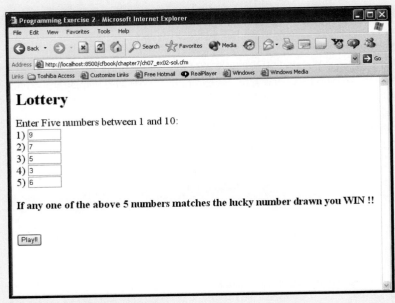

FIGURE 7.12A   Lottery—Form

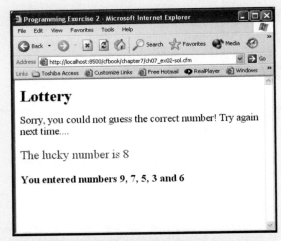

FIGURE 7.12B   Lottery—Nonwinner

  e. Find the first occurrence of any of the letters "aeiou".
  f. Find the position of the first "B" starting from the sixth character.
  g. Replace all occurrences of "B" with "b".
  h. Encrypt this string using the key "encrypt".
  See Figure 7.13 for sample output.
4. Correct the following erroneous code snippets:

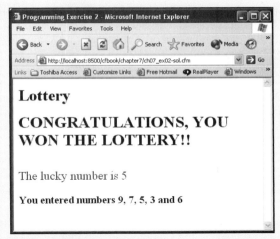

FIGURE 7.12C   Lottery—Winner

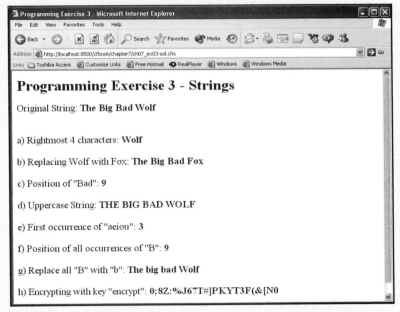

FIGURE 7.13   String Manipulation

a. `<cfif IsLeapYear(now())>`
   `This is a leap year`
   `</cfif>`
b. `<cfoutput>`
   `#ReplaceNoCase(stringToSearch, "the", "a", ONE)#`
   `</cfoutput>`

On completion of the Project Building Exercises given below, you should be done with Phase 1 of the shopping cart application. Your website should allow one item to be saved in each order. We will learn how to add multiple items in the shopping cart in the next chapter.

Order Review Page

In the Chapter 4 Project Building Exercises, you built a form to accept customer information. There you accepted billing and shipping addresses, shipping method, and payment type. On this page, when you click on the **Review Order** button, the Order Review page should appear. In this exercise, you will build this Order Review page for the shopping cart application.

In the Order Review page, display all the customer information from the form/session properly formatted as below.

1. If all the shipping address fields have data, then use the shipping address form fields as the shipping address.

2. If any shipping address field is empty, set the shipping address equal to the billing address (all billing address fields were required fields in the Customer Information page you built in Chapter 4, whereas shipping address fields were optional).

3. Based on the shipping method selected in the Customer Information form, calculate shipping cost as

   a. Ground costs 0.1 percent of the `OrderTotal` (i.e., `OrderTotal` * 0.001).

   b. Air costs 0.2 percent of the `OrderTotal` (i.e., `OrderTotal` * 0.002).

   c. Overnight costs 0.3 percent of the `OrderTotal` (i.e., `OrderTotal` * 0.003).

4. Tax was calculated in the Shopping Cart page that you built in Chapter 6. In the Shopping Cart page, you were asked to set `TotalOrderAmount = OrderTotal + Tax` where `OrderTotal = Price * Qty`.

5. Since `ShippingCost` is calculated in this page, at this point you should add the `ShippingCost` also to the `TotalOrderAmount` in the session.

6. Set billing and shipping address fields in the session.

7. Encrypt the credit card number using the key `"ccencryption"`.

8. Set the encrypted credit card number in the session.

9. Set the shipping method and shipping cost in the session.

10. Set order amounts (`OrderTotal` and `TotalOrderAmount`) in the session.

11. Display the Order Review page using session variables. Format dollar amounts appropriately.

    a. Product code, name, price, quantity ordered, total cost.

    b. `OrderTotal` (price * qty).

    c. Tax amount (as calculated in the Shopping Cart page).

    d. `ShippingCost` (as calculated above)

    e. `TotalOrderAmount` (`OrderTotal + ShippingCost + Tax`). In the Shopping Cart page, `TotalOrderAmount` was calculated as `OrderTotal + Tax`. Here you have to add the `ShippingCost` to that amount in the session.

    f. Show the selected shipping method next to the shipping cost.

    g. Billing address (first name, last name, address fields, email address).

    h. Shipping address (first name, last name, address fields, email address). Use the billing address if fields are left empty or are incomplete.

    i. Credit card type selected in the Customer Information page.

   j. Credit card number entered in the Customer Information page.

   k. Expiration date of the credit card as entered in the Customer Information page.

12. Implement the following changes in the code above:

   a. Capitalize the first letter of the first name, last name, and city.

   b. If the state is two letters, capitalize both; otherwise, capitalize the first letter of the state.

   c. Display only the last four digits of the credit card number and replace the remaining digits with XXXXX.

See Figure 7.14 for a sample Order Review page.

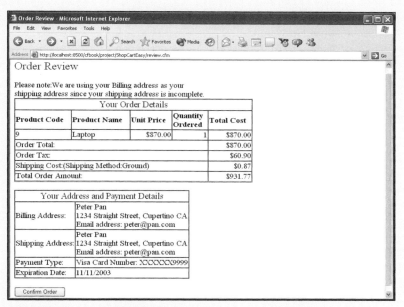

FIGURE 7.14   Order Review Page

Order Confirmation Page

We have built a Product Listing page through which we can add an item to our shopping cart. Next, we built a Shopping Cart page that calculates the totals and allows us to change the quantity ordered. Then, we built the Customer Information page that accepts the customer address and payment details. Finally, we built the Order Review page that allows us to review the order before finalizing it.

The final step in the shopping cart application is to confirm or save the order in the database and to give the customer his or her order number. In this Order Confirmation template, all the session variables should be consolidated into an order in the database. A confirmation should be given to the customer that his or her order has been received.

The sequence of steps to be performed is given here. All the following database steps should be performed within a single transaction so that if any step fails, the entire transaction is rolled back. See Chapters 5 and 6 for information on database transactions.

1. First insert the customer information. You will need to insert two sets of addresses—the shipping address and billing address—separately into the Customer table. Take all the address values from the session variables.
   a. Insert the billing address fields into the Customer table with `addressType = 'billing'`.
   b. Insert the shipping address fields into the Customer table with `addressType = 'shipping'`.
2. Get the address IDs of the addresses you just inserted so you can insert these IDs into the Order table.
   a. Query the maximum billing address ID from the Customer table. You need this to insert it into the Order table as a foreign key to the Customer table.
   b. Query the maximum shipping address ID from the Customer table. You need this to insert it into the Order table as a foreign key to the Customer table.
3. Insert the new order into the Order table. (Hint: Since `order` is a reserved word in MS Access, please refer to this table as [order] within square brackets in your queries.)
   a. `OrderDate`: use the current date.
   b. `BillingAddressId`: use the ID of the billing address you inserted into the Customer table.
   c. `ShippingAddressId`: use the ID of the shipping address you inserted into the Customer table.
   d. `OrderAmount`: use `TotalOrderAmount` from the session.
   e. `PaymentType`: use the value stored in the session.
   f. `CreditCardNumber`: use the value stored in the session.
   g. `ExpirationDate`: use the value stored in the session.
   h. `ShippingMethod`: use the value from the session.
   i. `ShippingCost`: use the value from the session.
   j. `Taxes`: use the value from the session.
   k. `OrderStatus`: use `'new'` to indicate a new order.
4. In a variable, get the ID of the order you just inserted. You need this to identify which order your line item belongs to in the OrderItem table. When you have multiple line items, this will make more sense. In the next few chapters, you will be inserting multiple items into the OrderItem table, but the shopping cart application that you have built will hold only one item.
5. Write an `Insert` query to insert the line item into the OrderItem table. There is only one item in the shopping cart, so this is simple.
   a. `OrderId`: use the order ID queried in part 4 above.
   b. `ItemNumber`: for now use 1 (since in this version of the shopping cart we have only one item per order).
   c. `ProductId`: use this from the session.
   d. `ProductQty`: use this from the session.
   e. `ItemTotal`: use this from the session.
6. Lastly, update the stock on hand in the Product table.
   a. Set `Productqty` to `Productqty - ProductQty` (the quantity ordered for the `ProductID` in the shopping cart.
7. Once all of the above have successfully executed, display the new order number to the user and thank the user for his or her order. It is a good idea to link the user to the product catalog from here so that the user can place another order if he or she wishes to.

See Figure 7.15 for a sample Order Confirmation page.

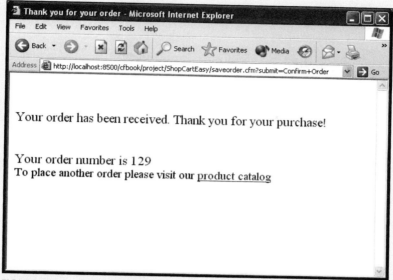

FIGURE 7.15   Order Confirmation Page

Complex Data Types

CHAPTER OBJECTIVES

1. Understand the purpose of complex data types.

2. Learn the usage of lists and their functions.

3. Use arrays and their functions to organize data.

4. Group and manipulate related data in memory using structures.

5. Combine the power of arrays and structures to build a shopping cart.

6. Understand the convenience of server-side scripting.

So far we have learned almost everything that a basic set of ColdFusion web pages should have. We know how to create a web page with dynamic content, process form data, use databases to access data, and use a number of built-in ColdFusion functions to present data to the user.

In this chapter we will learn about complex data types and some built-in functions that are commonly used with these data types. You also will see how you can combine complex data types to build a shopping cart. We will use session variables more extensively in this chapter when we build the shopping cart. This chapter also will give you an introduction to server-side scripting in ColdFusion.

Introduction to Complex Data Types

ColdFusion allows you to use complex data types to help you manage complex data. ColdFusion built-in **complex data types** include lists, arrays, structures, queries (Chapters 5 and 6), and XML document objects (Chapter 10). Using complex data types, you can make changes to your data in memory without repeated database transactions. The data are committed to the database only after the transaction in memory is complete and ready to be stored in the database.

This section explains how lists, arrays, and structures can be used within your applications to help you manage your data better and to enhance your application.

Lists

Tech Tip

Lists are useful when getting multiple values from form fields, like checkboxes or multiple-selection drop-down lists.

Lists are just strings that have delimiters. For example, a sentence is a list of words delimited by spaces.

You can create a list by simply assigning a value to a variable. Some examples are

```
<cfset namelist="Dave,Peter,Bob,Mary"
<cfset sentence="This list is a sentence">
```

List Functions

Specific functions are used in ColdFusion to simplify access and manipulation of list elements. The default delimiter for list elements is the comma. This can be changed within any of the list functions. All list functions have an optional delimiter parameter that you can use to change the default delimiter to another character. If you are sticking to the comma as the delimiter, you need not specify that parameter since comma is the default.

The table on page 283 lists some of the commonly used list functions. Let us use the list `namelist` declared above for the examples in the table. The initial value of `namelist` is `Dave,Peter,Bob,Mary`.

Example 8.1 shows how a sentence, which is a list of words, can be split into individual words using some of the above list functions. The code splits the sentence `The cow jumped over the moon` and lists each word on a separate line. Save the example code as `ex8-1.cfm`. The output of this code is shown in Figure 8.1.

Example 8.1   List Functions (ex8-1.cfm)

```
1. <!DOCTYPE html
2. PUBLIC "-//W3C//DTD XHTML 1.0 Transitional//EN"
3. "http://www.w3.org/TR/xhtml1/DTD/xhtml1-transitional.dtd">
4. <html xmlns="http://www.w3.org/1999/xhtml">
5. <head>
```

Syntax	Explanation	Example	Result/Output
ListFirst(*list* [, *delimiters*])	Returns the first element in a list	ListFirst(namelist)	Dave
ListLast(*list* [, *delimiters*])	Returns the last element in a list	ListLast(namelist)	Mary
ListLen(*list* [, *delimiters*])	Returns the number of elements in a list	ListLen(namelist)	4
ListAppend(*list*, *value* [, *delimiters*])	Appends a value to a list	ListAppend(namelist, "Paul")	**New list:** Dave, Peter, Bob, Mary, Paul
ListInsertAt(*list*, *n*, *value* [, *delimiters*])	Inserts a value in the nth position of the list	ListInsertAt(namelist, 5, "Tom")	**New list:** Dave, Peter, Bob, Mary, Tom, Paul
ListPrepend(*list*, *value* [, *delimiters*])	Inserts a value at the beginning of the list	ListPrepend(nameList, "Tim")	**New list:** Tim, Dave, Peter, Bob, Mary, Tom, Paul
ListGetAt(*list*, *n* [, *delimiters*])	Returns the nth element in a list	ListGetAt(namelist, 3)	Peter
ListDeleteAt(*list*, *n* [, *delimiters*])	Deletes the nth element in the list	ListDeleteAt(nameList,5)	**New list:** Tim, Dave, Peter, Bob, Tom, Paul

```
6.    <title>List example</title>
7.  </head>
8.  <body>
9.    <h2>List example</h2>
10.   <cfset sentence="The cow jumped over the moon">
11.   <cfoutput>
12.     <b>Sentence: </b> #sentence# <br />
13.     <b>Word count: </b> #listlen(sentence," ")#<br
        /><br />
14.     <b>List of Words:</b><br />
15.     <cfloop index="count" from=1
        to=#listlen(sentence," ")#>
```

```
16.              <cfset word = listGetAt(sentence,count," ")>
17.           #count#) #word#<br />
18.        </cfloop>
19.     </cfoutput>
20.  </body>
21.  </html>
```

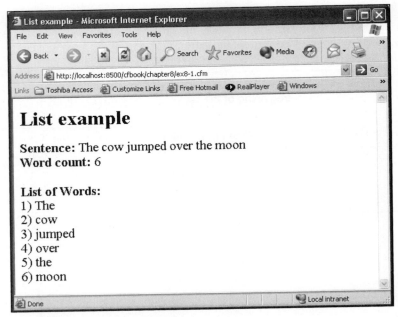

FIGURE 8.1   List of Words in a Sentence

How the Code Works

1. Line 10 sets a variable called sentence to the string The cow jumped over the moon.

2. Line 13 displays the length (number of elements or words) in the list.

3. Lines 15 through 18 loop through the list of words.

4. In line 16, for each list element, the variable word is set to that element using the function listGetAt() and this variable's value is displayed in line 17.

Arrays

Arrays are data types that hold related data temporarily in memory in a table-like format. An array is a list of related variables that each contains information. For example, a list of names can be stored in an array just as we can store it in a list. The elements of an array are called **array elements** and the position of an element in an array is identified by its **index**. The differences between an array and a list are that arrays do not have any delimiter and they can have **multiple dimensions**.

Array Dimensions

ColdFusion supports multidimensional, dynamic arrays with up to three dimensions. It differs from a traditional array where the array size is fixed.

A **one-dimensional array** is like a single row of elements in a table. For example, a list of names could be stored in a one-dimensional array.

A **two-dimensional array** is like several such rows arranged one below the other as in a spreadsheet. The calendar for one year can be represented by a two-dimensional array where the months in a year form a one-dimensional array and each month is itself an array of days.

Creating and Accessing Arrays

In ColdFusion you can create a new array of a specified dimension using the `ArrayNew(n)` function, where n is the dimension of the array. The following code snippet creates a one-dimensional array called `nameArray`.

```
<cfset nameArray = ArrayNew(1)>
```

You can refer to an array element by using the array name and enclosing the index within square brackets. For example, `nameArray[1]` accesses the first element of the one-dimensional array `nameArray`.

You can set the elements of an array using the array index. For example, to set the first element to `Peter` and the second to `Mary`, you use the following syntax:

```
<cfset nameArray[1] = "Peter">
<cfset nameArray[2] = "Mary">
```

To understand two-dimensional arrays, let us define an array called `calendar` that holds months in a year (first dimension) and days within a month (second dimension). The following code creates a two-dimensional array called `calendar`:

```
<cfset calendar = ArrayNew(2)>
```

The code `calendar[3][1]` refers to the first element (day) of the third element (month) of the above two-dimensional array. Now, let us set up `calendar` elements for five days in the month of March (11th to 15th of March).

Tech Tip

A dynamic array is an array that expands as you add data to it and contracts as you remove data from it.

Tech Tip

Array indices start from 1 in ColdFusion.

```
<cfset calendar[3][11]="Soccer Game">
<cfset calendar[3][12]="Orthodontic Appointment">
<cfset calendar[3][13]="Soccer Practice">
<cfset calendar[3][14]="Music">
<cfset calendar[3][15]="Art">
```

To access the 14th day in the third month, we would use `calendar[3][14]`; this would give us the value `Music`. We can loop through an array using `<cfloop>` to access or display the array elements. For example, the following code displays the days between the 11th and 15th of the third month:

```
<cfloop index="i" from="11" to="15">
  <cfoutput> #calendar[3][i]#</cfoutput><br />
</cfloop>
```

`<cfdump>` is a convenient way to display the entire contents of an array in a tabular form on the screen and is used as given below:

```
<cfdump var=#calendar#>
```

Array Manipulation Functions

Some common functions that can be used with arrays are listed in the table on page 287. To illustrate these with examples, we will use the array `nameArray` that we defined earlier with elements `Peter` and `Mary`.

There are many more functions that help manipulate arrays, but the table covers most of the commonly used functions. Example 8.2 creates an array called `colorArray` and sets the array elements to `Red`, `Blue`, `Green`, `Yellow`, `Orange`, `Pink`, `White`, and `Black`. This example uses some array functions and illustrates how array elements can be appended, deleted, and inserted at specific positions in the array. The contents of the array after manipulation are displayed using `<cfdump>`. Save the code example as `ex8-2.cfm`. Load this code into your browser; then try clicking on the array displayed by `<cfdump>` and see how it collapses and expands to show more or less detail. The output of this example can be seen in Figure 8.2.

Example 8.2　Array Manipulation (ex8-2.cfm)

1. `<!DOCTYPE html`

2. `PUBLIC "-//W3C//DTD XHTML 1.0 Transitional//EN"`

3. `"http://www.w3.org/TR/xhtml/DTD/xhtml1-transitional.dtd">`

4. `<html xmlns="http://www.w3.org/1999/xhtml">`

5. `<head>`

6. `  <title>Array Manipulation</title>`

7. `</head>`

Syntax	Description	Example	Result
ArrayAppend(`Array, Element`)	Creates a new array element at the end of an array	ArrayAppend(nameArray, "Bob")	"Peter" "Mary" "Bob"
ArrayPrepend(`Array, Element`)	Creates a new array element at the beginning of an array	ArrayPrepend(nameArray, "Dave")	"Dave" "Peter" "Mary" "Bob"
ArrayInsertAt(`Array, ArrayIndex, Element`)	Inserts an array element at the index position specified	ArrayInsertAt(nameArray, 3, "Jack")	"Dave" "Peter" "Jack" "Mary" "Bob"
ArrayDeleteAt(`Array, Index`)	Deletes an array element at a particular index	ArrayDeleteAt(nameArray, 3)	"Dave" "Peter" "Mary" "Bob"
ArrayIsEmpty(`Array`)	Returns true if the array has no data	ArrayIsEmpty(nameArray)	False (not empty)
ArrayLen(`Array`)	Returns the length of an array	ArrayLen(nameArray)	4
IsArray(`Array`)	Returns true if the parameter is an array	IsArray(nameArray)	True
ArrayToList(`Array, Delimiter`)	Converts an array to a list delimited with the specified character	ArrayToList(Array,"|")	"Dave | Peter | Mary | Bob"
ListToArray(`List, Delimiter`)	Converts a list delimited with the specified character to an array	ListToArray("Dave | Peter | Mary | Bob","|")	"Dave" "Peter" "Mary" "Bob"
ArrayClear(`Array`)	Clears all data in the array	ArrayClear(nameArray)	Empties nameArray

8. `<body>`

9.   `<h2>Array Manipulation</h2>`

10. `<cfset colorArray=arrayNew(1)>`

11.   `<cfset colorArray[1]="Red">`

12.   `<cfset colorArray[2]="Blue">`

```
13.    <cfset colorArray[3]="Green">

14.    <cfset colorArray[4]="Yellow">

15.    <cfset colorArray[5]="Orange">

16.    <cfset colorArray[6]="Pink">

17.    <cfset colorArray[7]="White">

18.    <cfset colorArray[8]="Black">

19.    <table border=1>

20.    <tr>

21.      <td><h4>Original Array</h4></td>

22.      <td><h4>Append "Grey"</h4></td>

23.      <td><h4>Prepend "Violet"</h4></td>

24.      <td><h4>Insert "Silver" at 5th position</h4></td>

25.      <td><h4>Delete 9th element </h4></td>

26.      <td><h4>Delete 4th element (final)</h4></td>

27.    </tr>

28.    <tr>

29.      <td><h2><cfdump var=#colorArray#> </h2></td>

30.      <td>

31.         <cfset var=#arrayAppend(colorArray,"Grey")#>

32.         <h2><cfdump var=#colorArray#> </h2>

33.      </td>

34.      <td>

35.         <cfset var=#arrayPrepend(colorArray,"Violet")#>

36.         <h2><cfdump var=#colorArray#> </h2>

37.      </td>

38.      <td>

39.         <cfset var=#arrayInsertAt(colorArray,5,"Silver")#>

40.         <h2><cfdump var=#colorArray#> </h2>

41.      </td>

42.      <td>

43.         <cfset var=#arrayDeleteAt(colorArray,9)#>
```

```
44.        <h2><cfdump var=#colorArray#> </h2>
45.    </td>
46.    <td>
47.        <cfset var=#arrayDeleteAt(colorArray,4)#>
48.        <h2><cfdump var=#colorArray#></h2>
49.    </td>
50.    </tr>
51.    </table>
52. </body>
53. </html>
```

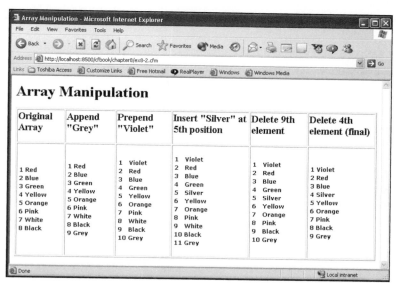

FIGURE 8.2   Array Functions

How the Code Works

1. Line 10 defines a new one-dimensional array called `colorArray`.

2. Lines 11 through 18 set each element of the array to the colors Red, Blue, Green, Yellow, Orange, Pink, White, and Black.

3. We use a table to show the transformation of the array depending on the manipulation functions we perform on it. Lines 20 through 27 display the headings of the table for each transformation.

4. Line 29 uses <cfdump> to show the original array. See Figure 8.2, column 1.

5. Line 31 appends Grey to the array. The transformed array is displayed using the <cfdump> statement on line 32. See Figure 8.2, column 2.

6. Line 35 prepends Violet to the array, which is displayed by the <cfdump> statement in line 36. See Figure 8.2, column 3.

7. Line 39 inserts the color Silver in the fifth position (between Green and Yellow). The transformed array is shown using the <cfdump> statement in line 40. See Figure 8.2, column 4.

8. Line 43 deletes the element at position 9 (White). The transformed array is displayed using the <cfdump> statement in line 44. See Figure 8.2, column 5.

9. Line 47 deletes the element at position 4 (Green). The final array is shown using the <cfdump> statement in line 48. See Figure 8.2, column 6.

Looping through One-Dimensional Arrays

There are many ways to populate an array in ColdFusion. Here we will discuss how to populate one- and two-dimensional arrays using the <cfloop> tag. In Example 8.3, the built-in ColdFusion function DayOfWeekAsString() has been used to populate an array with the names of the seven days of the week. The function DayOfWeekAsString() returns the day name in words depending on the number passed into it. Refer to Chapter 7 for date functions. Then the names of the days are displayed using <cfloop> to loop from the array created. Save the example code as ex8-3.cfm. Figure 8.3 shows the output of this code.

Example 8.3   One-Dimensional Array (ex8-3.cfm)

```
1. <!DOCTYPE html
2. PUBLIC "-//W3C//DTD XHTML 1.0 Transitional//EN"
3. "http://www.w3.org/TR/xhtml1/DTD/xhtml1-transitional.dtd">
4. <html xmlns="http://www.w3.org/1999/xhtml">
5. <head>
6.   <title>Looping through Arrays</title>
7. </head>
8. <body>
9.   <h2>Days of the week: </h2>
```

```
10.    <cfset weekDays=arrayNew(1)>
11.    <cfloop index="count" from=1 to=7>
12.       <cfset weekdays[count]=DayofWeekAsString(count)>
13.    </cfloop>
14.    <cfloop index="count" from=1 to=7>
15.       <cfoutput>#weekdays[count]#</cfoutput><br />
16.    </cfloop>
17. </body>
18. </html>
```

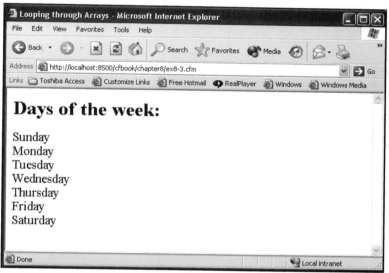

FIGURE 8.3   One-Dimensional Array

How the Code Works

1. Line 10 defines a new one-dimensional array called weekDays.

2. Line 11 loops from 1 to 7 through each element in array weekDays.

3. As you learned in Chapter 7, the function DayOfWeekAsString() returns the day of the week as a character string when passed a numeric day-of-week parameter. In line 12, the name of the day corresponding to the loop index is returned by the function DayofWeekAsString() and is assigned to the corresponding weekDays array element.

4. Line 14 loops through from 1 to 7 and line 15 displays each value of the weekDays array.

Looping through Multidimensional Arrays

To populate and display multidimensional arrays, you need to use **nested loops.** Nested loops are loops within loops. For each dimension, you use a separate loop that will maintain the counter for that dimension. Example 8.4 populates a two-dimensional array with the multiplication tables from 1 to 5. The code then displays the multiplication tables from 1 to 5, as you can see in Figure 8.4. The outer loop loops from 1 to 5 and the inner loop goes from 1 to 12 for each table. Save the example code as ex8-4.cfm.

Example 8.4   Multidimensional Array (ex8-4.cfm)

```
1.  <!DOCTYPE html
2.  PUBLIC "-//W3C//DTD XHTML 1.0 Transitional//EN"
3.  "http://www.w3.org/TR/xhtml1/DTD/xhtml1-transitional.dtd">
4.  <html xmlns="http://www.w3.org/1999/xhtml">
5.  <head>
6.     <title>Multi-dimensional Array Manipulation</title>
7.  </head>
8.  <body>
9.     <h2>Multi-dimensional Array Manipulation</h2>
10.    <cfset numArray=arrayNew(2)>
11.    <cfloop index="i" from=1 to=5>
12.      <cfloop index="j" from=1 to=12>
13.        <cfset numArray[i][j]=(i*j)>
14.      </cfloop>
15.    </cfloop>
16.    <table border=1 cellspacing=2 cellpadding=2>
17.    <tr>
18.      <cfloop index="i" from="1" to="#ArrayLen(numArray)#">
19.        <td>
20.          <cfloop index="j" from="1" to="#ArrayLen
             (numArray[i])#">
```

```
21.          <cfoutput><b>#i# X #j#</b> =
             #numArray[i][j]#<br></cfoutput>

22.        </cfloop>

23.      </td>

24.    </cfloop>

25.  </tr>

26. </table>

27. </body>

28. </html>
```

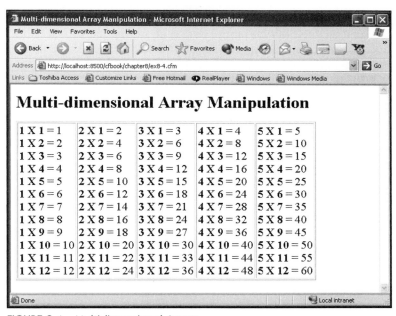

FIGURE 8.4   Multidimensional Arrays

How the Code Works

1. Line 10 defines a new two-dimensional array called numArray.

2. Line 11 is the outer loop that loops from 1 to 5 for multiplication tables 1 to 5.

3. For each value of the outer loop's index i, the inner loop on line 12 loops from 1 to 12 using the index j.

4. Line 13 sets each element numArray[i][j] of the array to the product (i*j) of the outer loop's index i and the inner loop's index j.

These two loops populate our array with the multiplication tables from 1 to 5.

5. To read and display our array elements, line 18 loops from 1 to 5 (the length of the array) and line 20 loops from 1 to 12 (the length of the first element).

6. Line 21 outputs the product in the format a X b = c for multiplication tables 1 to 5.

Structures

Structures provide a powerful and flexible mechanism for representing complex data by allowing you to group related data under a single entity. You can create a structure to hold employee data such as first name, last name, salary, age, and so forth. You can then refer to this set of data as a structure called employee instead of referring to each attribute separately.

It is better to have a structure in the session that contains related data than to have multiple global or session variables. ColdFusion structures consist of **key-value pairs**. The **key** must be a string and the value associated with the key can be a string, integer, array, or another structure. Structures are defined by assigning a new structure to a variable using the function StructNew(). The example code below creates a new structure called employee:

```
<cfset employee=structnew()>
```

Now we will look at ways to reference structures in ColdFusion to assign values to or display structure elements.

Property Notation

The **property notation** is used when you know the fields in the structure. Using this notation, you can add elements to the employee structure using the syntax *object.property* and you display the contents of a structure using the properties of the object as given below:

```
<!- setting employee properties ->
<cfset employee.firstname="Peter">
<cfset employee.lastname="Pan">
<cfset employee.salary="40000">
<cfset employee.age="40">

<!- displaying employee properties ->
<cfoutput>#employee.firstname#</cfoutput>
<cfoutput>#employee.lastname#</cfoutput>
<cfoutput>#employee.salary#</cfoutput>
<cfoutput>#employee.age#</cfoutput>
```

As you saw with arrays, <cfdump> can be used to output the contents of the structure, as shown below:

```
<cfdump var=#employee#>
```

Example 8.5 populates a simple address structure with data accepted through a form. The form submits to the same file (ex8-5.cfm), which executes the action as well. Figures 8.5A and 8.5B show the output of the form and action respectively.

Example 8.5   Populating Structures (ex8-5.cfm)

```
1.  <!DOCTYPE html
2.  PUBLIC "-//W3C//DTD XHTML 1.0 Transitional//EN"
3.  "http://www.w3.org/TR/xhtml1/DTD/xhtml1-transitional.dtd">
4.  <html xmlns="http://www.w3.org/1999/xhtml">
5.  <head>
6.    <title>Structure example</title>
7.  </head>
8.  <body>
9.    <h2>Structure example</h2>
10.   <cfif isDefined("form.submitButton")>
11.       <cfset address=StructNew()>
12.       <cfset address.name=#form.name#>
13.       <cfset address.street=#form.street#>
14.       <cfset address.city=#form.city#>
15.       <cfset address.state=#form.state#>
16.       <cfset address.zip=#form.zip#>
17.       Your address is <cfdump var=#address#>
18.   <cfelse>
19.     <form name="itemForm" action="ex8-5.cfm"
              method="post">
20.       Name: <input type="text" name="name"><br />
21.       Street: <input type="text" name="street"><br />
22.       City: <input type="text" name="city"><br />
23.       State: <input type="text" name="state"><br />
```

24.   `Zip: <input type="text" name="zip"><br />`

25.   `<input type="submit" name="submitButton"`
               `value="Submit"><br />`

26.   `</form>`

27. `</cfif>`

28. `</body>`

29. `</html>`

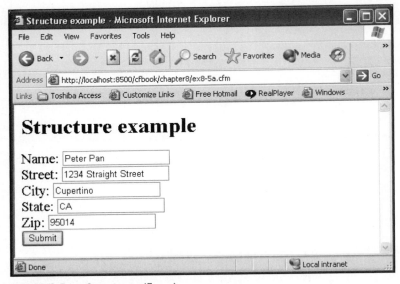

FIGURE 8.5A   Structures (Form)

How the Code Works

Note that this form is submitted to the same file, so conditional statements are used to check if the variable `form.submitButton` exists to determine whether or not to perform the action part of the code.

1. Initially, `form.submitButton` is not available. Since the form has not yet been submitted, lines 19 through 26 are executed. This is the code that creates the form that accepts the name, street address, city, state, and zip code from the user.

2. When the form is submitted, `form.submitButton` is defined and lines 11 through 17 are executed.

3. A new structure called `address` is created on line 11 and its elements are set on lines 12 through 16 using the form variables submitted.

4. Line 17 displays the structure using the `<cfdump>` tag.

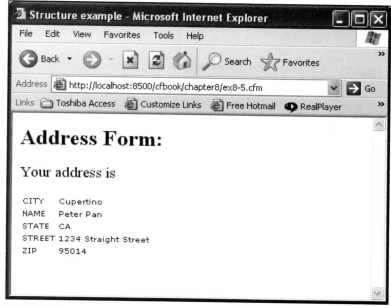

FIGURE 8.5B   Structures (Action)

Associative Array Notation

The property notation was used in the previous example because you knew the names of the elements or properties in your structure. You knew you wanted to store employee name and address. But if the properties of your structure are dynamic, you cannot use the property notation. Structures can be defined dynamically using **associative arrays.** Using this notation, you can use structures as arrays with **string indices** (keys) rather than integers.

For example, if you want to put names of students and their grades into a structure and you want to access each student's grade through the student's name, you can use the associative array notation. You do not know how many elements (students) there will be in the structure. The code snippet below creates a grade structure that holds the grades of students. Here, we use an associative array that matches student names with their grades. We retrieve the values associated with each key (name) by using that key within quotes, as given below.

> **Tech Tip**
>
> The key (index) in an associative array must be a string within quotes.

```
<!- Creating a new structure ->
<cfset grade=structNew()>

<!- Setting structure elements ->
<cfset grade["Mary"]="A">
```

```
<cfset grade["Peter"]="B">
<cfset grade["John"]="C">

<!- Displaying structure elements ->
<cfoutput>#grade["Mary"]#</cfoutput>
<cfoutput>#grade["Peter"]#</cfoutput>
<cfoutput>#grade["John"]#</cfoutput>
```

We also can use the associative array notation to build the `address` structure in Example 8.5 and we can display the structure elements using the associative array notation by referring to the properties as below:

```
<!- Creating a new structure ->
<cfset address=StructNew()>

<!- Setting structure elements ->
<cfset address["name"]=#form.name#>
<cfset address["street"]=#form.street#>
<cfset address["city"]=#form.city#>
<cfset address["state"]=#form.state#>
<cfset address["zip"]=#form.zip#>

<!- Displaying structure elements ->
<cfoutput>
   Your address is: <br />
   #address["name"]#<br />
   #address["street"]#<br />
   #address["city"]#<br />
   #address["state"]#<br />
   #address["zip"]#<br />
</cfoutput>
```

With the `address` structure, you know exactly how many elements you want to store in the array (`name`, `street`, `city`, `state`, `zip`). So here you could use either notation. With the `grade` structure, you do not know how many students there are to begin with. You keep adding to the structure as and when you get a new student's grade. Moreover, you want to access the grade using the student's name. In such a situation, the associative notation is necessary. This is called a **dynamic structure** created using associative arrays.

Structure Functions

ColdFusion provides us with built-in functions to build and manipulate structures. We can use the `StructInsert()` function to populate structures and `StructUpdate()` to update values of keys in the structure. Some of these functions are given in the table on page 299. The example used is the `grade` structure defined above.

Syntax	Description	Example	Return Value
StructClear(structure)	Deletes all data from the structure	StructClear(grade)	Returns yes after deleting the structure's data
StructInsert(structure, Key, value [, allowoverwrite])	Inserts a key-value pair into a structure	StructInsert(grade, "Paul", "A")	Returns yes if successful and no if not
StructUpdate(structure, Key, Value)	Modifies the value associated with a key	StructUpdate(grade, "Paul", "B")	Returns yes if successful and no if not
StructFind(structure, Key)	Returns the value associated with a key in the structure	StructFind(grade, Paul")	B
StructCount(structure)	Returns the number of keys in a structure	StructCount(grade)	Returns 1
IsStruct(variable)	Returns true if the variable is a structure	IsStruct(grade)	Returns true since grade is a structure

Collection Loops

Using a collection loop, we can loop through the elements in a ColdFusion structure or any collection object. A collection object is a set of similar items referenced as a group. A structure is a set of related items or an associative array referenced through a single object. To loop through a structure's elements or properties, we use the <cfloop> tag. The item attribute holds the value of the key or index in the loop. The loop executes until all properties are accessed, as shown below:

```
<cfloop collection=#grade# item="student">
  <cfoutput>#student# - #grade[student]#</cfoutput>
</cfloop>
```

Building a Multiple-Item Shopping Cart

The address structure in Example 8.5 allows us to store exactly one address in the structure. Every time we reassign the structure elements, it overwrites the previous data. This is useful if we want to store a structure at a time. But a shopping cart with a single item structure, for example, is of no use for an order in a real-life application. Until now, in our Project Building Exercises, our shopping cart has held only one item and our order has always been a single-item order. When we try to add a new item, the previous item is overwritten with the new item.

In this section, let us enhance our shopping cart to hold multiple line items. What we want to achieve is that if the customer presses the browser's **back** button to order another item, the customer's shopping cart should contain that item in addition to all the other items in his or her cart.

To enable this, we will combine the features of arrays and structures. We will populate an array with a list of shopping cart item structures. This array of shopping cart items will be stored in the session, where we can keep appending to it with new item structures each time the customer adds a new item to the shopping cart. See Figure 8.6A for a diagrammatic representation of the shopping cart in the session.

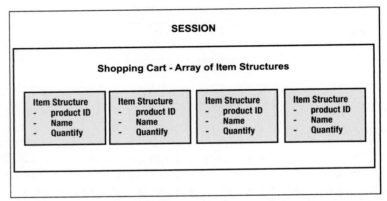

FIGURE 8.6A   Diagrammatic Representation of a Shopping Cart

Example 8.6 builds this shopping cart as described above. Save the example code as ex8-6.ccfm. Before you run this code, please check to see that your Application.cfm file has the setting sessionmanagement="Yes", since we are using session variables in this example. The output can be seen in Figure 8.6B.

Example 8.6   Combining Arrays and Structures (ex8-6.cfm)

1. `<!DOCTYPE html`

2. `PUBLIC "-//W3C//DTD XHTML 1.0 Transitional//EN"`

3. `"http://www.w3.org/TR/xhtml1/DTD/xhtml1-transitional.dtd">`

4. `<html xmlns="http://www.w3.org/1999/xhtml">`

5. `<head>`

```
6.      <title>Structure example</title>
7.  </head>
8.  <body>
9.      <h2>Shopping Cart</h2>
10.     <cfif isDefined("form.submitButton")>
11.         <cfif NOT(isDefined("session.sCartItems"))>
12.             <cfset session.sCartItems = arrayNew(1)>
13.         </cfif>
14.     <cfoutput>
15.         <cfset newItem=StructNew()>
16.         <cfset newItem.productID=#form.productid#>
17.         <cfset newItem.productName=#form.productName#>
18.         <cfset newItem.Qty=#form.qty#>
19.         <cfset var=#arrayAppend(session.sCartItems,
                newItem)#>
20.         <br />
21.         Your shopping cart has the following items:<br />
22.         <table border=1>
23.         <tr>
24.           <td><b>Product ID</b></td>
25.           <td><b>Product Name</b></td>
26.           <td><b>Quantity</b></td>
27.         </tr>
28.         <cfloop index="count" from=1
                to="#arraylen(session.sCartItems)#">
29.         <tr>
30.             <td>#session.sCartItems[count].
                  productid#</td>
31.             <td>#session.sCartItems[count].
                  productname#</td>
32.             <td>#session.sCartItems[count].qty#</td>
33.         </tr>
```

34.   `</cfloop>`

35.   `</tr>`

36.   `</table>`

37.   `<br />`

38.   `</cfoutput>`

39.   `</cfif>`

40.   `<form name="itemForm" action="ex8-6.cfm" method="post">`

41.   Product ID: `<input type="text" name="productID"><br />`

42.   Product Name: `<input type="text" name="productName"><br />`

43.   Quantity: `<input type="text" name="qty"><br />`

44.   `<input type="submit" name="submitButton" value="Show Order"><br />`

45.   `</form>`

46. `</body>`

47. `</html>`

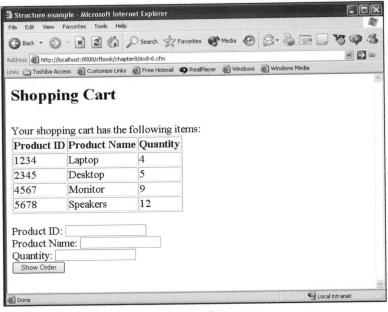

FIGURE 8.6B   Combining Structures and Arrays

How the Code Works

1. This form is submitted to the same template that handles the action part as well. Initially the variable `form.submitButton` is not defined, so lines 40 through 45 are executed to display a form with product ID, product name, and quantity.

2. When the form is submitted, lines 11 through 38 are executed.

3. Line 12 creates a new one-dimensional array called `sCartItems` in the session if `session.sCartItems` does not already exist.

4. Lines 15 through 18 set up a new structure called `newItem` and populate it with the submitted form variables.

5. Line 19 appends this newly created and populated structure to the `sCartItems` array in the session.

6. Lines 21 through 36 display the shopping cart items in a table. Lines 23 through 27 display table headings for the shopping cart items.

7. Line 28 loops through each element (each item) in the array.

8. Lines 30 through 32 display that element's product ID, product name, and quantity ordered. This is displayed for each item in the cart.

Server-Side Scripting

Client-side scripts (such as JavaScript) run on the client's browser. **Server-side scripts** interact with the server and output web pages. These are not browser dependent and are more flexible than client-side scripting languages. Cold-Fusion offers us the <cfscript> tag for server-side scripting. The syntax of this language is very similar to JavaScript but simpler to use. In CFScript we do not use the <cfset> tag for assignments or functions. We can assign variables and call functions directly. CFScript assignments are usually faster than <cfset> tags.

CFScript code can use all the ColdFusion functions and expressions and has access to all ColdFusion variables that are available in the script's scope. CFScript statements end with a semicolon (;) and multiple statements are enclosed in curly braces to group them. Comments are written with the // symbol or you can place comments between /* and */. CFScript variables can be of any ColdFusion type. This language is case insensitive.

Below are some assignment statements that can be used within <cfscript> tags:

```
A=b;
A = "teststring";
```

Tech Tip

CFScript is a server-side language. Unlike JavaScript, CFScript does not run on the client system. It runs on the ColdFusion server.

Tech Tip

All CFML expressions and functions are valid in CFScript, but you cannot use any CFML tags.

```
Arr[10] = 91;
Employee.firstname = "Peter";
```

CfScript code is used between the <cfscript> and </cfscript> tags. Some developers find it more convenient to use CFScript in their code. As you can see above, it can be used to replace multiple <cfset> statements. Example 8.7 is a simple example that shows how to use CFScript within a Cold-Fusion template. In it we will rewrite Example 8.5 (Address form) using <cfscript> tags. The example code populates an address structure using structure property notation. The output is no different from Figure 8.5, as you can see in Figures 8.7A (form) and 8.7B (action).

Example 8.7 CFScript (ex8_7.cfm)

```
1.  <!DOCTYPE html
2.  PUBLIC "-//W3C//DTD XHTML 1.0 Transitional//EN"
3.  "http://www.w3.org/TR/xhtml1/DTD/
      xhtml1-transitional.dtd">
4.  <html xmlns="http://www.w3.org/1999/xhtml">
5.  <head>
6.    <title>CFScript</title>
7.  </head>
8.  <body>
9.    <h2> CFScript</h2>
10.   <cfif isDefined("form.submitButton")>
11.     <cfscript>
12.       address=StructNew();
13.       address.name=form.name;
14.       address.street=form.street;
15.       address.city=form.city;
16.       address.state=form.state;
17.       address.zip=form.zip;
18.     </cfscript>
19.     <cfoutput>
20.       <br />Your address is: <br />
```

```
21.          #address.name#<br />
22.          #address.street#<br />
23.          #address.city#<br />
24.          #address.state#<br />
25.          #address.zip#<br />
26.      </cfoutput>
27.    </cfif>
28.    <form name="itemForm" action="ex8-7.cfm" method="post">
29.       Name: <input type="text" name="name"><br />
30.       Street: <input type="text" name="street"><br />
31.       City: <input type="text" name="city"><br />
32.       State: <input type="text" name="state"><br />
33.       Zip: <input type="text" name="zip"><br />
34.       <input type="submit" name="submitButton"
                value="Show"><br />
35.    </form>
36. </body>
37. </html>
```

How the Code Works

1. This form submits to the same template. Lines 28 through 35 display a form that accepts the name, address, city, state, and zip.

2. If the variable `form.submitButton` is defined—that is, if the form was submitted—then lines 11 through 26 are executed.

3. Lines 12 through 17 set up the address structure. Instead of the `<cfset>` tag, CFScript code is used between the `<cfscript>` and `</cfscript>` tags.

4. Lines 19 through 26 output the newly populated `address` structure. The output (Figures 8.7A and 8.7B) is similar to that of Example 8.5 (Figures 8.5A and 8.5B). The only difference is that here, instead of using `<cfdump>`, the structure is displayed using the property notation.

CFScript is an entire topic in itself, so we will only learn a few of the basics of this scripting language in this book.

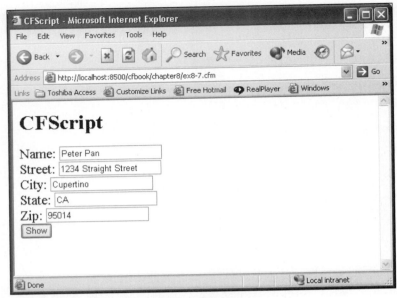

FIGURE 8.7A   Server-Side Scripting (Form)

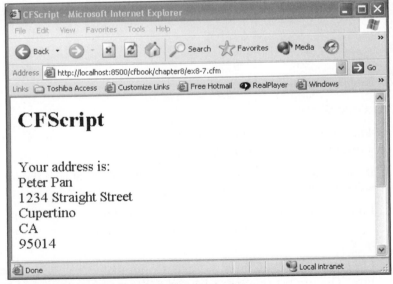

FIGURE 8.7B   Server-Side Scripting (Action)

The following table summarizes commonly used CFScript language constructs. We also can output data in CFScript using the WriteOutput() function as given below:

```
WriteOutput("Hello World!");
```

Construct	Examples	Explanation
| If/else | ```
if (marks GT 90)  {
   grade = "A";
} else if (marks GT 80) {
   grade = "B";
} else if (marks GT 70) {
   grade = "C";
} else if (marks GT "60") {
   grade = "D"
} else {
   grade = "F"
}
``` | The curly braces are needed here only if multiple statements exist between the `if` statement and the `else` statement |
| For loop | ```
for (loop=1; loop LT 5;
     loop=loop+1)  {
   a[loop] = loop;
}
``` | Curly braces are necessary only if multiple statements exist in the body of the loop |
| Do-while loop | ```
do {
   a[loop] = loop + 5;
   loop = loop + 1;
} while (loop LT 10);
``` | Note that the expression comes after the code, so this code is always executed at least once |
| Switch statement | ```
switch(grade) {
   case "A": { comment="Excellent";
      break;      }
   case "B": { comment = "Very good";
      break;      }
   case "C": { comment = "Fairly good";
      break;      }
   case "D": { comment = "Can do better";
      break;      }
   case "F": { comment = "No effort";
      break;      }
   default:    { comment = "Good Job";
      break;      }
}
``` | Note that a default case is added at the end to catch any values of grade that don't fall within the cases listed |
| Break | ```
do   {
   if (a[loop] gt 10) break;
   a[loop] = loop + 5;
   loop = loop + 1;
}   while (loop LT 10);
``` | The loop is executed at least once, but if `a[loop]` is greater than 10, then it exits the loop without continuing |
| Continue | ```
do {
   if (loop eq 1) continue;
   a[loop] = loop + 5;
}
``` | Continues with the next iteration of the loop |

This information is sufficient to start off on some basic scripts. Example 8.8 prints the number of days in each month of the year using `<cfscript>` looping constructs. Save the example code as `ex8-8.cfm`. The output can be seen in Figure 8.8.

Example 8.8   CFScripting (ex8-8.cfm)

```
1.  <!DOCTYPE html
2.  PUBLIC "-//W3C//DTD XHTML 1.0 Transitional//EN"
3.  "http://www.w3.org/TR/xhtml1/DTD/xhtml1-transitional.dtd">
4.  <html xmlns="http://www.w3.org/1999/xhtml">
5.  <head>
6.     <title>cfscript example</title>
7.  </head>
8.  <body>
9.    <cfscript>
10.       for (mon=1; mon lte 12; mon=mon+1) {
11.           thisDate = CreateDate(2002, mon, 1);
12.           writeOutput(monthAsString(mon) & " has " &
13.           daysInMonth(thisDate) & " days <br>");
14.       }
15.    </cfscript>
16.  </body>
17.  </html>
```

How the Code Works

1. Line 10 is a CFScript `for` loop that loops from 1 to 12.

2. Within the loop, line 11 creates a new date initialized to the first of each month. The loop index (1–12) is used as the month number and 2002 is used to initialize the year.

3. Lines 12 and 13 write out for each month: `Month has XX days`. Note the usage of date functions `monthAsString()`, used to get the month name, and `daysInMonth()`, used to get the number of days in the month.

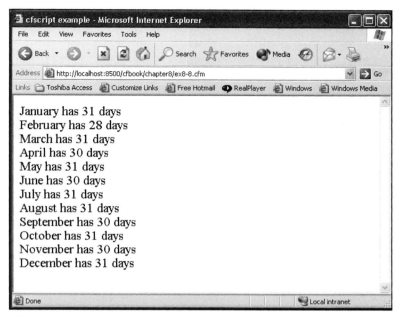

FIGURE 8.8   ColdFusion Scripting

As you can see, CFScript provides a compact and convenient way to code in ColdFusion. It is normally used when you want to set multiple variables, use JavaScript-like flow-control structures, or create user-defined functions. We will see how they are used in user-defined functions in the next chapter.

In this chapter we learned how to create and use complex data types such as lists, arrays, and structures. Lists are specialized strings. Arrays in ColdFusion are memory-efficient dynamic data types that expand and collapse depending on the number of elements. Structures are very useful to store related data in the session. Arrays and structures can be combined to create an array of structures.

We learned the basics of CFScript, a language based on JavaScript. Though it resembles JavaScript, it is a server-side scripting language, unlike JavaScript. Generally CFScript is quicker than using multiple `<cfset>` or `<cfparam>` tags.

Summary

Key Terms

array
array element
associative array
client-side script
collection loop
collection object
complex data type

dynamic structure
index
key
key-value pair
list
multiple dimensions
nested loop

one-dimensional array
property notation
server-side script
string index
structure
two-dimensional array

Review Questions

1. Name three complex data types in ColdFusion.
2. What is the advantage of using complex data types?
3. What is the default delimiter for list elements?
4. How do we create lists in ColdFusion? Give one example.
5. What is a dynamic array?
6. Which function creates a new array in ColdFusion? Give examples of how one-dimensional and two-dimensional arrays are created.
7. What are ColdFusion structures?
8. How are structures created in ColdFusion? Give an example.
9. What are the two notations that can be used to reference structures in ColdFusion? Give one example of each notation.
10. What is the server-side scripting language in ColdFusion?
11. Give an advantage of using this language.
12. Which function in CFScript is used to output values? Give an example.
13. What are the differences between client-side and server-side scripting?
14. What complex data type(s) would you use to store product details in the session if the fields to be stored are product name, price, stock on hand, and category?
15. Give an example (other than a shopping cart) where you would combine the power of arrays and structures.
16. What function do you use to update values in a structure?

True or False

State whether the following statements are true or false.

1. The default delimiter for list elements is a space. _____
2. Structures group related data. _____
3. CFScript is a client-side scripting language. _____
4. Using complex data types, related data can be held in memory until they are ready to be committed to the database. _____
5. ColdFusion does not support multidimensional, dynamic arrays. _____
6. Structures can be defined dynamically using associative arrays. _____
7. CFScript is a case-sensitive scripting language. _____

1. Write a ColdFusion template that reads 10 words with the help of a form. In the action part of the template, do the following:
   a. Append the words to a list.
   b. Display the number of elements in the list.
   c. Display the first and last values in the list.
   d. Display the fifth value in the list.
   e. Convert the above list to an array.
   f. Display the array using <cfdump>.

   Sample outputs can be seen in Figures 8.9A (form) and 8.9B (action).

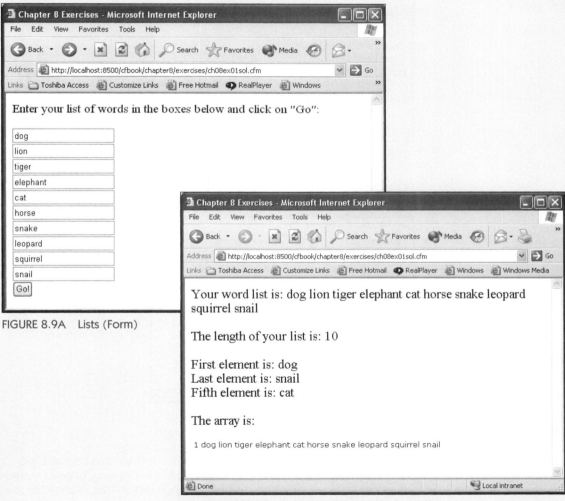

FIGURE 8.9A   Lists (Form)

FIGURE 8.9B   Lists (Action)

2. Design a form that accepts a course name, duration, and fees. Store all the course fields in a course structure in the action part of the form and display the structure. Example:

Course name = ColdFusion

Duration in months = 6

Fees = 100.00

Sample output can be seen in Figures 8.10A (form) and 8.10B (action).

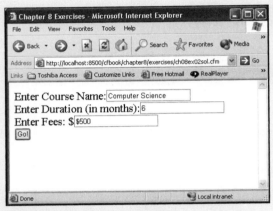

FIGURE 8.10A   Structures (Form)

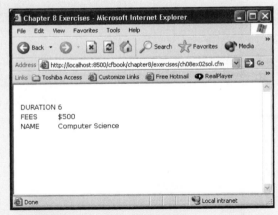

FIGURE 8.10B   Structures (Action)

3. Extend your solution for the previous exercise. Create an array of course structures so that if you hit the **back** button and refill the form, it appends to the array. Display the resulting array of course structures after each form submission. Use `<cfscript>` tags where appropriate. Hint: Make sure that `sessionManagement` is enabled in the Application.cfm file.

Sample output can be seen in Figures 8.11A (form) and 8.11B (action).

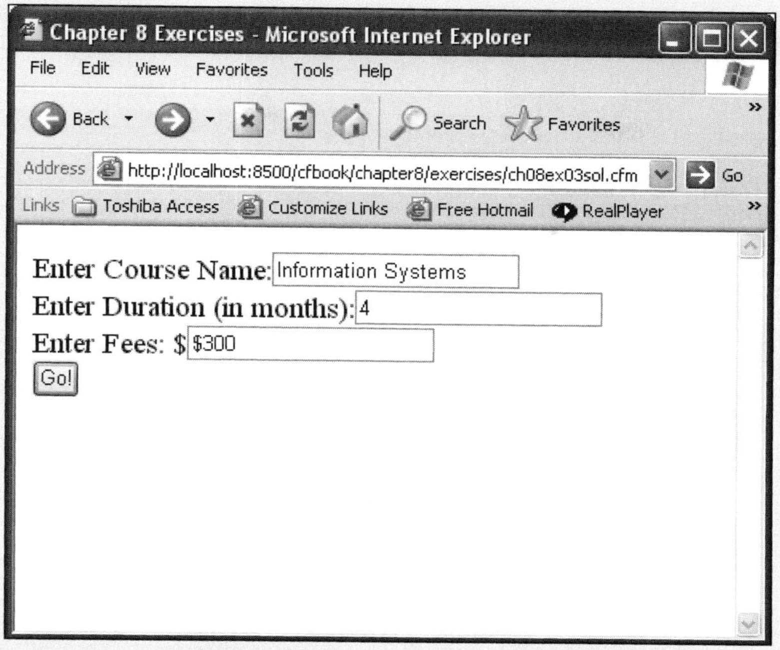

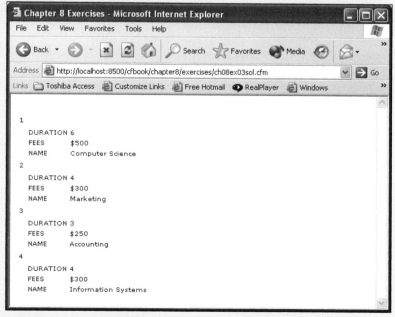

FIGURE 8.11A   Array of Structures (Form)

FIGURE 8.11B   Array of Structures (Action)

4. Using two-dimensional arrays, create the monthly calendar for the current year. Sample output can be seen in Figure 8.12.

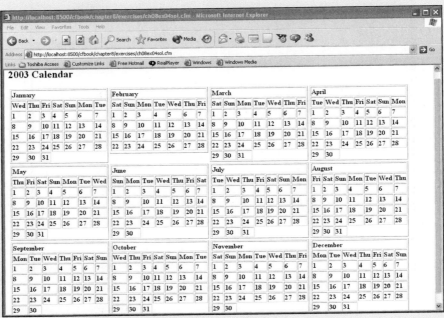

FIGURE 8.12   MULTIDIMENSIONAL ARRAY—CALENDAR

5. Correct the following erroneous code snippet:

   1. `<cfset session.courseList = arrayNew()>`

   2. `<cfset myCourse=StructNew()>`

   3. `<cfset myCourse.courseID="12">`

   4. `<cfset myCourse.courseName="Computer Science">`

   5. `<cfset myCourse.fee="1200">`

   6. `<cfset myCourse.months="3">`

   7. `<cfset var=#arrayAppend(session.courseList, myCourse)#>`

Shoppingcart.cfm

Use an array of structures to hold the shopping cart items in the session so that multiple items can be stored in the cart. Use CFScript where appropriate. See Figure 8.13.

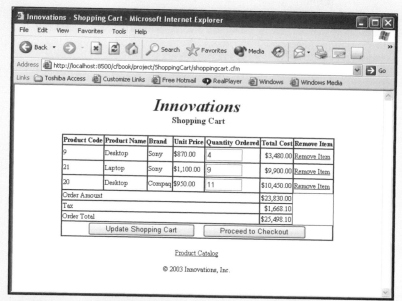

FIGURE 8.13   Multiple-Item Shopping Cart

Review.cfm

Use structures and `<cfscript>` to store address and payment details entered in the Customer Information page. Store this information in the shopping cart in the session in the Review Order page. See Figure 8.14.

SaveOrder.cfm

Store multiple line orders into the database using the line items from the shopping cart (array of structures) in the session. Hint: The changes should be made to the queries used to add orders and items into the database. The confirmation page will look the same as before, but the code will change.

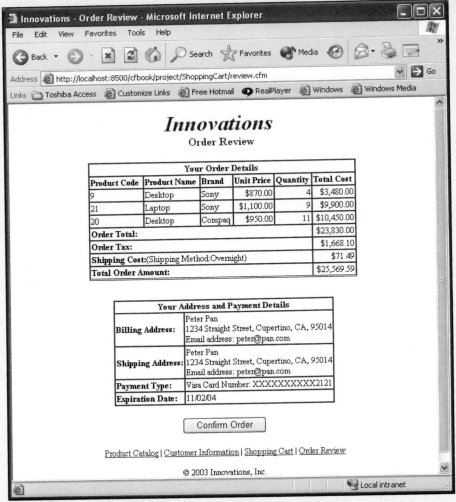

FIGURE 8.14   Order Review Page (Multiple Items)

Modular Code

CHAPTER OBJECTIVES

1. Modularize your code using include files within templates.

2. Write user-defined functions to modularize code.

3. Understand custom tags and paired tags.

4. Understand and write ColdFusion MX components.

5. Take a peek at object-oriented features of ColdFusion components.

You have now become really familiar with functions, complex data types, and other advanced ColdFusion programming techniques. You may have noticed by now that you sometimes have to repeat code in every page to reuse code, and this does seem to be a little inefficient.

This chapter will introduce you to a variety of advanced features of ColdFusion MX that can be used to make your code more efficient and modular. You will learn how to include other files within your templates. You will use user-defined functions, custom tags, and ColdFusion MX components to make your code more modular and manageable. The techniques in this chapter will help write more elegant code. We will also take a look at the new enhancements made to ColdFusion components in ColdFusion MX 6.1.

Modular Coding

ColdFusion lets you re-use code by allowing you to include other files within your templates. You can define custom tags and user-defined functions to perform tasks. These can be called within your applications. These techniques make your code more modular. ColdFusion MX also allows you to define **components** to group related functionality. You can develop large applications with dynamic web pages in ColdFusion with relative ease due to **modular coding.**

Using Include Files

The <cfinclude> tag allows you to embed other ColdFusion templates within your template. For example, you may have a standard header and footer on each of your pages. Usually company logos, page title and heading, header hyperlinks, and other top-of-the-page information are included in the header template. Contact information, terms of use, copyright information, and any footer hyperlinks are included as part of the footer template. This content usually needs to be included on every page. You would not want to repeat this code in each page on your website because it becomes very difficult to maintain and modify such pages. Instead, you can create a header template and a footer template and include these templates within your pages using the <cfinclude> tag as given below:

```
<cfinclude template="Header template name">
<cfinclude template="Footer template name">
```

A company logo image can be inserted into every page by including a header template with the logo image and other header content. This eliminates repeating header and footer code in every page. The contents of the included template get inserted into the main template that contains these tags when the main template is loaded. This way, you only maintain one header file and one footer file in your site.

The template attribute of the <cfinclude> tag contains the file name of the template to include. The path of the file is relative to the calling page. For example, if the calling page is c:/cfusionmx/test/mypage.cfm and you want to include the template c:/cfusionmx/test1/anotherpage.cfm, then you can use the relative path when including the template in mypage.cfm as given below:

```
<cfinclude template="../test1/anotherpage.cfm"
```

Different developers use include files in different ways. You should try to separate out any block of code that is repeated in multiple pages into a separate template and include that template in your pages using the <cfinclude> tag.

```
<cfinclude template="Queries template name">
<cfinclude template="Any other template name">
```

As you can see above, include files can be used to hold queries and functions that are written separately and included in templates that need them.

Example 9.1 shows how you can include separate header and footer templates in the top and bottom of a main template. Here we have three templates: header.cfm (header content), footer.cfm (footer content), and template.cfm (your page body). If you load the main template, you will see a page like Figure 9.1 with header content at the top and footer content at the bottom.

Tech Tip

`<cfinclude>` is a very important concept for developers and simplifies and modularizes code. It reduces code repetition and the necessity to modify multiple pages when changing templates. It also helps to separate out business logic from the program flow.

Example 9.1   Include Files (ex9-1.cfm)
Header Template (header.cfm)

```
1. <!DOCTYPE html
2. PUBLIC "-//W3C//DTD XHTML 1.0 Transitional//EN"
3. "http://www.w3.org/TR/xhtml1/DTD/xhtml1-transitional.dtd">
4. <html xmlns="http://www.w3.org/1999/xhtml">
5. <head>
6.   <title>CFInclude Example</title>
7. </head>
8. <body>
9. <b>Header content goes here ....</b>
```

Main Template (ex9-1.cfm)

```
1. <cfinclude template="header.cfm">
2. <br /><br /><b>Page content goes here ....
     </b><br /><br />
3. <cfinclude template="footer.cfm">
```

Footer Template (footer.cfm)

```
1.    <b>Footer content goes here ....</b>
2. </body>
3. </html>
```

How the Code Works
Header Template   In the header.cfm template, we have the XHTML header code, the `<html>`, `<head>`, and `<title>` tags including the opening `<body>`tag. These need not be repeated in the main template if the header template is included on the top of the main template.

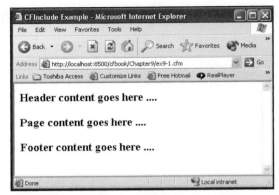

FIGURE 9.1   Including Files (Header and Footer Templates)

Main Template (ex9-1.cfm)

1. The main template is very simple. In line 1 it contains the `<cfinclude>` tag for the header at the top, so the main template need not worry about the XHTML header, title, and other things specific to the header. These are done only once in the header template.

2. After including the header, in the main template we have the content of the page as shown in line 2. In reality you would have much more content than we have here.

3. Finally, on line 3 we include the footer template at the bottom of the page.

Footer Template   The footer.cfm template contains the footer content and the closing `</body>` and `</html>` tags. This is so that your main template need not worry about anything other than the content that goes into that page.

User-Defined Functions

A **function** is a block of code that performs a task and returns some value. **User-defined functions (UDFs)** were introduced in ColdFusion 5. They are used to encapsulate business logic; for example, a frequently used algorithm (mathematical calculation, string manipulation, etc.) that returns a result. They are rarely used to output content. You can call these functions from within your template as long as the functions are within the scope of the page. You can either define functions within the page or include the template that contains the functions using the `<cfinclude>` tag. It is advisable to save frequently used functions in a separate template and include this template in all pages that use the functions.

As far as possible, you should avoid repeating the same code in multiple pages. Using UDFs you can reuse code that you write once. This will enable you to make global changes easily by modifying a single piece of code instead of modifying every page in which you wrote that code.

You can write user-defined functions using CFScript syntax or you can use the new <cffunction> tag. We will look at both these methods of writing UDFs.

CFScript Method for UDFs

In ColdFusion 5, you could write user-defined functions only with the help of <cfscript> tags. The following syntax is used to define a function using <cfscript> tags:

```
Function FunctionName( [parameter1 [, parameter2 ...]] )
{
    CFScript statements
}
```

FunctionName is the name of your function. It cannot be a ColdFusion built-in function name. No two functions can have the same name. *Parameter1* and *parameter2* . . . are names of required **parameters** or **arguments** that must be passed into the function by the calling program. All functions return a value. The Return statement makes the control leave the function and go back to the calling page with the value returned.

The simplest form of the UDF is given below. This is a function called AddThem() that adds two numbers.

```
<cfscript>
function addThem(n1, n2)  {
    var sum;
    sum = n1 + n2;
    Return (sum);
}
</cfscript>
```

The body of a function written using the CFScript method consists of CFScript statements. The function body begins with var statements to create local variables that exist only within the function as shown below:

```
var variableName = value;
```

Required parameters are parameters that are specified in the function definition. In the above function AddThem(), n1 and n2 are required parameters. Functions are called or used after they are defined. The **function call** cannot leave out any of the required parameters. The simplest form of the function call for AddThem() is given on page 322:

Tech Tip

Local variables should be defined using the var keyword and these statements should appear at the top of the UDF.

Tech Tip

Variables that are specified in the function definition are required parameters when calling the function. Additional arguments passed to the function in the function call are optional and are not specified in the function definition.

```
AddThem(num1, num2)
```

In the above call, num1 and num2 are values passed into n1 and n2 of function AddThem().

Optional arguments are arguments that are not specified as parameters in the function definition. These parameters can be passed into a function through the function call just like required parameters. Let us suppose that the function AddThem() supports one optional parameter. The optional argument num3 is not specified in the function AddThem() defined above but is passed to the function through the function call as given below:

```
AddThem(num1, num2, num3)
```

The required parameters n1 (which gets the value of num1) and n2 (which gets the value of num2) can be accessed directly within the function, whereas the optional parameter num3 cannot be accessed directly from within the function since it does not have a placeholder in the function definition. All functions have a built-in Arguments array that contains all arguments that are passed into the function (required and optional). Within the function, the two required parameters passed as num1 and num2 can be accessed directly as n1 and n2 or through the Arguments array as Arguments[1] and Arguments[2] since these are the first two arguments passed into the function. The optional argument num3 can be accessed within the function through the Arguments array as Arguments[3] since it is the third argument passed into the function, but it cannot be accessed directly since it is not specified in the arguments list of the function definition. The total number of arguments that have been sent into the function in the function call can be determined if you know the length of the Arguments array using the built-in array function ArrayLen(Arguments). Within the function, you could loop through the Arguments array and process all the arguments—required and optional.

Tech Tip

The length of the Arguments array determines the number of arguments passed to the function by the function call. If the function definition has fewer arguments than the number called, the remaining arguments are optional.

As explained above, using UDFs you can accept any number of parameters into a function. In the AddThem() function definition, the additional argument num3 passed to the function will be ignored because there is no code within the function that looks at the additional parameter. Let us look at Example 9.2 that defines a function that accepts any number of arguments and returns the sum of them all. The function iterates through the Arguments array to access all the arguments passed—required and optional. The result of this code is seen in Figure 9.2.

Example 9.2   UDF with CFScript (ex9-2.cfm)

```
1. <!DOCTYPE html

2. PUBLIC "-//W3C//DTD XHTML 1.0 Transitional//EN"

3. "http://www.w3.org/TR/xhtml1/DTD/xhtml1-transitional.dtd">

4. <html xmlns="http://www.w3.org/1999/xhtml">
```

```
5.  <head>
6.    <title>UDF - cfscript example</title>
7.  </head>
8.  <body>
9.    <cfscript>
10.     function addThem(n1, n2)  {
11.       var sum=0;
12.       var numargs = arrayLen(Arguments);
13.       for (i = 1; i lte numargs; i=i+1) {
14.         sum = sum + Arguments[i];
15.       }
16.       Return (sum);
17.     }
18.   </cfscript>
19 <cfoutput>
20.     Adding 2 numbers (12, 22): <b>#addthem
        (12,22)#</b><br />
21.     Adding 3 numbers (14, 21, 34): <b>#addthem
        (14,21,34)#</b><br />
22.   </cfoutput>
23. </body>
24. </html>
```

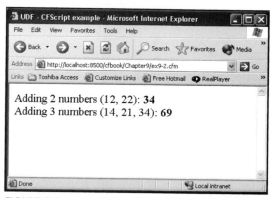

FIGURE 9.2   User-Defined Functions with CFScript

How the Code Works

1. Line 9 starts the <cfscript> tag within which line 10 defines the function addThem( ) that takes two required parameters: n1 and n2.

2. Line 11 defines a local variable sum to hold the sum of the numbers within the function.

3. Line 12 defines a local variable numargs to hold the number of arguments the function has been passed when called. The length of the Arguments array specifies the number of arguments passed into this function. The Arguments array holds all the arguments, required and optional.

4. Line 13 loops through the Arguments array and within the loop line 14 adds the value of each argument to the variable sum.

5. After the loop, line 16 returns the variable sum, which is the sum of all the arguments.

6. Line 20 calls the addThem( ) function with two arguments (both arguments are required).

7. Line 21 calls the addThem( ) function with three arguments. The first two arguments are required and the third one is optional.

Functions and Variable Scope

A function can access and change any variable available in the calling page using the variable's name or prefixed with the word variables; for example, variables.variableName. Any variable that is declared using the var declaration and any function parameters are local to that function, so they can be directly accessed within the function. When the control leaves the function, none of the function variables are available. If there is a variable myVar within a function with the same name as another variable in the main page, the variable within the function takes precedence inside the function. So if within the function you refer to myVar, the function's variable will be accessed. The variable in the main page must be referenced as variables.myVar from within the function.

<cffunction> Tag for UDFs

ColdFusion MX introduced the new <cffunction> tag enables us to use ColdFusion tags within our functions. This new tag enables you to take advantage of the power of CFML without limiting yourself to the functionality available in CFScript. One disadvantage of using CFScript to write UDFs is that you cannot use ColdFusion tags inside a <cfscript> block. Moreover, CFScript itself is a new syntax to learn.

The new <cffunction> tag can be used independently to create UDFs or it can be used within ColdFusion components (CFC) to define component methods. ColdFusion components are explained in a later section.

The `<cffunction>` tag is used to define the function and the `<cfargument>` tag is used to define the arguments that are passed into the function. The `<cfreturn>` tag defines the value that is returned from the function. Using these tags, the simple form of the addThem() UDF that takes two parameters and returns the sum of exactly two numbers would be as follows:

```
<cffunction name="addThem" returnType="numeric">
   <cfargument name="n1" type="numeric" required="true">
   <cfargument name="n2" type="numeric" required="true">
   <cfset sum=0>
   <cfset sum = n1 + n2>
   <cfreturn sum>
</cffunction>
```

Valid function calls are

```
AddThem(num1, num2)
AddThem(num1, num2, num3)
```

Since our function does not have any processing code for optional parameters, the additional parameter num3 passed by the second call above into the AddThem() function will be ignored by the function. Example 9.3 is similar to Example 9.2, but it uses the `<cffunction>` tag instead of the `<cfscript>` syntax. Any number of parameters can be passed into the function to be summed up and returned by the function. The output in Figure 9.3 is the same as the output of Example 9.2 (Figure 9.2).

Example 9.3   UDF with `<cffunction>` (ex9-3.cfm)

```
1.  <!DOCTYPE html
2.  PUBLIC "-//W3C//DTD XHTML 1.0 Transitional//EN"
3.  "http://www.w3.org/TR/xhtml1/DTD/xhtml1-transitional.dtd">
4.  <html xmlns="http://www.w3.org/1999/xhtml">
5.  <head>
6.     <title>cffunction example</title>
7.  </head>
8.  <body>
9.     <cffunction name="addThem" returnType="numeric">
10.        <cfargument name="n1" type="numeric" required="true">
11.        <cfargument name="n2" type="numeric" required="true">
12.        <cfset sum=0>
13.        <cfloop index="i" from="1" to="#ArrayLen(Arguments)#">
```

```
14.            <cfset sum = sum + Arguments[i]>
15.         </cfloop>
16.         <cfreturn sum>
17.     </cffunction>
18.     <cfoutput>
19.         Adding 2 numbers (12,22): <b>#addthem
                (12,22)#</b><br />
20.         Adding 3 numbers (14,21,34): <b>#addthem
                (14,21,34)#</b><br />
21.     </cfoutput>
22. </body>
23. </html>
```

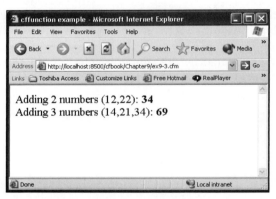

FIGURE 9.3   User Defined Functions with
<cffunction>

How the Code Works

1. Line 9 creates a function called addThem() that returns a numeric value as specified in the returnType attribute of the <cffunction> tag.

2. Lines 10 and 11 specify the two required numeric arguments for this function using the <cfargument> tag.

3. Line 12 declares a local variable to hold the sum and initializes it to 0.

4. Line 13 loops through all the arguments (required and optional) that have been sent into this function in the function call by using the length of the Arguments array.

5. Line 14 adds each argument value to the sum variable.

6. The function returns the sum of all the arguments in line 16 using the <cfreturn> tag.

7. Line 19 calls the addThem() function with two required arguments and outputs the sum of the two arguments returned by the function. If you passed only one argument, this function would not work since it has two required parameters. Since this function call used two arguments, there were no optional arguments passed into this function.

8. Line 20 calls the addThem() function with three arguments and displays the sum of these three arguments. The function AddThem() adds all the arguments (two required and one optional) in the Arguments array. The third argument is an optional argument since there are only two arguments in the function definition.

Reusing Code with Custom Tags

Custom tags allow you to extend the CFML language by adding your own tags. You also can use custom tags built by other developers to enhance your pages. Custom tags are similar to functions. They provide a way to reuse code and make applications modular. Using custom tags, templates can call other templates (called custom tags) to perform an action and output content. They are usually used for presentation (user interface, buttons, navigation, etc).

Where to Save Custom Tags

Custom tags are just like other .cfm templates. We save the custom tag in a .cfm file just like any other template. We use it within any template in an application just like any other ColdFusion tag with a cf_ prefix to the file name and without the .cfm suffix. For example, the tag name <cf_display> is used to call a custom tag saved in the file display.cfm. These tags are globally accessible when placed globally. If custom tag templates are saved in the same directory as the calling page, then they are only accessible to that page and to other pages in that directory. To share a custom tag among applications in multiple directories, and to enable custom tags to be globally accessible by any page in your application and in other applications, you would save them in the special directory called CustomTags in your ColdFusion installation directory C:\CfusionMX\CustomTags. ColdFusion first looks for custom tags in the directory of the calling page and then it looks in the CustomTags directory.

When custom tags are executed, they take control and return control to the caller when done. They can help you reduce repetition of code in your application.

Tech Tip

If you need to perform a task that does not necessarily return a result you need to work with, write a custom tag. If you need to write a routine that will help you set variables or evaluate to a single result, write a UDF.

IMPORTANT

You should avoid placing copies of a custom tag in different locations since that would make it difficult to maintain the tag.

Custom Tag Variables and Scope

Data are passed into and returned from the custom tag using `attributes`. Custom tags protect variables that are local to the custom tag and to the templates. Custom tags cannot directly refer to local variables created in the calling page unless they use the `caller.variablename` syntax to refer to these variables and override the protection. Similarly, local variables created in the custom tag cannot be used in the calling page. In other words, the custom tag is like a black box. Variables that are passed to the caller (URL, form, CGI, cookie) and global variables (session, client, application, server, request) are accessible from the custom tag. Local variables created in the caller need to be passed to the custom tag. Any ColdFusion element can be sent into a custom tag as an `attribute` (string, number, variable, array, structure, query, etc). Values are passed to a tag using `attribute=value` pairs. The custom tag can access these variables by using the `attributes.variablename` syntax. For example, the custom tag `cf_display` can be accessed using the following syntax:

```
<cf_display firstname="Peter" lastname="Pan">
```

Tech Tip

Attributes can be passed in any order to the tag since they are name-value pairs.

Within the custom tag, the `firstname` and `lastname` attributes are referred to as `attributes.firstname` and `attributes.lastname`.

Example 9.4 defines a simple custom tag Showname.cfm that displays a name that is passed into the tag by the caller template (ex9-4.cfm). In this example, you will see how the calling template accesses the tag and how the tag performs its task of displaying the name. Save the custom tag code as `Showname.cfm` in the `CfusionMX\CustomTags` directory and save the calling template in `ex9-4.cfm` within the subdirectory in which you have all of your application files. If you load this file in your browser, you will see a screen similar to Figure 9.4.

Example 9.4   Custom Tags (ex9-4.cfm)
Custom Tag (Showname.cfm)

```
1. <cfparam name="attributes.fname" default="">

2. <!DOCTYPE html

3. PUBLIC "-//W3C//DTD XHTML 1.0 Transitional//EN"

4. "http://www.w3.org/TR/xhtml1/DTD/xhtml1-transitional.dtd">

5. <html xmlns="http://www.w3.org/1999/xhtml">
```

6. `<head>`

7. `<title>Custom Tag example</title>`

8. `</head>`

9. `<body>`

10. `<cfoutput> Hello #attributes.fname#</cfoutput>`

11. `</body>`

12. `</html>`

Calling Template (ex9-4.cfm)

1. `<!DOCTYPE html`

2. `PUBLIC "-//W3C//DTD XHTML 1.0 Transitional//EN"`

3. `"http://www.w3.org/TR/xhtml1/DTD/xhtml1-transitional.dtd">`

4. `<html xmlns="http://www.w3.org/1999/xhtml">`

5. `<head>`

6. `<title>Custom tags example</title>`

7. `</head>`

8. `<body>`

9. `<cfset firstName = "Peter">`

10. `<cf_showname fname="#firstname#">`

11. `</body>`

12. `</html>`

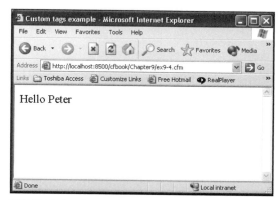

FIGURE 9.4   Custom Tags

How the Code Works
Custom Tag (showname.cfm)

1. Line 10 outputs the variable `#attributes.fname#` that is sent into the custom tag by the calling template.

2. Note that we have a `<cfparam>` tag at the top of this template in line 1 so that there is a default value to protect from the tag being invoked without the attribute.

Calling Template (ex9-4.cfm)

1. Line 9 sets a variable called `firstName` to the string `"Peter"`.

2. Line 10 invokes the custom tag to do the job of displaying the value of the variable `firstName`. The variable `firstName` is sent into the custom tag through attribute `fname`.

The above example gives you an idea about how custom tags are used. In this example, the display could have been done within the template without the custom tag. Custom tags are very useful when you have to do some processing repeatedly in each page. When your process does not return a single value, you should use a custom tag instead of repeating it in each template or using a UDF. The processing within your custom tag may differ depending on the values of the attributes sent into the custom tag by the calling template.

Paired Tags

Paired start and end tags enable us to pass data between the tags other than through attributes. Data between tags are passed in a variable called `thistag.generatedcontent` by which custom tags can access and change the results generated within the body of the tag. When paired tags are used, the custom tag runs twice: once when the tag starts and again when the tag is closed. Here is an example of paired tags:

```
<cf_tag>
   some coldfusion statements
</cf_tag>
```

When we use paired tags, we have access to another variable called `thistag.executionmode`. When the template is being run by the opening tag call, this variable has the value `start` and when it is run by the closing tag call, this variable has the value `end`. During the execution of the body of the custom tag, the `thistag.executionMode` variable is inactive.

The tag `thistag.generatedcontent` is available only in `end` mode. This variable is used to process the text between the tags, for example, to store data in a database. You can suppress displaying the text before the processing of the closing tag by assigning an empty string to the variable `thistag.generatedcontent` before the closing tag is processed. You may manipulate the text between the tags by assigning `thistag.generatedcontent` to the new text.

The tag `thisTag.hasendtag` is used to determine if a paired tag has a closing tag. It returns yes if there is a closing tag and no if there is no closing tag. This variable is available in both `start` and `end` modes.

Example 9.5 shows how paired tags can be used effectively. The code capitalizes the string `my name is peter` by performing a `ucase()` function on the generated content of the tag between the `start` and `end` states of the tag.

Example 9.5   Paired Tags (ex9-5.cfm)
Calling Template (ex9-5.cfm)

```
1. <!DOCTYPE html
2. PUBLIC "-//W3C//DTD XHTML 1.0 Transitional//EN"
3. "http://www.w3.org/TR/xhtml1/DTD/xhtml1-transitional.dtd">
4. <html xmlns="http://www.w3.org/1999/xhtml">
5. <head>
6. <title>Custom tags example</title>
7. </head>
8. <body>
9. <cf_ucase>
10. my name is peter
11. </cf_ucase>
12. </body>
13. </html>
```

Custom Tag (Ucase.cfm)

```
1. <!DOCTYPE html
2. PUBLIC "-//W3C//DTD XHTML 1.0 Transitional//EN"
3. "http://www.w3.org/TR/xhtml1/DTD/xhtml1-transitional.dtd">
4. <html xmlns="http://www.w3.org/1999/xhtml">
5. <head>
6.    <title>Custom Tag example</title>
7. </head>
8. <body>
```

```
9.     <cfif thistag.executionmode is "end">
10.        <cfset thistag.generatedcontent=ucase(thistag.
           generatedcontent)>
11.    </cfif>
12. </body>
13. </html>
```

The output of the text `my name is peter` is the capitalized text that you see in Figure 9.5.

FIGURE 9.5   Paired Tags

How the Code Works
Calling Template (ex9-5.cfm)

1. Line 9 uses the `<cf_ucase>` tag to call the custom tag.

2. Within the `start` and `end` tags in line 10 is the text `my name is peter`.

3. Line 11 closes the custom tag using `</cf_ucase>`.

Custom Tag—Ucase.cfm

1. Within the custom tag, the variable `thistag.generatedcontent` contains the text within the `<cf_ucase>` and `</cf_ucase>` tags in the calling template, that is, `my name is peter`.

2. Line 9 checks if the execution mode is `end`. In other words, it checks if the `</cf_ucase>` tag has been encountered in the calling template.

3. If so, it modifies `thistag.generatedcontent` by capitalizing `thistag.generatedcontent` in line 10. So the output is MY NAME IS PETER, as you can see in Figure 9.5.

ColdFusion MX Components

ColdFusion components (CFC) are a new feature in ColdFusion MX. They encapsulate business logic and data access logic and do not output content. Components are ideal for communicating with third-party products such as Flash movies and Web Services. Components encapsulate functionality and provide a standard interface to the client. The client can then access this functionality by invoking methods on the components. Components enable you to reuse code, so you need to modify only the component file when you want to change functionality. They also help you make your code more modular. For each component, ColdFusion can automatically generate the HTML documentation.

Component files are written like ordinary ColdFusion pages, but with the .cfc suffix. These files can be saved in the web root or web server directories or in any directory accessible through your ColdFusion mappings or with the custom tags.

To create ColdFusion components, we use the `<cfcomponent>` and `<cffunction>` tags. The `<cfcomponent>` tag contains one or more `<cffunction>` tags.

Example 9.6 is a very simple component example that shows you how to use this feature in ColdFusion MX. The role of the component in this example is to display Hello World. This example will be followed by a more complex business example using database queries within multiple functions. When you load the template file, you will see a page with the text Hello World, as in Figure 9.6.

> **Tech Tip**
> Components should encapsulate all the business logic and data access logic of an application in ColdFusion.

> **Tech Tip**
> Code that lies inside the `<cfcomponent>` tag but outside any methods or functions is called initialization code. It will be automatically called when the object is first created.

Example 9.6   ColdFusion Components (ex9-6.cfm)
Component File (helloWorld.cfc)

```
1. <cfcomponent>
2. <cffunction name="hello">
3. <cfreturn "Hello World">
4. </cffunction>
5. </cfcomponent>
```

Template File (ex9-6.cfm)

```
 1. <!DOCTYPE html
 2. PUBLIC "-//W3C//DTD XHTML 1.0 Transitional//EN"
 3. "http://www.w3.org/TR/xhtml1/DTD/xhtml1-transitional.dtd">
 4. <html xmlns="http://www.w3.org/1999/xhtml">
 5. <head>
 6. <title>Components example</title>
 7. </head>
 8. <body>
 9. <cfinvoke component="helloWorld" method="hello"
10. returnvariable="hellolocal">
11. <cfoutput>#hellolocal#</cfoutput>
12. </body>
13. </html>
```

FIGURE 9.6   ColdFusion Components

How the Code Works

Component File (helloWorld.cfc)   The above component code is saved in a file called helloWorld.cfc. Line 1 opens the <cfcomponent> tag within which there is a function or method called hello() on line 2 that returns the text Hello World on line 3.

Calling Template (ex9-6.cfm)

1. The template file uses the above component by invoking it in line 9 with the <cfinvoke> tag. It specifies the component by giving the

component file name without the .cfc extension as the value for the `component` attribute. It specifies the `method` name `hello()`. It also specifies the `returnvariable` name as `hellolocal`, which means that the value returned by the function is stored locally in a variable called `hellolocal`. The function returns the string `Hello World`, so the `hellolocal` variable contains this value.

2. The `helloLocal` variable is displayed in line 11 to show the text `Hello World`, which was the value the `helloWorld` component's `hello()` function returned.

Business Example Using ColdFusion Components

Now that you have understood how to use components, let us do a real-world example using components. The ideal example would be the shopping cart that we have been building. So far we have been saving orders, but we have no way yet to extract order information or view orders.

Example 9.7 will allow you to enter an order number to view the order details, shipping address, and billing address for that order. Before we start, you should refresh your memory by looking at the database design of the shopping cart application given in the Chapter 5 Project Building Exercises. In this example, we have used queries to extract orders from the shopping cart database.

Now, let us begin by creating a component file that will hold functions (methods) with queries to extract order details, given an order number. We will save this in a component file called `GetOrderDetails.cfc`. In this component, we define four user-defined functions using the `<cffunction>` tag. We first create the `getOrderDetails()` component and then use the methods of the component from within our template saved in `ex9-7.cfm`.

Example 9.7 ColdFusion Components—Business Example (ex9-7.cfm)
Component File (GetOrderDetails.cfc)

```
1. <cfcomponent>
2.    <cffunction name="getOrders" returnType="query">
3.       <cfargument name="orderId" type="numeric"
             required="true">
4.       <cfquery name="rsOrder" datasource="shoppingcart">
5.          select OrderId, OrderDate, ShippingMethod,
6.          BillingAddressId, ShippingAddressId,
                ShippingCost,
7.          Taxes, OrderAmount, OrderStatus
8.          from [Order]
```

```
9.          where orderId = #arguments.orderId#

10.      </cfquery>

11.      <cfreturn rsOrder>

12.   </cffunction>

13.   <cffunction name="getOrderItems" returntype="query">

14.      <cfargument name="orderId" type="numeric"
            required="true">

15.      <cfquery name="rsOrderItems"
            datasource="shoppingcart">

16.      select ItemNumber, ProductId,

17.      ProductQty, ItemAmount

18.      from OrderItem

19.      where orderId = #arguments.orderId#

20.      </cfquery>

21.      <cfreturn rsOrderItems>

22.   </cffunction>

23.   <cffunction name="getBillingAddress" returntype="query">

24.      <cfargument name="addressId" type="numeric"
            required="true">

25.      <cfquery name="rsBaddress"
            datasource="shoppingcart">

26.      select FirstName, LastName, Address, City,
            State, Zip

27.      from Customer

28.      where addressId = #arguments.addressId#

29.      </cfquery>

30.      <cfreturn rsBAddress>

31.   </cffunction>

32.   <cffunction name="getShippingAddress"
         returntype="query">

33.      <cfargument name="addressId" type="numeric"
            required="true">

34.      <cfquery name="rsSaddress"
            datasource="shoppingcart">
```

35.   select FirstName, LastName, Address, City,
            State, Zip

36.   from Customer

37.   where addressId = #arguments.addressId#

38.   </cfquery>

39.   <cfreturn rsSAddress>

40. </cffunction>

41. </cfcomponent>

Template File (ex9-7.cfm)

1. <!DOCTYPE html

2. PUBLIC "-//W3C//DTD XHTML 1.0 Transitional//EN"

3. "http://www.w3.org/TR/xhtml1/DTD/xhtml1-transitional.dtd">

4. <html xmlns="http://www.w3.org/1999/xhtml">

5. <head>

6.   <title>Components Business example</title>

7. </head>

8. <body>

9.   <cfif isDefined("form.submitbutton") and
        isnumeric(form.orderid)>

10.   <cfinvoke component="getOrderDetails" method="getOrders"

11.   orderId="#form.orderId#" returnvariable="myorder">

12.   <cfif myOrder.recordcount>

13.   <cfinvoke component="getOrderDetails"
            method="getOrderItems"

14.   OrderId="#myorder.orderId#"
            returnvariable="orderitems">

15.   <cfinvoke component="getOrderDetails"
            method="getBillingAddress"

16.   AddressId="#myorder.billingaddressid#"
            returnvariable="billingAddress">

17.   <cfinvoke component="getOrderDetails"
            method="getShippingAddress"

18.   AddressId="#myorder.shippingaddressid#"

```
19.          returnvariable="shippingAddress">
20.       <cfoutput>
21.       Order ID: <b>#myOrder.orderId#</b><br />
22.       Order Date:<b>#dateformat(myOrder.orderDate,
            "mm/dd/yyyy")#</b><br />
23.       Status: <b>#myOrder.orderStatus#</b><br />
24.       Shipping Method: <b>#myOrder.
            shippingmethod#</b><br />
25.       Order Items:
26.       <table border=1>
27.         <tr>
28.           <td>Item number</td>
29.           <td>Product ID</td>
30.           <td>Product Qty</td>
31.           <td>Item Amount</td>
32.         </tr>
33.         <cfloop index="count" from=1
            to=#orderitems.recordcount#>
34.         <tr>
35.           <td>#orderitems.itemnumber[count]#</td>
36.           <td>#orderitems.ProductId[count]#</td>
37.           <td>#orderitems.productQty[count]#</td>
38.           <td>#orderitems.itemamount[count]#</td>
39.         </tr>
40.       </cfloop>
41.       <tr>
42.         <td colspan=2>Billing Address:
43.           <br />#billingaddress.firstname#
              #billingaddress.lastname#
44.           <br />#billingaddress.address#
45.           <br />#billingaddress.city#
46.             #billingaddress.state# #billingaddress.zip#
47.         </td>
```

```
48.          <td colspan=2>Shipping Address:
49.             <br />#shippingaddress.firstname#
                 #shippingaddress.lastname#
50.             <br />#shippingaddress.address#
51.             <br />#shippingaddress.city#
                 #shippingaddress.state#
52.               #shippingaddress.zip#
53.           </td>
54.         </tr>
55.       </table>
56.       </cfoutput>
57.    <cfelse> Order not found. Please try again.
58.    </cfif>
59.  </cfif>
60.  <form name="componentsform" action="ex9-7.cfm"
       method="post">
61.    Please enter your order number:
62.    <input type="text" size="10" name="orderId">
63.    <br /><input type="submit" name="submitbutton"
         value="Get Details">
64.  </form>
65. </body>
66. </html>
```

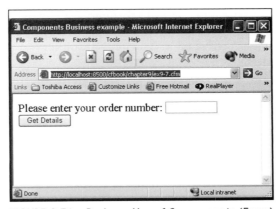

FIGURE 9.7A   Business Use of Components (Form)

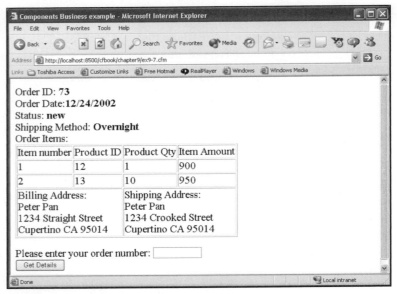

FIGURE 9.7B   Business Use of Components (Action)

How the Code Works
Component File (GetOrderDetails.cfc)

1. Line 1 uses the `<cfcomponent>` tag to open the component, and `</cfcomponent>` on line 41 closes the component.

2. Within the component four functions are defined that enclose queries and return result sets. The first function (lines 2 through 12) contains a query that takes one numeric argument, `orderID`. It queries the order details from the Order table. Among the fields queried are the `BillingAddressID` and `shippingAddressID`, which will help us retrieve the billing and shipping addresses later. The order result set is returned by this function.

3. The second function (lines 13 through 22) encloses a query that takes one numeric argument, `orderID`. It queries the order items from the OrderItem table. The items result set is returned by this function.

4. The third function (lines 23 through 31) encloses a query to retrieve the billing address. This function takes one numeric argument (`BillingAddressID` that was obtained from the Order table in the first function).

5. The fourth function (lines 32 through 40) encloses a query to retrieve the shipping address. This function has one numeric argument (`ShippingAddressID` that was obtained from the Order table in the first function).

Template File (ex9-7.cfm)

1. This form is submitted to the same template that does the action part also. The existence of `form.submitbutton` is checked in line 9. Initially this variable does not exist, so only the form is displayed (lines 60 through 64) to accept an order number. You will notice that line 9 also checks whether `form.orderID` is numeric. It allows the form action part to execute only if `form.orderID` is a number. Later you can enhance the error-handling part of this code to provide a user-friendly error message when a nonnumeric order ID is entered.

2. The `<cfinvoke>` tag in line 10 invokes the `getOrderDetails` component and calls the `getOrders()` method. In line 11, it passes `form.orderID` into the `orderID` argument of the method and stores the result of the `rsOrder` query in a local variable myorder.

3. Line 12 checks to see if the `getOrders()` method returned any data. If not, we don't want to proceed because the `orderID` was not found. So the code skips to line 57, where we tell the user that the order number could not be found.

4. The `<cfinvoke>` tag in line 13 invokes the `getOrderDetails` component and calls the `getOrderItems()` method. In line 14, it passes `myOrder.orderID` into the `orderID` argument of the method and stores the result of the `rsOrderitems` query in a local variable `orderitems`.

5. Line 15 invokes the `getOrderDetails` component and calls the `getBillingAddress()` method, passing `myorder.billingaddressid` in line 16 into the `AddressId` argument of the method. It stores the result of the `rsBAddress` query in a local variable `billingAddress`.

6. Line 17 invokes the `getOrderDetails` component and calls the `getShippingAddress()` method, passing `myorder.shipping addressid` in line 18 into the `AddressId` argument of the method. In line 19 it stores the result of the `rsSAddress` query in a local variable `shippingAddress`.

7. Through the variables `myorder`, `orderitems`, `shippingAddress`, and `billingAddress` we can access any of the fields in the returned record sets. Lines 21 through 24 display the `orderId`, `orderDate`, `orderStatus`, and `shippingmethod` through the `myOrder` variable.

8. Line 26 starts a table that holds the line items for the order. Lines 33 through 40 loop through all the order items to display the `itemnumber`, `ProductId`, `productQty`, and `itemamount` for each item through the `orderitems` variable.

9. Lines 43 through 46 display the billing address through the `billingaddress` variable.

10. Lines 49 through 52 display the shipping address through the `shippingaddress` variable.

CFC and Object-Oriented Technologies

Though CFML is not an object-oriented language, CFCs and object-oriented languages have some common features such as inheritance and encapsulation.

Inheritance allows one object to have all the properties of its parent. The parent or **superclass** is very generic (for example, Math) and the child or **subclass** is specific (for example, Algebra) and can be extended to include other behaviors. A CFC can inherit methods and properties of another CFC. This allows you to create multiple components without having to change the code on your basic component. ColdFusion MX allows you to use the `extends` attribute in your component to inherit all the methods and attributes of another component. ColdFusion MX 6.1 has introduced a new `super` scope to access methods that were overridden in the subclass.

Encapsulation means hiding some parts of a program that can be accessed using an **interface.** Encapsulation helps reduce the complexity of large programs. Components should be used to encapsulate business logic. The programmer writing the template should use the interface of the component to do what is needed. But the programmer need not know how the component is written. The component can be a black box for the programmer. An efficient interface is all that is required to be able to invoke the component methods and easily add functionality to pages. Components also can be shared among applications. CFCs are very powerful because of their ability to expose some of their methods as remote functions for Flash remoting or web services. You just need to add the `access="remote"` attribute to the `<cffunction>` tag.

ColdFusion components cover a vast topic and this book only skims the surface of this very interesting subject.

Summary

In this chapter, we learned how to modularize our code. Modular code helps reuse blocks of code, speeds up development, enables parallel development, helps code debugging, and is easier to maintain and modify. We can include files in our templates and reduce repetition of regularly used code such as headers, footers, queries, and user-defined functions. Custom tags are one of the easiest and most powerful ways to extend the functionality of ColdFusion and make code modular. User-defined functions can be created using `<cfscript>` tags and now with `<cffunction>` tags that are new to ColdFusion MX. The new ColdFusion MX components help us modularize and encapsulate code. Using CFCs we can extend the functionality of ColdFusion and share it with third-party applications.

Key Terms

argument
ColdFusion components (CFC)
components
custom tags
encapsulation
function

function call
inheritance
interface
modular coding
optional argument
paired start and end tags

parameter
required parameter
subclass
superclass
user-defined function (UDF)

Review Questions

1. Which tag allows you to embed other ColdFusion templates within your template? Give an example to include a template called myHeader.cfm.
2. What are two advantages of including files in templates?
3. Give two examples of files that you would include in templates.
4. State two ways that you can write user-defined functions.
5. What is the difference between required and optional arguments in ColdFusion functions?
6. What is the `var` section in user-defined functions used for?
7. When would you prefer to use a UDF to a custom tag?
8. When would you prefer to use a custom tag to a UDF?
9. How does a custom tag get data?
10. Where do you save custom tags if you want them to be accessed by all applications?
11. What are paired tags used for?
12. What is the code that is within a component but outside the functions called and what is the purpose of that code?

State whether the following statements are true or false.

True or False

1. `<cfinclude>` helps to reduce repeated code. _____
2. UDFs can be written in a separate template and included in templates that need them. _____
3. Custom tags are like black boxes because they protect data. _____
4. ColdFusion first searches for custom tags in the global Custom Tags directory. _____
5. Components should be used to encapsulate business logic and data access logic. _____
6. Components contain one or more functions. _____
7. When your process needs to return a single value, you should use a custom tag instead of a UDF. _____
8. ColdFusion component files are written like ordinary ColdFusion pages with the .cfm suffix. _____
9. The `<cfcomponent>` tag contains one or more `<cffunction>` tags. _____
10. When paired tags are used, the custom tag runs twice. _____

Use Figures 9.8A, 9.8B, and 9.8C for Exercises 1–3.

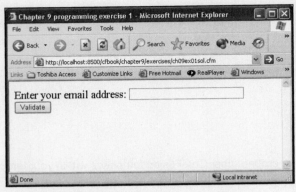

FIGURE 9.8A   Email Form

FIGURE 9.8B   Invalid Email Address

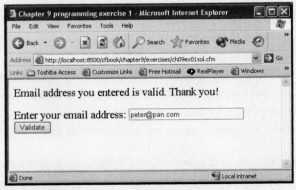

FIGURE 9.8C   Valid Email Address

1. Create a ColdFusion template that displays a form (Figure 9.8A) that accepts an email address from the customer and validates it. Use a UDF for the validation.

   UDF specifications:

   a. Write a UDF that validates the email address sent through the form.

   b. Validation should include searching for a period and an "@". Also, validate that no spaces are entered.

   c. The UDF should return 1 if the email address is valid and 0 if it is not valid.

   d. Save the UDF as a separate file and include it in your main template.

   Main template specifications:

   e. The main template should display the form with one text input box for email and a submit button. See Figure 9.8A.

   f. It should use the UDF to check if the email address is valid or not.

   g. Depending on the value returned by the UDF, an appropriate message should be displayed. See Figures 9.8B and 9.8C.

2. Write a custom tag that does the same as the above exercise.

   a. Let your main template display the form (Figure 9.8A).

   b. The purpose of the custom tag is to output the appropriate message to the customer depending on the validity of his email address. See Figures 9.8B and 9.8C.

   c. The validation code should be inside the custom tag.

   d. The custom tag should display the error message if the email address is invalid and thank the customer if the email address is valid.

   e. Modify your main template to invoke the custom tag to display the appropriate messages.

3. Modify your main template to use a ColdFusion component instead of a custom tag to process your form field.

   a. Write a ColdFusion component that contains a function that holds your email validation code and returns a Boolean value.

   b. Let your main template display the form (Figure 9.8A).

   c. Invoke the component from the main template with the appropriate parameter (email).

   d. Depending on the value returned by the function in the component, display the appropriate message to the user in your main template (Figures 9.8B and 9.8C).

4. Correct the following erroneous code snippet:

```
<cfscript>
    function add(num1, num2, num3) {
        return num1 + num2 + num3;
    }
</cfscript>
<cfoutput> #add(1,2)# </cfoutput>
```

Productlist.cfm

1. Use components with UDFs to execute queries to get the product list. The user interface will not change.

2. Create separate header and footer files for your application. Include these files in every page of your application. The user interface will not change.

3. For the header and footer, use custom tags instead of include files. Change the title and heading of each page depending on the page the customer is on. The user interface will not change.

CHAPTER 10

Cool Features

CHAPTER OBJECTIVES

1. Suppress output in ColdFusion templates.
2. Use ColdFusion's debugging features.
3. Throw and catch standard and custom exceptions.
4. Enable and use sitewise error-handling templates.
5. Log errors that may occur in your pages.
6. Abort processing of your ColdFusion page.
7. Relocate users to another page from your template.
8. Handle files and directories on the server.
9. Send email and attachments.
10. Send multipart email messages.
11. Create different types of graphs and charts including multiple series graphs.
12. Generate XML from database queries.

In the previous chapter, we learned modular programming techniques in ColdFusion MX. In this chapter we will learn some of the cool features that ColdFusion offers us to enhance our pages. There are a variety of techniques that are explained in this chapter. This chapter is light and easy to read and does not go into too much depth. Hopefully you will enjoy reading and using the functionality explained here.

You will get an introduction to output suppression, relocation, code debugging, and logging. In addition, you will learn exception handling, sitewise error handling, and how to abort processing. Finally, you will see how to send email, create charts, and generate XML using ColdFusion. You also will use the new enhancements made to the mail handling functionality in ColdFusion MX 6.1.

Suppressing Output

ColdFusion suppresses all output that is produced by the CFML within the `<cfsilent>` and `</cfsilent>` tags. This is a useful tag when you want to suppress output within your code. All HTML output is suppressed. It is a good practice to encapsulate within these tags any logic that does not need to output any HTML. Example 10.1 illustrates the `<cfsilent>` tags in ColdFusion that suppresses the output string `Within cfsilent`. Type the code and save it in a file called `ex10-1.cfm`. When you run the code, you should see an output like Figure 10.1. Note that the code only outputs the string `Outside cfsilent`, not `Within cfsilent`.

Example 10.1   CFSilent (ex10-1.cfm)

```
1.  <!DOCTYPE html
2.  PUBLIC "-//W3C//DTD XHTML 1.0 Transitional//EN"
3.  "http://www.w3.org/TR/xhtml1/DTD/xhtml1-transitional.dtd">
4.  <html xmlns="http://www.w3.org/1999/xhtml">
5.  <head>
6.      <title>CFSilent Example</title>
7.  </head>
8.  <body>
9.      <h3>CFSilent Example</h3>
10.     <cfsilent>
11.         <cfset x=10>
12.         <cfset y=20>
13.         <cfset z=x*y>
14.         <cfoutput>Within cfsilent: #z#</cfoutput>
15.     </cfsilent>
16.     <cfoutput>Outside cfsilent: #z#</cfoutput>
17. </body>
18. </html>
```

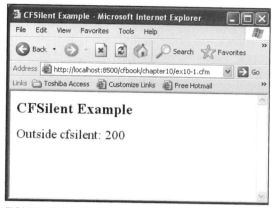

FIGURE 10.1   CFSilent

How the Code Works

1. Line 10 starts the $<$cfsilent$>$ tag and line 15 ends the $<$cfsilent$>$ tag.

2. Lines 11 through 13 set x to 10, y to 12, and z to the product of x and y, that is, z=200.

3. Any output that is within $<$cfsilent$>$ and $<$/cfsilent$>$ tags will be suppressed. Line 14 outputs the value of z. This output will be suppressed so you will not see the text Within cfsilent: 200.

4. Line 16 displays the value of z again, this time outside the $<$cfsilent$>$ tag. That is why you only see the text Outside cfsilent: 200 when you load this page.

Debugging

ColdFusion MX makes debugging easy. In the debugging and logging section of the ColdFusion Administrator, there is a subsection called **Debugging Settings.** Enabling **debugging** is the most basic setting in this page. This enables client machines to see debugging information unless you limit the IP addresses in the Debugging IP Addresses section. On the same page, checking the **Tracing Information** checkbox enables tracing information to be reported along with the debugging information for that page.

Using the $<$cftrace$>$ tag

One of the new features of ColdFusion MX is the $<$cftrace$>$ tag that helps developers to debug their applications. The $<$cftrace$>$ tag enables you to get information about the state of your application when the $<$cftrace$>$ tag

Tech Tip

The `<cftrace>` tag must be enabled in the ColdFusion MX Administrator Debugging and Logging section to execute successfully.

is executed. It conveniently displays values of all the variables you want to view including the execution time of your code. It also shows you the time taken for each piece of code to execute. ColdFusion MX also logs the `cftrace` output to the file `cftrace.log` in the logs directory of your server (usually `cfusionmx\logs\`).

The syntax of this tag is as follows:

```
<cftrace
    abort = "Yes or No"
    category = "string"
    inline = "Yes or No"
    text = "string"
    type = "format"
    var = "variable_name"
</cftrace>
```

This tag takes different attributes to help trace the code.

- `Abort` is an optional attribute that can take values `Yes` or `No` (default). If the value is `Yes`, it aborts processing by calling `<cfabort>` when the tag is executed.
- `Category` is an optional user-defined string used for identifying trace groups.
- `Inline` is an optional attribute that can take values `Yes` or `No` (default) and it specifies whether the tracing details should be logged on the cfm page or in the debugging output of the page.
- `Text` is an optional attribute that enables you to give a textual detail of what you are tracking.
- `Type` is an optional attribute that has a default value of `Information`. It is the output format that can have values `Information`, `Warning`, `Error`, and `Fatal Information`.
- `Var` is an optional attribute that specifies the name of the variable to be displayed at that trace point. A complex variable such as a structure is displayed in `<cfdump>` format.

Example 10.2 shows how `<cftrace>` is used. The example code displays a form that accepts two numbers and displays the maximum of the two values. Save this code in a file called `ex10-2.cfm`. The form is submitted to the same file that does the action part also. You will see that the `<cftrace>` tag enables you to trace the form variables that have been submitted. See figure 10.2.

Example 10.2   CFTrace (ex10-2.cfm)

1. `<!DOCTYPE html`

2. `PUBLIC "-//W3C//DTD XHTML 1.0 Transitional//EN"`

3. `"http://www.w3.org/TR/xhtml1/DTD/xhtml1-transitional.dtd">`

```
 4.  <html xmlns="http://www.w3.org/1999/xhtml">

 5.  <head>

 6.    <title>CFTrace example</title>

 7.  </head>

 8.  <body>

 9.    <h2>CFTrace example</h2>

10.    <form name="cftraceform" action="ex10-2.cfm"
          method="Post">

11.      Enter first number: <input type="text" name="num1"
            size="5"><br />

12.      Enter second number: <input type="text"
            name="num2" size="5"><br />

13.      <input name="submitbutton" type="submit"
            value="Find Maximum"><br />

14.    </form>

15.    <cfif isDefined("form.submitbutton")>

16.      <cftrace var="form" inline="yes" text="Form tag">

17.      <cfoutput>

18.        The numbers are: #form.num1# and #form.num2#<br />

19.        <cfset maxnum = max(form.num1, form.num2)>

20.        The bigger number is #maxnum#<br />

21.          <cftrace var="maxnum" inline="yes" text="After
              max">

22.      </cfoutput>

23.    </cfif>

24.  </body>

25.  </html>
```

How the Code Works

1. Lines 11 and 12 accept two numbers and line 13 submits this form to the action section.

2. Line 16 uses the `<cftrace>` tag to conveniently display the form variables after they have been submitted. Note that the `var` attribute has the value `form`, which tells `<cftrace>` to display all the form variables.

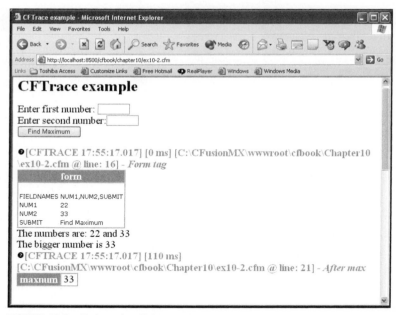

FIGURE 10.2   Debugging Using `<cftrace>`

3. Line 19 sets the variable `maxnum` to the maximum of the two numbers.

4. Line 20 outputs the value of `maxnum`.

5. Line 21 traces the value of `maxnum`. Note that `<cftrace>` also shows the time taken for each piece of code to execute.

Exception Handling

An **exception** is an event that disrupts the normal flow of any process. Exceptions are usually caused by errors, for example, failed database queries or missing include files. Normally, when ColdFusion encounters an error, it stops processing and throws an error page.

ColdFusion offers a way for developers to catch and process exceptions in their applications by using the `<cftry>`, `<cfcatch>`, and `<cfthrow>` tags within the code. If an error or exception occurs within a block of code that is within a `<cftry>` block, the `<cfcatch>` tag can catch the error before the code stops and crashes. The developer can add some code in the `<cfcatch>` block to be executed when the exception is caught so that the exit is graceful. The developer also can specify his or her own events on which to raise **custom exceptions** so that the developer can alter the flow of the code.

Since the idea of this section is to teach you the concept of exception handling in ColdFusion, only a few commonly used properties and their features will be discussed here, just enough to enable you to enhance your ColdFusion application with simple exception-handling code.

Exception-Handling Syntax

In order for ColdFusion to handle an exception, you should enclose your code block in a `<cftry>` block. Then you use a `<cfcatch>` block within the `<cftry>` block after your code block. The `<cfcatch>` block will catch any error that may occur in the code enclosed within the `<cftry>` block.

When ColdFusion encounters an error within the `<cftry>` block, it throws an exception, jumps to the `<cfcatch>` block, and starts executing the code within that block. The correct `<cfcatch>` block is identified by the `type` attribute that identifies the exception type of the `<cfcatch>` block. Within each `<cfcatch>` block will be code that will execute when the exception that occurs matches the `<cfcatch>` block's `type` attribute. This will be discussed in the following sections.

The syntax of the `<cftry>` and `<cfcatch>` blocks is as follows:

```
<cftry>
  <!--- code block --->
  <cfcatch type="exceptiontype">
    <!--- exception code --->
  </cfcatch>
</cftry>
```

Custom Exceptions

Sometimes, based on the occurrence of a particular event, you may want to raise or throw your own custom exception instead of using one of the standard ColdFusion exceptions. You can raise your own custom exceptions when an event occurs, so that you can alter the flow of your code. Custom exceptions are your own (user-defined) exceptions that can be explicitly thrown within the code block by using the `<cfthrow>` tag. These exceptions are caught in the `<cfcatch>` block having a matching `type` attribute just like standard exceptions. The `<cfthrow>` tag has a `type` attribute that identifies the exception it throws.

You can specify exception `type`, `message`, and other attributes in the `<cfthrow>` block that will be used in the `<cfcatch>` block.

```
<cftry>
  --- code block ---
  <cfthrow type="exceptiontype" message="error message"
    detail="error details">
  --- code block continues ---
```

```
        <cfcatch type="exceptiontype">
          --- exception processing code ---
        </cfcatch>
      </cftry>
```

Attributes of `<cfcatch>`

The `<cfcatch>` tag can access these specific details about the exception and the `<cfthrow>` tag is used to set specific details in custom exceptions. Standard exceptions have preset attributes. In custom exceptions, these attributes need to be set through the `<cfthrow>` tag. Only a few commonly used attributes and their features and values will be discussed here. The `type` attribute specifies what type of recoverable error occurred. This attribute is accessed by `<cfcatch>` and can be set by `<cfthrow>` for custom exceptions. The following table mentions a few of the commonly used exception types.

Exception Type	Explanation
Type="Application"	Application-defined exceptions, custom exceptions
Type="Database"	Database failures
Type="Template"	Template errors
Type="MissingInclude"	Missing include files
Type="Custom_exception_type"	Custom exceptions
Type="Any"	Any unexpected error that may not be caught by the other `<cfcatch>` blocks; for example, internal memory failures. If a `<cfcatch>` block is not defined for custom exceptions thrown, it is caught here.

When an error condition occurs, the ColdFusion server checks the `<cfcatch>` handlers. If it finds an appropriate handler, it will execute that code. The `type` attribute enables ColdFusion to find the correct exception handler.

`Message` **and** `Detail`

`Message` is the error message and `Detail` contains details about the exception that occurred. Detail helps you to identify the line and tag that threw the exception in your application. These attributes are preset in ColdFusion for standard exceptions. If you want to access these values, you use the following code within your `<cfcatch>` block.

```
<cfoutput>
  Error Message: #cfcatch.message#<br />
```

```
       Error Detail: #cfcatch.detail#
    </cfoutput>
```

For custom exceptions, you can explicitly set the message attribute using the
<cfthrow> construct. For example:

```
<cfthrow type="myException"
  message="Illegal user"
  detail="You do not have access to this page">
```

This exception can be caught in a <cfcatch> block like the one below:

```
<cfcatch type="myException>
  <cfoutput>
    Error Message: #cfcatch.message# <br />
    Detail: #cfcatch.message#
  </cfoutput>
</cfcatch>
```

If message and/or detail is not provided, these attributes will be empty
strings since they have no preset values in custom exceptions.

Example 10.3 uses the <cftry>/<cfcatch> block in ColdFusion to catch
different types of exceptions. Included is a <cfthrow> construct to show you
how to raise your own error condition and catch it so that you can process it.
Figure 10.3A is the output you get if you enter a name other than **Peter** in the
username input box and click **submit**. Figure 10.3B is the output you get if the
include file header.cfm is missing.

Example 10.3   Exception Handling (ex10-3.cfm)

```
 1. <!DOCTYPE html
 2. PUBLIC "-//W3C//DTD XHTML 1.0 Transitional//EN"
 3. "http://www.w3.org/TR/xhtml1/DTD/xhtml1-transitional.dtd">
 4. <html xmlns="http://www.w3.org/1999/xhtml">
 5. <head>
 6.   <title>Exception Handling Example</title>
 7. </head>
 8. <body>
 9.   <h3>Exception Handling Example</h3>
10.   <form name="exceptionform"
11.     action="ex10-3.cfm?department=Marketing"
          method="Post">
```

```
12.      Enter your name: <input type="text"
           name="username">

13.      <input type="submit" name="submitbutton"
           value="submit">

14.   </form>

15.   <cfif isDefined("form.submitbutton")>

16.   <cftry>

17.      <!--- Custom Exception --->

18.      <cfif form.username neq "Peter">

19.         <cfthrow type="myException"

20.         message="<cfoutput>#username#</cfoutput> is
              illegal!"

21.         detail="This user does not have access to
              this application">

22.      </cfif>

23.      <!--- Database Exception --->

24.      <cfquery name="somequery" datasource="shoppingcart">

25.         select FirstName, LastName

26.         from Customer

27.      </cfquery>

28.      <!--- Include File Exception --->

29.      <cfinclude template ="header.cfm">

30.      <!--- Other Exception --->

31.      <cfoutput>#url.department#</cfoutput>

32.      <!--- Exception Handling for missing include files --->

33.      <cfcatch type="MissingInclude">

34.         <h1>Include file is missing!</h1>

35.         <cfoutput>

36.            <ul>

37.               <li><b>Message:</b> #cfcatch.Message#

38.               <li><b>Detail:</b> #cfcatch.Detail#

39.               <li><b>File name:</b> #cfcatch.
                   MissingFilename#
```

```
40.          </ul>
41.          </cfoutput>
42.      </cfcatch>
43.      <!--- Exception Handling for database exception --->
44.      <cfcatch type="Database">
45.      <h1>Database Error Occurred!</h1>
46.      <cfoutput>
47.          <ul>
48.              <li><b>Message:</b> #cfcatch.Message#
49.              <li><b>Native error code:</b>
                    #cfcatch.NativeErrorCode#
50.              <li><b>SQLState:</B> #cfcatch.SQLState#
51.              <li><b>Detail:</B> #cfcatch.Detail#
52.          </ul>
53.      </cfoutput>
54.      </cfcatch>
55.      <!--- Exception Handling for any other exceptions
            not handled above --->
56.      <cfcatch type="Any">
57.      <h1>Unexpected Error Occurred!</h1>
58.      <cfoutput>
59.          <ul>
60.              <li><b>Message:</b> #cfcatch.Message#
61.              <li><b>Detail:</b> #cfcatch.Detail#
62.          </ul>
63.      </cfoutput>
64.      </cfcatch>
65.      <!--- Exception Handling for custom exceptions --->
66.      <cfcatch type="MyException">
67.      <h1>Illegal usage!</h1>
68.      <cfoutput>
69.          <ul>
```

70.   `<li><b>Message:</b> #cfcatch.Message#`

71.   `<li><b>Detail:</b> #cfcatch.Detail#`

72.   `</ul>`

73.   `</cfoutput>`

74.   `</cfcatch>`

75.   `</cftry>`

76.   `</cfif>`

77. `<body>`

78. `</html>`

FIGURE 10.3A   Custom Exception

How the Code Works

1. Lines 10 through 14 set up a form to accept username. Line 11 has the form action="ex10-3.cfm?department=Marketing".

2. Note that the URL variable department is being sent to the action part of the page. If this URL variable is not sent, then an exception will be thrown on line 31.

3. Line 16 opens the `<cftry>` tag that is closed in line 75 at the bottom of the code.

4. In lines 18 through 22, if form.username is not Peter, then the myException custom exception is thrown with the message that the

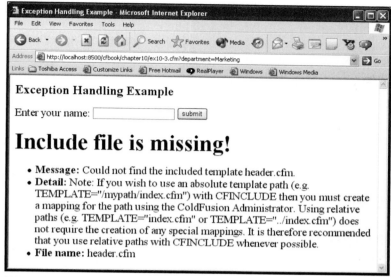

FIGURE 10.3B   Missing Include

user is illegal and `detail` that the user does not have access to the application. This exception is caught in the `<cfcatch>` block of type `MyException` in line 66. The `message` and `detail` are displayed for this exception on lines 70 and 71. To process this page correctly, enter **Peter** in the `username` field.

5. Line 24 starts up a query using the shopping cart database to get `FirstName` and `LastName` from the Customer table. This is a valid query so there is no exception. If you change the data source to be invalid or change the SQL query to be invalid, then the `Database` exception will automatically occur and ColdFusion will look for the appropriate `<cfcatch>` block. Lines 44 through 54 show the `<cfcatch>` block for the `Database` exception. Here, the predefined `message` and the `detail` are output. In addition, we also have available through the `<cfcatch>` object the `Native error code` and the `SQL state`, which give us more database-specific error codes.

6. Line 29 includes a file (`header.cfm`) in this template. ColdFusion will look for this file in the same directory as the current template on the server since no relative path has been mentioned. If this file cannot be found, then ColdFusion throws a `MissingInclude` exception. The appropriate `<cfcatch>` block, for `MissingInclude` is found on lines 33 through 42. In this block, we display the predefined `message`, `detail`, and `MissingFilename`. To get rid of this exception, check that the header.cfm template exists in the same directory as this template.

7. Line 31 tries to display the URL variable `url.department`. If this variable is not found in the URL, an exception is thrown and the appropriate catch block is executed. Since there is no specific catch block for this exception, the catch block of `type = "Any"` is executed. Line 56 shows the `<cfcatch>` block for any exception that was not handled by the other handlers. Here again we show the `message` and `detail`. To get rid of this exception, add the URL parameter by appending the query string `?department=Marketing` to your URL and reload the template.

Sitewise Error Handling

A common way to handle errors in ColdFusion applications is to specify a **sitewise** or **global error** template using the `<cferror>` tag for your entire site. This tag enables you to display your own error page when any error occurs within your application. This tag is generally used in the Application.cfm file so that it applies to every page in your application.

This is achieved by using the `<cferror>` tag. Instead of the ColdFusion standard error page, you can display a customized error page that belongs to your own application. If you load a page that has an error, and if ColdFusion finds a `<cferror>` tag that specifies an error template, it will display that template instead of the standard ColdFusion error template.

`<cferror>` Syntax

The syntax of the `<cferror>` tag is as follows:

```
<cferror type = "error type"
    template = "template_path"
    mailTo = "email_address"
    exception = "exception_type">
```

The following are the attributes of this tag:

- `Type` is the type of error being handled. Valid values are `Request`, `Validation`, or `Exception`. `Request` (default) handles errors during page processing. Request errors occur when a page having an error is requested. `Validation` handles data input validation errors that occur when form field validation rules are violated while submitting a form. `Exception` handles exception errors.

- `Template` is the relative path of the template that you want to display when an error occurs.

- `MailTo` is the email address of the person to inform when the error occurs.

- Exception is the exception that caused the page to be displayed. It is necessary only if type is exception.

The Error Object

The **error object** is created when an error occurs. This object has certain attributes that can be accessed by the error page to get details about the error that occurred.

Attributes	Explanation
Error.diagnostics	Detailed diagnostics from the ColdFusion server
Error.mailto	Email address you specified in the MailTo attribute of the <cferror> tag
Error.dateTime	Date and time when this error occurred
Error.browser	Browser and version that were running when this error occurred
Error.remoteAddress	IP address of the client on which this error occurred
Error.template	Name of the page that was running when this error occurred
Error.querystring	URL query string of the request

Example 10.4 has three files. First is the Application.cfm. This is where we will specify the <cferror> tag and its attributes so that it can be used for sitewise error handling. Next is the **error template.** This is the error page with the same look and feel as the rest of your site. This is where we pull the specific details about the error and display them to the user. Then there is the **application template.** This is any page within your application in which the error occurs. The <cferror> tag within the Application.cfm file will identify the error and call the error page automatically. The boxes below summarize the picture for you.

Application.cfm	**Template.cfm**	**Error.cfm**
Contains the <cferror> tag specifying the name of your error page.	Contains your web page with ColdFusion code that has the error on loading.	Contains your error page code. Uses the error object to display error details.

The code expects a URL parameter called firstname. If this parameter exists (append ?firstname=some_name to your URL), then you should see an output like Figure 10.4B. If your URL parameter is missing, then you will see the error template created below (see Figure 10.4A).

Example 10.4   Sitewise Error Handling (ex10-4.cfm)
Application File (Application.cfm)

```
1.  <cfsilent>
2.  <cfapplication
3.    name="cfexamples"
4.    applicationtimeout="#CreateTimeSpan(1,0,0,0)#"
5.    sessionmanagement="No"
6.    clientmanagement="No"
7.    setclientcookies="No"
8.    setdomaincookies="No">
9.    <cferror type = "request"
10.       template = "error.cfm"
11.       mailTo = "admin@yourcompany.com">
12. </cfsilent>
```

Error Template (error.cfm)

```
1.  <!DOCTYPE html
2.  PUBLIC "-//W3C//DTD XHTML 1.0 Transitional//EN"
3.  "http://www.w3.org/TR/xhtml1/DTD/xhtml1-
       transitional.dtd">
4.  <html xmlns="http://www.w3.org/1999/xhtml">
5.  <head>
6.    <title>CFError Example</title>
7.  </head>
8.  <body>
9.    <cfoutput>
10.       <b>Your Location:</b> #error.remoteAddress#<br>
11.       <b>Your Browser:</b> #error.browser#<br>
12.       <b>Date and Time the Error Occurred:</b>
           #error.dateTime#<br>
13.       <b>Page You Came From:</b> #error.
           HTTPReferer#<br><hr>
14.    <b>Message Content</b>: <br>The following error
           occurred: #error.diagnostics#
```

```
15.     <b><br>End of message content </b><br><hr><br>
16.     <b>Please send questions to:</b>
17.     <a href = "mailto:#error.mailTo#">#error.
        mailTo#</a><br>
18.   </cfoutput>
19. </body>
20. </html>
```

Template File (ex10-4.cfm)

```
1. <!DOCTYPE html
2. PUBLIC "-//W3C//DTD XHTML 1.0 Transitional//EN"
3. "http://www.w3.org/TR/xhtml11/DTD/xhtml11-transitional.dtd">
4. <html xmlns="http://www.w3.org/1999/xhtml">
5. <head>
6.    <title>cferror Example</title>
7. </head>
8. <body>
9.    <h3>cferror Example</h3>
10.   Url parameter <b>firstname</b> exists !
11.   <br> Firstname is: <b><cfoutput>#url.
       firstname#</cfoutput></b>
12. </body>
13. </html>
```

How the Code Works
Application File (Application.cfm)

1. Line 1 uses the `<cfsilent>` tag to make sure that nothing is output from within the Application.cfm file.

2. The main tag here is the `<cferror>` tag on lines 9 through 11, which specifies that the sitewise error template is error.cfm. The contact person to email errors to is admin@yourcompany.com.

Error Template (error.cfm)

1. Line 10 shows the location—that is, the IP address—of the client on which this error occurred.

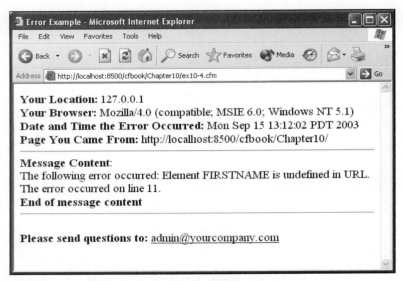

FIGURE 10.4A   Sitewise Error (Missing URL Variable)

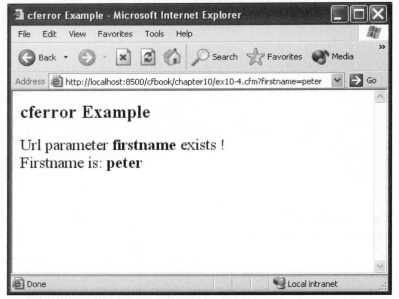

FIGURE 10.4B   URL Variable Exists

2. Line 11 shows the browser and version running when this error occurred.

3. Line 12 shows the date and time the error occurred.

4. Line 13 shows the referrer page.

5. Line 14 shows the error diagnostics from the ColdFusion server.

6. Line 17 displays the `mailTo` link set up in the Application.cfm file that can be clicked to send the error email.

Template File (ex10-4.cfm) Line 11 tries to display the URL variable `url.firstname`. If this variable does not exist, the error template error.cfm is displayed (see Figure 10.4A). If it does exist (i.e., your URL has the query string `?firstname=anyname`), then there is no error and you should see a page like Figure 10.4B.

Logging Messages

Log files are useful for debugging and for displaying error details as well as for logging status of an application, who has logged in, which process is running, and so forth. The `<cflog>` tag can be used to log entries into ColdFusion log files. These log entries are for internal use only. People who visit your site will not have access to these files. You could use this tag within the error page to log errors into the log file or you can use the tag within any template to log status entries. The log entry fields are written in the log file as comma-delimited lists of values enclosed in double quotes.

Tech Tip
The `<cflog>` tag can be disabled through the ColdFusion Administrator's Basic Security page.

The syntax of this tag is

```
<cflog text = "text"
    log = "log type"
    file = "filename"
    type = "message type"
    application = "application name yes or no">
```

The attributes of this tag are

- `Text` (required) allows you to specify the text you wish to log.
- `Log` (optional) can have the values `Application` or `Scheduler`. It allows you to specify whether you want to write to the Application.log file (application-specific messages) or the Scheduler.log file (scheduled tasks). If you are running the code as a scheduled task, you may want to specify `Scheduler` as the `Log` attribute.
- `File` allows you to specify the name of the file in which you want to log the messages. If you specify a value for this attribute, then the `Log` attribute is ignored. It must have a .log extension, for example, mylog.log. The file will be located in the logs directory.
- `Type` specifies the severity of the message. Valid values are `Information` (default), `Warning`, `Error`, and `Fatal`.

- `Application` specifies whether you want to log the application name or not. Valid values are `Yes` (default) or `No`.

The `Thread`, `Date`, and `Time` attributes all default to `Yes`. `ThreadID`, logged by default, helps you identify which request logged the message. The system date and time are also logged by default. These attributes are deprecated in ColdFusion MX; that is, they may become obsolete in future versions.

Example 10.5 shows how you could use `<cflog>` within any template for logging messages for debugging and/or other purposes using a minimum set of attributes. This is a very simple example that displays a form to accept `username` and displays the `username` accepted. Save this code in a file called `ex10-5.cfm`.

Example 10.5   CFLog (ex10-5.cfm)

```
1.  <!DOCTYPE html
2.  PUBLIC "-//W3C//DTD XHTML 1.0 Transitional//EN"
3.  "http://www.w3.org/TR/xhtml1/DTD/xhtml1-transitional.dtd">
4.  <html xmlns="http://www.w3.org/1999/xhtml">
5.  <head>
6.    <title> Logging Example</title>
7.  </head>
8.  <body>
9.    <cfif isDefined("form.submitbutton")>
10.       <h2>Hello <cfoutput>#form.username#</cfoutput></h2>
11.       <cflog file="myLog"
12.         text="#Form.username# logged on.">
13.    </cfif>
14.    <form name="cferrorform" action="ex10-5.cfm"
         method="Post">
15.      Enter your username: <input type="text"
          name="username">
16.      <input type="submit" name="submitbutton"
          value="go">
17.    </form>
18.  </body>
19.  </html>
```

Figure 10.5A shows the form displayed by the above code, and Figure 10.5B shows the log file entry created by the <cflog> tag on submission of the form. This log file is found in the ColdFusion logs directory (usually C:\CFusionMX\logs). You can view the mylog.log file using Notepad.

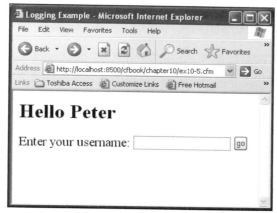

FIGURE 10.5A   Logging—Transparent to Visitors

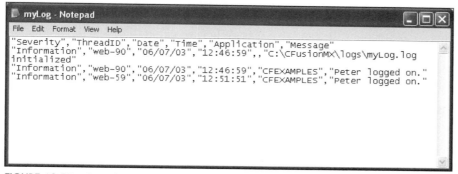

FIGURE 10.5B   Sample Log File

How the Code Works

1. Lines 14 through 17 display a form to accept the username. When you load this page, enter **username** and click on **Go**.

2. Line 10 executes when the form is submitted and welcomes the user using the username entered.

3. Lines 11 and 12 show how to use <cflog> to log that this user has logged on.

4. If you look at the log file, you'll see that the default value for type is Information. The ThreadID, Date, Time, and Application are logged by default even though you did not set them.

5. These log messages are logged in the log file you specified in the `<cflog>` tag. The log file is found in the ColdFusion logs directory `C:\CfusionMX\logs`.

Abort Processing

Sometimes, you may want to abort or stop processing a page midway. The `<cfabort>` tag stops processing of a template and exits at the location of the tag. Normally we use conditional processing to abort processing when a certain condition occurs. Unlike `<cferror>`, which redirects flow of the application to the custom error page, `<cfabort>` stops processing completely and exits.

The syntax of this tag is

```
<cfabort showerror = "error message">
```

This tag has no required attributes. `Showerror` is an optional attribute that holds the error message that you want to show after the application aborts. This error message is shown on the standard ColdFusion error page.

Example 10.6 shows the use of this tag by aborting processing midway. Type this code in a file called `ex10-6.cfm`. When you load this page in your browser, you will see only the output statements that execute before the `<cfabort>` tag and not the one following the tag.

Example 10.6   CFAbort (ex10-6.cfm)

```
1.  <!DOCTYPE html
2.  PUBLIC "-//W3C//DTD XHTML 1.0 Transitional//EN"
3.  "http://www.w3.org/TR/xhtml1/DTD/xhtml1-transitional.dtd">
4.  <html xmlns="http://www.w3.org/1999/xhtml">
5.  <head>
6.    <title>CFABORT Example</title>
7.  </head>
8.  <body>
9.    <h3>CFABORT Example</h3>
10.   Before Abort <br />
11.   Aborting process....
12.   <cfabort>
```

13.   `After Abort <br />`

14. `</body>`

15. `</html>`

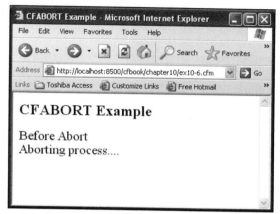

FIGURE 10.6   Aborting a Process

How the Code Works

1. Line 12 aborts the page before `After Abort` in line 13 can be displayed.

2. Line 13 cannot be displayed since the `<cfabort>` tag is on the previous line. That is why we see only the output statements before the `<cfabort>`, that is, `Before Abort` and `Aborting processing....`

Template Redirection

Sometimes, you may want to relocate the user to a new page after performing a task in your template. The `<cflocation>` tag is used to direct users to other templates. The syntax of this tag is

```
<cflocation
  url="another page"
  addtoken="yes or no">
```

The attributes are

- `Url` is a required attribute that specifies the URL to which to direct the users.

- `Addtoken` is an optional attribute that indicates whether client variables should be sent in the URL. Valid values for `Addtoken` are `Yes` (default) or No. If Addtoken="yes", ColdFusion appends the cfid and cftoken values to the URL that the <cflocation> tag sends the browser to. These variables track the client's session and are automatically set by ColdFusion for each user.

Example 10.7 displays a form that accepts username. Type this code into a file called ex10-7.cfm and load it in your browser. To run this code, you need to create two other templates that are Peter's and Paul's home pages. In this example, we just have two simple pages called ex10-7a.cfm (consisting of one line—Peter's Home Page) and ex10-7b.cfm (consisting of one line—Paul's Home Page). If you enter the username **Peter**, the code relocates you to Peter's home page (Figure 10.7A) and if you enter the username **Paul**, Paul's home page is displayed. Figure 10.7 shows an error because an invalid name (neither Peter nor Paul) was entered.

Tech Tip

You could create HTML pages instead of .cfm pages if there is no ColdFusion code on that page.

Example 10.7　CFLocation (ex10-7.cfm)

```
 1. <!DOCTYPE html
 2. PUBLIC "-//W3C//DTD XHTML 1.0 Transitional//EN"
 3. "http://www.w3.org/TR/xhtml1/DTD/xhtml1-transitional.dtd">
 4. <html xmlns="http://www.w3.org/1999/xhtml">
 5. <head>
 6.   <title>CFLocation Example</title>
 7. </head>
 8. <body>
 9.   <h3>CFLocation Example</h3>
10.   <form name="cferrorform" action="ex10-7.cfm"
        method="Post">
11.     Enter your username: <input type="text"
          name="username">
12.     <input type="submit" name="submitbutton"
          value="go">
13.   </form>
14.   <cfif isDefined("form.submitbutton")>
15.     <cfif form.username eq "Peter">
16.       <cflocation url="ex10-7a.cfm"
17.         addtoken="no">
18.     <cfelseif form.username eq "Paul">
```

19.   `<cflocation url="ex10-7b.cfm"`
20.   `addtoken="no">`
21.   `<cfelse>`
22.   `Invalid Name !`
23.   `</cfif>`
24. `</cfif>`
25. `</body>`
26. `</html>`

Example 10.7A   CFLocation (ex10-7a.cfm)

1. `<!DOCTYPE html`
2. `PUBLIC "-//W3C//DTD XHTML 1.0 Transitional//EN"`
3. `"http://www.w3.org/TR/xhtml1/DTD/xhtml1-transitional.dtd">`
4. `<html xmlns="http://www.w3.org/1999/xhtml">`
5. `<head>`
6. `<title>CFLocation Example</title>`
7. `</head>`
8. `<body>`
9. `<h3>Peter's Home Page</h3>`
10. `</body>`
11. `</html>`

Example 10.7B   CFLocation (ex10-7b.cfm)

1. `<!DOCTYPE html`
2. `PUBLIC "-//W3C//DTD XHTML 1.0 Transitional//EN"`
3. `"http://www.w3.org/TR/xhtml1/DTD/xhtml1-transitional.dtd">`
4. `<html xmlns="http://www.w3.org/1999/xhtml">`
5. `<head>`
6. `<title>CFLocation Example</title>`
7. `</head>`
8. `<body>`
9. `<h3>Peter's Home Page</h3>`

10. `</body>`

11. `</html>`

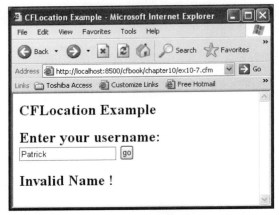

FIGURE 10.7   CFLocation, Depending on Form Variable Values

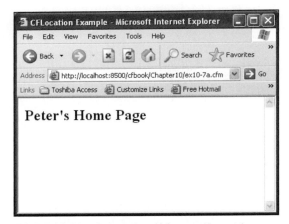

FIGURE 10.7A   Relocation Using `<cflocation>`

How the Code Works

1. In line 11 `username` is accepted in the form. The form is submitted to the same template as you can see in line 10.

2. Line 15 checks if the `username` entered is `Peter`. If it is, the user is relocated to Peter's home page (in this case, it is ex10-7a.cfm)— line 16.

3. Line 18 checks if the `username` is `Paul`. If it is, then the user is relocated to Paul's home page (in this case, it is relocated to ex10-7b.cfm)—line 19.

4. Line 22 displays an error message if the `username` entered is neither `Peter` nor `Paul`.

You also can use the `<cflocation>` tag to relocate to an external URL. For example:

```
<cflocation url="http://www.PetersWebsite.com"
  addtoken="no">
```

File Handling

The `<cffile>` tag helps you to perform file-handling tasks from within your application on files that are on the ColdFusion server. Using this tag, you can create, move, delete, and copy files, or append to files.

Depending on the tasks you want to perform, you use an appropriate `action` attribute. The other attributes of this tag vary depending on the `action` attribute's value. Though we will not cover all the attributes and actions, we will look at some of the common functions that can be performed with this tag.

`<cffile>` Action	Simplest Usage Example	Explanation

read	`<cffile action = "read"`
	`file = "path of file to read"`
	`variable = "Message">`
		Reads a file on the server into the variable

move	`<cffile action = "move"`
	`source = "source file path"`
	`destination = "destination directory path">`
		Moves a file from one location to another on the server

rename	`<cffile action = "rename"`
	`source = "sourcefile path"`
	`destination = "destination path">`
		Renames a file on the server to another name

copy	`<cffile action = "copy"`
	`source = "source file path"`
	`destination = "destination directory path">`
		Copies one file on the server to another on the server

delete	`<cffile action = "delete"` `file = "path of file to delete">`	Deletes a file on the server

Continued

<cffile> Action	Simplest Usage Example	Explanation (continued)

write	`<cffile action = "write"`
	`file = "name of file to write to"`
	`output = "some text">`
		Creates a file on the server and writes some text to it

append	`<cffile action = "append"`
	`file = "name of file to write to"`
	`output = "additional text">`
		Appends text to a file on the server

In Example 10.8, we will create a file called `c:\cfusionmx\cffile.txt` using the `write` action of the `<cffile>` tag. Then we'll move that file to another location, rename it, copy it, read it, append to it, and then delete it. This should make you really comfortable with simple file manipulation tasks. Figure 10.8 shows the output of this code.

Note: The directories `c:\temp` and `c:\cfusionmx` should exist on your machine before you run this code or you will get an error.

Example 10.8   File Handling (ex10-8.cfm)

```
1.  <!DOCTYPE html
2.  PUBLIC "-//W3C//DTD XHTML 1.0 Transitional//EN"
3.  "http://www.w3.org/TR/xhtml1/DTD/xhtml1-transitional.dtd">
4.  <html xmlns="http://www.w3.org/1999/xhtml">
5.  <head>
6.  <title>CFFile Example</title>
7.  </head>
8.  <body>
9.    <h2>CFFile Example</h2>
10.   Creating file c:\temp\cffile.txt....<br />
11.     <cffile action = "write" file = "c:\temp\cffile.txt"
            output = "The cat sat on the mat">
12.   Moving file c:\temp\cffile.txt to c:\cfusionmx\
          cffile.txt....<br />
13.     <cffile action = "move" source="c:\temp\cffile.
            txt" destination= "c:\cfusionmx\">
14.   Renaming file c:\cfusionmx\cffile.txt to c:\
          cfusionmx\cffile1.txt....<br />
```

```
15.    <cffile action = "rename" source="c:\cfusionmx\cffile.
       txt" destination= "c:\cfusionmx\cffile1.txt">
16.    Copying file c:\cfusionmx\cffile1.txt to c:\
       cfusionmx\cffile2.txt....<br />
17.    <cffile action = "copy" source="c:\cfusionmx\
       cffile1.txt" destination= "c:\cfusionmx\cffile2.txt">
18.    Deleting file c:\cfusionmx\cffile1.txt....<br />
19.    <cffile action = "delete" file="c:\cfusionmx\
       cffile1.txt">
20.    Reading file c:\cfusionmx\cffile2.txt into variable
       msg....<br /><br />
21.    <cffile action = "read" file="c:\cfusionmx\
       cffile2.txt" variable= "msg">
22.    Contents of the cffile2.txt :<h2><cfoutput>#msg#</
       cfoutput></h2>
23.    Appending to file c:\cfusionmx\cffile2.txt....<br />
24.    <cffile action = "append" file="c:\cfusionmx\cffile2.txt"
       output=" and the cow jumped over the moon!">
25.    Reading file c:\cfusionmx\cffile2.txt into variable
       msg....<br /><br />
26.    <cffile action = "read" file="c:\cfusionmx\
       cffile2.txt" variable= "msg">
27.    Contents of the cffile2.txt :<h2><cfoutput>
       #msg#</cfoutput></h2>
28.    Deleting file c:\cfusionmx\cffile2.txt....<br />
29.    <cffile action = "delete" file="c:\cfusionmx\
       cffile2.txt">
30. </body>
31. </html>
```

How the Code Works

1. Line 11 creates the file `cffile.txt` in the directory `c:\temp\` and writes the text `The cat sat on the mat` into the file. The directory `c:\temp\` must already exist for this command to work.

2. Line 13 moves the file from the `c:\temp` to the `c:\cfusionmx` directory. Now the file is no longer in the `c:\temp` directory. It has moved

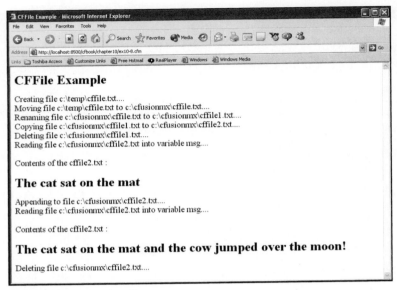

FIGURE 10.8   File Handling

to the `c:\cfusionmx` directory. You should use appropriate directories in your system to test out this code.

3. Line 15 renames the file in the `c:\cfusionmx` directory from `cffile.txt` to `cffile1.txt`. Now `cffile.txt` no longer exists. We have `cffile1.txt` with the same content.

4. Line 17 copies `cffile1.txt` to `cffile2.txt`. Now we have two files in the `c:\cfusionmx` directory: `cffile1.txt` and `cffile2.txt`.

5. Line 19 deletes `cffile1.txt`. We will now work only with `cffile2.txt`.

6. Line 21 reads `cffile2.txt` into the `msg` variable, which now contains the contents of that file.

7. Line 22 displays the value of `msg`, that is, the contents of `cffile2.txt`. The `cat sat on the mat` is displayed on the web page.

8. Line 24 appends the text `and the cow jumped over the moon!` to the file `cffile2.txt`.

9. Line 26 reads `cffile2.txt` again into variable `msg`. The variable now contains the contents of that file.

10. Line 27 displays the value of msg. Since we appended to that file, we now see the text The cat sat on the mat and the cow jumped over the moon! on the web page (see Figure 10.8).

11. Line 29 deletes the file cffile2.txt in the c:\cfusionmx directory.

You can comment out the delete statements, load the page, and then open Windows Explorer to see your files cffile1.txt and cffile2.txt in the c:\cfusionmx directory. Be sure to delete the files when you're done so you don't clutter your directories with unnecessary files.

Sending Email

ColdFusion MX 6.1 has greatly enhanced the mail handler by providing a mail server fail over capability, support for SMTP authentication, new character set encoding options, and support for creating multipart email. Cold Fusion MX 6.1 also has added the option to specify multiple mail servers in the ColdFusion Administrator console. This enables mail to be delivered even if the primary mail server is down. Before you are able to send out email through your applications, you need to set your mail SMTP server name or IP address in the ColdFusion Administrator screen under Server Settings.

Most business applications need the capability to send email to customers or users. Examples are order confirmations, invoices, newsletters, or greeting cards. The <cfmail> tag is used to send an email message from a ColdFusion template. The simplest usage of this tag is as follows:

```
<cfmail
  to = "recipient's email address"
  from = "sender's email address"
  cc = "recipient's email address"
  bcc = "recipient's email address"
  subject = "message subject"
  – more attributes –>
```

This tag has many more attributes, which we will not be covering in this book. For most of your applications, this simple usage will be sufficient. Attributes to, from, and subject are required; all the others are optional. A consolidated example for the <cfmail> tag is given in Example 10.9. The most basic use of this tag is given below:

```
<cfmail to="your@friend.com" from="your@self.com"
  subject="Keeping in touch!">
  Hello! How are you?
</cfmail>
```

Attaching Files and Headers to Email

The `<cfmailparam>` tag can be used to *attach a file* to an email or *add a header* to a message. This tag is nested within the `<cfmail>` tag. The syntax of this tag is

```
<cfmail .......>
  <cfmailparam file="file name">
  <cfmailparam name="header name" value="header value">
</cfmail>
```

Multipart Email Messages

ColdFusion MX 6.1 introduced a new tag called `<cfmailpart>` that can be used within the `<cfmail>` tag to separate parts of a **multipart email message.** A multipart message is a message that has more than one body section. Some email clients can accept email messages that use HTML and others accept only plain text messages. This new tag is useful to format email messages differently for different clients depending on whether or not they can accept HTML messages. That way, clients that can accept HTML see the HTML message and those that cannot accept HTML see the plain text message.

The syntax of this tag is

```
<cfmail .......>
  <cfmailpart
    type="mime type"
    charset="character encoding"
    wraptext="number">
  </cfmailpart>
</cfmail>
```

Type is a required attribute that specifies the MIME type of the message part. It can be text or plain (both specify MIME type text/plain) or html (specifies MIME type text/html). Charset is an optional attribute that specifies the character encoding for the message part (example utf-8). Wraptext specifies the maximum length of each line in the message. A line break is inserted at that point. `<cfmailpart>` is an optional tag.

The code below shows the simplest usage of this tag to help separate text and HTML messages:

```
<cfmail to="your@friend.com" from="your@self.com"
  subject="Keeping in touch!">
  <cfmailpart type="text">
    Hello!
      How are you?
  </cfmailpart>
```

```
        <cfmailpart type="html">
           <b>Hello!</b><br />
        <p>How are you?</p>
      </cfmailpart>
   </cfmail>
```

Example 10.9 creates a form that accepts an email greeting, from address, to address, and subject. It also accepts a file attachment to be emailed. The action part sends the email using the `<cfmail>` tag to the recipient(s) specified in the form. It uses the `<cfmailparam>` tag to attach a file and to add the header `reply-to`. It also uses the `<cfmailpart>` tag to separate HTML and plain-text messages. When you first load this page in the browser, you see the form as in Figure 10.9A; when you fill in the form and click **send**, then you see a page like Figure 10.9B that confirms that your greeting has been sent. Enter your email address in the form and click on **send** to send off the email.

Example 10.9   Sending Email (ex10-9.cfm)

```
1.  <!DOCTYPE html
2.  PUBLIC "-//W3C//DTD XHTML 1.0 Transitional//EN"
3.  "http://www.w3.org/TR/xhtml1/DTD/xhtml1-transitional.dtd">
4.  <html xmlns="http://www.w3.org/1999/xhtml">
5.  <head>
6.  <title>CFMail Example</title>
7.  </head>
8.  <body>
9.  <h2>CFMail Example</h2>
10.    <cfif isDefined("form.submitbutton")>
11.      <cfmail to="#form.to#" from="#form.from#"
              subject="#form.subject#">
12.        <cfmailparam name="Reply-To" value="#form.from#">
13.        <cfmailparam file="#form.attachment#">
14.        <cfmailpart type="text">
15.          Hello!
16.          This is a plain text message:
17.          #form.message#
18.        </cfmailpart>
```

```
19.        <cfmailpart type="html">
20.           <b>Hello!</b><br />This is an HTML message:
21.           <p>#form.message#</p>
22.        </cfmailpart>
23.     </cfmail>
24.     <br>The following email has been sent: <br />
25.     From: <cfoutput>#form.from#</cfoutput> <br />
26.     To: <cfoutput>#form.to#</cfoutput> <br />
27.     Subject: <cfoutput>#form.subject#</cfoutput> <br />
28.     Message: <cfoutput>#form.message#</cfoutput> <br />
29.     Attachment: <cfoutput>#form.attachment#</cfoutput>
           <br />
30.     Header: <cfoutput>Reply-To #form.from#</cfoutput>
           <br />
31.   <cfelse>
32.   <cfform name="emailForm" method="post"
           action="ex10-9.cfm">
33.     <table>
34.     <tr>
35.       <td class="blacksm">Your First Name: </td>
36.       <td><cfinput type="text" name="first"
             required="yes" size=30></td>
37.     </tr>
38.     <tr>
39.       <td class="blacksm">Your Last Name: </td>
40.       <td><cfinput type="text" name="last"
             required="yes" size=30></td>
41.     </tr>
42.     <tr>
43.       <td class="blacksm">Email Subject: </td>
44.       <td><cfinput type="text" name="subject"
             required="yes"
45.         value="Season's Greetings" size=30></td>
```

```
46.        </tr>
47.        </tr>
48.          <td class="blacksm">Your Email address:</td>
49.          <td><cfinput type="text" name="from"
               required="yes" size=30></td>
50.        </tr>
51.        <tr>
52.          <td class="blacksm">Recipient Email
               Address(es)<br />
53.          (comma-separated list):</td>
54.          <td><textarea rows=5 cols=30
               name="to"></textarea></td>
55.        <tr>
56.          <td class="blacksm">Your message:</td>
57.          <td><textarea rows=5 cols=30
               name="message">Happy Holidays!
58.          </textarea></td>
59.        </tr>
60.        <tr>
61.          <td class="blacksm">File to be attached (full
               path):</td>
62.          <td><input type="file" name="attachment"
               size="30"></td>
63.        </tr>
64.        <tr>
65.          <td colspan=2><input type="submit"
               name="submitbutton" value="send"></td>
66.        </tr>
67.        </table>
68.      </cfform>
69.    </cfif>
70.  </body>
71.  </html>
```

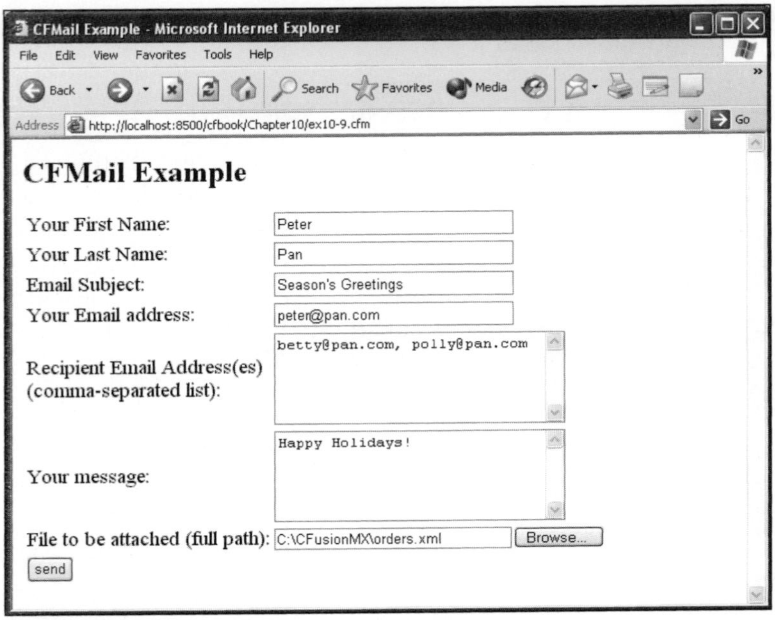

FIGURE 10.9A   Email Form

FIGURE 10.9B   Email Confirmation

How the Code Works

1. Lines 32 through 68 set up a form that accepts first and last name, email subject with a default value of Season's Greetings, your email address, recipient email address(es), and a message with a default value of Happy Holidays! In addition, it takes the name of a file to attach (note the use of input type="file" in order to browse the local directory). Select an existing file to attach.

2. When the form is submitted, line 11 sends an email using the <cfmail> tag to the recipient mentioned in the form, using the subject mentioned in the form, and from the sender mentioned in the form.

3. Line 12 uses the <cfmailparam> tag to specify the header to be included as Reply-To. The form.from variable is used to provide a value here.

4. Line 13 uses the <cfmailparam> tag to specify the file to attach. The form.attachment variable is used to provide this tag a value for the file attribute.

5. Lines 14 through 18 use the <cfmailpart> tag for text messages. Notice that there are no HTML characters in that message.

6. Lines 19 through 22 use the <cfmailpart> tag for HTML messages. Notice the HTML characters in the message.

7. Within the <cfmailpart> and </cfmailpart> tags is the body of the message. We put the form.message value here.

8. Lines 24 thtough 30 display a confirmation to the user giving him or her the details of the email sent.

Graphs and Charts

ColdFusion 5.0 enabled us to generate dynamic graphs and charts to include in web applications. ColdFusion MX offers greater flexibility and variety to create graphs and charts by using three new tags: <cfchart>, <cfchartseries>, and <cfchartdata>. Each of these tags is used for a specific purpose as described below.

The <cfchart> Tag

The <cfchart> tag is used to define general attributes of the graph such as the color, gridlines, appearance of X and Y attributes, font size of data series, axis titles, and other such properties. The syntax of this tag with some important attributes is

```
format = "flash, jpg, png"
scaleFrom = "integer minimum value specifying the starting
    scale"
scaleTo = "integer maximum value specifying the ending
    scale"
gridLines = "integer number of grid lines to draw"
xAxisTitle = "X-axis title text"
yAxisTitle = "Y-axis title text"
show3D = "yes/no"
rotated = "yes/no"
url = "onClick destination page"
— more optional attributes —
</cfchart>
```

> **Tech Tip**
>
> The `<cfchart>` tag in ColdFusion MX replaces the `<cfgraph>` tag of ColdFusion 5.0.

Most of these attributes are self-explanatory. There are many more optional attributes that will not be covered here.

- `format` determines the format in which to save the graph; `flash` is the default format.
- `scaleFrom` and `scaleTo` specify the Y-axis minimum and maximum values.
- `gridLines` specifies the number of gridlines to display.
- `xAxisTitle` and `yAxisTitle` specify the titles to use for the X-axis and Y-axis.
- `show3d` displays the chart with a 3D appearance.
- `xOffset` and `yOffset` determine the units by which to angle the 3D chart.
- `rotated` rotates the chart 90 degrees. Use this to create a horizontal bar chart.
- `url` specifies the URL to open if the user clicks an item in a data series.

The `<cfchart>` tag is a container that holds `<cfchartseries>` and `<cfchartdata>` tags within it. We will use some of the common attributes of this tag in our examples below.

The `<cfchartdata>` Tag

The `<cfchartdata>` tag is used to define the data points that must appear on the graph. The syntax of this tag is

```
<cfchartdata item = "data point name" value = "numeric
    value">
```

> **Tech Tip**
>
> Use the `<cfchartdata>` tag if you need to graph static data points. The `<cfchartdata>` tag is an optional tag within the `<cfchart>` tag.

This tag has two attributes:

- `Item`: This attribute takes the data point name (text).
- `Value`: This attribute takes the data point value (number).

The `<cfchartseries>` Tag

The `<cfchartseries>` tag specifies the type and style of the chart or graph's data series. This tag enables you to define multiple series of data in your graph, as you will see in the next section. The syntax of this tag is as follows:

```
<cfchartseries
   type="graph type (bar, line, pie etc.)"
   query="queryName"
   itemColumn="queryColumn"
   valueColumn="queryColumn"
   seriesLabel="Label Text"
   seriesColor="Hex value or Web color"
   paintStyle="plain, raise, shade, light"
   markerStyle="style"
   colorlist = "list">
</cfchartseries>
```

- `type` is a required attribute that specifies the type of the graph (bar, line, pie, etc.).
- `query` is an optional attribute and takes the name of a query. The data points to be used for the chart or graph can be generated by a query or set manually.
- `itemColumn` and `valueColumn` specify the query columns of the query named in the `query` attribute. In bar and line graphs, the X-axis in the graph refers to the `itemColumn` and the Y-axis refers to the `valueColumn`.
- `seriesColor` identifies the color you would like that series to have.
- `paintStyle` determines the display style of the data series.
- `colorlist` specifies the colors to use for pie charts.

> The `<cfchartseries>` tag in ColdFusion MX defines the style of the graph in which to display data.

Let us see how ColdFusion MX creates line, bar, pie, and area graphs from a query in Example10.10. The output of this code is shown in Figures 10.10A through 10.10D. This example queries the quantities of products from the products table. The graphs show the quantity of products (Y-axis) for each product name (X-axis).

Example 10.10 Graphs for a Single Data Series (ex10-10.cfm)

```
1. <!DOCTYPE html
2. PUBLIC "-//W3C//DTD XHTML 1.0 Transitional//EN"
3. "http://www.w3.org/TR/xhtml1/DTD/xhtml1-transitional.dtd">
4. <html xmlns="http://www.w3.org/1999/xhtml">
5. <head>
```

6.   `<title>CFChart Example - Single Data Series</title>`

7. `</head>`

8. `<body>`

9.   `<h2>CFChart Example <br>Single Data Series - Bar Graph</h2>`

10.   `<cfquery name = "getProducts" datasource="ShoppingCart">`

11.   `Select Products.ProductName, Products.ProductQty`

12.   `From Products`

13.   `</cfquery>`

14.   `<cfchart xAxisTitle="ProductName" yAxisTitle="ProductQty"`

15.   `scaleFrom=0 scaleTo=900 gridLines=10>`

16.   `<cfchartseries type="bar" query="getProducts"`

17.   `valueColumn="ProductQty" itemColumn="ProductName">`

18.   `<cfchartdata item="Keyboards" value="700">`

19.   `<cfchartdata item="Mice" value="700">`

20.   `</cfchartseries>`

21.   `</cfchart>`

22. `</body>`

23. `</html>`

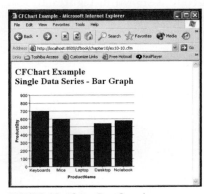

FIGURE 10.10A   Bar Graph

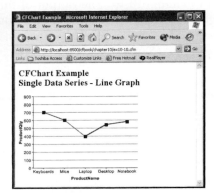

FIGURE 10.10B   Line Graph

FIGURE 10.10C   Pie Graph

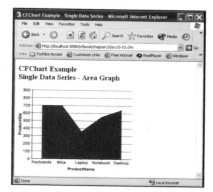

FIGURE 10.10D   Area Graph

How the Code Works

This example generates the data points for the graph from a query.

1. Lines 10 through 13 set up the query getProducts.

2. Line 14 starts the <cfchart> tag and includes the titles for the X and Y axes, which are the fieldnames from the query.

3. In line 15 we have set the scale from 0 to 900 with 10 grid lines.

4. Line 16 starts the <cfchartseries> tag and specifies the type of the graph. You can change this value and view the different types of graphs: bar (Figure 10.10A), line (Figure 10.10B), pie (Figure 10.10C), or area (Figure 10.10D). The query name getProducts is specified in this tag.

5. Line 17 is part of the <cfchartseries> tag and sets the value for attributes valueColumn to be ProductQty and itemColumn to be ProductName.

6. Lines 18 and 19 define two new data points using the <cfchartdata> tag for Keyboards and Mice. Note that this tag should appear within the <cfchartseries> tag.

7. Line 21 closes the <cfchart> tag.

Graphs with Multiple Data Series

Very often we want to compare sets of data in a single graph. ColdFusion MX makes this possible by allowing us to have multiple <cfchartseries> tags within the <cfchart> tag. Example 10.11 shows how this can be done. We will not use a query this time. Instead, we will use <cfchartdata> tags to specify the different data points in the graph for multiple series. In this example, we use three series. This example shows a survey conducted on the usage

Tech Tip

ColdFusion MX has introduced the ability to graph multiple data series in a single graph using the `<cfchartseries>` tag embedded within the `<cfchart>` tag.

of three different types of software by different age groups. The different types of software that this code surveys are computer games, educational software, and commercial software.

Example 10.11 Graph for Multiple Data Series (ex10-11.cfm)

```
1.  <!DOCTYPE html

2.  PUBLIC "-//W3C//DTD XHTML 1.0 Transitional//EN"

3.  "http://www.w3.org/TR/xhtml1/DTD/xhtml1-transitional.dtd">

4.  <html xmlns="http://www.w3.org/1999/xhtml">

5.  <head>

6.  <title>CFChart Example</title>

7.  </head>

8.  <body>

9.  <h2>CFChart Example <br>Bar Graph - Survey by
       age</h2>

10. <cfchart xAxisTitle="Age" yAxisTitle="Number Interested"

11.     scaleto="6000" scalefrom="0" gridlines="7">

12.     <cfchartseries type="bar" seriesLabel="Computer
           Games">

13.         <cfchartData item="1-20" value="5000">

14.         <cfchartData item="21-40" value="4000">

15.         <cfchartData item="41-60" value="2000">

16.         <cfchartData item="61-80" value="2000">

17.     </cfchartseries>

18.     <cfchartseries type="bar" seriesLabel="Educational
           Software">

19.         <cfchartData item="1-20" value="4500">

20.         <cfchartData item="21-40" value="3000">

21.         <cfchartData item="41-60" value="1300">

22.         <cfchartData item="61-80" value="400">

23.     </cfchartseries>

24.     <cfchartseries type="bar" seriesLabel="Commercial
           Software">
```

```
25.        <cfchartData item="1-20" value="300">
26.        <cfchartData item="21-40" value="5000">
27.        <cfchartData item="41-60" value="4000">
28.        <cfchartData item="61-80" value="1500">
29.     </cfchartseries>
30.     </cfchart>
31. </body>
32. </html>
```

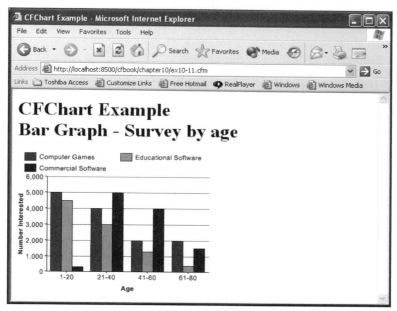

FIGURE 10.11   Bar Graph with Multiple Data Series

How the Code Works

1. The `<cfchart>` tag on line 10 starts off the graph with Age on the X-axis and Number interested on the Y-axis.

2. There are three series in this graph: one for Computer Games (line 12), the second for Educational Software (line 18), and the third for Commercial Software (line 24).

3. As you can see, the `<cfchartdata>` tag in each of the series creates the four data points for ages 1–20, 21–40, 41–60, and 61–80.

Generating XML

XML is the latest buzzword in the field of information exchange over the Internet. Some of the reasons for the popularity of XML are the abilities to define user-defined tags, separate content from presentation of the document, and also deal with graphical data. ColdFusion MX offers easy-to-use built-in functions to handle XML data. The new tag <cfxml> creates a new XML document. The <cfxml> tag has an attribute called variable that holds the ColdFusion XML document object. This document object is a Cold-Fusion structure that can later be accessed and modified.

The new function xmlparse() creates a ColdFusion structure from a valid XML string and the xmlsearch() function allows you to search for an XML file via the xpath.

Example 10.12 shows how to create an XML document from the results of a query. The resulting XML is displayed on the browser using the <cfdump> tag and also written to a file using the <cffile> tag. Figure 10.12 shows the XML output using the <cfdump> tag. The XML file output is shown in Figure 10.13.

Example 10.12 Generating XML (Static Table Columns) (ex10-12.cfm)

```
1.  <!DOCTYPE html PUBLIC
2.  "-//W3C//DTD XHTML 1.0 Transitional//EN"
3.  "http://www.w3.org/TR/xhtml1/DTD/xhtml1-transitional.dtd">
4.  <html xmlns = "http://www.w3.org/1999/xhtm">
5.  <head>
6.    <title>XML Example</title>
7.  </head>
8.  <body>
9.    <cfquery name="qryproducts" datasource="shoppingcart">
10.      SELECT productid, productname, productqty,
           productprice
11.      FROM products
12.    </cfquery>
13.    <cfxml variable = "xmlproducts">
14.      <products>
15.        <cfoutput query = "qryproducts">
16.          <product>
17.            <productid>#qryproducts.productid#</
             productid>
```

```
18.          <productname>#qryproducts.productname#</
             productname>

19.          <productqty>#qryproducts.productqty#</
             productqty>

20.          <productprice>#qryproducts.productprice#</
             productprice>

21.       </product>

22.      </cfoutput>

23.      </products>

24.    </cfxml>

25.  <cfdump var="#xmlproducts#">

26.  <cffile action="write" file="c:\cfusionmx\products.xml"

27.          output=#toString(xmlproducts)#>

28. </body>

29. </html>
```

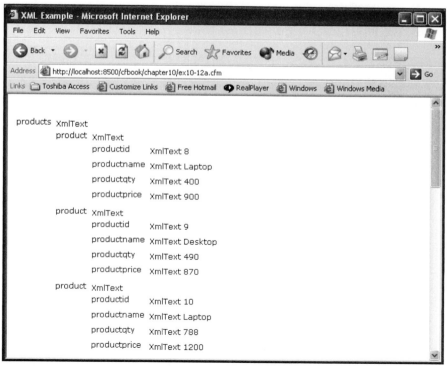

FIGURE 10.12   XML Output Using `<cfdump>`

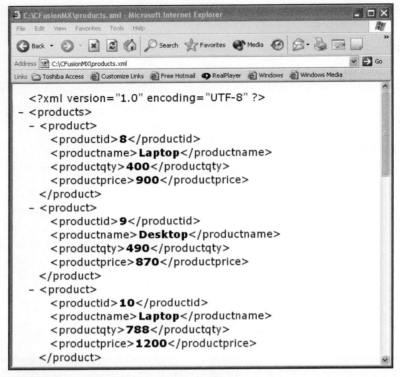

FIGURE 10.13   XML File Viewed by the Browser

How the Code Works

1. Lines 9 through 12 define a query that extracts `productid`, `productname`, `productqty`, and `productprice` from the Products table in the shopping cart database.

2. Line 13 uses the `<cfxml>` tag and creates the variable `xmlproducts`, which holds the ColdFusion XML document object.

3. Line 14 creates the root element `products` of the XML document.

4. Lines 15 through 22 loop through the query results and output, for each row, the child element `product` and its child elements—`productid`, `productname`, `productqty`, and `productprice` in XML format.

5. Line 25 uses the `<cfdump>` tag to display the contents of the XML document variable `xmlproducts` on the browser.

6. Line 26 writes out the XML to a file called `products.xml` using the `<cffile>` tag. Note that when we need to output XML to a file, we need to convert the variable to a string using the `toString()` function.

That was a very simple implementation of generation of XML in ColdFusion. We can make this code more dynamic by replacing lines 15 through 22 with code that dynamically generates the XML element names based on the fields it reads from the database. Example 10.13 shows you how to dump all the contents of the products table into XML without specifying any column names. This is very useful when you know the table name but don't know the column names. We do not hardcode the database fields in this example. The output of this code is the same as the previous example, Figure 10.12, and the XML file is like Figure 10.13 in the previous example.

Tech Tip

XMLFormat() is a function that returns a string that is safe to use with XML.

Example 10.13   Generating XML (Dynamic Table Columns) (ex10-13.cfm)

```
1.  <!DOCTYPE html PUBLIC
2.  "-//W3C//DTD XHTML 1.0 Transitional//EN"
3.  "http://www.w3.org/TR/xhtml1/DTD/xhtml1-transitional.dtd">
4.  <html xmlns = "http://www.w3.org/1999/xhtm">
5.  <head>
6.    <title>XML Example</title>
7.  </head>
8.  <body>
9.    <cfquery name="qryproducts" datasource="shoppingcart">
10.       SELECT *
11.       FROM products
12.   </cfquery>
13.   <cfxml variable="xmlproducts">
14.       <products>
15.       <cfloop query="qryproducts">
16.         <product>
17.           <cfloop list="#qryproducts.ColumnList#"
                  index="field">
18.             <cfoutput>
19.             <#field#>#xmlformat(qryproducts[field]
                  [currentrow])#</#field#>
20.             </cfoutput>
21.           </cfloop>
22.         </product>
```

```
23.        </cfloop>
24.        </products>
25.      </cfxml>
26.      <cfdump var="#xmlproducts#">
27.      <cffile action="write" file="c:\cfusionmx\products.xml"
28.              output=#toString(xmlproducts)#>
29.  </body>
30.  </html>
```

How the Code Works

1. Line 13 creates the XML object in the variable xmlproducts.

2. Line 15 uses the <cfloop> tag on the query qryproducts instead of the <cfoutput> that we used in Example 10.12. This is a loop through each row of the query's result set. Here, we are regarding the rows and columns of the result set as a two-dimensional array.

3. Line 16 creates the child element product.

4. Line 17 loops through all the fields of each row of the query qryproducts and displays each column or field of the query result set.

5. Line 19 creates the element with the same name as the field name of the column in the query. We use the ColumnList and the currentrow as indices to the query results (two-dimensional array) to access each field value.

6. Line 19 uses the code #xmlformat(qryproducts[field][currentrow])# to get the field value to use as the value of the element in the XML document. xmlformat() is a function that returns a string that is safe to use with XML.

7. Line 21 marks the end of the loop and proceeds to the next iteration of the loop (in this case, it would be the next field in the column list).

8. Line 26 uses <cfdump> to display the XML object on the web page.

9. Lines 27 and 28 write out the XML to a file called products.xml using the <cffile> tag. Note the conversion of the variable to a string using the toString() function.

In this chapter, we saw some cool features of ColdFusion MX. The <cfsilent> tag can be used to suppress output within your application. The debugging tag <cftrace> provides enhanced debugging facilities for your applications. Exception handling enables you to catch standard ColdFusion exceptions and developer-specified exceptions. The <cferror> tag helps you standardize your error pages. The <cflog> tag enables you to customize logs for your application and helps debug applications without displaying everything on the screen. Application pages can be aborted when an error occurs using the <cfabort> tag. The <cflocation> tag can be used to send users to other templates, HTML pages, or URLs. Files can be created, moved, deleted, copied, appended to, and renamed using the <cffile> tag. Emails can be sent out through ColdFusion applications using the <cfmail> tag. We saw some new features introduced in ColdFusion MX 6.1 that can enhance the mail-handling capability of your applications.

ColdFusion MX has new and enhanced tags for creating graphs and charts supporting multiple series of data. ColdFusion MX provides us with new tags for generating XML. There are more cool features of ColdFusion MX that have not been addressed in this book. You can refer to these online at www.macromedia.com.

With this chapter we have completed all the concepts that this book covers. The next chapter will help you complete your shopping cart project.

application template	error object	global error
custom exception	error template	multipart email message
debugging	exception	sitewise error

1. What is the purpose of the <cfsilent> tag?
2. Which new ColdFusion MX tag enables you to trace your code for debugging purposes?
3. Which tag is used to log errors in ColdFusion? What are the advantages of logging?
4. What is the difference between the tag used for logging and the tag used for tracing?
5. What is an exception?
6. What is the advantage of using exception-handling code in your ColdFusion pages?
7. What are custom exceptions? State one instance when you would throw a custom exception.
8. Which attribute in the <cfcatch> block helps ColdFusion identify the type of exception to catch?
9. What type of exception is thrown (a) when an include file is missing and (b) when a database error occurs?
10. When is the error object created? What kind of information can you get through the error object?
11. What are the advantages of using sitewise error handling?
12. In which file would you specify the sitewise error-handling tag and why?
13. Which tag would you use to abort processing of a ColdFusion template midway? Why would you do this?

14. Which tag is used to relocate the user to another template? Give one situation when you could use this tag.

15. Which tag would you use to copy files on the server? What action would you use to copy a file from one location to another on the ColdFusion server?

16. Which tag enables you to send email from within a ColdFusion template?

17. How would you attach a file in your email?

18. Which tag helps you to send multipart email messages?

19. Name and state the purpose of the three new tags in ColdFusion MX that enable you to create charts.

20. Which tag do you require to define multiple data series in a graph? Within which tag does this tag need to appear?

21. Name the new tag in ColdFusion MX that creates a new XML document.

True or False

State whether the following statements are true or false.

1. You would not enable debugging in the production environment. _____

2. Using `<cftrace>` you cannot see the time taken for the piece of code to execute. _____

3. Exception-handling tags do not enable you to recover from errors and resume processing normally. _____

4. In ColdFusion the developer can specify his own events on which to raise exceptions so that he can alter the flow of his code. _____

5. The `type="any"` for the catch block enables you to catch any error that is not caught by the other catch blocks. _____

6. The `<cferror>` tag should be in the `Application.cfm` file so that it is available to all pages in your application. _____

7. Thread, date, and time are depreciated attributes of `<cflog>` in ColdFusion MX. _____

8. The `<cffile>` tag cannot be used unless it is enabled in the ColdFusion Administrator. _____

9. In ColdFusion we can attach files to email using the `<cfmailparam>` tag. _____

10. The capability to separate multipart email messages is a new feature introduced in ColdFusion MX 6.1. _____

11. The data points to be used for a chart or graph can be generated by a query but not manually. _____

Programming Exercises

1. Write a code snippet that
   a. Executes a database query (use any table or query that has an error in it).
   b. Catches a database exception.
   c. Logs the error in a log file in the exception code.
   d. Generates an error page like Figure 10.14.

2. Write a ColdFusion template that
   a. Reads the contents of any file on your server.
   b. Displays the contents on your web page.
   c. Emails the contents of the file to you.

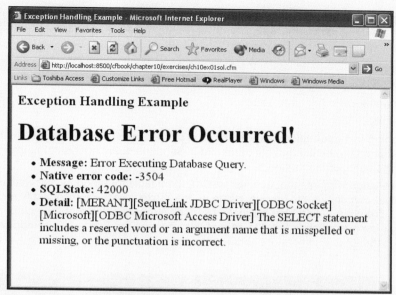

FIGURE 10.14 Database Exception

3. Write a ColdFusion template that
   a. Queries a table of your choice (for example, the Order table).
   b. Generates an XML file.
   c. Emails that file as an attachment to you.
   d. Dumps the XML output on the screen.
4. Correct the following code snippets:
   a.
   ```
   <cfmail subject="Your order has been received">
   Dear Customer,
   Thank you for your order. We appreciate your business.
   </cfmail>
   ```
   b.
   ```
   <cffile action="write" file="c:\test.txt">
   ```
   c.
   ```
   <cfparam name=username default="guest">
   <cftry>
      <cfif form.username eq "guest">
         <cfthrow type="illegalUserException"
         message="<cfoutput>#username#</cfoutput> does not have
            access to this page"
      </cfif>
      <cfcatch type="MissingInclude">
         <h1>Illegal user!</h1>
   </cfcatch>
   </cftry>
   ```

1. Implement sitewise error handling for your shopping cart application. Specify the `<cferror>` tag in your Application.cfm file and design an error page for your application. In your error template, display the following attributes of the error object:

   a. IP address of the client on which the error occurred.

   b. Browser and version number.

   c. Date and time when the error occurred.

   d. Error details.

2. In the shopping cart application, once the order is created, add code to send an email to the customer indicating that you have received his or her order. Send the customer his or her order number and order details including amounts due.

3. Write a ColdFusion template that queries the OrderItem table for products that were ordered until now. Create a chart that shows the product name on the X-axis and the total quantity ordered (to date) on the Y-axis. This chart would help business users analyze the sales that took place that month, so it should show the quantities ordered to date of each item on the Y-axis. Your graph should look similar to Figure 10.15.

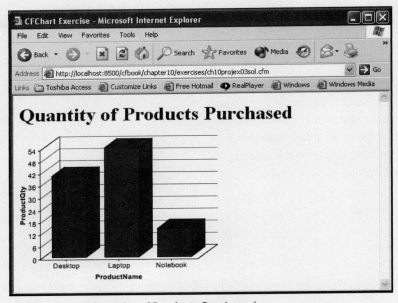

FIGURE 10.15   Quantity of Products Purchased

11

E-Commerce Shopping Cart Application

CHAPTER OBJECTIVES

1. Understand basic concepts behind e-commerce and shopping cart applications.

2. Review the flow diagram of the shopping cart application.

3. Understand the shopping cart data structures.

4. Understand the usage of session variables for this application.

5. Write the Application.cfm file for this application.

6. Create header and footer templates to include in all pages.

7. Implement sitewise error handling for this application.

8. Develop a Product Catalog page for the store.

9. Develop the Shopping Cart page to add products.

10. Develop the Customer Information page to get customer-related data.

11. Develop the Order Review page to allow the customer to confirm the order.

12. Develop the Order Confirmation page that sends email and saves the order.

13. Analyze and develop suggested shopping cart enhancements.

14. Analyze and develop new projects.

Throughout this book, you have been building a shopping cart application. By now, you must be almost done with this project and you have probably learned enough to build and complete this application.

This chapter gives you a sample solution for this application. It is based on what you have learned so far and is kept as simple as possible. This chapter may help clarify some of the concepts you learned in all the previous chapters. Almost every chapter is touched again in this chapter in this complete application.

At the end of this chapter, you will find some suggestions for other projects that you can build to enhance your knowledge of web development and ColdFusion.

E-Commerce and the Shopping Cart

E-commerce or **electronic commerce** refers to all online transactions. It gives you the ability to buy, sell, and market your products and services online. **B2C** stands for **business-to-consumer** transactions and refers to any business that sells its products or services to consumers online. Examples include selling books online, online banking, online travel services, auction websites, health information websites, real estate websites, and so forth. **B2B** stands for **business-to-business** transactions. It refers to businesses buying from and selling to each other, online.

In order to set up an e-commerce website, you need to have a website and something to sell. It can be either a product or a service. You would then set up an online store from which you will sell these goods or services, normally using a shopping cart application.

But just a shopping cart is not enough for you to have an e-commerce website. A shopping cart is only a small part of your site. You need to be paid for your orders when you ship products out. For this, you need a secure way to accept payments. You need an online **credit card authorization system** to process payments and a **merchant account** with a bank to deposit your payments automatically into your account for the goods or services you sell.

A shopping cart application will accept orders from customers, but it will not ship your orders. Normally, shipping is done through a **fulfillment system** that can mark products as shipped and charge credit cards once shipped.

Customer service is a very important part of an e-commerce application. It gives your customers a way to receive information, give feedback, and obtain customer support for the products they buy. A useful feature that helps boost customer service is an ability to view order status. Many e-commerce websites have a separate customer service application for the customer service personnel to view orders so that they can provide efficient service to their customers. Many e-commerce websites also provide a way for the customer to view his or her own orders so the customer knows the shipment's status. Another useful feature that some websites provide is a way for customers to return products they are not satisfied with and a way to cancel orders they have placed.

A good shopping cart application is vital for online selling. The shopping cart application allows customers to place orders for products online. Any shopping cart application should be robust enough to allow the customer to change his or her mind anytime during the ordering process. None of the customer's information should be committed to the database until the end when the customer confirms all his or her entries. That is the stage when the shopping cart becomes an order.

High-Level Flow Diagram

In the flow diagram in Figure 11.1, the enclosed boxes are the *web pages* that we will design for the shopping cart application. The open text boxes with no borders are **hyperlinks** that take you to other pages from the starting page. The arrows show the *direction* of flow. The shaded text boxes without borders are *buttons* that submit forms.

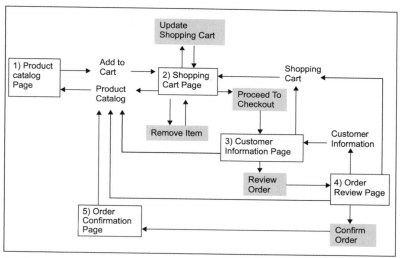

FIGURE 11.1   High-Level Flow Diagram (Shopping Cart Application)

There are five main pages in this application:

1. The **Product Catalog page** that lets customers view the products.

2. The **Shopping Cart page** that holds the items customers want to buy.

3. The **Address and Payment Information page** (or Customer Information page) where the customer enters his or her shipping and billing addresses and payment details and selects a shipping method.

4. The **Order Review page** where the customer can look at the order, addresses, and payment details before committing to the order.

5. The **Order Confirmation page** that confirms the order. Here the order will be saved in a database and the customer gets a confirmation on the screen and in an email.

Data Structures

In this project we are going to use one structure (called `ShoppingCart`). This structure contains an array of items (called `ItemList`), order totals, shipping and billing addresses, shipping method, payment information, totals, and other order-level information. The array of items contained within the shopping cart structure is an array of structures (called `NewItem`), each of which holds item-specific details such as product ID, name, brand, price, quantity ordered, available quantity, item totals, and so forth.

The Item Structure

Let us start from the lowest level: the item. The structure called `NewItem` represents an item that is being added to the cart. The Product Catalog page queries the Products and Suppliers tables to list the products. The `Add to Cart` hyperlink in this page sends the results in URL variables to the Shopping Cart page. Each time an item is added to the shopping cart, the Shopping Cart page checks to see if the item already exists in the cart. If it does, then the Shopping Cart page just increments that item's quantity. If it doesn't, then the Shopping Cart page creates the new item structure (`NewItem`) and appends it to the item array (called `ItemList`) of the `ShoppingCart` structure. The following table shows the item-specific details that we store in the `NewItem` structure.

Field Name	Explanation
`ProductID`	This is the ID of the product added to the shopping cart. This is passed from the Product Catalog page in a URL variable to the Shopping Cart page, where a new item is created with this ID if it does not already exist in the shopping cart and is appended to the `ItemList` array in the `ShoppingCart` structure.
`Qty`	This is the quantity of the product added to the shopping cart. Each time an item is added to the cart, the quantity is passed as 1 from the Product Catalog page in a URL variable to the Shopping Cart page. Here the `NewItem` structure is created with the quantity passed if the item does not already exist in the cart, and this new item is appended to the `ItemList` array. If the item already exists in the cart, this quantity is just added to the existing item in the `ItemList` array in the `ShoppingCart` structure.

Continued

Field Name	Explanation (continued)
ProductName	This is the name of the product added to the shopping cart. This is passed from the Product Catalog page in a URL variable to the Shopping Cart page. Here, the NewItem structure is created with this product name if the item does not already exist in the shopping cart and is inserted into the ItemList array in the ShoppingCart structure.
Brand	This is the brand of the product added to the shopping cart. This information is queried from the Suppliers table. The Products table has SupplierID as the foreign key to the Suppliers table so a simple join query gets us the brand from the Suppliers table. The brand is passed from the Product Catalog page in a URL variable to the Shopping Cart page, where, if the item does not already exist in the cart, a NewItem structure is created and appended to the ItemList array of the ShoppingCart structure.
Price	This is the price of the product ordered. This is passed from the Product Catalog page in a URL variable to the Shopping Cart page, where the NewItem structure is created if the item does not already exist in the ItemList array of the ShoppingCart structure.
ItemTotal	This is the total cost of the item added to the shopping cart. It is calculated (Price * Qty) in the Shopping Cart page and inserted into the NewItem structure in the ItemList array of the ShoppingCart structure. Remember, this total needs to be recalculated for an item every time the item is added to the cart or the quantity is updated in the cart.
QtyAvail	This is the total available quantity of the product added to the cart. This is needed to prevent overordering of the product. This is passed from the Product Catalog page in a URL variable to the Shopping Cart page, where the NewItem structure is created with this attribute if it does not already exist in the cart.

The Shopping Cart Structure

The shopping cart structure (called ShoppingCart) contains an array (called ItemList) of the above item structures. An item structure (called NewItem) is appended to the array every time a new product is added to the cart from the Product Catalog page. In addition, the shopping cart calculates the order total based on item totals and tax based on the order total. These amounts are all stored as elements in the shopping cart structure.

The Customer Information page gets shipping and billing addresses from the customer. These two addresses may be either the same or different. On this page, a checkbox is provided for the customer so that he or she need not reenter the address if the shipping address is the same as the billing address. Shipping method and payment details are also part of the Customer Information form. These are all submitted to the Order Review page, which stores these values in the ShoppingCart structure. The Order Review page also calculates the shipping charges and stores them in the ShoppingCart structure. It also recalculates the order amount by adding shipping charges to the total and updates this in the `ShoppingCart` structure. The following table shows the details stored in the shopping cart structure.

Field Name	Explanation
`Itemlist`	This is the array of item structures in the `ShoppingCart` structure. Each time a new item is created (as a `NewItem` structure), it is populated with the URL variables for that item, and then it is appended to the `ItemList` array in the `ShoppingCart` structure. The `NewItem` structure is created only if the `ShoppingCart` does not already have that item in its `ItemList` array. If the item exists, then all the other URL variables are ignored except the `Qty` (the quantity of the product added to the cart). This quantity is added to the existing item's quantity in the `ShoppingCart`'s `ItemList` array.
`OrderTotal`	This is the sum of all the item totals. This is calculated in the Shopping Cart page and inserted in the `ShoppingCart` structure.
`Tax`	`Tax = OrderTotal * 0.07`. This is calculated in the Shopping Cart page and inserted in the `ShoppingCart` structure.
`OrderAmount`	`OrderAmount = OrderTotal + Tax`. This is calculated in the Shopping Cart page and inserted in the `ShoppingCart` structure.
`ShipMethod`	This information is accepted in the Address and Payment Information form (the Customer Information page, getCustInfo.cfm). The Order Review page sets this information in the `ShoppingCart` structure from the Address and Payment form submitted. `ShipMethod` is the method the customer wants us to use for shipping his product. Options are `Ground`, `Overnight`, and `Air`. The shipping cost is calculated based on this selection.
`PaymentType`	The Order Review page sets this value in the `ShoppingCart` structure from the form submitted in the Customer Information page. This is the credit card name. Options in this solution are `Visa`, `Discover`, and `Mastercard`. You can add more if you like.
`ExpDate`	The Order Review page sets this value in the `ShoppingCart` structure from the form submitted in the Customer Information page. This is the credit card expiration date. At present, this date is accepted in the mm/dd/yyyy format, but you can modify this to accept only month and year.
`BillFirstName`	The Order Review page sets this value in the `ShoppingCart` structure from the form submitted in the Customer Information page. This is the first name that the customer uses for billing purposes.
`BillLastName`	The Order Review page sets this value in the `ShoppingCart` structure from the form submitted in the Customer Information page. This is the last name that the customer uses for billing purposes.
`BillAddress`	The Order Review page sets this value in the `ShoppingCart` structure from the form submitted in the Customer Information page. This is the street address that the customer uses for billing purposes.

Continued

Field Name	Explanation (continued)
BillCity	The Order Review page sets this value in the ShoppingCart structure from the form submitted in the Customer Information page. This is the city name for the customer's billing address.
BillState	The Order Review page sets this value in the ShoppingCart structure from the form submitted in the Customer Information page. This is the state name or code for the customer's billing address.
BillZip	The Order Review page sets this value in the ShoppingCart structure from the form submitted in the Customer Information page. This is the zip code for the customer's billing address.
BillEmail	The Order Review page sets this value in the ShoppingCart structure from the form submitted in the Customer Information page. This is the email address that the customer uses for billing purposes.
ShipFirstName	The Order Review page sets this value in the ShoppingCart structure from the form submitted in the Customer Information page. This is the first name of the person the customer wants the product shipped to.
ShipLastName	The Order Review page sets this value in the ShoppingCart structure from the form submitted in the Customer Information page. This is the last name of the person the customer wants the product shipped to.
ShipAddress	The Order Review page sets this value in the ShoppingCart structure from the form submitted in the Customer Information page. This is the street address of the person the customer wants the product shipped to.
ShipCity	The Order Review page sets this value in the ShoppingCart structure from the form submitted in the Customer Information page. This is the city for the shipping address.
ShipState	The Order Review page sets this value in the ShoppingCart structure from the form submitted in the Customer Information page. This is the state name or code of the shipping address.
ShipZip	The Order Review page sets this value in the ShoppingCart structure from the form submitted in the Customer Information page. This is the zip code of the shipping address.
ShipEmail	The Order Review page sets this value in the ShoppingCart structure from the form submitted in the Customer Information page. This is the email address of the person the product is being shipped to.
SameAddress	This is 1 if the shipping and billing addresses are same. This value need not be set in the ShoppingCart structure if you don't want to use it, but in this application it has been set. It can be used to recheck or uncheck the checkbox in the Customer Information page when the customer goes back to it from the Order Review page. If SameAddress is 1, then billing address fields are set to the shipping address that was submitted in the Customer Information page.

Continued

Field Name	Explanation (continued)
ShipCost	This is the charge for shipping based on the shipping method selected in the Customer Information page. For `shippingMethod = Ground`, we charge 0.1% of the order amount. For `shippingMethod = Overnight`, we charge 0.2% of the order amount. For `shippingMethod = Air`, we charge 0.3% of the order amount. This is inserted into the `ShoppingCart` structure.
OrderAmount	This is the same element as the one in the Shopping Cart page. Here we add the shipping cost to the `OrderAmount` and update this in the `ShoppingCart` structure.

Session Variables

Tech Tip

The default timeout for session variables is 20 minutes. We will use the default in this application.

A **session** refers to all requests that are made from a single client machine to the server in a continuous time period. No two users can access the same set of session variables. Each user has an independent session. Session-level data are stored in session variables that can be accessed from any page in your application.

To enable the shopping cart to be available across every page in our application, we need to save it in the session. That way, we need not pass URL or other parameters into every page. At the same time, we do not want all of the above variables to be floating around in the session independently. So we hold all of them under the shopping cart structure and place this structure in the session. You need to preface session variables with the scope name `Session` in order to use them. `Session` is itself a ColdFusion structure. The shopping cart, its attributes, as well as item details can be accessed through this structure using the property notation. For example, to access the order amount, we use the following code:

```
Session.ShoppingCart.OrderAmount
```

To access the first item's `ItemTotal`, we use the following code:

```
Session.ShoppingCart.ItemList[1].ItemTotal
```

The Application.cfm File

Tech Tip

Note: when you turn `sessionmanagement` on, you need to specify the application name as well.

The `Application.cfm file` is available across each page in your application. This file should be saved in the root folder of your application. For example, if your root folder is `c:\cfusionmx\wwwroot\shoppingcart`, your Application.cfm file also should be in that same directory. You should define application-level settings here, such as the application name, client state management options, application and session variables, default variables, sitewise error handling, data sources, and so forth.

Our Application.cfm file is very simple, as you can see below.

Application.cfm

```
1. <cfsilent>
2.      <cfapplication name="shopCart"
3.      sessionmanagement="Yes" >
4.      <cfset dsn = "shoppingCart">
5.   <cferror type = "request"
6.      template = "error.cfm">
7. </cfsilent>
```

How the Code Works

1. Line 1 shows the `<cfsilent>` tag since you don't want any output from this page.

2. The application name is mentioned in line 2 using the `<cfapplication>` tag.

3. We want to set `sessionmanagement` to `yes` as in line 3 since our shopping cart is going to be held in the session while it is being built before we commit it to the database.

4. Line 4 sets the `ShoppingCart` data source to a variable called `dsn`. This global variable can be accessed in every page of your application. The data source needs to be created in the ColdFusion Administrator's database section as you learned in Chapter 5.

5. Lines 5 and 6 use the `<cferror>` tag to specify the sitewise error-handling template `error.cfm`. This file will have code to display our standard error page throughout the site.

Include Files

Header File

Including a header file is a convenient way to reuse code that we need on the top of every page in our application.

Since the page name and title are different for each page, this should change from within the header file each time a page renders. In other words, the title should be dynamically generated. For example, the product catalog page will

Tech Tip

The XHTML header code, the page titles, and the name and logo of the company should all be part of the header file.

be called Product Catalog, whereas the shopping cart page will be called Shopping Cart.

To achieve this, we will set a variable in every page called `pagetitle` that indicates the page that it is part of. After setting this variable, we include the header file, which can read this variable and identify which page title and heading it should display. The following table contains the page title and file names for our five files.

Value of `pagetitle` Variable	File Name
Product Catalog	ProductList.cfm
Shopping Cart	ShoppingCart.cfm
Customer Information	GetCustInfo.cfm
Order Review	Review.cfm
Order Confirmation	SaveOrder.cfm

The code below shows the header file (`header.cfm`) that is included on the top of every page of our application.

Header.cfm

```
1. <!DOCTYPE html
2. PUBLIC "-//W3C//DTD XHTML 1.0 Transitional//EN"
3. "http://www.w3.org/TR/xhtml1/DTD/xhtml1-transitional.dtd">
4. <html xmlns="http://www.w3.org/1999/xhtml">
5. <cfparam name="pagetitle" default="Product Catalog">
6. <head>
7.     <title>Innovations - <cfoutput>
          #pagetitle#</cfoutput></title>
8. </head>
9. <body>
10.   <p align="center">
11.     <font size="+4" color="Blue">
12.       <b><i>Innovations </i></b><br />
13.     </font>
14.     <font size="+2" color="Blue">
15.       <b><cfoutput>#pagetitle#</cfoutput></b>
```

16.   `</font><br />`

17.   `</p>`

How the Code Works

1. Line 5 sets a default value for `pagetitle`.

2. We even open the `<body>` tag within the header.cfm file, as you can see in line 9.

3. On line 12 the company name is displayed.

4. Line 15 displays the `pagetitle` variable that is set in each page individually. In case the variable has not been set, it will display `Product Catalog`, which is the default.

Footer File

The footer file should contain everything that you want to include at the bottom of every page in your application. In addition to any copyright information, we can use the footer to provide hyperlinks to other pages in our site. The footer hyperlinks provided in the shopping cart pages will be different for every page. We want the customer to have access to different sets of pages depending on which stage of the ordering process he or she is in. The textboxes without borders in the flow diagram and the points below should clarify this requirement:

- The Product Catalog page needs access to no other pages since it is the first page.
- The Shopping Cart page needs a hyperlink to the Product Catalog page.
- The Customer Information page needs hyperlinks to the Shopping Cart and Product Catalog pages.
- The Order Review page needs hyperlinks to the Product Catalog, Shopping Cart, and Customer Information pages.
- The Order Confirmation page is a page that appears after the order is created. So here we need a hyperlink to go back to the Product Catalog page. The shopping cart should no longer exist at that point, so no other pages should be linked here.

In addition to the links, we need to display that the shopping cart is empty either when the session times out, when there are no items in the cart, or when the order has been created and the session is cleared. In the beginning, the shopping cart does not exist in the session, but we don't want to display the message `Your shopping cart is empty` because we don't want to distract the user from browsing through our product catalog. On any other page, if the shopping cart does not exist in the session or if the item list is empty, then we need to tell the user that so that the user doesn't wonder where his or her shopping cart suddenly disappeared. The code on page 410 is the footer (`footer.cfm`) that is added to the bottom of every page in our application. Figure 11.2 shows the empty shopping cart message that appears on any page other than the Product Catalog page. Here the Order Review page is accessed without having a shopping cart in the session. Note that a link to the Product Catalog page is displayed.

Footer.cfm

```coldfusion
1.  <cfif pagetitle neq "Product Catalog">
2.   <cfif not(isDefined("session.shoppingcart")) or
         arrayisempty(session.shoppingcart.itemlist)>
3.     <font color="Blue"><br />
4.     Your shopping cart is currently empty.<br />
5.     To place an order please visit our
6.     <a href="productlist.cfm">Product Catalog</a>
7.     </font>
8.   </cfif>
9.  </cfif>
10. <p align=center><span color="grey" align="center">
11.   <cfif pagetitle eq "Shopping Cart">
12.     <a href="productlist.cfm">Product Catalog</a>
13.   </cfif>
14.   <cfif pagetitle eq "Customer Information">
15.     <a href="productlist.cfm">Product Catalog</a> |
16.     <a href="shoppingcart.cfm">Shopping Cart</a> |
17.     <a href="GetCustInfo.cfm">Customer Information</a>
18.   </cfif>
19.   <cfif pagetitle eq "Order Review">
20.     <a href="productlist.cfm">Product Catalog</a> |
21.     <a href="GetCustInfo.cfm">Customer Information</a> |
22.     <a href="shoppingcart.cfm">Shopping Cart</a> |
23.     <a href="review.cfm">Order Review</a>
24.   </cfif>
25.   <cfif pagetitle eq "Order Confirmation">
26.     <a href="productlist.cfm">Product Catalog</a>
27.   </cfif>
```

28.   `<br /><br />`

29.   `&copy; <cfoutput>#Year(Now())#`
           `</cfoutput>Innovations, Inc.`

30. `</span></p>`

31. `</body>`

32. `</html>`

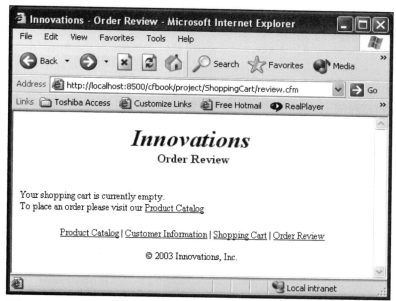

FIGURE 11.2   Footer (Empty Shopping Cart Message)

How the Code Works

1. Lines 1 through 9 tell the user that his or her shopping cart is empty. The user is offered a hyperlink to the Product Catalog page. This is displayed only under the following circumstances:

   a. Product Catalog is not the current page and the shopping cart does not exist in the session (see Figure 11.2).

   b. Product Catalog is not the current page and the shopping cart has an empty item list.

2. The next block of lines, lines 11 through 27, display the appropriate hyperlinks depending on the current page. The `pagetitle` variable is checked to determine the current page. The code displays the Product Catalog link for the Shopping Cart page. The Product Catalog and Customer Information links are displayed for the Customer

Information page. The Product Catalog hyperlink is displayed for the Order Confirmation page.

3. Lastly, the current year is displayed on line 29 using the function Year(Now()) to get the current year. In addition, any copyright information is displayed as part of the footer.

Sitewise Error Handing

Tech Tip

Alternatively, you could design an error template and specify it in the ColdFusion Administrator's Server Settings screen. Here you could specify a missing template error page and another sitewise error handler.

Sitewise error handling (discussed in Chapter 10) gives your site a consistent look and feel if any errors occur. The sitewise error file name is mentioned in the Application.cfm file using the <cferror> tag. In this application, a functional file, error.cfm, shown below, has been created just to show you how to use it (see Figure 11.3). You can enhance and modify it to suit your requirements. Generally, it should match the other pages in your site.

Error.cfm

```
1.  <!DOCTYPE html
2.  PUBLIC "-//W3C//DTD XHTML 1.0 Transitional//EN"
3.  "http://www.w3.org/TR/xhtml1/DTD/xhtml1-transitional.dtd">
4.  <html xmlns="http://www.w3.org/1999/xhtml">
5.  <cfparam name="pagetitle" default="Product Catalog">
6.  <head>
7.    <title>Innovations - Error</title>
8.  </head>
9.  <body>
10.    <p align="center">
11.    <font size="+4" color="Blue">
12.      <b><i>Innovations </i></b><br />
13.    </font>
14. <b>An error occurred! <br>#error.diagnostics#</b><br />
15. <cfoutput>
16. <cflog text="<B>Your Location:</B> #error.
       remoteAddress#<br>
17.    <B>Your Browser:</B> #error.browser#<br>
```

18. `<B>Date and Time the Error Occurred:</B> #error.`
     `dateTime#<br>`

19. `<B>Page You Came From:</B> #error.`
     `HTTPReferer#<br><hr>`

20. `<B>Message Content</B>: #error.diagnostics#`

21. `<br><br>"`

22. `file="shoppingcart.log">`

23. `</cfoutput>`

24. `</body>`

25. `</html>`

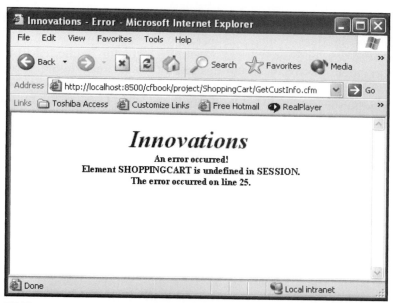

FIGURE 11.3   Sitewise Error Template

How the Code Works

1. The error object's diagnostics are displayed in line 14. You can have any other custom error message here. For debugging purposes, the diagnostics are very useful as you can see exactly what error occurred. But in a production environment, you would not like to publicize the problem with your site. Usually companies have a standard error message for their site such as "Sorry we are currently having technical difficulties. Please try again later."

2. Lines 16 through 22 log the error in a log file. You could do this in a production environment as well so that you know what is going on in

your site. Here we collect the IP address, browser version, date and time, referrer URL, and error details. These are all saved in the log file called `shoppingcart.log`. This file is created in the ColdFusion logs directory, usually `c:\cfusionmx\logs`.

Product Catalog

The first page the customer sees is the Product Catalog. This is where he or she will spend time browsing through your product catalog and will be tempted to buy items. So an attempt should be made to make this page as easy to use and friendly as possible. You could add pictures of your products in this page and present hyperlinks to product features. Another cool feature you can add is a comparison chart so that customers can compare different models of your products to help them make a selection.

The simplest Product Catalog page would need to display a list of products, their description, and their prices. All this information is queried from the Product table in the database. On this page, the customer should be able to see whether the item is in stock or out of stock. He or she also should be able to add an item to the shopping cart from the Product Catalog. If a product is out of stock, that should be indicated on this page, and the customer should not be able to add it to the shopping cart. Once the customer adds an item to the cart, he or she should see the Shopping Cart page with the newly added product in the cart.

You may need to group your items according to category or cost depending on your requirements. Sometimes you may want the user to decide how he or she wants the list sorted. That is what we have done in this project. Since we just have a simple list of products, we will sort the list by the product name field and provide the capability for the customer to click on any field name to sort by that field.

ColdFusion Component to Get the Product List

`GetList.cfc` is the component that has been created to help us query the Products table and populate the Product Catalog. Following this is another listing of the template that uses the component's methods called `productList.cfm`.

GetList.cfc

1. `<cfcomponent>`
2. `  <cffunction name="getproductlist" returntype="query">`
3. `    <cfargument name="sortorder" type="string" required="true">`

```
4.      <cfargument name="dsn" type="string"
           required="true">

5.      <cfquery Name = "qryproductlist" DataSource =
           "#arguments.dsn#">

6.         SELECT Products.ProductID, Products.ProductName,

7.            Suppliers.SupplierName, Products.ProductQty,

8.            Products.ProductPrice, Products.
               ProductDescription

9.         FROM Suppliers, Products

10.        WHERE Suppliers.SupplierID = Products.SupplierID

11.        ORDER BY

12.        <cfqueryparam cfsqltype="cf_sql_varchar"
              value="#arguments.sortorder#">

13.     </cfquery>

14.     <cfreturn qryproductlist>

15.  </cffunction>

16. </cfcomponent>
```

How the Code Works

1. Line 1 opens the `<cfcomponent>` tag.

2. Line 2 defines a function using the `<cffunction>` tag. This function returns a query.

3. Lines 3 and 4 indicate that this function takes two arguments: `sortorder` and `dsn`. `Sortorder` will determine how to sort the product list and `dsn` is the data source to use for the query.

4. Lines 5 through 13 define a query to get the product details and brands from the database. This query is a join between the Products and Suppliers tables. The join is on the `supplierID` field, which is a foreign key in the Products table. The Suppliers table contains the `brand` or supplier name of each product.

5. Line 14 returns this result set to the calling template.

Displaying the Products

In the previous section, we created a component called getlist.cfc. Now, `productlist.cfm`, listed below, will use that component and populate the HTML table. Figure 11.4 shows the Product Catalog page created by the code listed below. Notice that the list of products in the figure is sorted by price. The company name and page name come from the header include; the product listing in the table comes from productlist.cfm, which gets the query results from the getlist.cfc component; and the footer copyright information comes from the footer include.

Productlist.cfm

```
1.  <cfset pagetitle = "Product Catalog">

2.  <cfinclude template="header.cfm">

3.  <cfparam name="url.sortorder" default="productname">

4.  <cfinvoke component="getlist" method="getproductlist"

5.  sortorder="#url.sortorder#" dsn="#dsn#"
        returnvariable="products">

6.  <cfif products.recordcount gt "0">

7.    <table border = "1" cellspacing = "0"
          bordercolor="red" align="center">

8.      <tr>

9.        <td><b><font color="Blue">

10.         <a href="productlist.cfm?sortorder=
              productname">

11.         Product Name</a></font></b></td>

12.       <td><b><font color="Blue">

13.         <a href="productlist.cfm?sortorder=
              suppliername">

14.         Brand</a></font></b> </td>

15.       <td><b><font color="Blue">

16.         <a href="productlist.cfm?sortorder=
              productdescription">

17.         Product Desription</a></font></b></td>

18.       <td><b><font color="Blue">

19.         <a href="productlist.cfm?sortorder=
              productqty">

20.         Stock</a></font></b></td>

21.       <td><b><font color="Blue">
```

```
22.          <a href="productlist.cfm?sortorder=
                productprice">

23.          Price</a></font></b></td>

24.       <td><b><font color="Blue">

25.          <a href="productlist.cfm?sortorder=
                productqty">

26.          Buy</a></font></b></td>

27.     </tr>

28.     <cfoutput query ="products">

29.     <tr>

30.       <td>#products.ProductName#</td>

31.       <td>#products.SupplierName#</td>

32.       <td>#products.ProductDescription#</td>

33.       <td>#products.ProductQty# </td>

34.       <td align="right">#dollarformat(products.
             ProductPrice)#</td>

35.       <td> 

36.         <cfif products.productqty gt 0>

37.           <a href="shoppingcart.cfm?productid=#products.
                 productid#&productname=#products.
                 productname#&brand=#products.
                 suppliername#&price=#products.
                 productprice#&qty=1&qtyAvail=#products.
                 ProductQty#&action=add">Add to Cart</a>

38.         <cfelse>

39.           Out of stock!

40.         </cfif>

41.       </td>

42.     </tr>

43.     </cfoutput>

44.   </table>

45. </cfif>

46. <cfinclude template="footer.cfm">
```

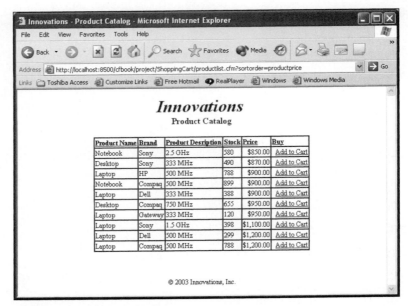

FIGURE 11.4   Product Catalog

How the Code Works

1. Line 1 sets the page title in the `pagetitle` variable.

2. Line 2 includes the file header.cfm to get the page title and header code.

3. Line 3 sets a default value for the variable `url.sortorder`. This variable is sent to the getlist.cfc component's `getProductList()` method to sort the records by a particular field in lines 4 and 5.

4. Lines 4 and 5 use the `<cfinvoke>` tag to call the `getproductlist()` method in the getlist.cfc component. It sends as parameters into that method `sortorder="#url.sortorder#"` and `dsn="#dsn#"`. The returning record set will be stored in the variable `products`.

5. Line 6 checks if the record set is empty. If so, nothing is displayed.

6. Otherwise, a table is created on lines 7 through 44 to hold the product catalog.

7. The column headings are displayed first in lines 8 through 27.

8. As mentioned earlier, we want to sort by any field by clicking on the column headings. To enable this, we create the heading as a hyperlink to the Product Catalog page (for example, line 10) and we pass the URL parameter `sortorder` and give it the value of the database field that it represents. The database query in the component gets the `sortorder` variable as an argument that it can use to sort the records.

9. The result of the query is displayed in lines 28 through 43. Note that the `<cfoutput>` tag's query name is the same as the return variable name in the `<cfinvoke>` tag.

10. `ProductPrice` in line 34 is formatted with the dollar sign and two decimal places.

11. On lines 36 through 40, if the product has quantity available, the `Add to Cart` hyperlink (to add that product to the shopping cart) is displayed. Otherwise, the `Out of Stock!` string is displayed on line 39. This suppresses the add-to-cart functionality for out-of-stock items.

12. The `Add to Cart` hyperlink, the most important functionality on this page on line 37, is a hyperlink to shoppingcart.cfm with URL variables `productid`, `productname`, `brand`, `price`, and `ProductQty` (quantity available), all of which come from the query result for that item through the component we created earlier. Note that we are sending one additional URL variable called `action` with value `add`. This variable indicates that this item needs to be added to the shopping cart. Since from the Product Catalog page the only functionality we can perform on the shopping cart is to add items to the cart, we can safely always send the value `add` in this variable from this page. You will see later that we can remove items and update quantities as well, so we need to differentiate between each action.

13. On line 46 we include the `footer.cfm` file that has our standard footer code.

Shopping Cart

This page shows the shopping cart or list of products added to the cart so far. This is presented in a neat table along with the quantity ordered, item totals, tax, and order totals. The item and order totals and tax amount are calculated and displayed in the shopping cart.

You should provide the ability to add multiple line items, change quantities, update totals, and remove unwanted items from the shopping cart. In other words, provide the customer with flexibility in case the customer changes his or her mind about selected items.

Your shopping cart should not accept any quantities that are greater than the maximum quantity available for that product. From this page, the customer should have a hyperlink to the Product Catalog page so that he or she can order other items. If the customer orders the same item again, the item should not be added as a new item. Instead, the shopping cart should detect that the item already exists and should increment the quantity of that item. If the customer orders a new item, then he or she should see the additional item in the cart.

Lastly, the customer should be able to proceed with his or her order and go to the Customer Information page. The following code listing shows the shopping cart template `ShoppingCart.cfm`. Figure 11.5 shows the Shopping Cart page and Figure 11.6 shows the shopping cart error alert if you try to add more than the available quantity on hand of a product.

Shoppingcart.cfm

```
1.  <cfparam name="url.productid" default="">
2.  <cfparam name="url.productname" default="">
3.  <cfparam name="url.brand" default="">
4.  <cfparam name="url.price" default="0">
5.  <cfparam name="url.qty" default="1">
6.  <cfparam name="url.action" default="">
7.  <cfparam name="total" default="0">
8.  <cfset itemFound=0>
9.  <cflock scope="session" throwontimeout="No"
        type="exclusive" timeout="30">
10. <cfif NOT(isDefined("session.shoppingcart"))>
11.   <cfset session.shoppingcart = structNew()>
12.   <cfset session.shoppingcart.itemlist = arrayNew(1)>
13.   </cfif>
14. <cfscript>
15.   for(thisItem=1; thisItem lte ArrayLen(session.
        shoppingCart.itemlist);
16.     thisItem=thisItem+1) {
17.   if (isDefined("form.update") or isDefined("form.
        proceed")) {
18.     thisitemqty=Evaluate("form.qty_" & thisitem);
19.     if (thisitemqty gt 0) {
20.       session.shoppingcart.itemlist[thisitem].
          qty = thisitemqty;
```

```
21.        session.shoppingcart.itemlist[thisitem].itemTotal=

22.        (session.shoppingcart.itemlist[thisitem].price *

23.        session.shoppingcart.itemlist[thisitem].qty);

24.     } else {

25.       arrayDeleteAt(session.shoppingcart.
              itemlist,thisitem);

26.         continue;

27.       }

28.     }

29.    if (session.shoppingcart.itemlist[thisItem].
          productid eq url.productid) {

30.       itemFound=1;

31.       if (url.action eq "add") {

32.         session.shoppingcart.itemlist[thisitem].qty =

33.           session.shoppingcart.itemlist[thisitem].qty
                + #url.qty# ;

34.           session.shoppingcart.itemlist[thisitem].
                itemTotal =

35.           (session.shoppingcart.itemlist[thisitem].
                price *

36.           session.shoppingcart.itemlist[thisitem].
                qty);

37.         break;

38.        }

39.       if (url.action eq "delete") {

40.         arrayDeleteAt(session.shoppingcart.itemlist,
              thisitem);

41.         break;

42.        }

43.      }

44.    }

45.   if (url.action eq "add" and not itemFound) {

46.     newitem=structNew();

47.     newitem.productid = #url.productid#;
```

```
48.      newitem.qty = #url.qty#;

49.      newitem.productname = #url.productname#;

50.      newitem.brand = #url.brand#;

51.      newitem.price = #url.price#;

52.      newitem.itemTotal=#url.price# * #url.qty#;

53.      newitem.qtyavail = url.qtyAvail;

54.      arrayAppend(session.shoppingcart.itemlist, newitem);

55.   }

56.   for(thisItem=1; thisItem lte ArrayLen(session.
         shoppingCart.itemlist);

57.        thisItem=thisItem+1) {

58.      total = total+session.shoppingcart.itemlist[thisitem].
         itemtotal;

59.   }

60.   session.shoppingcart.orderTotal = total;

61.   session.shoppingcart.tax = session.shoppingcart.
         orderTotal * 0.07;

62.   session.shoppingcart.orderAmount = session.
         shoppingcart.orderTotal +

63.          session.shoppingcart.tax;

64. </cfscript>

65. </cflock>

66. <cfif isDefined("form.proceed")>

67.    <cflocation url="GetCustInfo.cfm" addtoken="no">

68. </cfif>

69. <cfset pagetitle = "Shopping Cart">

70. <cfinclude template="header.cfm">

71. <cflock timeout="30" throwontimeout="Yes" type="readonly"
       scope="session">

72.    <cfset variables.shoppingcart=Duplicate(session.
         shoppingcart)>

73. </cflock>

74. <cfif not arrayisempty(variables.shoppingcart.
         itemlist)>
```

```
75.   <cfform action="shoppingcart.cfm" method="post"
      name="shoppingcart">

76.   <table border = "1" cellspacing = "0"
      bordercolor="red" align="center">

77.   <tr>

78.     <td><b><font color="blue">Product
        Code</font></b></td>

79.     <td><b><font color="blue">Product
        Name</font></b></td>

80.     <td><b><font color="blue">Brand</font></b>
        </td>

81.     <td><b><font color="blue">Unit
        Price</font></b></td>

82.     <td><b><font color="blue">Quantity
        Ordered</font></b></td>

83.     <td><b><font color="blue">Total
        Cost</font></b></td>

84.     <td><b><font color="blue">Remove
        Item</font></b></td>

85.   </tr>

86.   <cfloop index="thisitem" from="1"

87.       to="#ArrayLen(variables.shoppingCart.
          itemlist)#">

88.   <tr>

89.   <cfoutput>

90.     <td>#variables.shoppingCart.itemlist[thisitem].
        productid#</td>

91.     <td>#variables.shoppingCart.itemlist[thisitem].
        productname#</td>

92.     <td>#variables.shoppingCart.itemlist[thisitem].
        brand#</td>

93.     <td>#dollarformat(variables.shoppingCart.
        itemlist[thisitem].price)# </td>

94.     <td><cfinput type=text size="5"

95.       value="#variables.shoppingCart.
          itemlist[thisitem].qty#"
```

```
96.            range="0,#variables.shoppingcart.
                  itemlist[thisitem].qtyAvail#"

97.            message="Please enter quantity between 0 and
                  #variables.shoppingcart.itemlist[thisitem].
                  qtyAvail# for #variables.shoppingcart.
                  itemlist[thisitem].brand# #variables.
                  shoppingcart.itemlist[thisitem].productname#"

98.            name="qty_#thisitem#">

99.        </td>

100.    <td align="right"> #dollarformat(variables.
            shoppingcart.itemlist[thisitem].itemTotal)#
            </td>

101.    <td><a href="<cfoutput>shoppingcart.
            cfm?productid=#variables.shoppingcart.
            itemlist[thisitem].productid#&action=delete
            </cfoutput>">Remove Item</a></td>

102.    </cfoutput>

103.    </tr>

104.    </cfloop>

105.    <tr><td colspan=5 align="left">Order Amount</td>

106.      <td align=right> <cfoutput> #dollarformat
            (variables.shoppingcart.orderTotal)#
            </cfoutput></td>

107.    </tr>

108.    <tr>

109.      <td colspan=5 align="left">Tax</td>

110.      <td align=right> <cfoutput> #dollarformat
            (variables.shoppingcart.tax)#
            </cfoutput></td>

111.    </tr>

112.    <tr>

113.      <td colspan=5 align="left">Order Total</td>

114.      <td align=right> <cfoutput> #dollarformat
            (variables.shoppingcart.orderAmount)#
            </cfoutput></td>

115.    </tr>

116.    <tr>
```

```
117.        <td colspan="7" align="center">
118.          <input type="submit" name="update"
                value="Update Shopping Cart">    
119.          <input type="submit" name="proceed"
                value="Proceed to Checkout">
120.      </td>
121.      </tr>
122.      </table>
123.    </cfform>
124. </cfif>
125. <cfinclude template="footer.cfm">
```

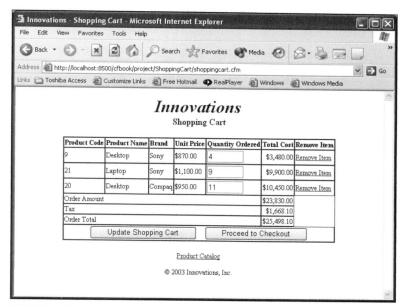

FIGURE 11.5   Shopping Cart

How the Code Works

1. Lines 1 through 6 set default values for all the URL variables expected by this page.

2. Line 7 sets the value of total to 0. This will accumulate the total amount of the order as we add items to the shopping cart.

3. Line 8 sets the value of the variable itemFound to 0. This variable identifies whether the item already exists in the cart, in which case

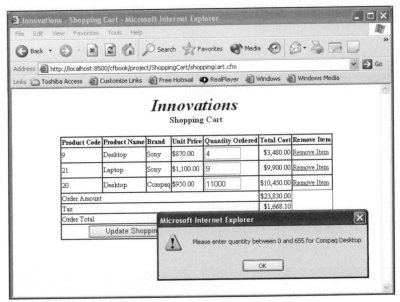

FIGURE 11.6   Shopping Cart—Protect against Overordering

we can just increment the quantity of the existing item. If `itemFound` is 0, it is a new item and will be freshly created and added to the cart.

4. Since we are accessing session variables, we lock the session on line 9.

5. If the shopping cart structure does not exist in the session, we need to create it at this point. Line 11 creates a new structure called `shoppingcart` in the session. In addition, in line 12, a new array is created for the shopping cart's `itemlist`.

6. When a new item is added to the cart, the `itemlist` array is empty. The loop on line 15 is not entered initially. Control goes directly to line 45 (right after the loop). Since we are passing the URL parameter `action=add` and initially `itemFound` is 0, the conditional code on line 45 is true, and the code block on lines 46 through 54 is executed. Line 46 creates a `newitem` structure for the newly added item. Lines 47 through 53 initialize all its elements using the URL parameters sent. `ItemTotal` is calculated and set in the structure in line 52. Line 54 appends the completed `newitem` structure to the shopping cart's `itemlist` array.

7. Lines 56 through 59 accumulate `itemtotal` into the local variable `total`. We did not put this along with the main loop because some items are deleted and others updated, so the totals can get tricky.

8. Line 60 sets the `orderTotal` (total of the items) in the shopping cart.

9. Line 61 calculates the `tax` amount in the shopping cart as 7 percent of `orderTotal`.

10. Line 62 sets `orderAmount` to the `orderTotal` + `tax`.

11. When an existing item is added to the cart, the `itemlist` array of the shopping cart is not empty. So the loop on line 15 is executed. It loops through each item in the shopping cart's `itemlist`. Since no form has been submitted, `form.update` and `form.proceed` are not present, so line 17's conditional code is skipped. Control goes to line 29, which checks if the `productid` passed through the URL variable is the same as the `productid` of the shopping cart's line item. If they are the same, then the code within that condition is executed. In this case, since we are adding an existing item, `url.productId` will match with an existing one in the cart. The variable `itemFound` is set to 1 in line 30. If you remember, when products are added from the Product Catalog page, we sent a URL variable called `action=add`. So the code between lines 31 and 38 is executed. This code adds `url.qty` to the existing item's quantity and recalculates the `itemtotal`. The next step is to break out from the loop since we add only one item at a time, so we don't need to complete the loop.

12. Now for the scenario when we add a product that does not exist in the shopping cart but the shopping cart is not empty. Control starts on line 15, which loops through the `itemlist` array in the shopping cart. No form has been submitted, so the conditional code on lines 17 through 28 is skipped. Line 29 checks each shopping cart item to see if it matches with the `productid` sent in the URL. Since none match, the loop is exited on line 44, normally without executing any of that code. Now `itemFound` has the original value of 0. Control then goes to line 45 with `itemFound = 0`. Since `action=add` and `itemfound=0`, this code is executed (same as adding a new item). The `newitem` structure is created and initialized with URL variable values on lines 46 through 53. Then this item structure is appended to the shopping cart's `itemlist` array in line 54. Again we loop through the items to get the total of all item amounts—lines 56 through 59. These amounts are set in the shopping cart on lines 60 through 63. The tax and order amount also are calculated and set in the shopping cart.

13. The next scenario is when the `remove item` hyperlink is clicked. Control starts at line 15, which loops through each item in the `itemlist`. Since no form is submitted, there is no `form.update` or `form.proceed` defined. So the conditional code for line 17 is skipped until line 28. Control goes to line 29. Here, if the appropriate `productid` that needs to be deleted is found, then the `url.action` variable's value is checked. Line 39 evaluates to true since the value of `url.action` is `delete` when we click on Remove

Item. As you can see in line 101, the Remove Item hyperlink passes the URL parameter action=delete to the shopping cart page along with the productid to delete, so line 40 is executed. Deletion is simple; we use the arrayDeleteAt() function and pass the itemlist array and the itemlist array's loop index as parameters to delete that item from the shopping cart.

14. Now, what if we **change** the quantities in the shopping cart and click update? Control starts at line 15, which loops through each item in the itemlist array. Since form.update is defined, line 18 gets the new quantity from the form. The quantity fields are numbered sequentially, as you can see in line 98, as qty_#thisitem#, where thisitem is the array index of the item list. So we can evaluate form.qty_#thisitem# to get the correct value from the form. If the quantity of that item in the cart is greater than 0, the item's quantity is replaced with the new quantity from the form for each item in the shopping cart in line 20. Then itemTotal is calculated and set in the item structure in the shopping cart's itemlist array in lines 21 through 23. If the quantity is not greater than 0, then the item is deleted from the shopping cart in line 25. Since action is not add or delete, control skips to line 56, where total is recalculated in line 58.

15. Note that this form is submitted to itself, as you can see in line 75. Form.proceed is available when the shopping cart is submitted using the Proceed to Checkout button. This is a backup trick. Just in case the user changed quantities and forgot to click on the Update Shopping Cart button before proceeding to checkout, this trick does a quick update to the cart values before it relocates the user to the customer information page. Control starts on line 15, which loops through the itemlist array. Since form.proceed is defined, the quantity is evaluated in line 18, which evaluates form.qty_#thisitem# to get the correct value from the form. The quantity fields are numbered sequentially, as you can see in line 98, as qty_#thisitem#, where thisitem is the array index of the item list. If the new quantity is greater than 0, then lines 20 through 23 reset the quantity in the item structure to the new quantity and totals are recalculated. If the quantity is not greater than 0, then the item is deleted from the cart in line 25. Lines 56 through 59 accumulate the new item totals. Lines 60 through 63 calculate the order level totals and tax and set them in the shopping cart.

16. We no longer need the exclusive lock, so we close the <cflock> tag in line 65.

17. Line 67 sends the customer to the Customer Information page since the shopping cart update is now complete.

18. Now let us see how we create the shopping cart. Line 69 sets the value of the `pagetitle` variable to `Shopping Cart` and line 70 includes the header.cfm file.

19. We now display the shopping cart structure. Since we are going to read from the session, we need a `readonly` lock as in line 71. We don't want to hold the lock unnecessarily, so we copy the session's shopping cart into `variables.shoppingcart` and close the lock. We can use this new local variable to access shopping cart elements.

20. The table is displayed only if there are items in the shopping cart, checked in line 74.

21. A form is created that submits to itself in line 75.

22. Lines 77 through 85 display table headings for the shopping cart table.

23. Line 86 loops through the item list in the shopping cart.

24. Lines 90 through 93 show all the item level attributes— `productid`, `productname`, `brand`, and `price`—from the item structure in the `itemlist` array in the shopping cart structure.

25. Lines 94 through 98 display an input box that is populated with the current item's quantity ordered. The `range` of this field is 0 to the quantity available of that item. Line 97 shows the `message`, which contains the product name, brand, and quantity available. This shows up as a JavaScript alert when the range is violated. Be sure not to split the `message` attribute's value into multiple lines; otherwise you will get a JavaScript error. Line 98 sets the name of this input field. Note the naming convention is `qty_#thisitem#`. This is dynamic and depends on the index of the loop so that the name will be different for different items in the cart.

26. The item total is displayed on line 100 formatted with a dollar sign.

27. Line 101 shows the `Remove Item` hyperlink that takes the customer to this page again (Shopping Cart page) with additional URL variables: `action=delete` and current `productid` to be deleted.

28. Line 104 closes the loop. All item level display is done.

29. Now for the order level display from the shopping cart structure. Line 106 displays the `orderTotal` (without tax or shipping costs); line 110 displays the `tax` amount; and line 114 displays the `orderAmount` (with tax and shipping costs).

30. Line 118 shows the `Update Shopping Cart` button (update quantities). This enables the customer to change quantities and recalculate totals.

31. Line 119 shows the submit button, `Proceed to Checkout`. This allows the customer to proceed with his or her order. But it first takes the customer back to the Shopping Cart page to do a quick update. Then the customer is redirected to the Customer Information page. All that is transparent to the customer, who feels as if he or she goes directly to the Customer Information page as soon as the button is clicked.

32. Line 125 includes the footer template footer.cfm.

Customer Information Page

This page displays a form to accept billing and shipping addresses from the customer. It also accepts the customer's email address so that we can communicate with the customer about his or her order. We would also like to know how the customer wants the order shipped and we should display the amounts we would charge for each shipping method to help the customer make a selection. We then need the customer's payment details: credit card number and expiration date. All these fields should be validated so that we have good data in our database. If the customer came here from the Order Review page, that is, with the shopping cart already populated with these fields in the session, then we should pre-populate the appropriate form fields with those values.

What if the customer came to this page but is not yet prepared to pay for his or her order and wants to take another look at the shopping cart before entering the credit card number? To make sure that the customer does not get stuck on this page if he or she is not ready to proceed, we should provide the customer a hyperlink to go back to the Shopping Cart page to change any selections. We also should provide the customer a link directly to the Product Catalog page so more products can be ordered if the customer so wishes. Most importantly, we should provide the customer with a button to enable him or her to proceed to the Order Review page after entering information in the customer information form.

What about validation? We should make sure that all required fields contain information. The customer should not enter invalid data such as incorrect dates, credit card number, and so on. For the customer's convenience, we should indicate required fields with an `asterisk` * beside them. The code listing on the next page shows the customer information code `GetCustInfo.cfm`. Figure 11.7 shows the customer information screen that this code generates.

GetCustInfo.cfm

```
1.  <cfset pagetitle="Customer Information">
2.  <cfinclude template="header.cfm">
3.  <cfparam name="bfirstname" default="">
4.  <cfparam name="blastname" default="">
5.  <cfparam name="baddress" default="">
6.  <cfparam name="bcity" default="">
7.  <cfparam name="bstate" default="">
8.  <cfparam name="bzip" default="">
9.  <cfparam name="bemail" default="">
10. <cfparam name="sfirstname" default="">
11. <cfparam name="slastname" default="">
12. <cfparam name="saddress" default="">
13. <cfparam name="scity" default="">
14. <cfparam name="sstate" default="">
15. <cfparam name="szip" default="">
16. <cfparam name="semail" default="">
17. <cfparam name="ccard" default="">
18. <cfparam name="edate" default="">
19. <cfparam name="url.msg" default="">
20. <cfif len(url.msg)>
21.    <p align="center">
22.    <font color="red"><cfoutput>** #msg#</cfoutput>
       </font></p>
23. </cfif>
24. <cflock timeout="30" throwontimeout="Yes" type=
       "READONLY" scope="SESSION">
25. <cfset variables.shoppingcart=Duplicate(session.
       shoppingcart)>
26. </cflock>
27. <cfif isDefined("variables.shoppingcart")>
```

```coldfusion
28.   <cfform action="review.cfm" method="post"
        name="GetCustInfo">

29.    <cfoutput>

30.      <table border=1 bordercolor="red" cellspacing=0
           align="center">

31.       <tr>

32.        <td align=left>

33.          <table border=0>

34.          <tr>

35.            <td colspan="2" align="left">

36.              <font size="+1" color="Blue"><b>

37.                Your Billing Address:</b></font>
                   <br><br>

38.            </td>

39.          </tr>

40.          <tr>

41.            <td align="left">First Name:<font
                 color="red">*</font></td>

42.            <cfif isDefined("variables.shoppingcart.
                 billfirstname")>

43.              <cfset bfirstname="#variables.
                   shoppingcart.billfirstname#">

44.            </cfif>

45.            <td align="left">

46.              <cfinput name="billFirstName" type="text"

47.                size="20" required="yes"

48.                value="#bfirstname#"

49.                message="Please enter billing first
                     name">

50.            </td>

51.          </tr>

52.          <tr>
```

```
53.        <td align="left">Last Name:<font
           color="red">*</font></td>
54.        <cfif isDefined("variables.
           shoppingcart.billlastname")>
55.        <cfset blastname="#variables.
           shoppingcart.billlastname#">
56.        </cfif>
57.      <td align="left">
58.        <cfinput name="billLastName" type="text"
59.          size="20" required="yes"
60.          value="#blastname#"
61.          message="Please enter billing last
             name">
62.      </td>
63.    </tr>
64.    <tr>
65.      <td align="left">Street Address:<font
         color="red">*</font></td>
66.        <cfif isDefined("variables.
           shoppingcart.billaddress")>
67.        <cfset baddress="#variables.
           shoppingcart.billaddress#">
68.        </cfif>
69.      <td align="left">
70.        <cfinput name="billaddress" type="text"
71.          size="30" required="yes"
72.          value="#baddress#"
73.          message="Please enter billing
             address">
74.      </td>
75.    </tr>
76.    <tr>
```

```
77.            <td align="left">City:<font
                 color="red">*</font></td>

78.              <cfif isDefined("variables.
                   shoppingcart.billcity")>

79.              <cfset bcity="#variables.shoppingcart.
                   billcity#">

80.              </cfif>

81.            <td align="left">

82.              <cfinput name="billcity" type="text"
                   size="20" required="yes"

83.              value="#bcity#"

84.              message="Please enter billing city">

85.            </td>

86.          </tr>

87.          <tr>

88.            <td align="left">State:<font color=
                 "red">*</font></td>

89.              <cfif isDefined("variables.
                   shoppingcart.billstate")>

90.              <cfset bstate="#variables.
                   shoppingcart.billstate#">

91.              </cfif>

92.            <td align="left">

93.              <cfinput name="billstate" type="text"

94.                size="20" required="yes"

95.                value="#bstate#"

96.                message="Please enter billing state">

97.            </td>

98.          </tr>

99.          <tr>

100.           <td align="left">Zip:<font
                 color="red">*</font></td>
```

```
101.        <cfif isDefined("variables.
              shoppingcart.billzip")>

102.        <cfset bzip="#variables.shoppingcart.
              billzip#">

103.        </cfif>

104.      <td align="left">

105.        <cfinput name="billzip" type="text"
              size="20" required="yes"

106.        value="#bzip#" message="Please enter
              billing zipcode">

107.      </td>

108.    </tr>

109.    <tr>

110.      <td align="left">Email:<font
            color="red">*</font></td>

111.        <cfif isDefined("variables.
            shoppingcart.billemail")>

112.        <cfset bemail="#variables.
            shoppingcart.billemail#">

113.        </cfif>

114.      <td align="left">

115.        <cfinput type="text" name="billemail"

116.          size="30" required="yes"

117.          value="#bemail#"

118.          message="Please enter billing email
              address">

119.      </td>

120.    </tr>

121.    </table>

122.  </td>

123.  <td  align="right">

124.    <table border=0>
```

```
125.        <tr>
126.          <td colspan="2" align="left"><font
                size="+1" color="Blue"><b>
127.            Your Shipping Address:</b></font><br>
128.            <input type="checkbox" name="sameaddress"
                value="1"
129.            <cfif isDefined("variables.shoppingcart.
                sameaddress")
130.              and variables.shoppingcart.sameaddress
                  eq 1>
131.              checked
132.            </cfif>>
133.            <font color="Blue">Use Billing
                Address</font><br>
134.          </td>
135.        </tr>
136.        <tr>
137.          <td align="left">First Name:</td>
138.            <cfif isDefined("variables.shoppingcart.
                shipfirstname")>
139.            <cfset sfirstname="#variables.
                shoppingcart.shipfirstname#">
140.            </cfif>
141.          <td align="left">
142.            <input name="shipFirstName" type="text"
143.            size="20" value="#sfirstname#">
144.          </td>
145.        </tr>
146.        <tr>
147.          <td align="left">Last Name:</td>
148.            <cfif isDefined("variables.shoppingcart.
                shiplastname")>
```

```
149.            <cfset slastname="#variables.
                shoppingcart.shiplastname#">

150.            </cfif>

151.        <td align="left">

152.            <cfinput name="shipLastName" type="text"

153.            size="20" value="#slastname#">

154.        </td>

155.      </tr>

156.      <tr>

157.        <td align="left">Street Address:</td>

158.            <cfif isDefined("variables.shoppingcart.
                shipaddress")>

159.            <cfset saddress="#variables.
                shoppingcart.shipaddress#">

160.            </cfif>

161.        <td align="left">

162.            <cfinput name="shipaddress" type="text"

163.            size="30" value="#saddress#">

164.        </td>

165.      </tr>

166.      <tr>

167.        <td align="left">City:</td>

168.            <cfif isDefined("variables.
                shoppingcart.shipcity")>

169.            <cfset scity="#variables.
                shoppingcart.shipcity#">

170.            </cfif>

171.        <td align="left">

172.            <cfinput name="shipcity" type="text"

173.            size="20" value="#scity#">

174.        </td>
```

```
175.        </tr>
176.        <tr>
177.          <td align="left">State:</td>
178.            <cfif isDefined("variables.shoppingcart.
               shipstate")>
179.            <cfset sstate="#variables.shoppingcart.
               shipstate#">
180.            </cfif>
181.          <td align="left">
182.            <cfinput name="shipstate" type="text"
183.            size="20" value="#sstate#">
184.          </td>
185.        </tr>
186.        <tr>
187.          <td align="left">Zip:</td>
188.          <cfif isDefined("variables.shoppingcart.
             shipzip")>
189.          <cfset szip="#variables.shoppingcart.
             shipzip#">
190.          </cfif>
191.          <td align="left">
192.            <cfinput name="shipzip" type="text"
               size="20" value="#szip#">
193.          </td>
194.        </tr>
195.        <tr>
196.          <td align="left">Email:</td>
197.          <cfif isDefined("variables.shoppingcart.
             shipemail")>
198.          <cfset semail="#variables.shoppingcart.
             shipemail#">
199.            </cfif>
```

```
200.            <td align="left">
201.              <cfinput type="text" name="shipemail"
202.                size="30" value="#semail#">
203.            </td>
204.          </tr>
205.          </table>
206.        </td>
207.      </tr>
208.      <tr>
209.        <td valign="top">
210.        <table border="0">
211.          <tr>
212.            <td colspan=2 align="left">
213.            <font size="+1" color="Blue"><b>Your
                  Shipping Method:</b></font>
214.            </td>
215.          </tr>
216.          <tr>
217.            <td valign=top align="left">
218.              <br><input name="shipMethod" type="radio"
                    value="Ground"
219.              <cfif isDefined("variables.shoppingcart.
                    shipmethod")
220.              and variables.shoppingcart.shipMethod eq
                    "ground">checked
221.              </cfif>>Ground
222.              <br><br><input name="shipMethod"
                    type="radio" value="Air"
223.              <cfif isDefined("variables.shoppingcart.
                    shipmethod")
224.              and variables.shoppingcart.shipMethod eq
                    "air">checked
```

```
225.            </cfif>>Air

226.            <br><br><input name="shipMethod"
                  type="radio" value="Overnight"

227.            <cfif not isDefined("variables.
                  shoppingcart.shipmethod")

228.              or isDefined("variables.shoppingcart.
                    shipmethod")

229.              and variables.shoppingcart.shipMethod eq
                    "overnight">checked

230.            </cfif>>Overnight

231.                <br>

232.          </td>

233.          <td valign=top align="left">

234.            <br>(0.1% * Order Value)

235.            <br><br>(0.2% * Order Value)

236.            <br><br>(0.3% * Order Value)

237.              <br>

238.            </td>

239.        </tr>

240.        </table>

241.      </td>

242.      <td>

243.        <table border="0">

244.        <tr>

245.          <td colspan=2 align="left"><font size="+1"
                color="Blue">

246.              <b>Your Payment Details:</b></font></td>

247.        </tr>

248.        <tr><td align="left">Credit Card Type:</td>

249.          <td align="left">

250.              <br><input name="paymentType" type="radio"
                    value="Visa"
```

```
251.        <cfif not isDefined("variables.
               shoppingcart.paymenttype") or
               isDefined("variables.shoppingcart.
               paymenttype") and variables.
               shoppingcart.paymenttype eq
               "visa">checked</cfif>>Visa Card

252.        <br><input name="paymentType"
               type="radio" value="Discover"

253.        <cfif isDefined("variables.shoppingcart.
               paymenttype") and variables.
               shoppingcart.paymenttype eq
               "discover">checked</cfif>>Discover Card

254.        <br><input name="paymentType"
               type="radio" value="Master"

255.        <cfif isDefined("variables.shoppingcart.
               paymenttype") and variables.
               shoppingcart.paymenttype eq
               "master">checked</cfif>>Master Card

256.        <br>

257.        </td>

258.     </tr>

259.     <tr>

260.        <td align="left">Credit Card ##:<font
               color="red">*</font></td>

261.        <cfif isDefined("variables.
               shoppingcart.creditcard")>

262.          <cfset ccard = "#decrypt(variables.
               shoppingcart.creditcard,
               'encryptionkey')#">

263.          </cfif>

264.        <td align="left"><cfinput name=
               "creditCard"

265.        type="text" value="#ccard#"

266.          required="yes"

267.          validate="creditcard"

268.          message="Please enter a valid credit
               card number"></td>
```

```
269.          </tr>
270.          <tr>
271.            <td align="left">Expiration Date:<font
                   color="red">*</font></td>
272.              <cfif isDefined("variables.
                     shoppingcart.expDate")>
273.                <cfset edate="#variables.
                     shoppingcart.expDate#">
274.              </cfif>
275.            <td align="left"><cfinput name="expDate"
276.                type="text" required="yes"
                      validate="date"
277.                value="#edate#"
278.                message="Please enter a valid
                      future expiration date"></td>
279.          </tr>
280.        </table>
281.      </td>
282.      </tr>
283.      <tr>
284.        <td colspan="2" align="center">
285.          <input type="submit" name="submitbutton"
                 value = "Review Order">
286.        </td>
287.      </tr>
288.    </table>
289.    </cfoutput>
290.  </cfform>
291. </cfif>
292. <cfinclude template="footer.cfm">
```

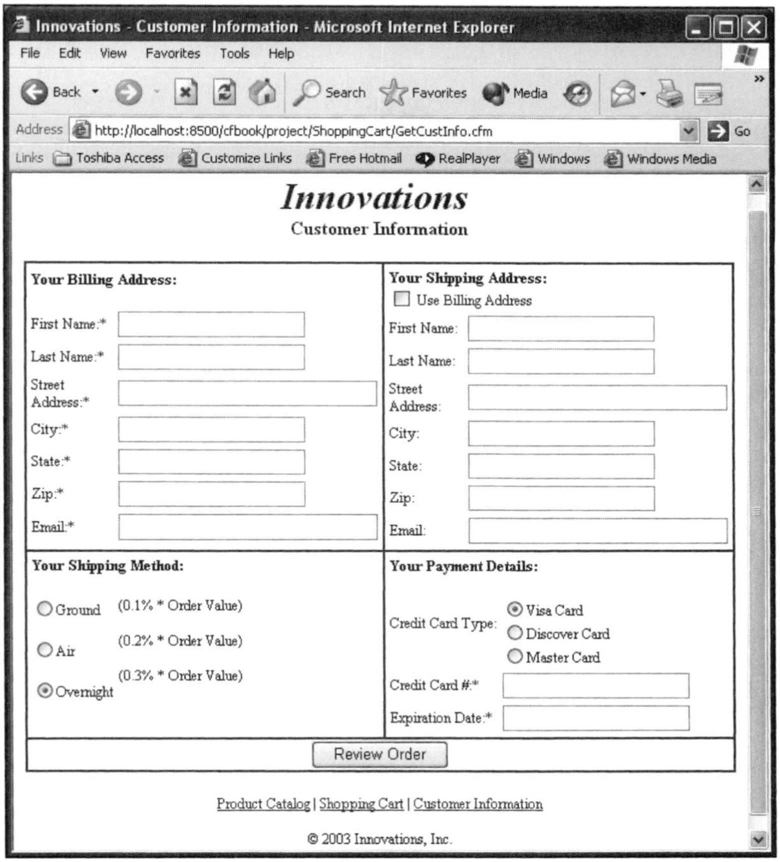

FIGURE 11.7   Customer Information Page

How the Code Works

1. Line 1 sets the `pagetitle` as Customer Information.

2. Line 2 includes the `header.cfm` file.

3. Lines 3 through 18 set variables with default values. These variables are going to be used for populating the form fields with shopping cart values if they exist. Line 19 initializes the variable `url.msg`. This variable holds any error messages that may occur on validating the form on the server side. This is currently being used to validate the credit card expiration date. Lines 20 through 23 display the message held in the variable `msg` in red if it is not empty.

4. Line 24 locks the session scope while it duplicates the session's shopping cart into `variables.shoppingcart` in line 25. This is because we don't want to keep the session locked unnecessarily.

5. Line 27 checks if the shopping cart exists in the session. If it does not exist, then the Customer Information page is not displayed. Line 28 starts a form that, when submitted, takes the customer to the Review page `review.cfm`.

6. The Billing Address section is set up in a table starting on line 30 and ending on line 121. Each field is populated with the values from the shopping cart in the session if it exists. The variables initialized for this purpose on lines 3 through 18 are used here. For example, in line 43, if the shopping cart has a `billfirstname` element, then the local variable `bfirstname` is set to the shopping cart's `billfirstname` for that session. Line 46 is an input text box used to accept billing first name. It is populated with the value of `bfirstname`. Required field validation is done for this field. If this field is left blank, then the message `Please enter billing first name` is displayed as a JavaScript alert box. This is because we used the `<cfinput>` tag for client-side validation. The same goes for all billing address fields.

7. The Shipping Address section starts on line 124 and ends on line 205. Line 128 is a checkbox that sets the value `1` for the variable `sameaddress` if checked. The user checks this checkbox if the billing and shipping addresses are the same. Next, the shipping address values are populated from the session just like the billing address fields are.

8. The Shipping Method is accepted in the table created on line 210 and ending on line 240. Lines 218 through 221 display a radio button for shipping method `Ground`. The button is selected if the session's shopping cart's shipping method is `Ground`. Lines 222 through 225 display a radio button for shipping method `Air`. The button is selected if the session's shopping cart's shipping method is `Air`. Lines 226 through 230 display a radio button for shipping method `Overnight`. If the session's shopping cart's shipping method is `Overnight`, or if no shipping method exists in the session, then this value is selected. In other words, `Overnight` is selected by default. Lines 234 through 236 display the percentage that will be charged for each shipping method: `0.1%` for `Ground`, `0.2%` for `Air`, and `0.3%` for `Overnight`.

9. The Payment Details are accepted next in a table starting on line 243 and ending on line 280. Line 250 displays a radio button for `Visa`

credit card. Just as for shipping method, if the shopping cart's payment type is `Visa`, then this is selected. `Visa` is also selected by default. Line 252 displays a radio button for `Discover` credit card. If the shopping cart's payment type is `Discover`, then this is selected. Line 254 displays a radio button for `Master` credit card. If the shopping cart's payment type is `Master`, then this is selected. Line 262 decrypts the encrypted credit card if it exists in the session. Line 264 displays an input text box to accept the credit card number. It is populated with the decrypted credit card if it exists. Required field validation and credit card validation are performed here. On lines 272 through 274, if the credit card expiration date exists in the session, then the input box on lines 275 through 278 is populated with this value. Required field validation is done here. Date validation to check that the expiration date is a future date is done in the Order Review page and that is why we need the `msg` variable.

10. Line 285 has a `submit` button to take the customer to the Order Review page.

11. Line 292 includes the `footer.cfm` file.

Order Review Page

The Order Review page is the page where the customer looks at all the information he or she has entered and all the items that have been selected. In this page the shipping cost is calculated based on the shipping method selected earlier.

On this page, the customer sees the entire order with the final order totals after shipping cost and tax are added. This is the amount the customer will be charged for this order. The customer can review all the information entered and commit his or her order if satisfied. The customer should be able to change any selections at this point so that the shopping cart can be populated with items that he or she is totally satisfied with. To achieve this, from this page it is very important that we offer the customer options to go back and modify any entries. The customer may just want to make changes to the quantities or remove items. For that a hyperlink to the shopping cart is needed. Maybe while reviewing the order the customer found that his or her email address was typed incorrectly. To help the customer modify this, we need to provide a link to the Customer Information page, through which the customer can make changes to the address, payment, and shipping information. Lastly, we need to provide the customer with a way to confirm his or her order when totally satisfied. The code listing below shows the Order Review code (`review.cfm`). Figure 11.8 shows the Review Order screen.

Review.cfm

```
1.  <cfparam name="form.billfirstname" default="">
2.  <cfparam name="form.billlastname" default="">
3.  <cfparam name="form.shipfirstname" default="">
4.  <cfparam name="form.shiplastname" default="">
5.  <cfparam name="form.shipmethod" default="">
6.  <cfparam name="form.paymenttype" default="">
7.  <cfparam name="form.creditcard" default="">
8.  <cfparam name="form.expdate" default="">
9.  <cfparam name="form.shipaddress" default="">
10. <cfparam name="form.shipcity" default="">
11. <cfparam name="form.shipstate" default="">
12. <cfparam name="form.shipzip" default="">
13. <cfparam name="form.billaddress" default="">
14. <cfparam name="form.billcity" default="">
15. <cfparam name="form.billstate" default="">
16. <cfparam name="form.billzip" default="">
17. <cfparam name="form.billemail" default="">
18. <cfparam name="form.shipemail" default="">
19. <cfparam name="form.sameaddress" default="">
20. <cfset encryptionkey="encryptionkey">
21. <cfset pagetitle="Order Review">
22. <cfinclude template="header.cfm">
23. <cfif isDefined("session.shoppingcart")>
24.    <cflock scope="session" throwontimeout="No"
          type="exclusive" timeout="30">
25.       <cfscript>
26.          session.shoppingcart.shipmethod = form.shipmethod;
```

```
27.     session.shoppingcart.paymenttype = form.
           paymenttype;
28.     session.shoppingcart.creditcard =
           encrypt(form.creditcard,encryptionkey);
29.     session.shoppingcart.expdate = form.expdate;
30.     session.shoppingcart.billfirstname = form.
           billfirstname;
31.     session.shoppingcart.billlastname = form.
           billlastname;
32.     session.shoppingcart.billaddress = form.
           billaddress;
33.     session.shoppingcart.billcity = form.billcity;
34.     session.shoppingcart.billstate = form.billstate;
35.     session.shoppingcart.billzip = form.billzip;
36.     session.shoppingcart.billemail = form.billemail;
37.     if (form.shipfirstname eq "" or form.
           shiplastname eq "" or
38.       form.shipaddress eq "" or form.shipaddress eq
             "" or
39.       form.shipcity eq "" or form.shipstate eq "" or
40.       form.shipzip eq "" or form.sameaddress eq 1) {
41.         session.shoppingcart.shipfirstname =
               form.billfirstname;
42.         session.shoppingcart.shiplastname =
               form.billlastname;
43.         session.shoppingcart.shipaddress = form.
               billaddress;
44.         session.shoppingcart.shipcity = form.billcity;
45.         session.shoppingcart.shipstate = form.
               billstate;
46.         session.shoppingcart.shipzip = form.billzip;
47.         session.shoppingcart.shipemail = form.
               billemail;
```

```
48.          session.shoppingcart.sameaddress =
                form.sameaddress;
49.        } else {
50.          session.shoppingcart.shipfirstname =
                form.shipfirstname;
51.          session.shoppingcart.shiplastname =
                form.shiplastname;
52.          session.shoppingcart.shipaddress =
                form.shipaddress;
53.          session.shoppingcart.shipcity = form.
                shipcity;
54.          session.shoppingcart.shipstate = form.
                shipstate;
55.          session.shoppingcart.shipzip = form.shipzip;
56.          session.shoppingcart.shipemail =
                form.shipemail;
57.        }
58.        if (form.shipMethod eq "overnight")
59.          session.shoppingcart.shipcost = session.
                shoppingcart.ordertotal * 0.003;
60.        else if (form.shipMethod eq "air")
61.          session.shoppingcart.shipcost = session.
                shoppingcart.ordertotal * 0.002;
62.        else if (form.shipMethod eq "ground")
63.          session.shoppingcart.shipcost = session.
                shoppingcart.ordertotal * 0.001;
64.        session.shoppingcart.orderAmount =
                session.shoppingcart.orderAmount
65.          + session.shoppingcart.shipcost;
66.      </cfscript>
67.    </cflock>
68.    <cflock timeout="30" throwontimeout="Yes"
          type="readonly" scope="session">
```

```
69.     <CFSET variables.shoppingcart=Duplicate
            (session.shoppingcart)>

70.  </cflock>

71.  <cfset comparison = DateCompare(form.expdate, now(),
        'm')>

72.  <cfif comparison lt 0>

73.    <cfset msg="Credit Card expiry date must be a
            future date">

74.    <cflocation url="GetCustInfo.cfm?msg=
            <cfoutput>#msg#</cfoutput>">

75.  </cfif>

76.  <cfoutput>

77.    <table border = "1" cellspacing = "0" width=65%
            bordercolor="red" align="center">

78.    <tr>

79.      <td colspan=6 align=center>

80.        <font size="+1" color="Blue"><b>Your Order
            Details</b></font>

81.      </td>

82.    </tr>

83.    <tr>

84.      <td><b>Product Code</b></td>

85.      <td><b>Product Name</b></td>

86.      <td><b>Brand</b></td>

87.      <td><b>Unit Price</b></td>

88.      <td><b>Quantity</b></td>

89.      <td><b>Total Cost</b></td>

90.    </tr>

91.    <cfloop index="thisitem" from="1"

92.      to="#ArrayLen(variables.shoppingCart.itemlist)#">

93.    <tr>
```

```
94.        <cfoutput>

95.        <td>#variables.shoppingCart.itemlist[thisitem].
           productid#</td>

96.        <td>#variables.shoppingCart.itemlist[thisitem].
           productname#</td>

97.        <td>#variables.shoppingCart.itemlist[thisitem].
           brand#</td>

98.        <td align=right> #dollarformat(variables.
           shoppingCart.itemlist[thisitem].price)#</td>

99.        <td align=right>#variables.shoppingCart.
           itemlist[thisitem].qty#</td>

100.       <td align="right"> #dollarformat(variables.
           shoppingcart.itemlist[thisitem].itemtotal)#
           </td>

101.       </cfoutput>

102.   </tr>

103.   </cfloop>

104.   <tr>

105.     <td colspan=5><b>Order Total:</b></td>

106.     <td align=right> <cfoutput> #dollarformat
           (variables.shoppingcart.orderTotal)#
           </cfoutput></td>

107.   </tr>

108.   <tr>

109.     <td colspan=5><b>Order Tax:</b></td>

110.     <td align=right> <cfoutput>#dollarformat
           (variables.shoppingcart.tax)# </cfoutput> </td>

111.   </tr>

112.   <tr>

113.     <td colspan=5><b>Shipping Cost:</b>(Shipping
           Method: #variables.shoppingcart.shipmethod#)
           </td>

114.     <td align=right> <cfoutput> #dollarformat
           (variables.shoppingcart.shipcost)#
           </cfoutput> </td>
```

```
115.    </tr>
116.    <tr>
117.      <td colspan=5><b>Total Order Amount:</b></td>
118.      <td align=right> <cfoutput> #dollarformat
           (variables.shoppingcart.orderAmount)#
           </cfoutput> </td>
119.    </tr>
120.    <tr>
121.   </table>
122.   <br /><br />
123.   <table border=1 bordercolor="red" cellspacing=0
          align="center">
124.   <tr><td colspan=6 align=center>
125.   <font size="+1" color="Blue"><b>Your Address and
          Payment Details </b> </font> </td>
126.   </tr>
127.   <tr>
128.     <td><b>Billing Address:</b></td>
129.     <td colspan=2>
130.        #variables.shoppingcart.billfirstname#
              #variables.shoppingcart.billlastname#<br />
131.        #variables.shoppingcart.billaddress#,
132.        #variables.shoppingcart.billcity#,
133.        #variables.shoppingcart.billstate#,
134.        #variables.shoppingcart.billzip# <br />
135.        Email address: #variables.shoppingcart.billemail#
136.     </td>
137.   </tr>
138.   <tr>
139.     <td><b>Shipping Address:</b></td>
140.     <td colspan=2>
```

```
141.        #variables.shoppingcart.shipfirstname#
               #variables.shoppingcart.shiplastname# <br />

142.        #variables.shoppingcart.shipaddress#,

143.        #variables.shoppingcart.shipcity#,

144.        #variables.shoppingcart.shipstate#,

145.        #variables.shoppingcart.shipzip# <br />

146.        Email address: #variables.shoppingcart.
               shipemail#

147.     </td>

148.   </tr>

149.   <tr>

150.     <td><b>Payment Type:</b></td>

151.     <cfset displaycc = "">

152.     <cfset ccright = right(form.creditcard,4)>

153.     <cfloop index=i from=1 to="#len(form.
             creditcard)-4#">

154.        <cfset displaycc = displaycc & "X">

155.     </cfloop>

156.     <cfset displaycc = displaycc & ccright>

157.     <td>#variables.shoppingcart.paymenttype# Card
             Number: #displaycc#</td>

158.   </tr>

159.   <tr>

160.     <td><b>Expiration Date:</b></td>

161.     <td>#variables.shoppingcart.expdate#</td>

162.   </tr>

163.   </table>

164. </cfoutput>

165. <form action=saveorder.cfm name="confirmorder">

166.   <p align="center"><input type="submit"
           name="submitbutton" value="Confirm Order"></p>

167. </form>
```

168. `</cfif>`

169. `<cfinclude template="footer.cfm">`

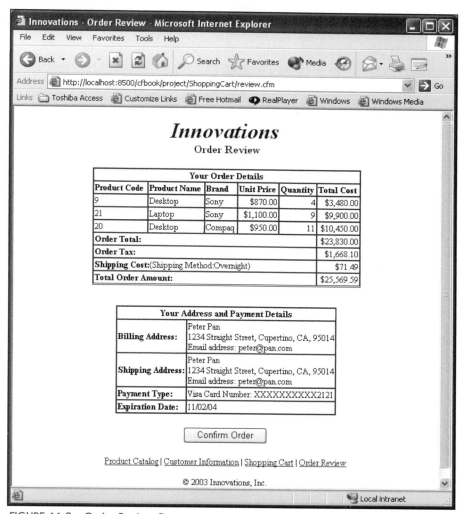

FIGURE 11.8   Order Review Page

How the Code Works

1. All the form fields are given default values to protect from errors (lines 1 through 19).

2. `Encryptionkey` is set to the value `encryptionkey` in line 20. This value should actually be read from a database table in real-life appli-

cations and should contain a value that is decided by your organization. Here we have hard-coded the value for simplicity.

3. Line 21 sets `pagetitle` to the value `Order Review` and line 22 includes the `header.cfm` file.

4. This page is rendered only if the shopping cart exists in the session, checked in line 23.

5. On line 24 we need an exclusive lock on the session while we are writing all the form variables from the Customer Information page to the session.

6. Lines 26 through 36 set the billing address fields into the session's shopping cart.

7. The variable `Sameaddress` is sent over as `1` if the checkbox was checked in the Customer Information page indicating that the shipping and billing addresses are the same. If `sameaddress` is `1` or if the shipping address fields are missing or incomplete, then we need to set the session's shipping address to the form's billing address fields (lines 41 through 48). If shipping address is complete, then the shipping address fields in the shopping cart are set to the shipping address fields from the form (lines 50 through 56).

8. `Shipcost` (shipping cost) is calculated and set in the shopping cart (lines 58 through 63) based on the shipping method selected in the customer information page. Charges are `0.1%` for `Ground`, `0.2%` for `Air`, and `0.3%` for `Overnight`. Shipping cost is added to `orderAmount` in line 64.

9. On line 67 we close the lock because we're done setting the shopping cart elements. Line 68 reopens a lock, this time `readonly` because we want to store the shopping cart locally in `variables.shoppingcart` so we can use it for display.

10. Expiry Date validation: On lines 71 through 75, the credit card expiry date entered in the form is compared with the current date with month precision. If the credit card expiry date is less than the current date, then the variable `msg` is set to an error message. The customer is relocated back to the Customer Information page to correct this. In the Customer Information page, this message is displayed in red if it exists.

11. Order Details are displayed in a table. First the item headings are displayed (lines 84 through 89). Line 91 loops through the `itemlist array` and lines 95 through 100 display elements of the `item structure` including item totals.

12. Line 106 displays the order total. Line 110 displays the tax, line 113 displays the shipping method, line 114 displays the shipping cost, and line 118 displays the total order amount.

13. The billing address is displayed on lines 130 through 135. The shipping address is displayed on lines 141 through 146.

14. The credit card is masked with XXXX so that it shows only the last four digits in line 157. Line 152 extracts the last four digits of the credit card number. The loop on lines 153 through 155 displays X's for first part of the credit card number. The credit card expiry date is displayed on line 161.

15. We have a form that contains a `submit` button on lines 165 to 167. This takes the customer to the Confirmation page, which saves the order.

16. Line 169 includes the `footer.cfm` file.

Order Confirmation Page

This page displays a confirmation to the customer. The customer is given his or her new order number. An email should be sent to the customer to confirm all the details of the order. The order should be saved in the database along with all the ordered items, quantities, shipping cost, tax, totals, shipping and billing addresses, payment details, and shipping method. This page also should update product stock so that the quantity on hand is reduced by the quantity ordered. To encourage the customer to continue shopping with us, we should provide a hyperlink to go to the Product Catalog again. An important thing to remember is to clear the session at this point. We also must not make any other hyperlinks available here, as the order that the customer has just confirmed cannot be modified at this point. The code listing below shows the order confirmation code (`saveorder.cfm`); Figure 11.9 shows the confirmation screen.

SaveOrder.cfm

```
1. <cfset pagetitle="Order Confirmation">
2. <cfinclude template="header.cfm">
3. <cfif isDefined("session.shoppingcart")>
4.        <cflock timeout="30" throwontimeout="Yes"
             type="readonly" scope="session">
```

```
5.            <cfset variables.shoppingcart=
                 Duplicate(session.shoppingcart)>

6.        </cflock>

7.    <cfif isDefined("variables.shoppingcart")>

8.      <cftransaction>

9.        <cfquery Name = "savebillingAddress" DataSource
             = "#dsn#">

10.         insert into customer

11.         (addresstype, firstname, lastname, address,
               city, state, zip, email)

12.         values

13.         (<cfqueryparam cfsqltype="cf_sql_varchar"
               value="billing">,

14.         <cfqueryparam cfsqltype="cf_sql_varchar"
               value="#variables.shoppingcart.
               billfirstname#">,

15.         <cfqueryparam cfsqltype="cf_sql_varchar"
               value="#variables.shoppingcart.
               billlastname#">,

16.         <cfqueryparam cfsqltype="cf_sql_varchar"
               value="#variables.shoppingcart.
               billaddress#">,

17.         <cfqueryparam cfsqltype="cf_sql_varchar"
               value="#variables.shoppingcart.billcity#">,

18.         <cfqueryparam cfsqltype="cf_sql_varchar"
               value="#variables.shoppingcart.billstate#">,

19.         <cfqueryparam cfsqltype="cf_sql_varchar"
               value="#variables.shoppingcart.billzip#">,

20.         <cfqueryparam cfsqltype="cf_sql_varchar"
               value="#variables.shoppingcart.billemail#">)

21.       </cfquery>

22.       <cfquery name="getBillingAddressID" DataSource =
             "#dsn#">

23.         select max(addressid) as billAddressID

24.         from customer
```

```
25.        where addresstype=<cfqueryparam
               cfsqltype="cf_sql_varchar" value="billing">

26.      </cfquery>

27.      <cfquery Name = "saveShippingAddress" DataSource
            = "#dsn#">

28.        insert into customer

29.        (addresstype, firstname, lastname, address,
               city, state, zip, email)

30.        values

31.        (<cfqueryparam cfsqltype="cf_sql_varchar"
               value="shipping">,

32.        <cfqueryparam cfsqltype="cf_sql_varchar"
               value="#variables.shoppingcart.shipfirstname#">

33.        <cfqueryparam cfsqltype="cf_sql_varchar"
               value="#variables.shoppingcart.shiplastname#">,

34.        <cfqueryparam cfsqltype="cf_sql_varchar"
               value="#variables.shoppingcart.shipaddress#">,

35.        <cfqueryparam cfsqltype="cf_sql_varchar"
               value="#variables.shoppingcart.shipcity#">,

36.        <cfqueryparam cfsqltype="cf_sql_varchar"
               value="#variables.shoppingcart.shipstate#">,

37.        <cfqueryparam cfsqltype="cf_sql_varchar"
               value="#variables.shoppingcart.shipzip#">,

38.        <cfqueryparam cfsqltype="cf_sql_varchar"
               value="#variables.shoppingcart.shipemail#">)

39.      </cfquery>

40.      <cfquery name="getShippingAddressID" DataSource
            = "#dsn#">

41.        select max(addressid) as shipAddressID

42.        from customer

43.        where addresstype=<cfqueryparam cfsqltype=
               "cf_sql_varchar" value="shipping">

44.      </cfquery>

45.      <cfquery Name = "saveOrder" DataSource =
            "#dsn#">
```

```
46.        insert into [order]

47.        (orderDate, billingAddressID, shippingAddressID,

48.        orderAmount, paymentType,

49.        creditCardNumber, expirationDate,
              shippingMethod,

50.        shippingCost, taxes, orderStatus)

51.        values (now(),

52.        <cfqueryparam cfsqltype="cf_sql_integer"
              value="#getBillingAddressId.billAddressId#">,

53.        <cfqueryparam cfsqltype="cf_sql_integer"
              value="#getshippingAddressId.shipAddressID#">,

54.        <cfqueryparam cfsqltype="cf_sql_money"
              value="#variables.shoppingcart.orderAmount#">,

55.        <cfqueryparam cfsqltype="cf_sql_varchar"
              value="#variables.shoppingcart.paymentType#">,

56.        <cfqueryparam cfsqltype="cf_sql_varchar"
              value="#variables.shoppingcart.creditcard#">,

57.        <cfqueryparam cfsqltype="cf_sql_date"
              value="#variables.shoppingcart.expDate#">,

58.        <cfqueryparam cfsqltype="cf_sql_varchar"
              value="#variables.shoppingcart.shipmethod#">,

59.        <cfqueryparam cfsqltype="cf_sql_money"
              value="#variables.shoppingcart.shipcost#">,

60.        <cfqueryparam cfsqltype="cf_sql_money"
              value="#variables.shoppingcart.tax#">,

61.        <cfqueryparam cfsqltype="cf_sql_varchar"
              value="new">)

62.     </cfquery>

63.     <cfquery Name = "getOrderID" DataSource = "#dsn#">

64.        select max(orderid) as thisorderid

65.        from [order];

66.     </cfquery>

67.     <cfloop index="thisitem" from="1"
```

```
68.          to="#ArrayLen(variables.shoppingCart.
               itemlist)#">

69.      <cfquery Name = "saveOrderItems" DataSource =
               "#dsn#">

70.          insert into [orderItem]

71.          (orderId, itemnumber, productid, productqty,
               itemamount)

72.          values (

73.          <cfqueryparam cfsqltype="cf_sql_integer"
               value="#getorderid.thisorderid#">,

74.          <cfqueryparam cfsqltype="cf_sql_integer"
               value="#thisitem#">,

75.          <cfqueryparam cfsqltype="cf_sql_integer"
               value="#variables.shoppingcart.
               itemlist[thisitem].productid#">,

76.          <cfqueryparam cfsqltype="cf_sql_integer"
               value="#variables.shoppingcart.
               itemlist[thisitem].qty#">,

77.          <cfqueryparam cfsqltype="cf_sql_integer"
               value="#variables.shoppingcart.
               itemlist[thisitem].itemtotal#">)

78.      </cfquery>

79.      <cfquery Name = "updateStock" DataSource =
               "#dsn#">

80.          update [products]

81.          set productQty = productQty -

82.          <cfqueryparam cfsqltype="cf_sql_integer"
               value="#variables.shoppingcart.
               itemlist[thisitem].qty#">

83.          where productid =

84.          <cfqueryparam cfsqltype="cf_sql_integer"
               value="#variables.shoppingcart.
               itemlist[thisitem].productid#">

85.      </cfquery>

86.    </cfloop>
```

```
87.     </cftransaction>
88.     <cfmail to="#variables.shoppingcart.billemail#"
89.       from="Innovations" subject="Order Confirmation">
90.       <cfmailpart type="text">
91.         Dear #variables.shoppingcart.billFirstname#,
92.
93.         This is a confirmation that your order was
              received at Innovations today!
94.         Here are your order details:
95.
96.         Order Number #getorderid.thisorderid#
97.
98.         Bill To: #variables.shoppingcart.billFirstname#
              #variables.shoppingcart.billLastname#,
              #variables.shoppingcart.billaddress#,
              #variables.shoppingcart.billcity#,
              #variables.shoppingcart.billstate#
              #variables.shoppingcart.billzip#
99.
100.        Ship To: #variables.shoppingcart.shipFirstname#
              #variables.shoppingcart.shipLastname#,
              #variables.shoppingcart.shipaddress#,
              #variables.shoppingcart.shipcity#,
              #variables.shoppingcart.shipstate#
              #variables.shoppingcart.shipzip#
101.
102.        Items Ordered:
103.        Item        Quantity            Total
104.        <cfloop index="thisitem" from="1"
              to="#ArrayLen(variables.shoppingCart.
              itemlist)#">
105.          #variables.shoppingcart.itemlist[thisitem].
                productname# #variables.shoppingcart.
                itemlist[thisitem].qty#
```

```
             #numberformat(variables.shoppingcart.item
             list[thisitem].itemtotal,"$____.__")#
106.      </cfloop>
107.
108.      Order Tax        : #numberformat(variables.
             shoppingcart.Tax,"$____.__")#
109.      Shipping Cost    : #numberformat(variables.
             shoppingcart.shipCost,"$____.__")#
110.      Order Total      : #numberformat(variables.
             shoppingcart.orderAmount,"$____.__")#
111.      Shipping Method : #variables.shoppingcart.
             shipMethod#
112.      Payment Type     : #variables.shoppingcart.
             PaymentType# Card
113.
114.      Thank you for your order!
115.    </cfmailpart>
116.    <cfmailpart type="html">
117.      Dear #variables.shoppingcart.
             billFirstname#,<br /><br />
118.      This is a confirmation that your order was
             received at Innovations today!<br />
119.      Here are your order details:<br /><br />
120.      <b>Order Number #getorderid.thisorderid#
             </b><br /><br />
121.      <table border=0 cellspacing=0 cellpadding=0>
122.      <tr><td valign="top"><b>Bill To:</b> </td>
123.        <td>#variables.shoppingcart.billFirstname#
             #variables.shoppingcart.billLastname#, <br />
124.        #variables.shoppingcart.billaddress#,
125.        #variables.shoppingcart.billcity#,
126.        #variables.shoppingcart.billstate#
             #variables.shoppingcart.billzip#</td>
```

```
127.        </tr>

128.        <tr></tr>

129.        <tr><td valign=top><b>Ship To:</b></td>

130.          <td>#variables.shoppingcart.shipFirstname#
                 #variables.shoppingcart.shipLastname#, <br />

131.            #variables.shoppingcart.shipaddress#,

132.            #variables.shoppingcart.shipcity#,

133.            #variables.shoppingcart.shipstate#
                 #variables.shoppingcart.shipzip#</td>

134.        </tr>

135.        <tr></tr>

136.        <tr><td><b>Item Name</b></td><td><b>
               Quantity</b></td><td><b>Total</b></td>
               </tr>

137.        <cfloop index="thisitem" from="1" to="#ArrayLen
               (variables.shoppingCart.itemlist)#">

138.          <tr>

139.            <td>#variables.shoppingcart.
                   itemlist[thisitem].productname#</td>

140.            <td>#variables.shoppingcart.
                   itemlist[thisitem].qty#</td>

141.            <td align="right"> #numberformat(variables.
                   shoppingcart.itemlist[thisitem].
                   itemtotal,"$____.__")#</td>

142.          </tr>

143.        </cfloop>

144.        <tr><td>Order Tax:</td><td></td><td
               align="right">#numberformat(variables.
               shoppingcart.Tax,"$____.__")#</td></tr>

145.        <tr><td>Shipping Cost:</td><td></td><td
               align="right">#numberformat(variables.
               shoppingcart.shipCost,"$____.__")#</td></tr>

146.        <tr><td><b>Order Total:</b></td><td></td>
               <td align="right"><b>#numberformat
```

```
                  (variables.shoppingcart.orderAmount,
                  "$____.__")#</b></td></tr>
147.              <tr></tr>
148.              <tr><td><br />Shipping Method:</td><td>
                  <br /> #variables.shoppingcart.shipMethod#
                  </td></tr>
149.              <tr><td>Payment Type:</td><td>#variables.
                  shoppingcart.PaymentType# Card</td></tr>
150.              </table>
151.              <p>Thank you for your order!</p>
152.            </cfmailpart>
153.          </cfmail>
154.          <br /><b>Your order number is
155.          <cfoutput>#getorderid.thisorderid#</cfoutput></b>
156.          <br /><br />You will receive an email with your
                  order details shortly.<br>
157.          Thank you for your purchase!<br /><br />
158.          <cfset clearsession=StructClear(session)>
159.        </cfif>
160. </cfif>
161. <br>
162. <cfinclude template="footer.cfm">
```

How the Code Works

1. Line 1 sets the pagetitle to Order Confirmation. Line 2 includes the header.cfm file.

2. Line 4 locks the code that accesses the shopping cart in the session. We need a read-only lock as we just want to save the shopping cart as a local variable for display purposes. This page is executed and rendered only if the shopping cart exists in the session.

3. Line 8 starts a transaction. We want all the queries to succeed before we commit any part of the order to the database. If there is any failure, we want all the queries to roll back so that the data are consistent.

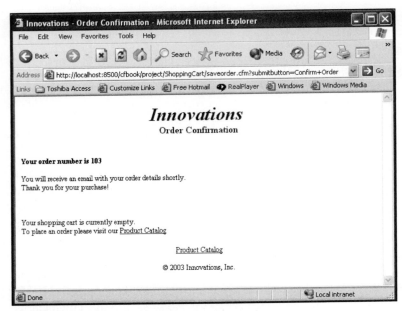

FIGURE 11.9   Order Confirmation Page

4. Lines 9 through 21 save the billing address fields into the Customer table with `addresstype = billing`. Lines 22 through 26 get the `billingAddressID` of the billing address just inserted.

5. Lines 27 through 39 save the shipping address into the Customer table with `addresstype = shipping`. Lines 40 through 44 get the `shippingAddressID` of the address just inserted.

6. Lines 45 through 62 insert the order into the Order table. The `orderDate` is sent as `now()`, which is the current date. The `shippingAddressId` and `billingAddressId` are inserted as foreign key values for the Customer table into the Order table. The `orderStatus` is inserted as `new`. Lines 63 through 66 get the `OrderID` of the order just inserted.

7. Now we save order items. Lines 67 and 68 loop through all the items in the shopping cart's `itemlist`. For each item, lines 69 through 78 insert the order item details from the shopping cart into the OrderItem table. Note that the `itemnumber` is set as the array index of the `itemlist` array. For each item, lines 79 through 85 update the quantity of the product in the Products table by subtracting the ordered quantity from the available product quantity.

8. The transaction ends on line 87 after all the items are successfully inserted.

9. An email is sent to the customer's billing email address to confirm his order (lines 88 through 153). All the order details are sent in this email to the customer. Notice the **multipart** email feature used. The <cfmailpart> tag on line 90 formats the email for text-only email clients. This tag is closed on line 115. The <cfmailpart> tag on line 116 formats the email in HTML for email clients that can accept HTML email. This tag is closed on line 152.

10. A confirmation page is displayed with the new orderid and a short thank-you message informing the customer that he or she will receive confirmation by email shortly (lines 154 through 157).

11. Line 158 clears the session so that the shopping cart is no longer available in the session. So now, if you hit the Back button and try to submit again, the shopping cart will not be available and you will not be able to duplicate your order. Instead, you get a message saying that your shopping cart is empty with a link to the Product Catalog page.

12. Line 162 includes the footer.cfm file.

Shopping Cart Enhancements

You can perform the following suggested simple improvements to the shopping cart application. You also can add to this list of enhancements and do something on your own.

Product Catalog Page

1. Add a company logo image to your header include file. The logo should appear on every page of the site.

2. Hyperlink the product names to a page showing details of the product. Pass the productID as a URL variable to the Product Details page so that the page knows which product to get details for. Add a field in the Products table to store details about each product.

3. Add images to the Product Catalog page. Add a field in the Products table to store an image path for a small image of the product. Show an image for each product in the product listing and a larger image in the Product Details page.

4. Modify the method in the CFC used by the Product Catalog page and get the product image path and display the product image.

5. Add a method to the component used by the Product Catalog page to get the product description for the Product Details page. Also get the large image for that page through that query.

6. Use a custom tag to display the Add to cart button or link.

Customer Information Page

1. Create a database table of states. Display and populate the drop down list of state names from the database for address fields in the Customer Information page. This would look better than expecting the customer to key in the state name. Use components (you can use the same component as product catalog and add a new method) to query the state names from the States table.

2. The expiration date of the credit card is currently accepted in the format mm/dd/yy. Since we need to accept only the month and year, use date functions to provide drop-down lists for month and year so that the customer just needs to select.

3. Using the value that we set for sameaddress in the shopping cart, check or uncheck the checkbox for same shipping and billing address depending on the value of this element.

Order Review Page

1. Combine the month and year accepted in the Customer Information page (as drop-down lists for month and year) and modify the date compare() function to compare the entered date with the current date so that it compares only month and year.

2. Create a table called Parameters and save shipping costs for each type of shipping in that table: Shipping-Ground = 0.001, shipping-air = 0.002, and shipping-overnight = 0.003. Also store tax in the same table. Use a component for your query.

3. The Encryption key should come from the database. So create a table called Key, put the encryption key there, and read it from there. We use a separate table for this so that it can have restricted access. Again use a component for your query.

Order Confirmation Page

1. Use a component with functions that save the order, items, and customer information and update the product quantity.

Other Suggested Projects

Project 1: Online Customer Service Application

A customer service interface can be designed to allow customer service representatives to view orders by searching specific criteria. Here are the guidelines. You can build it as you think best.

Ship Orders

Allow the customer service representative to change the status of the orders. Once the status is changed from New to Shipped, an email should go to the customer telling him or her that the product has been shipped. Normally it is at this time that the credit card is charged.

Cancel Orders

Allow the customer service representative to cancel orders that have not yet been shipped. You would have a new status called Canceled. Do not allow the status of canceled orders to be changed to Shipped status. Also, do not allow canceling of shipped orders.

Order Search

Design an order search form that helps you serve your customers better. The form will access the Order, OrderItems, and Customer tables and retrieve orders matching some criteria. Some search criteria can be a combination of one or more of the following:

- Order number.
- First and last names (shipping and/or billing address).
- Order date range.
- Credit card number.
- Order status.

Graphs and Charts

Generate charts and graphs of the number of orders each month or the total number of individual products ordered.

Project 2: Online Student Course Registration

Design software that would allow students to register for online courses. Please go ahead and add more or less complexity based on the guidelines on the following page.

Database Design

1. `Courses table`. Fields: course ID, course name, start date, end date, maximum number of students, instructor ID, class number, course description, fees.

2. `Instructor table`. Fields: instructor ID, instructor name (any other instructor-related attributes).

3. `Student table`. Fields: studentID, student name, address, telephone number, email address, date of birth, credit card number, expiration date.

4. `StudentCourses table`. Fields: student ID, course ID, grade.

Course Listing Page

Display a list of courses to the student using a component. Show course ID, name, start date, end date, max number of students, instructor name, class number, and fees. Hyperlink course name to course description. Use components. Give an `Add to Cart` functionality so that students can select courses.

Shopping Cart Page

Allow the student to remove selected courses. Do not allow overlapping courses. Allow only one course per date range. Hint: Check start date and end date. If end-date of first course is less than start-date of second course, then display, "You already selected a course during that period". Display total fee per course and total for all selected courses. Don't have a quantity field (does not apply here). Have a **Proceed** button. Provide a hyperlink to the course list page.

Student Profile Page

Accept student's name, address, email address, telephone number, credit card number, expiration date, and date of birth. Provide a Review button. Provide hyperlinks to the shopping cart and to the course list page.

Review Page

Display selected course lists, amounts, and student profile. Allow modification of all items displayed on this page. Provide a `Confirmation` button.

Confirmation Page

Add student details to the Student table. Add selected courses with student ID to the StudentCourses table. Email the student with his student ID and courses information including fees that will be charged to his credit card.

Add any further enhancements and features that you like to this application.

Summary

In this chapter, you learned about e-commerce and the various parts of an e-commerce website. You learned that just a shopping cart is not enough to build an e-commerce website. You need a payment processor, fulfillment house, customer service applications, and much more.

In this chapter, the shopping cart application has been completed for you. The code has been presented in detail with screen shots and explanations of how each program works.

You were given some suggestions for enhancing the shopping cart application. You should implement these so that you have experience with such real-world applications. You also could think of more enhancements to this software and implement them.

Finally, you were given two projects that you can work on independently: Online Customer Service Application and Online Student Course Registration. Implement these to practice and enhance your knowledge.

Key Terms

business to business (B2B)	e-commerce	hyperlink
business to consumer (B2C)	electronic commerce	merchant account
credit card authorization system	fulfillment system	session
customer service		

SQL | Commands

The purpose of this appendix is to provide students with a list of commonly used SQL commands. Please see the following online references for additional information: http://www.w3schools.com/sql/default.asp, http://www.htmlcenter.com/tutorials/tutorials.cfm/157/General/, and http://www.aspalliance.com/habal/sql/default.asp.

Name	Description	Example
ALL_VIEWS	Shows all views accessible to a user.	ALL_VIEWS
ALTER TABLE	Adds a column to a table. Here we add a column—Address—to the Customer table.	ALTER TABLE Customer ADD Address varchar2(20)
AVERAGE	Used for finding the average in a data set. Supposing we want to find the average hours worked by employees, we use the AVG function and select the attribute hours from the Employee table.	SELECT AVG(Hours) FROM Employee;
COMMENTS	We can include comments in SQL to enhance readability.	/* first comment style */ -- second comment style
COUNT	Lets you view the number of rows in the result set. We may also count the occurrences of attributes.	SELECT COUNT(*) FROM student; SELECT COUNT(class) FROM Student;
CREATE SYNONYM	Creates a synonym for a table.	CREATE SYNONYM x FOR y;
CREATE TABLE	Allows you to create a table in which you may store information.	CREATE TABLE employee [name CHAR(8), wage NUMBER(10)];

Continued

Name	Description	Example (continued)
`DBA_CONSTRAINTS`	Shows constraint definitions on all tables.	`DBA_CONSTRAINTS`
`DELETE`	Used to delete rows in a table. Deletes rows where customer balance is zero.	`DELETE FROM Customer` `WHERE Balance < 0;`
`DESCRIBE`	Sees what attribute names are in a table.	`DESC table_name`
`DISTINCT`	Used to select distinct values. Here we select all distinct grades.	`SELECT DISTINCT Grade FROM` `grade_report`
	We can use this command to count distinct grades.	`SELECT COUNT(DISTINCT` `grade) FROM grade_report`
`DROP SYNONYM`	Drops a synonym.	`DROP SYNONYM synonym_name`
`GRANT`	Allows other views use tables you have created. Here we grant public access on the Student table.	`GRANT SELECT` `ON student TO PUBLIC;`

`GROUP BY`	This is a clause in a `SELECT` statement that is designed to be used in conjunction with aggregate functions.
	Here we find the sum of room capacities for rooms that have no overhead projectors (N), rooms that do (Y), and rooms where the overhead projector capacity is unknown (NULL).
		`SELECT ohead,`
		`   SUM(capacity)`
		`FROM room`
		`GROUP BY ohead`

`HAVING`	Used as a find filter on a `SELECT`.
	Here we are only interested in classes that have more than a certain number of people.
		`SELECT COUNT (*)`
		`FROM student`
		`GROUP BY class`
		`HAVING COUNT(*) 6;`

`IN`	Used to find the objects from set A that are also in set B.
	Here we find all student names from the Student table where the class is in the set (3,4).
		`SELECT sname`
		`FROM student`
		`WHERE class IN (3,4);`

`INSERT INTO SELECT`	Inserts multiple rows and values from the Employee table into New Employee.	`INTO new_employee`
		`SELECT *`
		`FROM employee;`

`INSERT INTO VALUES`	Inserts values into a row of a table. Note: The attribute order must be correct.
	Here the values for name and wage are inserted into the Employee table.
		`INSERT INTO Employee`
		`   (Name, Wage)`
		`VALUES ('John Smith',`
		`   '18.00');`

Continued

Name	Description	Example (continued)

JOIN	Joins tables with the use of the SELECT command and the FROM and WHERE clauses. SELECT requests a result set that contains only those resultant rows that have the same field value in two tables; for example, jobc (jobcode) in the Jobs table equal to jobcode in the Employee table.	`SELECT *`
		`FROM emps, jobs`
		`WHERE emps.jobcode =`
		`    jobs.jobc;`

	We also can use table aliases to join tables.	`SELECT *`
		`FROM emps e, jobs j`
		`WHERE e.jobcode = j.jobc;`

LIKE	Lets us find whether a character string exists in an attribute. Here it finds any pattern with SMITH in sname. This is done by putting % on both sides of the string.	`SELECT * FROM student` `WHERE sname LIKE '%SMITH%'`
	Here it finds any pattern starting with SMITH in sname. This is done by putting % at the end.	`SELECT * FROM student` `WHERE sname LIKE 'SMITH%'`
	LIKE also can be used with a positioned match and a wildcard. Here it matches any character in the first four positions, then matches a 2, and then any character in the last three positions.	`WHERE Course_num` `LIKE '____2___';`

LIKE using UPPER	Converts strings to all uppercase (we can use LOWER to convert strings to lowercase).	`SELECT * FROM student`
		`WHERE UPPER(sname) LIKE`
		`    'SMITH%'`

MAX	Used to find the maximum value in a data set. Suppose we want to find the maximum wage paid to an employee. We use the MAX function and select the attribute WAGE from the Employee table.	`SELECT MAX(WAGE)` `FROM Employee;`

MINUS	Finds the students only in class (3,4). This example might seem useless, but we are trying to show the use of MINUS here.	`SELECT sname`
		`FROM student`
		`WHERE class IN (2,3,4);`
		`MINUS`
		`SELECT sname`
		`FROM student`
		`WHERE class IN (2);`

NOTIN	Here we find all student names from the Student table where the class is not in the set (2).	`SELECT sname`
		`FROM student`
		`WHERE class NOTIN (2);`

Continued

Name	Description	Example (continued)
ORDER BY	Orders the display, apart from showing the contents of a table.	```SELECT wage, hours FROM employee ORDER BY wage;```
	Orders the display in descending order apart from showing the contents of a table.	```SELECT wage, hours FROM employee ORDER BY wage DESC;```
REVOKE	Disallows access to a table, here the Student table.	```REVOKE SELECT ON student FROM PUBLIC;```
ROLLBACK	Used to undo the last command.	```ROLLBACK```
ROWNUM	Manipulates result sets by rows. It selects the Rownum and sname from the Employee table where the Rownum < 5. Note that Rownum = 5 will not work.	```SELECT Rownum, sname FROM Student WHERE Rownum < 5```
SELECT "attribute" FROM "table name"	Selects attributes from a table.	```SELECT * wage, hours FROM employee```
SELECT * FROM	Displays a table called x.	```SELECT * FROM x```
	Displays a table called Employee where the employee name is John.	```SELECT * FROM employee WHERE e_name = 'John';```
SUM	Used to sum values in a data set. Suppose we want the sum of hours worked by all employees. Use the SUM function and select the attribute Hours from the Employee table.	```SELECT SUM(Hours) FROM Employee;```
TABS	Gives you information of all the tables and synonyms you have created.	```SELECT * FROM tabs```
UNION	A set operation on two sets where the result contains all the elements of both sets. The resulting display here contains the names of students who are majoring in either MATH or COSC.	```SELECT sname FROM student WHERE major = 'COSC' UNION SELECT sname FROM student WHERE major = 'MATH'```
UPDATE	Used to update the values in a table. Here it updates the values in the Customer table and sets all balances to zero.	```UPDATE Customer SET Balance = 0;```

Continued

Name	Description	Example (continued)

	Here it updates the values in the Customer table and sets all balances to zero for customer number 101.	`UPDATE Customer`
		`SET Balance = 0`
		`WHERE Cno = 101;`

USER_SYNONYMS	Lets you see all the synonyms you have created.	`SELECT * FROM` `user_synonyms`
USER_TAB_COLUMNS	Gives you information on all the tables you have created.	`SELECT * FROM` `user_tab_columns`
USER_TABLES	Holds tables created by a USER. With this command, we can view all the USER tables.	`USER_TABLES`

VIEW	Used to break up a query into parts or to restrict a set of users from viewing a part of a database.
	Here a simple view (namemaj) is shown. Once the view is created, it is used in a SELECT statement.
		`CREATE OR REPLACE`
		`  VIEW namemaj AS`
		`SELECT  sname, major`
		`FROM student;`
		`SELECT * FROM namemaj`

WHERE	Restricts the output of rows in the result set.	`SELECT wage, hours`
		`FROM employee`
		`WHERE wage < 18.00;`

B

XHTML versus HTML Tags
Ordered by Function

XHTML	HTML	Comparison	Description
Basic Tags			
`<!->`	`<!->`	S	Defines a comment
`<!DOCTYPE>`	`<!DOCTYPE>`	S	Defines the document type
`<body>`	`<body>`	S	Defines the body element
` `	` `	D	Inserts a single line break; include a backslash in XHTML
`<html>`	`<html>`	S	Defines an HTML document
`<h1>` to `<h6>`	`<h1>` to `<h6>`	S	Defines header 1 to header 6
`<hr />`	`<hr>`	D	Defines a horizontal rule; include a backslash in XHTML
`<p>`	`<p>`	S	Defines a paragraph
Block Tags			
`<acronym>`	`<acronym>`	S	Defines an acronym
`<abbr>`	`<abbr>`	S	Defines an abbreviation
`<address>`	`<address>`	S	Defines an address element
`<blockquote>`	`<blockquote>`	S	Defines a long quotation
`<center>`	`<center>`	S	Defines centered text
`<cite>`	`<cite>`	S	Defines a citation
`<del>`	`<del>`	S	Defines deleted text
`<ins>`	`<ins>`	S	Defines inserted text

Continued

477

XHTML	HTML	Comparison	Description (continued)
`<q>`	`<q>`	S	Defines a short quotation
`<s>`	`<s>`	S	Defines strikethrough text
Character Formatting Tags			
`<b>`	`<b>`	S	Defines bold text
`<bdo>`	`<bdo>`	S	Defines the direction of text display
`<big>`	`<big>`	S	Defines big text
`<em>`	`<em>`	S	Defines emphasized text
`<font>`	`<font>`	S	Defines the font face, size, and color of text
`<i>`	`<i>`	S	Defines italic text
`<small>`	`<small>`	S	Defines small text
`<strong>`	`<strong>`	S	Defines strong text
`<sub>`	`<sub>`	S	Defines subscripted text
`<sup>`	`<sup>`	S	Defines superscripted text
`<u>`	`<u>`	S	Defines underlined text
Frame Tags			
`<frame>`	`<frame>`	S	Defines a subwindow (a frame)
`<frameset>`	`<frameset>`	S	Defines a set of frames
`<iframe>`	`<iframe>`	S	Defines an inline subwindow (frame)
`<noframes>`	`<noframes>`	S	Defines a noframe section
Image Tags			
`<area />`	`<area>`	D	Defines an area inside an image map; include a backslash in XHTML
`<img />`	`<img>`	D	Defines an image; include a backslash in XHTML
`<map>`	`<map>`	S	Defines an image map
Input Tags			
`<button>`	`<button>`	S	Defines a push button
`<fieldset>`	`<fieldset>`	S	Defines a fieldset
`<form>`	`<form>`	S	Defines a form
`<input>`	`<input>`	S	Defines an input field

Continued

XHTML	HTML	Comparison	Description (continued)
`<label>`	`<label>`	S	Defines a label
`<legend>`	`<legend>`	S	Defines a title in a fieldset
`<optgroup>`	`<optgroup>`	S	Defines an option group
`<option>`	`<option>`	S	Defines an item in a list box
`<select>`	`<select>`	S	Defines a selectable list
`<textarea>`	`<textarea>`	S	Defines a text area
Link Tags			
`<a>`	`<a>`	S	Defines an anchor
`<link>`	`<link>`	S	Defines a resource reference
List Tags			
`<dd>`	`<dd>`	S	Defines a definition description
`<dfn>`	`<dfn>`	S	Defines a definition term
`<dir>`	`<dir>`	S	Defines a directory list
`<dl>`	`<dl>`	S	Defines a definition list
`<dt>`	`<dt>`	S	Defines a definition term
`<menu>`	`<menu>`	S	Defines a menu list
`<li>`	`<li>`	S	Defines a list item
`<ol>`	`<ol>`	S	Defines an ordered list
`<ul>`	`<ul>`	S	Defines an unordered list
Meta Info Tags			
`<base />`	`<base>`	D	Defines a base URL; include back-slash in XHTML
`<basefont />`	`<basefont>`	D	Defines a base font; include back-slash in XHTML
`<head>`	`<head>`	S	Defines information about the document
`<meta>`	`<meta>`	S	Defines meta information
`<title>`	`<title>`	S	Defines the document title
Output Tags			
`<code>`	`<code>`	S	Defines computer code text
`<kbd>`	`<kbd>`	S	Defines keyboard text
`<pre>`	`<pre>`	S	Defines preformatted text

Continued

XHTML	HTML	Comparison	Description (continued)
`<samp>`	`<samp>`	S	Defines sample computer code
`<tt>`	`<tt>`	S	Defines teletype text
`<var>`	`<var>`	S	Defines a variable
Programming Tags			
`<applet>`	`<applet>`	S	Defines an applet
`<noscript>`	`<noscript>`	S	Defines a noscript section
`<object>`	`<object>`	S	Defines an embedded object
`<param>`	`<param>`	S	Defines a parameter for an object
`<script>`	`<script>`	S	Defines a script
Style Tags			
`<div>`	`<div>`	S	Defines a section in a document
`<span>`	`<span>`	S	Defines a section in a document
`<style>`	`<style>`	S	Defines a style definition
Table Tags			
`<caption>`	`<caption>`	S	Defines a table caption
`<col>`	`<col>`	S	Defines attributes for table columns
`<colgroup>`	`<colgroup>`	S	Defines groups of table columns
`<table>`	`<table>`	S	Defines a table
`<tbody>`	`<tbody>`	S	Defines a table body
`<td>`	`<td>`	S	Defines a table cell
`<tfoot>`	`<tfoot>`	S	Defines a table footer
`<th>`	`<th>`	S	Defines a table header
`<thead>`	`<thead>`	S	Defines a table header
`<tr>`	`<tr>`	S	Defines a table row

Notes: D = Tags in HTML and XHTML are slightly different.
    S = Tags in XHTML and HTML are the same.

For additional information, see the following online references: http://www.w3schools.com/default.asp and http://www.mindbuilders.net/xhtml_tutorials.html.

Index

485